The Way to the Western Sea

LEWIS AND CLARK ACROSS THE CONTINENT

DAVID LAVENDER

University of Nebraska Press
Lincoln and London

First Bison Books printing: 2001

Library of Congress Cataloging-in-Publication Data
Lavender, David Sievert, 1910–
The way to the western sea: Lewis and Clark across the continent / David
Lavender.
p. cm.
Originally published: New York: Harper & Row, c1988.
Includes bibliographical references (p.   ) and index.
ISBN: 978-0-8032-8003-8
1. Lewis and Clark Expedition (1804–1806)   2. Lewis, Meriwether, 1774–1809.
3. Clark, William, 1770–1838.   4. West (U.S.)—Discovery and exploration.
5. West (U.S.)—Description and travel.   I. Title.
F592.7 .L38   2001
917.804′2—dc21   2001033592

To M. M. L.
*Always gallant,
no matter how hard the way*

Contents

List of Maps		xi
Acknowledgments		xiii
One	Beginner's Luck	1
Two	Preparing for the Future	22
Three	Grappling with Logistics	40
Four	Trial Run	52
Five	Facing Reality	73
Six	Smoky Water	94
Seven	Emphasis on Indians	116
Eight	Into Winter	134
Nine	The Grand Plan	149
Ten	Forty Below—and Far to Go	168
Eleven	Hazards by Water	189
Twelve	The Great Portage	211
Thirteen	The Great Divide	229
Fourteen	Hunger	251
Fifteen	Wild Water	275
Sixteen	The Farthest Reach	298

Seventeen	Against the Flow	316
Eighteen	Peace Mission to the Blackfeet	336
Nineteen	Hurrying Home	356
Twenty	Endings	372
Appendix I:	Jefferson's Instructions to Lewis	389
Appendix II:	The Permanent Party	395
Appendix III:	Much Ado About Little—The Case of the *Lydia*	397
Notes		401
Bibliography		425
Index		433

List of Maps

The Lewis and Clark Expedition, 1803–6   xiv–xv

Winter Camp at Fort Mandan   156–157

The First Months on the Missouri   194–195

Portage Around the Missouri's Great Falls   222–223

Across the Continental Divide   260–261

From the Headwaters of the Missouri River to the
   Pacific Ocean   278–279

The Farthest Reach   300–301

The Two Routes Back   344–345

Acknowledgments

In one way or another, the following people, listed alphabetically, contributed significantly to making this book work: Christian Brun, Department of Special Collections, University of California at Santa Barbara; Cort Conley, boatman and outdoorsman of Cambridge, Idaho; Sherm and Claire Ewing, ranchers and fliers of Great Falls, Montana; Howard Foulger, now of St. George, Utah, with whom, when he was a U.S. Forest Ranger, I tramped over much of western Montana; Eugene Gressley, American Heritage Center, University of Wyoming, Laramie, Wyoming; Curtis Johnson of Fort Clatsop National Memorial, Oregon; Mildred Lavender; Denise Miller, librarian, Thacher School, Ojai, California; and Marcia Staigmiller of the Lewis and Clark Trail Heritage Foundation, Inc., Great Falls, Montana, chapter.

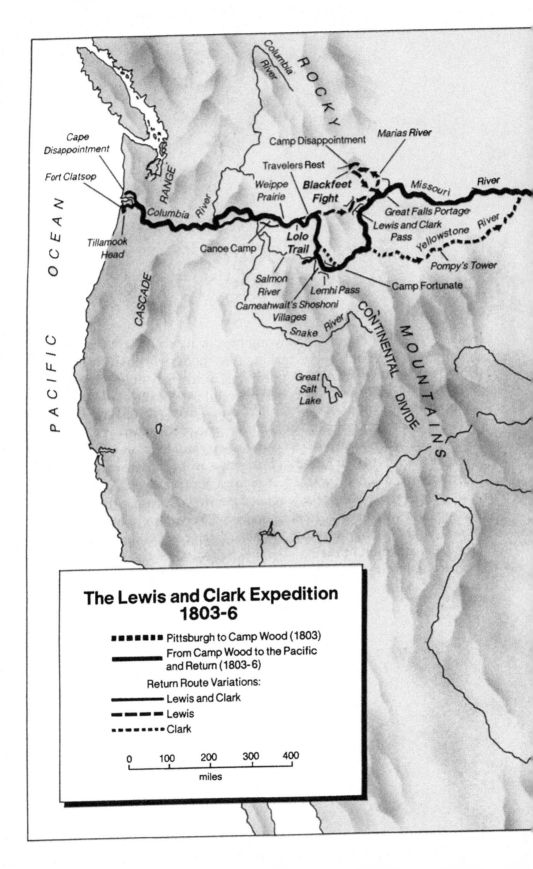

The Lewis and Clark Expedition 1803-6

CANADA

Fort Mandan

*Confrontation with
Teton Sioux*

Mississippi River

Sgt. Floyd's Gravesite

Pittsburgh

Wheeling

Marietta

Cincinnati

St. Charles

La Charette

Camp
Wood

Ohio River

*Falls of
the Ohio*

Louisville

Cahokia

St. Louis

Fort Kaskaskia

Fort Massac

GULF OF MEXICO

The Way to the Western Sea

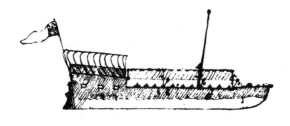

ONE

Beginner's Luck

Luck! It began for Captain Meriwether Lewis, paymaster of the First Infantry Regiment, United States Army, when he reached his regimental headquarters in Pittsburgh on March 5, 1801, after a rough trip from Detroit, and found in his mail a letter from Thomas Jefferson, recently elected president of the United States.

His thin, long-nosed face must have shown his mingled delight and astonishment. Jefferson needed a private secretary with unusual qualifications. "Your knolege of the Western country," he wrote, "of the army and of all it's interests and relations have rendered it desirable for public as well as private purposes that you should be engaged in that office."[1]

Pay would be five hundred dollars a year. Not much even then, but Lewis could retain his rank as job insurance and save living expenses as a member of the president's household. Now, that was exciting! Lewis, who was given to quick exhilarations and, balancing them, occasional deep depressions, dashed off a boastful note to an army friend—he would now be in a position to "inform you of the most important political occurrences of our government or such of them as I may feel myself at liberty to give"[2]—and then wrote a more circumspect letter to Jefferson accepting the appointment. After settling his accounts, he requisitioned three fresh horses, one for riding and two for packing, and shortly after March 10 started for the new federal city of Washington. It was a miserable trip. Flat gray skies, leafless trees, the *plop-suck, plop-suck* of hooves in the thawing mire, followed by long nights in dreary wayside inns.

Some of the phrases in Jefferson's letter kept returning to puzzle him. Knowledge of the Western country, of the army and all its interests and relations . . . He knew army procedures and could get along in the wilderness, but surely there was nothing in that to command national interest. Indian affairs? Hardly. The tribes of the Northwest had been quiet since their crushing defeat at Fallen Timbers in 1794 by General Anthony Wayne. Military defense? That seemed just as unlikely. British fur traders were no longer occupying posts on American soil and stirring up trouble. Another tension had ended in 1795 when Spain had opened the Mississippi to the flatboats of the pioneers surging across the Allegheny Mountains. The undeclared naval war with revolutionary France was winding down. Peace, in short, seemed assured for many years.

Yet Jefferson wanted his special talents. Strange, strange. Well, he'd learn eventually. On he plodded, losing still more time because one of his horses went lame.

He reached Washington shortly after April 1, to find that Jefferson had departed for a short rest at his home, Monticello, in Albemarle County, Virginia. He had left behind, in the leaky, unfinished hull of the President's House (now called the White House), a steward, a housekeeper, and three servants whose chief responsibility, until Jefferson returned, would be taking care of Meriwether Lewis.[3] Gratifying enough after a winter on the Northern frontier. Yet probably Lewis would rather have gone south, too, for Albemarle County was home to him as well as to the president.

The Lewis plantation, Locust Hill, named for the big locust trees that sheltered the main buildings, was only eight or nine miles from Monticello. Meriwether had been born there August 18, 1774, the second child and first son of William and Lucy Meriwether Lewis. He scarcely remembered his father, for William Lewis, a lieutenant in the Continental Army, had died in November 1779 from injuries and exposure suffered when his horse fell in an icy stream while he was homeward bound on leave.

The death left Lucy with three small children to raise, a thousand-acre plantation to manage, additional lands in the wilderness to fret about, and sharp worries over British raiders in the vicinity. She solved the problems in part by marrying, six months after her husband's death, another army officer and a man she had known for some time, Captain John Marks. By him she bore two more children.

In 1784 a friend of Marks's persuaded him and his family to join a speculative land rush to the Broad River in the wilds of northern Georgia. There is no direct evidence that young Meriwether did not get along with the stepfather who had twice changed his life. Still, he became, during those years, a moody lad who often went alone into the woods with his dogs, frequently at night to hunt raccoons and opossums. He had an eye for plants and one way or another taught himself a good deal about the vegetation he encountered. His mother probably encouraged him. She was a noted herb doctor, and it is not hard to imagine them going into the forest together on collecting trips.

Almost certainly Lucy Marks taught her children the rudiments of writing, reading, and doing sums. Within three years, however, Meriwether had surpassed his mother's capabilities and those of the neighborhood schools. Whether at her urging or his, he was sent back to Locust Hill in 1787. For a little more than two years he attended a sequence of schools run by impoverished divines. The uncles who were acting as his guardians then set him to work on the plantation at the age of fifteen or so. It was an exacting practical education—learning to oversee the slaves who performed the labor in the almost self-sufficient plantation. Herding, butchering, milling, planting; spinning thread and making clothes; erecting buildings and fences; extemporizing repairs, hauling. Setting up goals and schedules. Keeping accounts. Learning the jargon of the neighboring planters who stopped by to trade news.

After Marks died either late in 1791 or early in 1792, Meriwether went to Georgia and brought the family back to Locust Hill, using for the journey a carriage said to have been built by Jefferson's slaves at Monticello.[4] Apparently he stayed restless, however, and if Thomas Jefferson is to be believed, he tried to seize the first big opportunity for adventure that came his way.

The circumstances are suggested in a letter Caspar Wistar, a professor of anatomy at the University of Pennsylvania, wrote to the American botanist Moses Marshall. Thomas Jefferson, Wistar said, and "some other gentlemen," mostly members of the American Philosophical Society, were proposing to raise a prize of one thousand guineas to be awarded to anyone who, after following the Missouri River to its source, brought back proof that he had continued to the Pacific.[5]

Years later, on August 18, 1813, the anniversary of Lewis's birth and four years after his death by suicide, Jefferson, then seventy, wrote a short memoir of the young man's life. In it he stated that Lewis, who in 1792 had been stationed in Charlottesville, Virginia, on recruiting service for the army, somehow learned of the transcontinental proposal and "warmly solicited me to obtain for him the execution of that object." Jefferson declined, implying the venture was too dangerous for a youth of eighteen.[6]

There are problems with this recollection. Lewis had not yet joined the army in 1792 and would not be stationed in Charlottesville until 1798. Donald Jackson, who has studied the Lewis and Clark expedition as deeply as anyone, is inclined to believe the aging Jefferson made a mistake and the episode may, in fact, never have occurred. Certainly there is no mention of it in any other surviving document.[7]

Be that as it may, another candidate soon appeared. This was the highly trained French botanist, André Michaux, aged forty-six. Michaux had been in the United States since 1785, searching for useful plants he could introduce into France. He established one nursery near Charleston, South Carolina, and another at Hackensack, New Jersey, and stocked them with specimens he found in the mountains of the Carolinas and the hazardous swamps of Florida. In 1792 he traveled with Montreal fur traders into the harsh lands near the southern tip of Hudson Bay. In Montreal, quite possibly, he learned that Alexander Mackenzie of the North West Company had just passed through the city on an exciting errand—crossing Canada to the Pacific by canoe in order to show that far western trading posts could be supplied from harbors on the distant coast.

The thought was bound to stir a man of Michaux's temperament. And though there is no evidence to prove this, he may well have heard of the thousand-guinea prize from his fellow botanist, Moses Marshall. In any event he applied to Jefferson for the position.

Jefferson and the Pacific: we need to digress in order to place his interest in perspective. Heritage, predilections, and circumstances all inclined him that way, though he himself never traveled physically more than fifty miles west of Monticello. His father had been a pioneer land speculator and mapmaker. The son had touched on the West in one of the few books he wrote, *Notes on Virginia.* While in France from 1784 to 1789 as American minister to the court of Louis XVI, he began assiduously collecting books on the West until he owned more volumes on the topic than any other collector in the world.[8]

That the West would be peopled by Americans, though Spain then owned almost all of it, Jefferson had no doubt. Even during the Revolution, citizens of the eastern regions and immigrants from Europe had persisted in crossing the Alleghenies in defiance of violent Indian opposition. When the war ended, the stream became a flood. In 1785, for a single instance, a thousand river craft, scores of them huge flatboats loaded with entire families, their goods, and livestock, went down the Ohio. Roads split the forests: the Forbes Road through Pennsylvania, the Wilderness Trail blazed through Cumberland Gap by Daniel Boone, and a dozen more. By 1800, three hundred thousand people lived in the trans-Allegheny region, as compared to thirty thousand at the close of the Revolution.

In Jefferson's fanciful moments the Mississippi disappeared as the boundary with Spain, and the human tide flowed unrestrained. In 1786 he wrote in a private letter, "Our confederacy must be viewed as the nest from which all America, North and South, is to be peopled." Others, stirred by the same prospect, shared the view. Jedediah Morse, writer of geography textbooks, proclaimed in 1789, "We cannot but anticipate the period, as not far distant, when the AMERICAN EMPIRE will comprehend millions of souls, west of the Mississippi." The poet Timothy Dwight sang, "Soon shall thy sons across the mainland roam / And claim on far Pacific shores their home."[9]

Savants of the American Philosophical Society, of which Jefferson was a member, loved to speculate on what venturesome settlers might find in the uncharted landmass. Did mammoths, long extinct in Europe, still wander there? How far north did the strange llamas of Peru range? Were there active volcanoes, as rumored? Mountains of undissolved salt? Above all, was there a central "height of land" from which the West's principal rivers extended like rays—the Red-Nelson system toward Hudson Bay, the Rio Grande southward, the Missouri eastward, and, interlocking with the headwaters of the Missouri, a navigable, west-flowing stream already named "Oregon" by two early army officers and traders, Robert Rogers and Jonathan Carver?

Should members of the Philosophical Society foster private attempts to find a westward crossing? Some thought so. In 1783, when garbled rumors reached Philadelphia that a group of Britons proposed to explore the country from the Mississippi to California, Jefferson wrote George Rogers Clark, the military hero of the trans-Allegheny West and one of William Clark's elder brothers, that "some of us here are talking in a feeble way of making the attempt to search that country. How would you like to lead such a party?" The offer was too feeble, and Clark declined. No Britons appeared, either.

John Ledyard came next. He was a Connecticut Yankee who had been with England's great navigator, James Cook, as a corporal of marines when Cook had visited the Northwest Coast of America in 1778 on his last voyage of discovery. Ledyard had seen how easily sea-otter pelts could be obtained from the natives and then resold in China at an enormous profit. Eager to set up trading posts in the region, he sought backing first in the East and then in France. After every financial prospect had failed him, he sought out Jefferson, then residing in Paris. To the minister the would-be explorer expounded one of the zaniest ideas in the history of exploration. He would cross Siberia to the Kamchatka Peninsula and embark for Alaska on a Russian fur ship. From there he would walk to the Mississippi, buoyed by two large hunting dogs, an Indian peace pipe, and a hatchet for chopping firewood. What he hoped to achieve by the incredible effort, beyond publicity and material for another book, is impossible to say.

There was no chance he could succeed. "He has too much imagination," Jefferson wrote, and added wistfully that if he should get through, "he will give us new, curious & useful information."[10] On Ledyard's behalf he wrote the empress of Russia for a passport. She refused it; the notion, one of her officers explained, was wholly chimerical. Grimly Ledyard went ahead anyway and came within seven hundred miles of the Pacific before he was arrested and dragged back.

Now hardly five years later, here was André Michaux, eager for fame and a thousand guineas. Embarrassed—apparently the talk of the prize had been only talk—a few members of the Philosophical Society scrambled to rectify matters. On January 22, 1793, they drew up an agreement about payments: one-fourth down and other installments according to the explorer's progress. Simultaneously they set about trying to raise the necessary funds.[11]

The arrival of Citizen Edmond Charles Genêt, France's new minister to the United States, at Charleston, South Carolina, on April 8, 1793, put a severe crimp in the program. By then it was known in America that France had just abolished the monarchy and war had broken out again between that country and most of the rest of Europe. Genêt's assignment was to stir up trouble in the New World for France's principal enemies by outfitting privateers in American harbors to prey on British shipping and by forming an army of insurgents to attack Spanish Louisiana.

The reception Washington and the pro-British Federalists in the cabinet granted Genêt, who reached Philadelphia on April 22, was noticeably cool. The Francophile Jefferson, then serving as secretary of state, was more amiable. He listened to the schemer's bombast and, although the Frenchman was already in contact with Michaux, went ahead with plans for the exploration. He drew up, under the date of April 30, detailed instructions, the main one of which was for Michaux to "seek for & pursue that route which shall form the shortest & most convenient communication between the higher parts of the Missouri & the Pacific ocean." Another society member was appointed to collect the first installment of the subscriptions specified in the agreement. Results are suggestive. Only twenty persons paid up. Amounts ranged from $2.00 to $25.00 from George Washington, who had subscribed the previous January. Jefferson paid $12.50, as did his enemy Alexander Hamilton. Total: $128.25.[12] Hardly enough for crossing the continent (he surely planned to take a crew along), and it is difficult to suppose that France's flagrant breaches of neutrality did not help account for the shortage.

On July 15, 1793, Michaux started West to further Genêt's plans, not the Philosophical Society's. It was not a fruitful trip. On Washington's demand, the French government recalled Genêt, Michaux drifted back to Philadelphia, and the disturbance lost its punch, although George Rogers Clark, whom Genêt had commissioned "Major General of the Independent and Revolutionary Legion of the Mississippi," kept fussing with it well into 1794.[13]

The episode left scars, for it exacerbated the feuding between Federalists and Antifederalists (Jeffersonian Republicans) in Congress and in the cabinet. Weary of turmoil, Jefferson resigned as secretary of state on December 31, 1793, and returned home to restore his neglected plantation and to resume work on his domed, pillared, airy mansion. He would not return officially to the capitol at Philadelphia until he challenged John Adams for the presidency in 1796.

To jump ahead: In those days voters cast their ballots for electors pledged to the presidential candidate of one party or the other. Those chosen then met in Philadelphia (later in Washington) and voted according to their pledges. The man who received the most electoral votes became president and the runner-up vice-president. In 1796, John Adams, a Federalist, won. Jefferson, a Republican, became his putative successor, an uneasy situation. Well, there would be another election in 1800 and Jefferson was determined that then he would be second to no one. That, too, became part of Meriwether Lewis's luck.

Lewis, meanwhile had let his yearning for adventure draw him into military service. The proximate cause was an excise tax of seven cents a gallon on distilled spirits, which commonly retailed on the frontier for twenty-five cents a gallon. Since making whiskey was almost the only way backwoods farmers had of disposing of their surplus grain, the West was outraged, particularly since no tax was imposed on any Eastern product. Antitax riots—the so-called Whiskey Rebellion—erupted in western Pennsylvania; revenue agents were tarred and feathered.

To demonstrate that the federal government could not be trifled with, Washington, at Hamilton's behest, asked the governors of Virginia, Maryland, New Jersey, and Pennsylvania to provide thirteen thousand militiamen for restoring order. Meriwether Lewis joined the Virginia contingent and quickly became an ensign, the equivalent today of a second lieutenant. The oversized force—a blunderbuss to kill a flea—marched through the brilliant reds and golds of fall to the Pittsburgh area. The ringleaders among the insurgents fled. Only eighteen protesters were captured and tried. Two were convicted, and Washington pardoned them. In spite of the clemency, the overkill turned many resentful frontiersmen into voters—Antifederalist voters—for the first time in their lives.

At the expiration of his enlistment, Lewis transferred, still an ensign, into what became the First Regiment of the regular army. Either late that year (1795) or early the next, he served for a few months at Fort Greenville, Ohio, in a rifle company commanded by Lieutenant William Clark, four years older than he and a veteran of the ferocious Indian wars of the first half of the 1790s. A strong friendship developed between them, but actual association ended, except for occasional letters, when Clark left the service to salvage what he could of the muddled affairs of his alcoholic brother George.

Unlike Clark, Lewis saw no action in the army. He drilled his men punctiliously in the Northwest's dreary stockades and supervised the building of Fort Pickering on a bluff above the Mississippi where Memphis now stands. Then, in 1798, he was placed on recruiting duty at Charlottesville, Virginia, near his home—and Jefferson's. He stayed there well into 1799. Certainly he saw the vice-president during that period. They could hardly have been close friends, for there was a thirty-one-year difference in their ages. Still, they were neighbors. Jefferson bought beautifully cured hams from Lucy Marks, and the presidential aspirant would have enjoyed talking to the younger man about the mood of the settlers in the Northwest, and about the region's natural history, a subject that fascinated both. Before long Jefferson would have sensed that Lewis was an ardent Republican, though most of his fellow officers were Federalists.

As the new century approached, Lewis was moved back to the Northwest. Late in 1800, aged twenty-six, he was promoted to captain and stationed at Detroit. Shortly thereafter he was made regimental paymaster, an assignment that involved arduous journeys down the Ohio by boat and through the dense forests by horse. Or, more accurately, it would have involved many such journeys if the election of 1800 had not intervened.

When the campaign, the most slanderous in American history, was over, the Federalists had been defeated—but two Republicans, Jefferson and Aaron Burr, were tied at seventy-three votes each. This threw the contest into the House of Representatives. Thirty-six ballots, each preceded by intense maneuvering, were cast before the deadlock splintered, with Jefferson as president and Burr as vice-president.

The triumph came February 17, only two weeks before the inauguration. A whole new administration had to be given shape, and yet Jefferson, ignoring qualified applicants near at hand, took time enough to reach out into the wilderness and hire Captain Meriwether Lewis as his private secretary.

For a long time many people have wondered why. Because Lewis eventually did lead the first American expedition to reach the Pacific by land, some historians have assumed the choice was in Jefferson's mind before the election.[14]

The conjecture just won't wash. It is true Jefferson had speculated at length about what lay beyond the Mississippi. It is true he envisioned a continental destiny for the United States. As a *private* individual, acting generally on behalf of the American Philosophical Society, he had involved himself in three ill-conceived plans. But there is no evidence that as a *public* leader, whether as secretary of state or vice-president, he had endeavored to set into motion a government-sponsored, carefully prepared enterprise.

Consider. The Spanish empire was losing its grip. Maintaining Louisiana even in a halfhearted way was endured only in the hope that the vast region would serve as a topographical buffer protecting New Mexico and, especially, Mexico, rich in silver. But that hope, Jefferson believed, was fatuous. The Mississippi Valley was filling with aggressive, energetic Americans. Some, taking advantage of Spain's offer of land grants to adult males who would embrace Spanish citizenship and Roman Catholicism (no inconvenient attention was paid to the way the "converts" observed their new faith), were already crossing the river. Daniel Boone's family was among them. So were Moses Austin and his young son Stephen, later the "fathers" of American Texas. Spain hoped, of course, that these and other rugged, naturalized Spaniards would leap to the defense of their property in case of invasion.

Jefferson thought not. The emigrants, he believed, would remember their origins and work for eventual annexation by the United States. So why stir up a hornet's nest by sending a government-sponsored expedition into alien territory? Why rouse French and British curiosity: what *were* those Americans doing? Better let nature take its course. Let the plum ripen until it was ready to fall without friction into American hands.

Then why did he hire Meriwether Lewis? The reasons were immediate, pragmatic, and political. Dressed in a dark uniform crisscrossed with white belts, and wearing a cocked hat with an eagle medallion in its front, the captain would lend dignity to the confidential messages he carried. He could serve as a decorative and charming host at presidential dinners—a real need, for Jefferson was a widower and his daughters could not often leave their own growing households to help. More important, Lewis was a stalwart Republican. The spoils system of appointing party faithful to government positions had not yet attained the lush growth it would achieve under Andrew Jackson, but it was on the way. The excise tax had provided openings for Federalist agents, and just before leaving office John Adams had created several "midnight" judges. During the expansion of the armed forces while the undeclared naval war with France was under way (1798–1800), most officers had been picked according to party allegiance. Now it was the Republicans' turn. One of Jefferson's campaign promises had been to cut the size of the army, but he wanted to be careful not to remove dependable Republicans.[15] Lewis, whom he knew to be trustworthy, could guide the endeavor and also work over long, dull lists of postmasterships.[16]

Toward the end of April 1801, Jefferson returned to swampy Washington (population 3,210) from Monticello and, with his new secretary, tackled the problem of making the huge, white-painted sandstone presidential mansion habitable. Its twenty-three rooms were big and cold; Abigail Adams had said it was impossible to keep warm in such a place. Because the Adamses had removed most of the furniture—it was their own property—more had to be provided. An unsubstantial partition was built in the East Room, on the second floor, to provide Lewis with two chambers. Jefferson had more suitable quarters in the west wing. The unkempt grounds were tidied up and surrounded by a rail fence, but little could be done about the approach to the entry hall; the outside steps and porch were still made of planks.[17]

Because the new secretary of state, James Madison, and his wife, Dolley, were temporarily without housing, Jefferson invited them to stay in the mansion until their own quarters were ready. Madison was wizened and sharp-eyed; Dolley, plump, pretty, and addicted to snuff.[18] Both were sparkling conversationalists and lent élan to the dinner parties the president launched as soon as a proper cook had been found for him by the Marqués de Casa Yrujo, the Spanish ambassador. Yrujo was a dashing, handsome, curly-haired cavalier given to resplendent uniforms. Fluent in English, he had married the daughter of that sound Republican, Thomas McKean, the governor of Pennsylvania, and was a favorite of Jefferson's.

Though Jefferson, six feet tall, angular, red-headed, and always poised, could have matched the sartorial splendor of some of his guests, he chose not to. He saw himself as the representative of the nation's sturdy tillers of the soil. He dressed accordingly, appearing at his own parties in ordinary clothing, occasionally wearing slippers. The food he served did not match his costume. One diarist, Mahlon Dickerson, who became a close friend of Meriwether Lewis, wrote after one dinner that "however [Jefferson] may neglect his person, he takes good care of his table. No man in America keeps a better." It should have been good. Jefferson, whose salary as president was $25,000 a year, spent that first year $6,508 on groceries and provisions, $2,797.28 on wine, and $2,700 on servants, some of them in livery.[19] Laborers, it might be pointed out, earned, at that period, $10.00 a month.

After several weeks, the Madisons moved to their own house, and the president and his secretary were left, Jefferson wrote one of his daughters, as lonely as two mice in a church.[20] Did that lonesomeness break down some of his habitual reserve? "Secrecy," according to his biographer Saul Padover, "was his strategy and his predilection."[21] Still, it would be strange if he did not let slip, during that summer, occasional remarks that revealed to his secretary some of his uneasiness about French intentions in the West.

The matter began innocuously. Shortly after the inauguration Louis André Pichon, French chargé d'affaires in Washington, told the president that Napoleon was planning to retake the island of Santo Domingo from Toussaint L'Ouverture and black insurrectionists. Could the French government count on American help?

The proposal awoke Jefferson's strongest biases—his love for France, where he had spent some of his happiest years; his desire not to ruffle the new Convention of 1800, which had ended America's undeclared naval war with that nation; and his dread, as a Southern slaveholder, of an independent black republic near the borders of the United States. If the spirit of black rebellion spread . . . Chilled by the thought—his own state of Virginia had just authorized the arming of fifteen thousand men as a defense against possible insurrection—Jefferson told Pichon the United States would halt shipments of food to Santo Domingo, hoping this would help starve Toussaint into submission.

So far, so good. But then rumors leaked across the Atlantic that Spain had retroceded all Louisiana to France![22] If they were true, America's hope of eventually absorbing the vast territory by slow and peaceful osmosis from moribund Spain was ended.

Rumor. But as Jefferson paced his office, talking to his cabinet members and with Meriwether Lewis quite possibly listening, he found it a rumor all too easy to believe. France had long dreamed of reclaiming her lost colonial empire in the New World. The Genêt–Michaux–George Rogers Clark conspiracy of 1792–93 had been part of the cloak-and-dagger game. Later, in 1796, the French general, George Victor Collot, had traveled through the Mississippi Valley, studying its topography in more detail than befitted an ordinary tourist. And now Santo Domingo.

Plus other matters that Jefferson could not have known at the time, though the outlines soon enough took shape. In 1798, France's lame, shrewd, unscrupulous foreign minister, Talleyrand, had baldly told his Spanish counterpart that Spain could not hold the westward-pushing Americans away from Mexico's silver mines, but France could. So why not let Napoleon take over Louisiana, together with East and West Florida, and create from them "a wall of Brass forever impenetrable to the combined efforts of England [working out of Canada] and the Americans"?[23]

Carlos IV of Spain refused to negotiate—until Bonaparte so thoroughly mauled an Austrian army at Marengo, Italy, in 1800 that the Austrian-Russian-British coalition pledged to subduing him began to break apart. Arrogantly then he put more pressure on Carlos, helped by the Spanish king's wife, who wanted a duchy for her brother's then-propertyless family. At San Ildefonso, on October 1, 1800—one day after Napoleon's ministers had removed another roadblock by signing the convention that brought peace with the United States—he promised to give Carlos the Grand Duchy of Tuscany with its bejeweled cities of Florence, Pisa, and Siena. In exchange he was to receive six warships and the territory of Louisiana, its boundaries only fuzzily known even along the lower Mississippi. (Whether or not West Florida could be considered a part of the territory would trouble American policymakers for years.)

Secretary of State James Madison carried the administration's worries to Louis Pichon. What, exactly, was going on in Europe? The French minister smiled blandly. Why the excitement? Was the United States planning to cross the river into territory it did not own? Not at all, Madison said, just as blandly. He was concerned over the free navigation of the Mississippi and the right of deposit at New Orleans—rights, granted by Spain, that allowed the entire export business of the valley to flow smoothly to docks and warehouses in the southern city. Sailing ships then landed at the same docks to pick up the merchandise for ocean transport. The lifeline was vital. The Mississippi, Madison would write later, was as important in the American view of things as "the Hudson, the Delaware, the Potomac, and all the navigable rivers of the Atlantic states formed into one stream."[24]

Would France observe Spain's customs?

Pichon's hands described a Gallic spread. How could Mr. Madison ask such a question when not a Frenchman was anywhere near Louisiana?

The maddening uncertainties were still plaguing Jefferson—and, by association, Meriwether Lewis—when Robert Livingston, the new American minister to France, sailed for Paris on November 11, 1801. His instructions were to block the retrocession if it was actually contemplated. If the exchange had taken place he should try to obtain land in West Florida where an American port could be built. At the very least he should obtain a guarantee of free navigation and unimpeded deposit—all without offending the French.

Confirmation of the retrocession did not have to wait on Livingston's report. Rufus King, minister to Great Britain, passed on the news in a letter to Madison dated November 20, 1801. Two days later General Charles Leclerc sailed for Santo Domingo with twenty thousand soldiers jammed into thirty transports. And England, the last holdout of the coalition that had begun crumbling after the battle of Marengo, signed the Treaty of Amiens with France. At least it was called a treaty, although most observers believed it was a truce only and would end as soon as the British had recuperated. Finally—Jefferson was back in the field of rumor again—fresh reports said that a second French fleet was slowly assembling in Holland. British strategists feared it was aimed at Canada, or perhaps even at England itself. American informants said no: its goal was Louisiana.

Furious, Jefferson realized he had been tricked. France, it seemed now, was attacking Santo Domingo not for itself but for use as a staging area for further adventures in the Caribbean and, probably, for a push against New Orleans. By occupying the city, through which three-eighths of America's commerce passed, Napoleon could make the young United States dance to whatever tune he called. He could push upstream against Canada. He might even persuade the impatient American West to detach itself from the Union and thus destroy one of the world's great experiments in the viability of self-government.

A grim Jefferson worked out his responses slowly, carefully, and secretly—secretly lest his political enemies, the Federalists, disturb the country by crying out that his plans were inadequate and that they could do better. The key element he proposed was a colossal bluff that he outlined on April 18, 1802, in a long letter to Robert Livingston. The minister, Jefferson directed, should convince Bonaparte that France would be sealing her own doom by trying to take possession of New Orleans. For the United States would immediately counter by seeking an alliance with Great Britain and creating a naval force strong enough to keep France from reinforcing whatever settlements Napoleon sought to plant in the New World—a world that was henceforth to be held "for the common purposes of the United British and American nations." The only way out, for France, would be the ceding of New Orleans and the Floridas to the United States. (Other letters suggested that in return for those critical areas the U.S. would assume two million dollars in claims American shipowners held against France for damages sustained in the quasi war just ended.)

Negotiating with the French while groping toward an alliance with the British would take time, the president admitted to Livingston. But time would be available. The French could not move into the Mississippi until Santo Domingo was subdued, and that, Jefferson predicted, "will not be a short work."[25]

Just contemplating an alliance with Great Britain was a wrench for Jefferson, for he despised that nation as an insufferable aristocracy. He could not be certain, moreover, that the self-centered Anglos, as he considered them to be, would play his game for him —or that Napoleon would be swayed by the bluster if a treaty did appear. So, though he was hoping to avoid war with his bluff, he had to prepare for war as best he could—still secretly because of the Federalists.

One of his long-range plans was to gain, as quickly as possible, title to Indian lands bordering the east bank of the Mississippi. White settlers pouring into the vacated areas would automatically create a strong defensive militia and relieve him of the necessity of reneging on his campaign promise to reduce the size of the country's standing army. He also ordered Governor William C. C. Claiborne of newly formed Mississippi Territory to ready other militia units strong enough to swarm across the border and seize New Orleans at the first sign the French were moving into the river. Still other contemplated steps included strengthening Fort Adams, which overlooked the Mississippi just north of the point where West Florida's northern boundary touched the river, and the building of an entirely new fort at Cahokia, across the stream from St. Louis.[26]

So much for a French invasion. But what of the powder keg he was proposing to cuddle up to—Great Britain? Its redoubtable fur traders, turned out of their posts south of the Great Lakes, were finding rich new sources of beaver in what is now the Minnesota-Iowa region and along the upper Missouri in North Dakota. Spain had not been able to check the trespasses, though its governors in St. Louis had tried after a fashion, but the French would have more muscle. To get the jump on them in the event of war, the Britishers might come swarming out of the north, take possession of all northern Louisiana, and then sit back to dicker about territorial divisions.

They'd not use an army for the invasion: logistics were too formidable. Small ranger forces led by men who knew the Indians would be more logical. And so small forces were what Jefferson prepared to meet them with. During the planning, Meriwether Lewis's "knolege of the Western country, of the army and all it's interests and relations" surely proved useful.

First, the secretary of war, Henry Dearborn, was directed to study means of stockpiling supplies and enlisting reinforcements for the forts along the Great Lakes frontier. But the big gap was in the unmapped wilderness farther west. Certainly it would be prudent for the Americans to learn something about its transportation routes, sites for army posts, and places where the topography made ambushes possible. Even more important would be convincing the Indians that the Americans would make better allies than the grasping Britons.

As the talk went on, the president's glance, it can be surmised, rested more and more speculatively on his young secretary. He was aware of Lewis's faults, particularly his tendency to give way at times to deep depressions, a characteristic Jefferson, who knew the Lewis family, attributed to heredity. But he also knew, as he wrote later, that Lewis was "brave, prudent, habituated to the woods & familiar with Indian manners & character."[27] He had served six years in the frontier army. He knew discipline and as a captain could presumably handle a group of soldiers specially selected for a military reconnaissance in foreign territory. Why search farther for a leader? And at that moment the seed that would grow into the Lewis and Clark expedition was planted.[28]

(Assumptions. Nearly three years later, on April 7, 1805, at the beginning of the final push to the Pacific, Lewis wrote exultantly in his journal of what had been "a da[r]ling project of mine for the last ten years." If taken literally "ten years" could not refer to the Michaux scheme of 1792–93, which he supposedly tried to join, but it could refer to his early years in the regular army when he served for a time with Lieutenant William Clark. Probably, though, the "ten" was a general statement. As we have noted, a refrain of the 1790s told of an American nation reaching from sea to sea. As soon as the Spanish barrier vanished, and most people believed the time was near, the army would take its place in the vanguard of the western surge. Speculation filled the barracks, and that may be what Lewis meant. But since neither he nor Jefferson left a word about the actual genesis of the darling project, we can only speculate in our turn. Anyway, Meriwether Lewis was still lucky—the right man in the right place.)

In spite of the leaky post office and slow communications of the time, no political enemy detected what was up. Smugly Jefferson wrote James Monroe some months later, "They [the Federalists] would be truly mortified if they could see our files. . . . They would see that though we could not say when war would take place, yet we said with energy what would take place when it should arise."[29]

The jolt, when it came, was from the outside. On November 23, 1802, couriers raced into Washington with word that the Spanish intendant of New Orleans, Juan Ventura Morales, had revoked the right of deposit the previous October 18. (Spain still held sway; Carlos had refused to sign the treaties of retrocession because of Napoleon's dilatoriness in handing over Tuscany.) Morales justified his action on the grounds of blatant bribery and smuggling by American shippers. Corruption existed, of a certainty. But few Americans accepted the explanation. French trickery, many thought, lay behind the revocation.

The angry surmise was wrong. Many years later scholars learned that Carlos himself had sent the order across the Atlantic to Morales as a final way to embarrass the French before he signed the treaties giving up Louisiana. But at the time no one knew this truth. Roars went up for retaliatory measures—meaning, as far as the more jingoistic Federalists were concerned, an immediate declaration of war against France.

To keep from disturbing the country more than it already was, Jefferson went about his ordinary business as if nothing untoward had occurred. Privately, however, he pushed his defense measures. One of his first moves was to visit his longtime friend, the Marqués de Casa Yrujo (the Spaniard might be more amenable than the French representative who would soon replace him) and ask permission for a small "literary" expedition—today we would call it a scientific trip—to cross Spanish Louisiana to the Pacific slope.

The request, which he had invented to disguise the group's military errand, was logical. Yrujo knew, and so told Spain's minister of foreign affairs in Madrid, that Jefferson had long fantasized about the day when America might extend its influence to the South Sea, as Spaniards often called the Pacific.[30] Immediacy had been lent to the dream by the great accomplishment of Alexander Mackenzie, who had crossed Canada to those distant shores in 1793 with a single canoe manned by eight or ten voyageurs. Since then an account of Mackenzie's voyages had been published, first in London in 1801 and in the United States a year later. Mackenzie closed his narrative by urging the British government to take steps that would place the beaver and sea-otter commerce of the far Northwest firmly in the hands of private Canadian traders, to the exclusion of the Boston seafarers who were already scouring those distant, fog-shrouded waters for pelts that could be sold in China.

One way for Jefferson to hold a line on the British would be to strengthen the American claim to the Columbia River, whose mouth had been discovered in May 1792 by the Yankee sea captain Robert Gray. For that matter, Spain also had shadowy claims to the region, based on a handful of landings made along the coast by its own early navigators. Other nations paid little heed to these Spanish pretensions. Still, Yrujo reasoned, they might be of some deterrence if the British, the Russians (already busy in Alaska), or the Americans developed notions of advancing on Mexico through Spanish-occupied California. Why weaken the Spanish position by facilitating the approach of Americans into the region?

As for letting a scientific expedition thread Louisiana by way of the Missouri River—well, Yrujo was no fool. Whatever scientific knowledge about Indians or geography its personnel gleaned could easily be adapted to military purposes if the need ever arose. Suavely he turned down the president's request.

Jefferson remained unruffled. He had done what protocol demanded. Now he would follow the dictates of necessity. He called Meriwether Lewis into his office and told him the expedition would go ahead regardless, providing Congress appropriated enough money to get it started. Inasmuch as the Constitution gave the lawmakers no expressed right to finance exploration outside the nation's own boundaries, he would lay the project before them as a preliminary step to extending commerce in furs. Lewis should start the ball rolling by drawing up a cost estimate not to exceed $2,500. A larger amount might frighten the legislators and would not sit well with Jefferson's repeated statements about economizing. Both men realized the voyage's costs would soar far higher than $2,500 (eventually the amount reached $38,722.25, not counting services and materials furnished by the War Department) but at the time that was not the point.

Lewis must have felt like a blindfolded child trying to pin the tail on the donkey. He could count on very few givens. For instance, he could avoid paying wages by recruiting army personnel whose pay and rations would continue wherever they were. As far as the Mississippi, army posts would render some assistance in the way of transportation and lodgings. But otherwise . . . what could he draw on, except things he remembered from his experiences as a regimental paymaster and from reading Alexander Mackenzie's book about crossing the continent far to the north in 1793?

Stabbing blindly, the captain produced such items as $217 for scientific instruments, $255 for "camp equipage," $430 for transportation, $696 (the largest item) for Indian presents, $55 for medicine, $87 for contingencies, and so on—$2,500 right on the button.

Congress convened on December 15. Jefferson's original plan had been to spring the adventure on the legislators during his annual message. His secretary of the treasury, the tall, balding, brilliant Albert Gallatin, though enthusiastic about the expedition itself, talked him out of a public declaration.[31] Such exposure would draw the world's attention to the fact that the United States was planning a deliberate trespass on alien territory. Surmise would fly. Would it not be wise to ask for funds behind closed doors? Jefferson complied and presented a public State of the Union address so bland that the leading Federalist war hawk, Alexander Hamilton, denounced it as a "lullaby."[32]

He next placated the angry voters west of the Allegheny Mountains by appointing James Monroe, who was popular in that turbulent region, as special envoy to Paris to help Robert Livingston's quest for the Floridas and New Orleans. The negotiators were authorized to offer France as much as ten million dollars for the desired lands.

He scheduled his secret message for January 18, 1803. He began it with an indirect approach to another of his defensive measures, obtaining more land along the east bank of the Mississippi from the Indians. Some years earlier, he reminded Congress, the government had established trading houses among the tribes. Their purpose was to defend the Indians against unscrupulous white traders. The question now was whether or not the act authorizing the government houses should be renewed.

He recommended an affirmative vote. Augmenting the trading-house program would create a desire in uncivilized breasts for many items of "domestic comfort." The yearners would realize they would have more goods to trade if they embraced agriculture and simple manufacturing. The need for hunting grounds would vanish, and they would be happy to dispose of the excess acres to the government at a favorable price. The U.S. would then parcel out the acquisitions to land-hungry Americans, who would promptly form themselves into militia units. In that way the country could plant "on the Missisipi itself the means of its own safety."

Only a few envious white traders, he continued, would object to this governmental interference with private enterprise, and their losses could be more than offset by extending the fur trade beyond the Mississippi, perhaps as far as the Pacific. The ultimate aim would be to make friends and allies of the far Western Indians while at the same time diverting valuable pelts from the rugged northern routes used by another nation—obviously Great Britain, though not named in the message—and bringing the harvest down the Missouri to the Mississippi and thence eastward by a variety of routes. In the process the explorers would gain much information about the continent's geography.

In this elucidation Jefferson did not say a word about military reconnaissance, and probably none was needed by his listeners. Unctuously he finished, "The nation claiming this territory [Spain] regarding this as a literary pursuit . . . would not be disposed to view it with jealousy, even if the expiring state of its interest did not render it a matter of indifference"[33]—a surprising statement in view of Yrujo's flat refusal only a few weeks before.

Bemused by Jefferson's adroit presentation, Congress over-whelmingly authorized an inquiry whose extraordinary scope they could not yet anticipate. From then on matters would rest largely in the hands of Meriwether Lewis, mostly because good fortune had brought him onto the scene, with his particular talents, when the opportunity was in the making.

TWO

Preparing for the Future

Fortunately Meriwether Lewis was able to put together the expedition as Jefferson then visualized it, almost free from the bedevilments of urgency. As the future would show, he could not handle certain harassments. But the breaking point did not come during the Napoleonic crisis. First, military pressure in the Mississippi Valley dwindled. The initial contingent of French troops in Santo Domingo was scythed down by yellow fever and frenzied black resistance. Because of the disaster, the fleet Napoleon had designed for occupying New Orleans was shifted to Santo Domingo. The French, it seemed clear, were not likely to move into the Mississippi in the near future. That being true, the British might not be tempted to counterattack out of Canada. And so the need for immediate reconnaissance faded.

Another benison was the cooling off of the Federalists in Congress. Hoping to undercut Jefferson in his political stronghold beyond the Appalachians, the minority party scorned as too little and too late the administration's handling of the deposit affair at New Orleans. They'd end the matter once and for all, they boasted. With Senator Ross of Pennsylvania leading the charge, they introduced resolutions calling for the raising of five million dollars and fifty thousand militiamen for seizing New Orleans from Spain before the transfer to France could be completed.

Appalled, Jefferson's Republicans retorted that so thoughtless an action would precipitate a general war. Besides, the proposal was doubly illegal. It usurped the president's prerogative to handle foreign affairs, and it ignored laws that stated militia could not be sent outside the nation. After considerable hot rhetoric, the resolutions were voted down. At snail's pace Congress returned to discussing the acts Jefferson had recommended in his secret message of January 18—acts for extending both the Indian trading houses and the external commerce of the United States. The measures were passed late in February.[1]

Officially this left Meriwether Lewis preparing to take ten or twelve chosen men westward to test the possibility of drawing furs out of Canada into the United States. There was no tearing hurry about it—not now that military needs had relaxed—but there was a marvelous increase in kinetics. The moment Congress agreed to send a cohesive body of American troops, however small, into the ambiguously held lands beyond the Mississippi, possibilities multiplied. An *American* West: fantasy's new Garden of the Hesperides, where sturdy yeomen would hold true to Jefferson's vision of democracy. Scientific inquiry: the range of the wonders that might be found would set the American Philosophical Society on fire. Commerce: not only in the interior of the continent, but also with busy ports at the far end of some Western river—the fabled passage to India, dreamed of ever since the unexpected land barriers of the New World had frustrated Columbus. All this Jefferson had contemplated for years without making an overt move. Now the time had arrived. Lewis, the expeditor, must have shared the excitement of these almost boundless expectations.

Boundless, but never impulsive, never ill-considered. Even as his ideas grew, Jefferson continued speaking in terms of fewer than a dozen explorers. As late as July 2, 1803, when Henry Dearborn, secretary of war, formally authorized the project, he specifically limited the size of the party, officers included, to twelve.[2] It was Lewis who fudged upward in the memo of requirements he wrote out for himself—fifteen rifles, fifteen knapsacks, fifteen overcoats, and (multiples of fifteen) thirty shirts, thirty pairs of socks, and so on.[3]

The fifteen men would have to be, by his definition, unmarried, robust, persevering, and dependable. Some would have to be hunters, for the party would live almost entirely off the land. Carpenters, ironworkers, and gunsmiths would be welcome, if such talents were available. They might not be. The nation's shrunken army paid its private soldiers five dollars a month, plus another five dollars as a clothing allowance. Such rates did not appeal to skilled men.

Lewis wrote of his requirements to the commanding officers of Fort Massac on the Ohio, Fort Kaskaskia on the Mississippi, and South West Point, near Nashville, Tennessee. (For some unstated reason he thought South West Point would turn out to be the most fruitful source.)[4] To tempt good men into his special service he authorized his correspondents to offer double pay fortified by a promise that those who made the trip could leave the army as soon as the journey was over, though the normal enlistment period was five years. On being mustered out, each would also receive several hundred acres of Western land. If these inducements failed to produce qualified applicants within the army itself, the officers could recruit civilians, offering each the standard twelve-dollar bonus the army paid men who joined the ranks. Except possibly for interpreters, no one could stay a civilian and go along. This was a military undertaking, a hangover perhaps of the original nature of the project. Besides, Meriwether Lewis, professional soldier, believed that success could be guaranteed best by men working under tight army discipline. It was the beginning of a long series of military explorations launched by the United States government.

Finally, Lewis insisted on the right to interview and turn down the volunteers who had been conditionally signed on by the other officers. These choices were vital, and ultimate decisions had to be his.

Having set the size of the party, he made out, over and over again, shopping lists for equipment. Hunting shirts, kettles and cutlery, powder, axes, adzes, chisels, "muscato curtains" (mosquito netting). There had to be barrels and boxes for storage, each with its waterproof covering, and forty yards of oiled linen cut in such a way that it could be used for either tents, coverings for canoes, or sails for a keelboat.

Medicinal supplies were another essential. There was no thought of taking a doctor along. Army regulations allowed only one "surgeon" to each forty-five men. Though the president might have bent the rule, he chose not to. He had lost several of his family, including his wife, to diseases that the doctors had seemed, in his mind, to aggravate rather than cure. Nature, he wrote his friend Caspar Wistar, was the best physician. Men should not experiment "on a machine so complicated and unknown as the human body and a subject so sacred as human life."[5] He would make an appointment for Lewis to consult with Dr. Benjamin Rush of Philadelphia about health rules, but once the group was in the field Meriwether and his ensign, if any, would have to diagnose, prescribe, and administer on their own.

Indian presents clearly would consume more of his initial funds than any other class of supplies. The gifts were not bribes, but unconditional statements, in the Indians' minds, of goodwill and friendship.[6] So down went itemized notations about blue beads and brass buttons, favored as ornaments by the natives; kettles, knives, awls, rings, and burning (magnifying) glasses; tobacco, cloth, and sewing needles; ear trinkets, vermilion, and strips of copper and sheets of tin that could be converted into adornments. He also planned to take along three hand-turned mills for grinding corn, a first step in the civilizing process. Plus several peace and friendship medals of varying sizes and designs, to be passed out to deserving chiefs as tokens of esteem from President Jefferson. The more powerful the chief, the bigger the medal.

For transporting this material he planned on obtaining, at South West Point, a keelboat about sixty feet long, with an eight-ton burden. This would be backed up by a forty-foot "canoe." (He meant *pirogue—canoe* was a misnomer he used consistently. Pirogues were hewn from huge tree trunks; they were far heavier and harder to maneuver than the Indians' birchbark canoes or the nimble craft used by today's recreationists.)

He would float his pirogue and keelboat, loaded with soldiers and supplies, down the Cumberland River to the Ohio, continue to the Mississippi, and ascend that stream to the Missouri, long regarded as *the* gateway to the West.[7]

After his keelboat and pirogue had ascended the Missouri as far as possible, then what? Some theoretical geographers believed that only a short portage—perhaps as little as half a mile—separated the headwaters of the Missouri from those of the Columbia. If that proved true, the pirogue (though not the big keelboat) could be carried and skidded across the divide. The pirogue alone, however, might not be enough for moving the men and supplies to the Pacific. If trees were available along the portage, additional dug-outs could be constructed wherever needed. If ... but he had read somewhere that many miles of treeless plains bordered the upper Missouri. As a precaution he therefore lovingly designed an iron boat frame that could be disassembled into sections and carried in the keelboat until needed. The pieces could then be portaged, along with the pirogue, to the nearest west-flowing stream and there sheathed with either bark or buffalo hide, according to availability. If the portage proved unexpectedly long, then the iron boat alone would have to suffice for the last leg of the journey.

So far he had contemplated, in the main, physical equipment only. But he also had to acquire skills so that during the trip he could gather the kind of scientific knowledge Jefferson wanted. As an example, let us use a book to which the president and his secretary gave concentrated attention: Alexander Mackenzie's *Voyages from Montreal . . . through the continent of North America to the frozen and Pacific Oceans in the years 1789 and 1793 . . .* The two volumes were not published until 1801. Another edition, slightly revised, appeared in Philadelphia in 1802. Quite possibly neither version would have been written if Mackenzie had not felt the need of a powerful propaganda weapon for forcing the British government into revising the nation's fur trade. The point was not lost on Jefferson, but our consideration of the book's ax grinding needs to wait until after we look at some of Mackenzie's intellectual successes—and failures—in fields that deeply concerned the American president.

The Scottish-born trader's primary goal was commercial. (So, ostensibly, was Lewis's.) Hauling supplies by birchbark canoe from Montreal to the foot of the Canadian Rockies was costly and laborious. Great savings would result if Mackenzie could find a navigable river opening into the Pacific, one that could be used for importing trade goods and exporting fur. He made his start, in 1789, from Fort Chipewayan, built near the chill west end of Lake Athabasca primarily for this purpose. Unhappily for himself, he picked the wrong river to probe—today it bears his name, the Mackenzie—and he ended, completely dismayed, among ice floes in the Arctic Ocean. Though he carried a sextant with him, he was not adept at determining latitude with it, and he could not measure longitude at all. Consequently he returned to Fort Chipewayan with only the haziest ideas of where he had been, scientifically speaking. He had learned, however, that between Lake Athabasca and the Arctic Ocean there was no feasible outlet to the Pacific.

To remedy his navigational deficiencies he put his trade in order and then spent the winter of 1791–92 in London studying surveying. He returned to Fort Chipewayan during the spring and summer of 1792 (as André Michaux may well have learned while in Montreal that same season). As soon as the ice broke in 1793, he would try again, this time along a more southerly river, the Peace.

His crew was about the same size as the one Jefferson later proposed—six French voyageurs, two Indians, and an able second-in-command, Alexander Mackay. (Jefferson may well have picked up his notions about size from Mackenzie's account.) Crowded with their supplies in a twenty-five-foot birchbark canoe, the group fought their way up the howling Peace, crossed a high, narrow divide, and descended to a mighty river the local Indians called Tacoutche Tesse. It ran wildly south. Today we know it as the Fraser. But when Mackenzie learned, a little later, that an American seaman named Robert Gray had sailed his ship *Columbia*, on May 11, 1792, into a regal stream farther south, Mackenzie thought he had stumbled onto a higher reach of the same river, named Columbia after Gray's ship.

Warned by the Indians that he could not negotiate the crushing rapids of the Tacoutche Tesse's lower gorge in a canoe, Mackenzie cached the fragile craft for use on his return journey and led his men west, walking at first and then using an Indian canoe. When at last they reached salt water—not the open sea but a long sound—he melted some animal fat he had with him and stirred in a generous pinch of the kind of vermilion Indians used for painting their faces and the parts in their hair. With this red mixture he inscribed on a cliff face, "in large characters, 'Alexander Mackenzie, from Canada, by land, the twenty-second of July, one thousand seven hundred and ninety three,'" a statement Jefferson and Lewis must have read with envy.

More to the point, Mackenzie used his astronomical instruments and skills to find and report, in the *Voyages*, the approximate location of his vermilion boast. Before that, he had fixed the latitude and longitude of Montreal; of Fort William on the northwest shore of Lake Superior, where his boisterous fellow traders of the North West Company held their annual rendezvous; of Fort Chipewayan; and of the narrow divide—a mere 817 paces, or about half a mile—that separated the watershed of the Peace from that of the Tacoutche Tesse (the Columbia, as he believed). After defining those points and hundreds in between he had been able to draw, and publish in the *Voyages*, a map that anyone who wished to cross the continent by canoe that far north could follow.

Jefferson wanted Lewis to produce an equally reliable map of a more southerly and, the president hoped, a far less difficult crossing to the Pacific, for by that time the western sea had ceased being a target of opportunity and was emerging as the expedition's primary goal. This meant training the young man, as Mackenzie had been trained, in the arts of celestial observation. Jefferson could have served as tutor. His book *Notes on Virginia* had contained a map originally produced by his father and later revised by the son. He had been chairman of the committee that had prepared the first draft of the Continental Congress's famed Ordinance of 1784, which had laid down the patterns by which the public lands of the United States were to be surveyed before being opened for sale to purchasers. Of necessity he had done rough and ready surveying around his plantation. We are told, moreover, that out of sheer intellectual curiosity, he often lugged his instruments onto the roof at Monticello, took sightings on a nearby mountain, and, using that as a focal point, happily calculated the latitude and longitude of the surrounding points of interest.[8]

Skills, then, he had. Time was something else. His presidential duties were pressing, and his instruments—none could be had in those days in the nation's swampy capital—were at Monticello. Rather than have them wrapped and sent to him, he taught Lewis theory out of books and invented problems whose solutions depended on the young man's mastery of the printed tables and abstruse formulas used by navigators. Actual practice would have to come later, under the critical eyes of trained astronomers located in busier intellectual centers than Washington.[9]

Alexander Mackenzie's scientific education had gone no farther than practical astronomy. Candidly he stated in the preface to his *Voyages*, "I do not possess the science of the naturalist." Moreover, the toils and perils of his traverse had not given him time "to dig in the earth [or] . . . to collect the plants which nature might have scattered on the way." Lewis would do things differently. He already was gifted with acute powers of observation and a knack for describing in accurate detail what he saw. He knew enough of the flora and fauna in the eastern part of the United States to ignore similar items in the West and thus could concentrate on what was new and different. But he had a folk approach to natural history, not the scientific one that philosophers would expect when he discoursed on the new world's climate, soils, minerals, birds, animals, plants, forests, fishes, and fossils.

Again Jefferson could have served as tutor if time had allowed.

His interest in the physical scene, like that of many cultured men of the time, was obsessive. The philosophy of the Age of Enlightenment pervaded his thinking. The universe, he believed, was an orderly place. A scientist's job (and there was more than a mite of elitism in this, a factor that appealed to Lewis) was to discover that order and fit it into the systematized patterns being developed by the learned men of the time—for example, by the great Swedish botanist and taxonomist, Karl Linné, who Latinized his name to Carolus Linnaeus so that it would accord with the Linnaean system of classification he had originated.

Jefferson fit the mold. He solicited, planted, and carefully noted the development of seeds and cuttings sent him by as many acquaintances in different parts of the world as he could reach. On being elected president of the American Philosophical Society in 1797, he took to his inaugural meeting, as exhibits for his address, a parcel of ancient bones that had been exhumed in western Virginia and sent him for study. He had deduced from the creature's claws that it had been a mighty feline, and he proposed naming it *Megalonyx:* big lion. Actually, as his friend Caspar Wistar showed, the remains were those of a huge, extinct ground sloth. No matter. Because of Jefferson's pioneering work in paleontology, the species was given his name, *Megalonyx jeffersonia,* much as he had been honored a few years earlier by having an American species of the European twinleaf called *Jeffersonia diphylla.* [10] But occasion did not serve for presidential tutoring, and Lewis was scheduled to receive instead a series of crash courses from some of the country's leading savants in Philadelphia.

Finally, underlying and informing all else was the psychological problem of maps. For the sake of his logistics, Lewis needed to accumulate all possible data about distances, topography, and potential enemies he would face on his way west. With Jefferson offering suggestions from time to time, he pored over charts purporting to contain enlightenment. Yet at the very moment of doing this he knew that much of what was offered was based on nothing more than guesswork, dimly understood Indian tales, or academic logic concocted as a substitute for actual observation. On occasion he must have felt completely adrift: how could he stake his success on the reliability of the very charts he was supposed to correct during his travels?

He began his course in map reading with a geographic preconception that had long been a fundamental in American thinking:

The gateway to the setting sun was the Missouri River. This axiom had sprung in part from the sheer power of the river as it flooded into the Mississippi—"like a conqueror," to borrow the words of the early French commentator, Pierre Francois Xavier Charlevoix, who had passed the junction in 1721. Surely such a river came from distant sources, gathering power as it moved east.[11]

Logic added its persuasions. The majestic Ohio and the twin tributaries that formed it, the Monongahela and the Allegheny, provided natural highways, broken by only minor carrying places, from the Mississippi Valley to the Atlantic seaboard. Did it not stand to reason that the equally majestic Missouri would provide comparable routes to the Pacific?

There were Indian tales as well. A notable one occurred in a *History of Louisiana* written by the Charlevoix cited above. In the spring of 1721, at the tiny French mission of Notre Dame de Cascasquios (Kaskaskia) on the Illinois bank of the Mississippi, he encountered a woman of the Missouris tribe who told him, "The Missouri rises from very high and very bare mountains, behind which there is another river, which probably rises there also and runs westward." Charlevoix's *History* was a popular book and went through several French editions and some in English. Jefferson considered the account necessary for good libraries to own, and it is easier to believe that Lewis read it than to suppose he did not.[12]

Once the far western river entered men's imaginings, it began receiving names. An early one came from the pages of a different *History of Louisiana,* this one published in 1763 by Antoine Simon le Page Du Pratz, who had lived beside the Mississippi for twenty-five years. During part of that time an Indian whom he called Moncacht-Apé enthralled him with tales of traveling far up the Missouri and then disembarking to wander happily north across a fertile plain, or perhaps over a low plateau, to a beautiful river flowing gently to the Pacific. (The Ohio, perhaps not coincidentally, was also called La Belle Rivière by the French.)

Now note: Moncacht-Apé did not go *west* over a height of land to La Belle Rivière, as one might assume. No, he walked north, at right angles to the Missouri, until he reached the dreamy river. In other words he (or Du Pratz) acted on the ancient concept of interlocking rivers, that is, the existence of neighboring, parallel streams that flow in opposite directions. Thus if a traveler discovered a short portage from an upbound course to a downward one, he could save many weary upstream miles. No wonder Moncacht-Apé called his "discovery" La Belle Rivière. Jefferson read about the adventure in a copy of Du Pratz's *History* he purchased in Paris. Meriwether Lewis picked up an English edition in Philadelphia and carried it with him to the Pacific and back.[12]

Du Pratz's name La Belle Rivière for the Great River of the West (which itself is a name) was soon supplanted by Ourigan, or Ouragan, or Aurigan, or (as it eventually became) Oregon. The source was Jonathan Carver's *Travels through the Interior Parts of North America in the Years 1766, 1767, and 1768,* published first in 1778. Carver had fought in the French-Indian Wars under the famed ranger Robert Rogers, and afterwards the two had gone to the Great Lakes area to embark in the fur trade. Out of their work came Indian rumors (so Rogers claimed) of a great Pacific-bound river called Ouregan. Carver swiped the name and fitted it into his *Travels,* which sold several editions on both sides of the Atlantic. Jefferson read the tales avidly, and Lewis was surely familiar with them.[13]

But was there really such a river or was it the product of centuries of vaporing? Alexander Mackenzie's 1793 discovery of the Tacoutche Tesse seemed to be the first solid evidence. Hadn't he been knighted for his work? Besides, corroboration came belatedly from two more sources, an English captain, George Vancouver, and an American ship trader, Robert Gray. In 1792 while coursing the Northwest coast in search of sea-otter pelts that could be exchanged in China for tea, spices, and porcelain, Gray had noticed through the mist a set of formidable breakers crashing across a bar that masked the entrance to what was probably a large estuary. Other traders and official explorers, both Spanish and English, had noticed the same tumult but had not wanted to confront it. Gray, though, bulled across and found himself in the mouth of a huge river that he named Columbia, after his ship. He spent upwards of a profitable week trading with the river's Chinook Indians and then sailed north to the west coast of Vancouver Island. There he encountered one of Britain's great navigators, George Vancouver, for whom the island would be named, and told him about the river. Vancouver was one of those who had seen the breakers but had sailed by. Now he decided that as an official explorer of Great Britain, he had better take a more careful look.

The rough waves and shallow water of the bar beat his flagship back, but a small tender commanded by Lieutenant W. R. Broughton broke through. This was October 1792, and the water was low. Gray had been in the estuary during the high water of spring five months earlier, and his descriptions did not tally with what Broughton saw. Convincing himself that the Yankee had never left the saltwater estuary and hence could not be credited with discovering whatever river entered the huge sound (actually Gray had sailed thirty-six miles upstream), Broughton decided to take a hand in the expansion of the British Empire. He ordered some of his men to lower a longboat and row him a hundred miles east and south to the approximate vicinity of today's Portland, Oregon, well within sight of the magnificent snow cones of Mount Saint Helens and Mount Hood, which he named. In the bright moonlight of October 30, 1792, he landed and claimed possession of the entire watershed for his king and country.[14]

Jefferson and Lewis learned all this when the six liberally illustrated volumes of Vancouver's *Voyage of Discovery to the North Pacific Ocean* were published in 1801, the same year Mackenzie's book appeared. They had heard of Gray's discovery, of course, but details were maddeningly vague, for neither the trader nor his mate, John Boit, had yet published a word or drawn a map. Vancouver's work removed the uncertainties and convinced the president and his secretary that a great River of the West did exist, its mouth scientifically located by a trained navigator. Meriwether Lewis was excited enough that he copied, from Vancouver's book, charts depicting the course Broughton had covered in reaching a landmark he had named Point Vancouver.[15]

An unspoken but unsettling corollary followed. The River of the West, La Belle Rivière, the Oregon, the Tacoutche Tesse, the Columbia—whatever it was called—was up for grabs. Spain definitely owned California and might insist that its province extended far enough north to embrace the stream. Mackenzie, it was generally thought, had established a British claim to the upper river and Broughton to its lower reaches. Though Gray had preceded both Britons by a small margin, the effectiveness of his short stays was disputable. A visit by a party traveling overland might help strengthen the American claim to the Northwest, even though occupation rather than mere declarations of possession were considered paramount in disputes over sovereignty.[16]

Another fragment of reality was added to the continent's geography by definite proof, published in 1801 and 1802, that the Missouri River extended much farther north than had been supposed. The key was the earthen, riverside villages occupied by the Mandan and Hidatsa Indians. Bold French explorers, led by the brothers Vérendrye, had visited those settlements in 1738, during a very premature attempt to reach the Pacific overland. After their withdrawal, darkness closed in until a small, loosely organized trade based on Canada's Assiniboine River was introduced during the late 1780s. By chance, Spanish traders out of St. Louis reached the villages shortly thereafter (more of that later) and conflict developed. In order to determine whether the villages lay in Spanish or English territory, the North West Company of Canada sent its chief astronomer, David Thompson, south to make the necessary observations.[17]

He started out in December 1797 with nine men, "fine, hearty, good humoured . . . fond of full feeding, willing to hunt for it, but more willing to enjoy it"—eight pounds of fresh deer, elk, or buffalo meat per man per day. Hoping to do some independent trading, the nine took along four or five heavily laden sleds pulled by thirty wolfish dogs. (Thompson rode a horse.) Temperatures that fell to 32°F below zero stretched a ten-day journey to thirty-three days. For Thompson there were compensations. He had his instruments with him and used the delays to determine "the latitude of six different places and the longitude of three, on the Road to the River."[18]

During his short stay with the Mandanes, as he spelled the name, he grew disgusted with their sexual practices (not so his men; they had agreed to make the trip partly so they could enjoy the rewards of the flesh), but he swallowed his scruples, made anthropological notes about everything he saw, and questioned his hosts in detail about the course of the Missouri above and below the villages. In the process he determined to his own satisfaction that the villages lay in Spanish territory. Whether or not his English superiors would thereafter keep their men out of the area was not his to determine. In February 1798, he returned with his party to their starting point.

Copies of the charts Thompson drew were sent by his company to London. Alexander Mackenzie saw them and used them to indicate, on the map he issued with his *Voyages* in 1801, the short stretch of the Missouri with which Canadian traders were in contact. Another recipient of a copy was Aaron Arrowsmith, a conscientious and able British cartographer who had made a huge map of North America in 1795 and who published thoroughly revised versions in 1801 and 1802. Finally, Edward Thornton, British chargé d'affaires in Washington, apparently got hold of yet another copy of Thompson's map of the Mandan area and loaned it to Thomas Jefferson. Almost certainly Meriwether Lewis traced the chart while waiting for Congress to pass the appropriation bill that would launch the Western reconnaissance.[19]

Those maps, obtained almost simultaneously, gave Lewis the approximate longitude and latitude of three key points along his hypothetical route: St. Louis, the Mandan villages, and the mouth of the Columbia . . . handles on space, so to speak. Because Arrowsmith had known the direction of the Missouri's flow as it left the Indian towns and also as it drove across the present-day state of Missouri into the Mississippi, he had felt free to draw the rest of its lower course with confident, if generalized, strokes. West of the villages, however, Lewis was faced with tantalizing choices that derived, in large part, from an Indian called The Feathers.

The Feathers was a Piegan of the Blackfoot Confederacy. Somewhere in the wastelands he had run into Peter Fidler, a surveyor for the Hudson's Bay Company, who himself was supposed to have ranged south along the Rockies as far as the forty-fifth parallel of latitude, the present boundary between Wyoming and Montana. Using primitive media of some sort—a twig in the earth, a charred stick on a buffalo hide—The Feathers drew for Fidler a chart of the headwaters of the Missouri. It was a crude representation of many channels flowing east, like the veins of a leaf, into one main stem.[20] Fidler sent this data, along with his own observations, to the Hudson's Bay Company. The company allowed Arrowsmith to see them. He refined them to fit his conception of how a river should take shape and transferred the result to the revised 1802 map that Meriwether Lewis studied with almost agonizing care.

A little above the Mandan towns, according to Arrowsmith's conjectures (which he labeled as such by using dotted instead of solid lines), the river forked into two tributaries fed by several smaller streams, as The Feathers had suggested. The tributaries gradually spread apart like the legs of a large, reclining isosceles triangle. A ridge, already known as the Rocky or Stony Mountains, formed the base of the triangle. High points along this mountain base were named: the King in the north, the Heart midway, the Bear's Tooth in the south. The ridge as a whole was represented as rising, on the average, 3,520 feet above the plain.

The altitude was comparable to that of the Blue Ridge Mountains of Virginia, and Lewis probably visualized them as such—heavily forested and creased by many steep-sided rills. It is unlikely that he imagined even the King or the Bear's Tooth as barren peaks, like those described to Charlevoix by the Indian woman at Kaskaskia. Yet did he never wonder why the Western uplift was called the Rocky Mountains?

The Missouri's northern tributary, to which Arrowsmith gave no name, headed at the peak called the King. This brought it close to one of the branches of the South Saskatchewan; this meant it might be used to further Jefferson's plan of siphoning furs out of Canada. On the western side of the King and drawn with a solid line was a fragmentary rendition of a stream called Great Lake River. A dotted line suggested that the Great Lake River continued southwest to join the southern reaches, also portrayed with dots, of Alexander Mackenzie's Tacoutche Tesse. After continuing south for some distance, the combined rivers bent east to join the Oregan (*sic*), whose lower course had been charted for Vancouver by Lieutenant Broughton and hence had been given a solid line by Arrowsmith.

An exciting legend appeared beside the presumed lower reaches of the Great Lake River: "The Indians say they sleep 8 Nights in descending the River to the Sea." Only eight nights after crossing a pass north of the King—a pass that probably did not exceed the half-mile portage Mackenzie had found up where the land was reputedly sterner. Here, indeed, was a way to the Pacific!

But was it any better than the southern branch?

Arrowsmith believed the southern fork to be the main one and had labeled it "River Mississury." If it carried more water than the unnamed north fork, it might be more easily navigated. There was another point. Though the River Mississury ran due west from the Mandan villages to the Bear's Tooth, it received several large southern branches that flowed out of a section bearing the note, "Hereabouts the Mountains divide into several low ridges." So it might be possible for Lewis's party to work through those low hills to some southern tributary of the Oregan. This would enable the explorers to stay in American territory, whereas following the north fork might cause them to trespass on British soil. And if reaching the Oregan by the southern branch proved impossible, they might try the Colorado River instead—it was shown as rising no great distance to the south—and float down it to the Gulf of

California and the Pacific, an option Jefferson himself had suggested.[21]

Secretary of the Treasury Albert Gallatin added to the uncertainties. If Lewis carried with him all the available maps of the trans-Mississippi region, the packet would be unwieldy. Why not have Nicholas King, official surveyor of the city of Washington, combine all relevant data into a single master chart?[22]

King agreed, but in transferring Arrowsmith's data to his own map, he made several revisions. Some arose from different interpretations of the David Thompson material, and some, it would appear, from King's (and Lewis's?) own flights of fancy. He thought the north tributary, left unnamed by Arrowsmith, was the main one, for he labeled it "Missesourie" (it, too, was portrayed with dotted lines) and he shifted the Great Lake River far enough south so that a portage between the two streams would not encroach on British territory. He renamed the dotted southern tributary, which Arrowsmith called the main stem, as the "Lesser Missesourie." He wiped out the low hills south of the Bear's Tooth. Most intriguing of all, he showed a conjectural great southern fork of the Oregan (even he, an American, disdained Gray's name Columbia) sweeping around the southern foothills of the Bear's Tooth, to rise well east of the Lesser Missesourie's headwaters. That is, the Lesser Missesourie and the south fork of the Oregan (if it existed) now interlocked. Lewis's explorers, following the example of Du Pratz's Indian, Moncacht-Apé, could walk readily from one stream to the other without crossing a major divide. Moncacht-Apé, of course, had walked north from the Missouri to La Belle Rivière, but it is not beyond the realm of possibility that the nature of the feat was in King's mind when he produced a similar situation south of the Bear's Tooth. And it was probably thoughts of the Oregan's southern tributary and of possible approaches to the Colorado River that led Jefferson to urge, in his instructions, that Lewis keep a sharp eye on the Missouri's southern confluences.[23]

Choice. Meriwether Lewis had at his fingertips two speculative maps prepared by two of the world's best cartographers from the latest information available. He could not ignore them. Yet which route, if any, could he depend on to take him and his party safely and successfully to their destination? Had not the great Alexander Mackenzie made an almost fatal choice that had spun him off to the sterile ice of the Arctic in 1789? Lewis could afford nothing like that.

These plans for transcontinental exploration were more daring in 1803 than they seem now. France still owned Louisiana and might continue to do so; America's envoys, Livingston and Monroe, had been instructed to dicker only for New Orleans and West Florida. Yet Jefferson wanted to push an American commercial highway across that foreign territory into another area—the Oregon country—to which title was by no means clear. More complications arose from Alexander Mackenzie's recently published *Voyages*. The Scot was less interested in obtaining book royalties than in bending the British government to his will. He concluded his tale by urging Parliament to charter a huge monopoly that could control the entire fur trade of Canada. The proposed firm would introduce goods into the heart of the continent by way of Hudson Bay in the East and the Columbia, over which Britain must spread its sovereignty, in the West. The new company would have the right to dispose of its Western fur harvest in the profitable markets of the Orient without interference from the South Sea or East Indian monopolies. Faced with so much power, America's exploitive ship captains, currently the dominant force in the sea-otter trade of the Northwest Coast, "would instantly disappear," or so Mackenzie argued. Even the beaver trade of the upper Missouri would be lost, for Mackenzie also proposed moving Canada's boundary with Louisiana Territory south from the forty-ninth parallel to the forty-fifth. If all this came to pass what point would there be in the American president and his secretary nosing along speculative river courses and over dreamed-of portages, searching for the Pacific?

There is no way to explain the president's audacity except to believe he was deliberately playing the odds. If the French did occupy Louisiana, there was a possibility they would send the same kind of expedition to the Pacific he was contemplating—and he certainly wanted to beat them to that, for the sake of American glory if nothing else.[24] But there was a much better chance that Napoleon would be unable to move into Louisiana. His armies were stalled in Santo Domingo, and he faced, in Europe, a renewal of his desperate wars against England, as Jefferson correctly sensed. (The new conflict broke out in May 1803.) So the president

was willing to move ahead on the assumption France would not
—could not—interfere.

What of Spain? No formal transfer of territory had taken place.
Hoping perhaps that none would because of Napoleon's other
involvements, the Spanish government might prove as intransi-
gent as Yrujo had predicted when Jefferson had approached him
earlier. In that event, Madrid's longstanding policy of using Louisiana as a buffer to protect Mexico might lead the officials in New
Spain to disregard France's ownership and resist Lewis's "invasion" with force. But New Spain was, in the main, lethargic, and
Jefferson was willing to take that chance, too.

Then there were the Britons, whom Mackenzie was trying to
stir into more empire building in the Northwest. The British were
not averse to such thinking, but in order to turn Mackenzie's
blueprint into actuality, Parliament would have to tread on the
toes of three powerful monopolies, the Hudson's Bay, South Seas,
and East India companies. That the government would do this for
a private entrepreneur's hustling company seemed unlikely to
Jefferson. Furthermore, Mackenzie's own partners in the North
West Company were reluctant, as the president may have known,
to support the Scot's expensive dream, even though some of their
traders were already groping for a new way across the Rockies
from the headwaters of the Saskatchewan.[25] So Jefferson did not
look for immediate objection there, either, and, in fact, probably
warmed himself with the thought that by getting Americans to the
Columbia ahead of the British, he could throw yet another roadblock in Mackenzie's way.

He concealed his audacity by lying about his purposes. Immediately after Congress had passed and he had signed, on February 28,
1803, the act appropriating money for extending the commerce of
the United States, he asked the British and French ministers to
grant passports to Lewis's party.[26] He assured both diplomats that
only the language of the act was devious. Lewis was furthering
science, not commerce or territorial acquisition, and would carry
with him only such merchandise as he needed to mollify suspicious
Indians. The act spoke of commerce, the president said, only because the American Constitution forbade the government's fi-
nancing enterprises devoted to advancing science or promoting
geographical discoveries.

Such statements were a calculated deception. Though Jefferson
did earnestly wish to promote science and geographical knowl-

edge, he also hoped to draw as many furs out of the British area of influence as possible. Developing good will among the Indians while learning trade routes and navigable river systems was essential to the realization of that mercantile goal.

Only the French minister, Louis André Pichon, raised an eyebrow. Inasmuch as Spain still administered Louisiana, he said, was its minister, Carlos Martínez, Marqués de Casa Yrujo, also granting passage? Jefferson evaded the question, saying only, *"Qu'il devait le donner"*: he ought to grant it. He went on with a great show of candor, tracing out Lewis's proposed route on Arrowsmith's map and then lending Pichon the British passport so he could use it as a model in preparing his own.

A final and very strange bit of camouflage was his telling, and ordering Lewis to tell, anyone who noted preparations for the expedition and wondered about its goal that it was bound up the Mississippi.[27] The French and British ministers knew better, as did the Federalists in Congress who had seen the enabling act passed. So why this last cover? No one can be sure. Possibly the president hoped to keep Federalist newspaper editors from raising a commotion about the true nature of the exploration. Perhaps he worried lest Western frontiersmen, feeling they could go wherever an official government party went, might create an incident by trying to follow Lewis into Louisiana. Or perhaps he believed, with his usual predilection for secrecy, that any questionable enterprise needed concealment as a matter of course and acted accordingly.

Whatever the reason, seldom has an expedition of such momentous potentials been prepared for with so little fanfare.

THREE

Grappling with Logistics

After weeks of paperwork, Meriwether Lewis at last felt the touch of the future when, in mid-March, 1803, he reached the U.S. arsenal at Harpers Ferry, Virginia (now West Virginia). There, on the rifle range, above the placid junction of the Shenandoah and Potomac rivers, he was handed one of the brand-new Model 1803, short-barreled, .54-caliber flintlocks that Jefferson's secretary of war, Henry Dearborn, had just adopted as the army's official rifle. He hefted it. Good balance. He tamped in powder, dropped in a ball. Quick, easy loading. Aim. Fire. Commendable accuracy in spite of the short barrel. He must have nodded satisfaction, for the livelihood of his party might depend in large part on the rifles the men carried.

He ordered fifteen guns for fifteen men, together with powder horns, pouches, bullet molds, wipers, and, of utmost importance, spare parts and the special tools needed for repairs. To this requisition he added two dozen large knives and three dozen pipe tomahawks, some for his own party, some as gifts for important Indians. The tomahawks could be used for a peaceful smoke as well as for splitting heads. Handles were hollow and a tobacco bowl was molded solidly onto the heel of the hatchet blade.[1]

What turned into a real monster was the iron boat frame he had designed earlier in Washington. The problem revolved around the detachable sections forming bow and stern. Each had to curve inward to a point while also creating the "sheer line," a curve that runs from the end of a boat's keel up to the tip of the bow and, in the case of the iron nightmare, to the tip of the stern as well. The keel of Lewis's boat was thirty-two feet long. The overall length was thirty-six feet. Therefore each sheer line had to rise two feet two inches, the depth of the boat, within a horizontal distance of two feet even. He used a cord suspended in a curve between two points to show the arsenal boatwrights the line to strive for.

The blacksmiths heated bars of wrought iron until they glowed cherry red and then hammered out long, thin slats that would be supported at intervals by iron stanchions. Bolt holes had to fit exactly so the sections could be assembled and disassembled. Eyelets were also bored along the gunwales and other parts of the frame. After the craft had been put together at a launching point, a lattice of sticks could be added to the frame as support for a cover of bark and/or buffalo hides; the whole could then be drawn tight by cords run through the eyelets. Whether or not the boat was also fitted for a mast, as wooden pirogues were, does not appear.

The construction demanded more time and care than Lewis had anticipated. He hovered anxiously around the arsenal's foundry while the workmen built and fit together one curved end section and one semicylindrical midsection, the latter four feet ten inches of beam and twenty-six inches wide at the bottom. From this partial work he calculated that the completed frame would weigh, without a sheathing, a mere ninety-nine pounds, an easy carriage. Feeling cocky, he named the boat *Experiment*, ordered it finished, and moved on.[2] But in the meantime he had not written a single line to the man who was most interested in hearing from him.

One wonders about the six weeks' delay. Jefferson, and hence Lewis, hoped the expedition would be several hundred miles up the Missouri before winter set in. With that as a goal, they had allotted one week for the work at Harpers Ferry. The president would be expecting regular reports, and Lewis knew it. He sent none, perhaps because he did not wish to create worries while success seemed elusive. He may have feared, too, that if Jefferson learned of the setbacks he would order the experiment abandoned. Or conceivably, the troubles may have put him into such a fit of depression that for a time he could not rouse himself to do much of anything.

Whatever the cause, the president was worried. On April 23, expecting Lewis would be in Philadelphia by then, he addressed a letter to him there, complaining of not having had word of him since March 7. "I have no doubt you have used every possible exertion to get off, and therefore we have only to lament what cannot be helped, as a delay of a month now may lose you a year in the end."[3]

By that time Lewis was in Lancaster, Pennsylvania, home of the surveyor Andrew Ellicott. His first move on arriving was to write Jefferson a long explanation of what he had been up to. Among other things, he stated, he had written many long, important memos to boat builders, recruiting officers, supply agents. (But none to the president.) He had, moreover, triumphed over the difficulties of the iron boat. Yes, he was late, but there was no need to worry. "I still think it practicable to reach the mouth of the Missouri by the 1st of August."[4]

His host, Andrew Ellicott, was one of the friends Jefferson had called on to prepare Lewis for what lay ahead. He was an able cartographer. When Virginia and Maryland had ceded the District of Columbia to the United States to be the new seat of government, Ellicott had surveyed and mapped the area. He had acted as assistant to the city's planner, Pierre Charles L'Enfant, and afterwards had taken several trips to the Mississippi, whose course from the mouth of the Missouri to the gulf he had surveyed more accurately than it had been done before. St. Louis had learned its definitive place on the globe from his calculations.

He did not believe in the kind of crash course Jefferson wanted him to give Lewis. The young man would need patience and practice, he told Jefferson—lots of practice, especially with the instruments used for determining latitude and longitude. This practice he proceeded to give him, working him hard for seventeen days, often after dark. Once again this was more time than Lewis had counted on when drawing up his schedule. And Philadelphia, where he would purchase the bulk of his supplies and receive more tutoring in different subjects, still lay ahead.

He reached the thriving city about May 9 and straightaway began spending the twenty-five hundred dollars Congress had appropriated for the trip. His indispensable helper was Israel Whelen, the government purchasing agent stationed in the city. Working together, they bought upwards of two hundred different items from twenty-eight vendors. More material came from the Schuylkill arsenal just outside the city. Altogether, it was a staggering accumulation, including a $250 chronometer needed for calculating longitude, rough clothing for his men, books on botany and navigation for himself, tools and gun flints, and articles for the

Indians they would meet. Though the last-named items were ostensibly good-will offerings, the heterogeny (its total cost came to $669.50) would also serve as a traveling showcase of the wares the United States was prepared to deliver to the Western tribes in exchange for furs[5]—2,800 fishhooks, 12 dozen pocket mirrors, 22 yards of scarlet cloth, 130 rolls of tobacco, 73 bunches of assorted beads (not enough of them blue, the Indians' favorite color), and on and on. Packing it properly for equitable distribution among an unknown number of potential customers would turn out to be a major problem.

The whites would take along a few specialties of their own. One was 193 pounds of soup concentrate, ordered from cook Francois Baillet at a cost of $289.50. Baillet boiled hunks of beef down to a thick liquid, clarified it with the whites of eggs, added chopped vegetables, and continued boiling until he had obtained a thick paste. He then sealed the stiff goo into lead canisters; after the contents were diluted and eaten, the containers could be melted down and molded into bullets.

Another of Lewis's inspirations was an air rifle specially made for him by Isaiah Lukens, manufacturer of machine tools, dies, medals, watches, and so on. Though the weapon, novel at the time (but not to boys with BB guns today), looked like a long-barreled Kentucky rifle, it was activated by air pumped under pressure into a reservoir in the gun's butt. Firing produced no smoke and only a pop—useful characteristics if one wished to be secretive or to awe the Indians with what seemed another example of "white man's powerful medicine."[6]

Even more curious than soup or airguns to modern readers are the medical supplies on which Lewis spent $94.49, for they reveal the abysmal state of medicine at the opening of the nineteenth century. The captain's adviser in this field was Jefferson's friend, Dr. Benjamin Rush. A native of Pennsylvania, Rush had graduated from Princeton at the age of fifteen. After a hard five-year apprenticeship under a Philadelphia doctor, he crossed the Atlantic to the University of Edinburgh, where he won his M.D. at the age of twenty-two. Returning home, he became the first professor of chemistry in the United States. His institution: the College of Philadelphia, soon to be absorbed by the University of Pennsylvania, which appointed him head of its medical department. He was one of the four doctors who signed the Declaration of Independence; he helped found the country's first antislavery league and was a leading member of the American Philosophical Society. He wrote prodigiously on all manner of subjects. A fluent and popular lecturer, he helped prepare an estimated three thousand doctors for the young United States. The harm they inflicted on the populace is incalculable.[7]

In those days no one had the foggiest notion of bacterial or viral infective agents. An ailing body was cured by draining away the morbidities that had invaded it. "Bad" blood was Rush's particular *bête noir*, as it had been for most physicians since the days of ancient Greece. Using a lancet (a small, sharp-edged, folding knife), he slit a sufferer's vein and let the blood flow into a bowl, where he studied its "diseased" state. Very ill patients were bled until they fainted. Bleeding was also resorted to in the case of dislocated and broken bones; it supposedly reduced muscular tension, thereby making manipulations easier. He practiced what he preached. During Philadelphia's yellow fever epidemic in 1793, he ranged heroically through the city's hospitals, a knife-wielding technician at his heels. When he caught the disease, he bled himself. On other occasions he bled one of his daughters when she was six weeks old and had twice bled a son by the time the infant was two months old. Both children survived—because of the remedies, Rush was sure.[8]

He treated syphilis by applying mercury compounds to lesions in the mouth. (Mercury, we now know, is a poison.) The resulting painful salivations, he believed, took away the ailment. Making a patient vomit was a cure for a wide variety of ills, and was often accompanied by bleeding. He ended constipation with his famed bilious pills, compounded out of calomel (which contains mercury) and jalap. The concoctions were popularly, and appropriately, known as Rush's Thunderbolts.

In following his recommendations, Lewis filled a specially made chest with 1,300 doses of physic, 1,100 doses of emetics designed to induce vomiting, 3,500 pills to cause sweating, and various drugs for increasing salivation and kidney output. Less harmful were 15 pounds of pulverized Peruvian bark, at a cost of $30 (it contained quinine for soothing malaria), and 30 gallons of strong spirit wine that could be diluted and spooned into patients as medicine. Instruments included lancets, a clyster syringe for enemas, and four pewter penis syringes for urethral irrigations for the relief of gonorrhea.[9]

To these cures Rush added written suggestions for maintaining health. Do not march when indisposed (though the men had a continent to cross) but rest in a *horizontal* position (Rush's emphasis). Use spirits for washing tired feet; take internally no more than three tablespoonfuls of liquor to refresh a chilled or weary body. At mealtime try water laced with molasses and a few drops of sulphuric acid. During difficult and laborious enterprises, *eat sparingly*. Wash your feet every morning with *cold* water. Beware of constipation.[10] In the event, the last admonition was the only one followed.

Rush also suggested, at Jefferson's request, some of the things Lewis should concentrate on while studying Indians. What diseases did they have? ("Is the bilious fever ever attended by a black vomit?") What remedies do they use? At what age do women begin and cease to menstruate? Take a sampling of pulse rates of both children and adults morning, noon, and night. What about their bathing habits? Do they ever commit suicide for love? Is murder common? Do they sacrifice animals during their worship? How do they dispose of their dead?[11]

Robert Patterson's advice about surveying—he was professor of mathematics at the University of Philadelphia—was far more practical than Rush's about health. Only a hint of it has survived, however, in a problem in astronomy he sent Jefferson, saying it was a sample of the training he would give Lewis. Elementary, he described it, "easy even to boys or common sailors of but moderate capacity," whereupon he filled several sheets of paper with figures and formulas. He also recommended certain statistical tables the explorer should take with him to speed his calculations.[12] Just learning to use those was something of a feat for a young man already overloaded with considerations.

At Jefferson's behest two more of the university's professors added their bits, Dr. Benjamin Smith Barton, a physician and naturalist, and Caspar Wistar, the professor of anatomy. Barton presumably helped Lewis with taxonomy and recommended texts, including his own famed *Elements of Botany*, which Lewis purchased for six dollars, a high price for a book in those days. Wistar perhaps made suggestions about fossils, a field in which he was skilled, but since neither man's offerings were put into writing, this is mostly guesswork. Nor is it written anywhere that Lewis visited, for purposes of study, Charles Willson Peale's natural history museum, the first of its kind in the United States and located, at that time, in Independence Hall, but it would be most uncharacteristic if he had overlooked the opportunity.

In spite of, perhaps because of, his busy days, Lewis enjoyed Philadelphia. He was associated with important men who clearly liked him, and he was in charge of an enterprise whose successful completion conceivably could bring him lasting fame. When night fell, he was able to turn to diversions he had grown accustomed to in Jefferson's household—stimulating company, handsome women, good talk. His guide to Philadelphia's social scene was Mahlon Dickerson, an entertaining young lawyer and future senator (1817–33) whom he had first met at the White House. They dined together several times, paid calls on various young ladies, and were guests two or three times at the home of Thomas McKean, governor of Pennsylvania. There Lewis again encountered McKean's handsome, curly-haired son-in-law, the Marqués de Casa Yrujo, Spain's minister to the United States.[13]

Undoubtedly Lewis learned that largely through Yrujo's efforts the right of shippers to deposit their cargoes at New Orleans, a right whose revocation had helped precipitate the expedition, had been restored. It is less certain whether Yrujo learned from Lewis that the expedition into Upper Louisiana, for which he had refused to grant passports, was going ahead anyway. In time to come the ambassador would object so constantly to Jefferson about his actions concerning Louisiana that the exasperated president would demand his recall.[14] Affairs had not reached that pass in May, however, and the meetings passed without jangle, though perhaps with cat-and-mouse games for information that Lewis, holding the upper hand, would have enjoyed.

Another satisfaction came from the solution of a nagging problem about transportation. His initial plan had been to launch the expedition from South West Point, Tennessee, close to the Cumberland River, a major tributary of the Ohio. But Congressman William Dickson of Tennessee, whom he had counted on to arrange for a keelboat and pirogue, had not answered his letters, and Major William McRae, who had been delegated to enlist, on approval, personnel for the expedition, wrote that a sufficient number of qualified men could not be found among the riffraff at the Point.

Meanwhile supplies were piling up in Philadelphia—twenty-seven hundred pounds, with another eight hundred or so waiting to be picked up at Harpers Ferry for transport across the mountains. The agent responsible, under government contract, for moving all public freight from the Atlantic to the trans-Appalachian area was one William Linnard. He knew roads, boatyards, and military installations. During discussions about the supplies, Lewis and he decided to switch the expedition's departure point from Tennessee to Pittsburgh, where the Allegheny and Monongahela rivers join to form the Ohio. Lewis ordered a five-horse outfit for the hauling, and dashed off a letter to the boatyard Linnard recommended, specifying the kind of craft he wanted and asking, overoptimistically, that it be ready for departure by July 20.[15]

By this time he was eager to be on the move. Except for a few more astronomical lessons from Robert Patterson, he had completed what he had been ordered to do, and instructions from Jefferson about the aims of the expedition as a whole were already at hand. Ostensibly a guide for Lewis as he marched west, this remarkable document was also the president's statement to history about the purpose of the quasi-secret, quasi-illegal mission he was about to send on its way. Into it he poured all that had piqued his encyclopedic curiosity during decades of interest in the American West. He did not let the orders rest on his musings alone. Having finished a rough draft, he sent copies to his cabinet members for suggestions.

Only Albert Gallatin and Levi Lincoln, the attorney general, had responded at length. Gallatin, remembering military reconnaisance as the original motive behind the expedition, did not want that element dropped, even though the right of deposit had been restored. The antagonistic nations of Europe still might carry their warfare into the Mississippi Valley. Lewis, therefore, should acquire "a perfect knowledge of the posts, establishments & force kept by Spain in upper Louisiana," and of the trails British traders used in reaching the Missouri. For the day might come when the United States would have to seize the area from its French owners and Spanish caretakers to "prevent G.B. from doing the same." His reasoning? The Missouri country was bound to be settled eventually "by the people of the U. States." It followed that Lewis should determine the area's boundaries, particularly southward toward Spanish New Mexico, and then examine the land not only for military purposes and scientific knowledge but also for its ability to support a large population. Here indeed was the voice of manifest destiny, unnamed yet but ringing clear.[16]

Levi Lincoln was more concerned with practical politics. Jefferson's opponents, the Federalists, remained "perverse, hostile, and mali[g]nant." To blunt their barbs, which would be especially sharp if the expedition failed, Lewis's instructions should be given, so far as was possible, a high moral tone. He should be advised, for instance, to determine how the Indians' religious and ethical standards could be improved—that is, made more like those of white Protestants. Who could fail to approve of that? Then he added a cautionary note. Meriwether Lewis was inclined to be rash and stubborn. He should be warned that if crises arose along the way, he should retreat rather than charge headlong.[17]

After incorporating both men's ideas into a new draft, Jefferson sent it to Philadelphia for further comments by Lewis's tutors and by Lewis himself. Reactions were enthusiastic. The only suggestion from any Philadelphian, and that one by implication only, was for the addition of Dr. Rush's queries to the other Indian material.

The primary object of the mission, the president wrote (his instructions are printed in full in appendix I) was to explore the Missouri and any adjoining Pacific stream that offered "direct and practicable communication across the continent for the purpose of commerce." Mapping was to be detailed and exact. To prevent loss of valuable material, copies of the celestial observations were to be entrusted to several trustworthy men; ". . . one of those copies [should] be on the paper of the birch, as less liable to injury from the damp than common paper." (There is no indication that such a copy was made; birch bark was not handy in the regions the men traversed.)

Since another aim of the expedition was to lay the groundwork for a profitable commerce with the Western Indians, Lewis should take pains to learn as much as he could about them—tribal names, vocabularies, populations, tribal boundaries, relations with other groups of Indians, occupations, diseases, life styles, and morals. He should always deal with the natives in a conciliatory manner, assuring them of the desire of the United States "to be neighborly, friendly & useful to them. . . . Confer with them on the points most convenient as mutual emporiums"—by which the president meant government-operated trading factories. He should arrange, if possible, to have influential chiefs visit the United States to see for themselves its power and richness. He should take with him "kine pox," a vaccine for smallpox, a disease to which Native Americans were particularly susceptible, and explain its use. In event of opposition by any "nation" (did Jefferson mean Spain or England as well as Indian tribes?) he must give way. "In the loss of yourselves, we should lose also the information you will have acquired."

Back to commerce: Lewis should investigate the possibility of diverting down the Missouri and into the U.S. the furs currently being sent to the West Coast for barter with ship traders. Most of those fur gatherers were Americans, but a cross-country route would be preferable to the long sea voyages around Cape Horn or the Cape of Good Hope.

And the end was not yet. Lewis was to bring back scientifically oriented reports on the topography, soil, climate, vegetation, animals, and minerals of the land he crossed. He should learn what he could of the southern tributaries of the Missouri and their connection, if any, with the Rio Grande and the Colorado River. He should discover, too, the routes Canadian traders used in reaching the Missouri.

As for getting home again, he should consider retracing his outward path, checking his original observations along the way, but only after sending two couriers East by sea—if a ship turned out to be available. If the outward journey had been "eminently dangerous," all could return by sea, again if a trading ship could be contacted. He would be given open letters of credit with which to buy fresh new clothes for his men and pay for the long ocean voyage. Lastly, after becoming acquainted with his group, he should name the most dependable among them to be his successor in the event of his being incapacitated or dying along the way.

With those awesome charges in mind—the final draft would be drawn up after the last suggestions had been received—Lewis returned to Washington, arriving sometime in early June.[18] There he learned of astounding news from France, where the American ambassador, Robert Livingston, and Jefferson's special envoy, James Monroe, had been seeking to obtain New Orleans and West Florida from Napoleon. During the talks the Duc de Talleyrand and François de Barbé-Marbois, head of the French treasury, had suddenly asked whether the United States would be interested in acquiring not pieces of Louisiana but *all* of it.

Napoleon's affairs had come to a crisis. His Santo Domingo adventure, during which his brother-in-law, General Charles Leclerc, had died of yellow fever, had collapsed. A renewal of war with England was imminent. Finally, Bonaparte wanted to impress history by reforming the unwieldy structure of the French government. Restoring France's New World empire, in short, had become irrelevant, and the first consul was willing to give up the enormous territory he had wrenched from Spain only two and a half years earlier for a mere one hundred and twenty million francs—this despite his promise to Carlos IV that he would never sell the territory, least of all to the United States.

Unable to conceal their astonishment, the American envoys stammered they had no authority to make such a purchase. How sad, Barbé-Marbois murmured to Livingston. For when war broke out, as assuredly it would, British naval forces in the Caribbean most probably would seize New Orleans for their nation, as a step toward Canada and the eventual boxing in of the Americans between the Atlantic and the Mississippi. In order to prevent such a disaster would it not be well to seize the initiative—and quickly, since Napoleon would not wait?

Late in the night of April 12, 1803, Livingston hurried to his desk in the American legation, and, writing feverishly until 3:00 A.M. on the 13th, described the situation in a long dispatch to Secretary of State James Madison. He and Monroe, he said in effect, had no choice but to go ahead with the negotiations, holding the price to as low a figure as they could.[19]

So affairs stood when Meriwether Lewis reached Washington. Luck again! Pure, shining luck! His expedition, which had been designed to pussyfoot ambiguously around in someone else's territory, showing off its wares to Indians attached commercially to other nations, suddenly was on the edge of achieving real historic status as the first Americans to explore officially the almost totally unknown lands beyond the Mississippi. American lands, for surely Jefferson would not repudiate the negotiations now. The purchase completed, a new gloss would inform every mile Lewis traveled. Every item of knowledge he acquired would be American knowledge, for the use of generations of Americans still to come.

Americans as far west as the Pacific? Why not? Louisiana certainly embraced the headwaters of the Missouri in the north and possibly reached even to the Rio Grande in the south. Territory beyond these limits might well fall into his country's hands through what was sometimes called the principle of contiguity—especially if he and his handful of men found a river that would let them link their overland discoveries to those made eleven years earlier by Robert Gray, when he had sailed his ship into the mouth of the Columbia on May 11, 1792.

Sea to shining sea! And he was on hand with his head crammed with astronomical formulas, his medicine chest with pills, and his packing boxes with Indian goods, ready to make the most of his fortune . . . provided something had not happened in Paris to end the negotiations before the purchase was completed. Suspense gnawed at him. If only transatlantic communications weren't so slow!

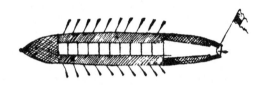

FOUR

Trial Run

The agreement whereby the United States obtained "the Colony or Province of Louisiana, with the same extent that it now has in the hands of Spain," was completed on April 30, 1803. Since mail took, on the average, six weeks to travel from Paris to Washington, the first unofficial word of the transfer presumably reached the White House about the middle of June. Its arithmetic was startling. Livingston and Monroe had whittled Napoleon's asking price down from 120 million francs to 80 million—60 for the territory itself plus another 20 million to be paid by the U.S. Treasury to American citizens who held claims against France for damages incurred during the undeclared naval war of 1798–1800.

This amounted, in U.S. money, to about $11,250,000 for Napoleon and $3,750,000 in claims. Total, $15 million, in round figures, for roughly 828,000 square miles—or a little under 3 cents an acre. During the same period the U.S. Land Office was selling off the public domain to settlers and speculators for $2 per acre. (There are 640 acres in one square mile.) So it was a dazzling bargain. Even counting interest payments on the bonds issued to Napoleon in payment for the territory, the full cost for doubling the size of the nation came to only $23,213,567.73.[1]

The extraordinary value of the purchase was, of course, scarcely glimpsed at the time. The Federalists, Jefferson correctly surmised, would argue strenuously that Louisiana was not worth the price. To cast ahead: one disgruntled New Englander complained that $15 million was the equivalent of 433 tons of solid silver; a wagon train capable of moving the mass would stretch out 5 1/3 miles. Senator Harrison Gray Otis of Massachusetts brayed, "I would rather the Mississippi were a running stream of burning lava, over which no human being could pass, than that the treaty should be ratified."[2]

More prescient Northeasterners pointed out that the acquisition could be divided into so many states that political power would shift west and south, to the detriment of the Atlantic seaboard. Of more import to Jefferson, a strict Constitutional constructionist, was the argument that the Constitution nowhere provided for the purchase of foreign territory or its incorporation into the body of the union. Finally, there was Spain, concerned not with the monetary value of the province, but with the loss of a buffer against avaricious Americans. Predictably, the Spanish minister, Jefferson's one-time friend, the Marqués de Casa Yrujo, reiterated over and over that the transfer was illegal: Napoleon had promised not to let any part of Louisiana fall into American hands.

Jefferson sought for and found rebuttals to the contentions. A main part of his political base was in the West and South, and he did not grieve over the New Englanders' discomfiture. Yrujo was brushed aside with the retort that agreements made between France and Spain were of no concern to the United States. (Nevertheless, the possibility that resistance to the transfer might boil up in New Orleans led the administration to ask the governors of Mississippi, Tennessee, Kentucky, and Ohio to have their militia ready if need be.)[3] Meanwhile Jefferson's cabinet talked away his worries about the Constitution: the right to govern a territory surely implied the right to acquire it, and Jefferson was pragmatic enough not to let philosophic scruples prevent him from securing for the nation a good that might never again be attainable.[4] As for value, he was personally convinced that the West would eventually be peopled by Americans devoted to his style of agrarian democracy. Yet he wanted to justify the purchase by pointing to a more immediate gain. One notion that occurred to him was the possibility of using Louisiana to help solve the stubborn Indian problem in the region north of the Ohio River and east of the Mississippi.

The Indians there still held title to hundreds of thousands of acres that white tillers of the soil were eyeing with increasing covetousness. He had hoped that once the Native Americans had learned agriculture and such handicrafts as weaving and sewing, they would realize they did not need great expanses of hunting grounds and would be willing to cede part of it, at a fair price, to the nation. Not all the red men were willing to abandon their old ways, however, and they exerted enough influence on the rest to block the signing of the necessary treaties. Louisiana might end this impasse. Let the Indians who wanted to retain their hunting culture swap Eastern lands for others beyond the Mississippi. Jefferson grew so enthralled with the notion that he envisioned the northern reaches of Louisiana as a huge reservation protected from white trespassers by an Indian cavalry patrolling the west bank of the great river. In short, get the East solidly settled first, with both red and white families, and then slowly duplicate the program west of the Mississippi in a wilderness so extensive he thought it could not be filled for centuries.[5]

Before the program could be initiated, all whites—French, Spanish, and Americans—currently living in St. Louis and other towns and farms of the Missouri country would have to be persuaded to vacate their homes and find, with government aid, new dwellings east of the Mississippi. Examining the feasibility of this exchange became yet another chore the president heaped, on the spur of the moment, onto the already overburdened shoulders of Meriwether Lewis—overburdened because what had begun as a reconnaissance had abruptly ballooned into a diplomatic mission charged with carrying word of the shift in sovereignty to every Indian tribe and foreign trader within reach from the Missouri River.

As the president and his secretary grew aware of the expedition's increased significance, they reexamined the paragraph in Lewis's instructions that directed him to appoint a possible successor from his party's ranks, after it was already on the march. Reports from recruiting officers indicated that there might not be anyone among the volunteers qualified for leadership. Would it not be wise to select a suitable second-in-command before the group set out?

Whether Jefferson or Lewis first proposed William Clark cannot be said with certainty. They both knew him. He was the sixth son and ninth child of a family of ten children.[6] Clarks had long farmed and soldiered in Virginia, part of the time in Albemarle County, home of both Jefferson's and Lewis's progenitors. Before William's birth, however, his family had moved close to tidewater on the Rappahannock River. Red-headed William Clark was born there on August 1, 1770, which made him four years and two and a half weeks older than Meriwether Lewis.

Five of the Clark boys fought in the Revolution. The one best remembered now was George Rogers Clark, who commanded Virginia's troops in the Kentucky region while Thomas Jefferson was serving as Virginia's governor. In 1784, after the war was over, the entire Clark family crossed the Allegheny Mountains and floated down the Ohio to Mulberry Hill, just outside of Louisville. During and after the migration a strong bond developed between George Rogers and William, with the older training the younger meticulously in natural history and wilderness skills but failing signally to do much about his grammar and spelling.

In 1789, aged nineteen, six feet tall, and heavily muscled, William joined the Kentucky militia. Afterwards he transferred to the regular army. It was a strenuous time. As a lieutenant he drilled his men hard, and learned how to build forts, draw maps, lead pack trains through enemy country, and fight the Indians on their ground. Twice he was sent on secret missions to spy on the Spanish, who during the first half of the 1790s were pushing their fortifications and wooing the Indians as high up the east bank of the Mississippi as they dared go. On his return from the last of these missions, in November 1795, Lieutenant Clark was put in charge of a select company of riflemen at Fort Greenville, Ohio. Shortly thereafter, Ensign Meriwether Lewis, fresh from the lackluster contention known as the Whiskey Rebellion, joined the group.

The two learned to respect each other while keeping their blue-ribbon company smartly drilled. During off-hours they undoubtedly went hunting together and, as dark closed in, swapped stories, revealed ambitions, and on occasion perhaps drank too much in the officers' quarters. But not for long. Peace, boredom, ill health, and his brother George's losing struggles with alcohol and debt led William to resign his commission and rejoin his brother at Clarksville, Indiana, just across the river from Louisville.

Lewis and he kept their contact alive by occasional letters and rare visits while Meriwether was still serving in the Ohio country and later in Washington when Clark dropped by on family business. On one of those visits the Westerner was introduced by Secretary Lewis to President Jefferson. Surely, too, the president remembered receiving, on January 7, 1803, a letter from doughty old George Rogers Clark, answering certain military questions. On closing, George recommended young William as "well quallified almost for any business of Honor and profit in this [Western] country.... I am sure it gives you pleasure to have it in your power to do me a Service ..."—a remark certain to remind the president of how shamefully the state of Virginia had treated George Rogers by refusing to honor drafts he had signed during the Revolution. So five months later, when the question of a second-in-command arose, the name William Clark was close to both men's tongues.

Whatever the details, Lewis did make an offer to Clark on June 19. The letter's structure is worth noting.[7] After touching first on a personal business matter, he threw out a hook to keep Clark reading: *what follows is secret.* Congress had sanctioned the exploration of North America, and the president had entrusted him, Meriwether Lewis, with the enterprise. "I have the most ample and hearty support the government can give," plus "liberal passports from the Ministers both of France and England." (Nothing about Spain.) He outlined his personnel needs and urged Clark to keep an eye open for likely recruits. He summarized his travel plans—"I do not calculate on geting further than two or three hundred miles up the Missourie before the commencement of the ensuing winter." He mentioned, again with adjurations of greatest secrecy, the expectation that the United States would obtain the entire western watershed of the Mississippi, including the Missouri, "in less than 12 Months from this date." It was vital, therefore, to achieve "an early friendly and intimate acquaintance with the tribes that inhabit that country, that they should be early impressed with a just idea of the rising importance of the U. States." Scientific goals, he added, were also involved.

And then, having presumably excited Clark with envy over the great good fortune that had befallen him, Lewis came to the point. "If therefore there is anything ... in this enterprise, which would induce you to participate with me in it's fatiegues, it's dangers and it's honors, believe me there is no man on earth with whom I should feel equal pleasure in sharing them as with yourself." He meant sharing in its fullest sense. The president, he wrote, promised Clark a permanent commission as captain, with all the benefits that went with the rank. "Your situation will in all respects be precisely such as my own."

The guarantee was Lewis's way of handling a ticklish situation.

Clark was his friend. Lieutenant Clark had also been his commanding officer at Fort Greenville on the Ohio seven years earlier. It
would be awkward for both if Lewis suddenly became his superior
during a long journey with a small group of enlisted men who
would be quick to notice each nuance of feeling, however small,
between the commanders. To obviate the friction before it developed, Lewis won Jefferson's promise to jump Clark a full rank
above the one he had held on leaving the army. Precise equality—
if Clark accepted. He might not. Therefore, when Jefferson issued
Lewis his final draft of instructions on June 20, he let stand the
provision about choosing a second-in-command from among the
enlisted men.[8] As a matter of collateral interest, it is clear from the
president's later letters to the expeditionary force that he never
really considered Clark to be Lewis's military equal. This expedition, which he had conceived and put into motion, stayed Lewis's
in the president's mind. Just as clearly, Lewis himself never felt the
least superiority.

The offer made, Lewis asked Clark to reply to him at Pittsburgh,
where a specially built keelboat would be waiting. Using seven or
eight soldiers being transferred to the South as crewmen, he would
float downstream to the Falls of the Ohio, between Louisville and
Clarksville. There he would pick up Clark and whatever recruits
for the Northwest his new co-captain had enlisted. He expected to
arrive early in August.

On May 30, the Boston newspapers broke the story of the Louisiana Purchase. The *National Intelligencer* of Washington followed
on July 4, giving a special fillip to that holiday. But newspapers
weren't treaties, and until Jefferson held the actual documents in
his hands he was not going to move openly. When Lewis left
Washington on July 5, there was no fanfare, and he still acted as
if he were bound for the upper Mississippi with no more than the
dozen men authorized by Secretary of War Dearborn on July 2.
But there was another order, also dated July 2, wherein the secretary directed the commanders at Fort Kaskaskia, Illinois, "to furnish a Sergeant and Eight good men who understand rowing" to
haul some of Lewis's provisions as high up the Missouri as they
could go and still return before the onset of ice.[9] This authorization of an additional boat, even if it went only partway to the
Pacific, is the first concrete sign that the administration was begin-

ning to realize that Lewis's assignment was going to demand more muscle than the small reconnaissance party first contemplated could produce.

Lewis's long road West led him first to Harpers Ferry—and a good thing it did. The teamster who was supposed to pick up the iron boat frame, new-model rifles, knives, tomahawks, and other material waiting there had failed to do so. Lewis had to spend two days finding substitute transportation. But there was compensation. During the wait he tested the rifles. They performed beautifully, and he was relaxed as he rode on to Pittsburgh—two hundred and fifty miles in six and a half days, his new, 150-pound, black Newfoundland dog, Seaman, trotting beside his horse.[10]

He approached the town in high anticipation, for Pittsburgh was, in a very real sense, the true start of his journey of exploration. Here the supplies he had ordered in the East would be brought together for embarkation. Here, if he was lucky, he might pick up two or three enlisted men who met the exacting qualifications he had in mind—young, unmarried, enduring men, powerfully muscled for the work of pushing the keelboat upstream with oars, setting poles, and tow rope.

Much depended on that keelboat. Lewis had sent his order to Pittsburgh—the name of the contractor does not appear in the records—as soon as he had decided not to make South West Point, Tennessee, his jumping-off place, and he expected the boat to be all but ready for loading when he reached the headwaters of the Ohio. There is some evidence that he had even specified two masts, a highly unusual feature for a keelboat[11]—just as the iron boat he had ordered at Harpers Ferry was unusual in its way. Otherwise the boat was standard: fifty-five feet long, eight feet, four inches wide. A high cabin in the stern would house some of the men and some of the goods. Another covered hold filled the bow. The rowers would occupy the open space amidships.

After finding his lodgings about 2:00 P.M. on July 15, Lewis dashed off a note to Jefferson and wandered off in search of Lieutenant Moses Hooke, who, as assistant military agent for supplies, was to receive the material from the East and oversee its transfer to the keelboat. A good man, young Hooke. He was a member of Lewis's own regiment, the First Infantry, and the two had grown friendly during Hooke's recent tour of duty in Washington. Quite likely he was the one who told Lewis that the keelboat, ordered for July 20, was nowhere near completion.

Lewis stormed to the boatyard. True enough: only a skeleton stood on the ways. Two rows of timbers curved up a few feet, like a whale's ribs, from the four-by-four beam, the keel, that ran down the boat's center line and was sturdy enough, supposedly, to absorb the shock of hitting submerged rocks and logs. A few planks had been nailed and tied to the ribs on one side. That was all.

The contractor, his breath fetid with whiskey, met him with that impression of mingled candor and offended dignity that habitual drunks know so well how to use. He'd had trouble getting good timber, he said. But depend on it, Lewis would have the boat by the end of the month. The captain silently added five days to the estimate, eyed the dropping levels of the water—1803 was a drought year; no one in town could recall such low water—and settled back to wait as patiently as he could.

Pittsburgh in those days was not conducive to patience. Summer doldrums lay on the brick houses lining the narrow, grubby streets, on the boatyards and warehouses crowded close to the banks of the uniting Allegheny and Monongahela rivers, and on the small inns and dark grogshops that catered to teamsters who hauled in Eastern merchandise for transshipment down the Ohio to the Mississippi. During spring, when the rivers were high, farmers poured in with corn, flour, hams, salted butter, whiskey, and brandy, all in demand at New Orleans. Hammers rang on bar iron of local make, and visitors stopped by to see the town's nail factory, the first in America.

Little of that activity was visible in July. Every morning Lewis visited the boatyard, trying to keep the contractor sober and his workers busy. He made sure each timber destined for the boat was sound, and held forth at length on the need for thorough caulking. When he could no longer endure that, he wandered through the town, yarned with Hooke, climbed a nearby hill to see a prehistoric Indian mound, and read until it was threadbare a copy of *The Navigator*, a pilot's manual for the Ohio, updated annually by an enterprising Pittsburgh printer, Zodak Cramer.[12]

Glumly he received, on time, the wagonload of supplies from Harpers Ferry and the seven soldiers who were to act as his crew as far as Fort Massac. (Called Fort Massacre by troops for no particular reason except the sound of the word, Massac was located on the Illinois side of the Ohio, and eight miles downstream from the mouth of the Tennessee River, where many years later William Clark would lay out the town of Paducah, Kentucky.) The bitterness caused by the timely arrivals for whom no boat awaited was increased on July 22 by a letter from Jefferson. Copies of the Louisiana Purchase treaty, the president wrote, had reached Washington.[13] The agreement still had to be confirmed by the Senate, and the House still had to authorize bonds enough to pay for the acquisition, but history was marching—and there Lewis sat, the captive of a drunken boatbuilder.

Even harder on his nerves was the lack of word from Clark, to whom he had written more than a month earlier. Fearful that some disaster might have befallen his friend, he decided that while there was still time to exchange letters with Washington, he should seek authority to enlist Moses Hooke to take Clark's place. But then the sun brightened. On July 29 in came the letter Clark had written in response to Lewis's offer—a letter that had gone to Washington before overtaking Lewis in Pittsburgh. Another note soon followed. Clark was delighted: "My friend I do assure you no man lives with whome I would perfur to undertake Such a Trip &c as your self." Moreover, he was already recruiting a few men of the caliber he assumed Lewis would want.[14]

On August 3 Lewis responded with equal fulsomeness: "I could neither hope, wish, or expect from a union with any man on earth, more perfect support or further aid . . . than that, which I am confident, I shall have from being associated with yourself." He predicted, overoptimistically, that he would greet Clark at the Falls of the Ohio by the end of the month.[15]

Not a chance—not with that boatbuilder. Balked by the man's apparent immovability, Lewis contemplated buying enough pirogues to float his supplies downstream until he could find another keelboat he could buy. Local merchants dissuaded him; the odds were strongly against a suitable craft being available at that time of year, even in St. Louis. In order to make sure of going up the Missouri at all, he would have to wait on the man he had unfortunately chosen by mail.[16]

The contractor's drinking and constant wrangling with his shifting crew of workers dragged on and on. To make use of his time, Lewis let slip word of his undertaking. (Until then he had been using the fabrication of a trip up the Mississippi.) Volunteers began applying for places. After telling each one that enlistment in the army was a prerequisite—it carried a twelve-dollar bonus with it—Lewis carefully interviewed those who agreed to accept the condition. Finally he chose three to go downriver with him on a trial run—no guarantees attached.

One of the three probably was George Shannon, either sixteen or eighteen years old. (His birth year is given variously as 1785 and 1787; in either event, he turned out to be the youngest member of the expedition.) His father, an Ohioan, had recently died and George seems to have been on his reluctant way to Pennsylvania to join his mother's family when the prospect of adventure in the West diverted him. Another of the Pittsburgh trio may have been that future maker of heroic mountain-man legends, John Colter, then about thirty years old, as strong as and considerably more nimble than an ox.[17] The indefiniteness about these men and the others who would be enlisted later is frustrating, and it reaches to the Pacific and back. Neither Lewis nor Clark wrote much about their men, or, for that matter, about each other, perhaps because they were oppressed by too many other duties.

Lewis's unrelenting persistence finally speeded up the boatmen. Meanwhile water levels dropped and dropped. According to reports from farther downstream, only six inches covered some of the bars he would have to cross, yet his keelboat, when loaded, would draw close to three feet. To lighten it, he hired two wagons to haul part of the cargo as far as Wheeling, where he expected to find better depths.[18] When the wagons proved insufficient, he added a third carrier, a craft he called a "canoe," probably a dugout made from the trunk of a cottonwood tree, but possibly a batteau, an oversized rowboat nailed together from planks.

At 10:00 A.M. on August 31, the travelers cast off for the start of their eleven-hundred-mile journey to the Mississippi. In addition to Lewis, the keelboat and its auxiliary craft carried the three volunteers whose suitability for the larger adventure was being tested, seven soldiers bound via Fort Massac to Fort Adams in Mississippi Territory, and a pilot hired for seventy dollars to take the boat through the river's shallow, shifting channels as far as the Falls of the Ohio, near Louisville.[19]

As Lewis had been warned to expect, the hardest part of the journey was the hundred miles (sixty-five by wagon) to Wheeling. The Ohio is indeed a beautiful river, but its course is serpentine and it is dotted with many islands, some of which in Lewis's day were the sites of prosperous orchards. Immense forests broken by frequent natural clearings covered the banks. Oaks, ash, and a scattering of pines flourished on the upper terraces; willow, honey locust, and hickory filled the bottoms, intermingled here and there with white-barked sycamores as much as sixteen feet in circumference. According to Zodak Cramer's *The Navigator*, potential feasts abounded: turkeys, partridges, bear and deer in the forests, ducks, pike, sturgeon, and, notably, catfish weighing up to a hundred pounds each along the river.

The islands were the travelers' bane. They "drew up" sand and small gravel at their heads. These accumulations gathered driftwood; bars began to reach toward the outer banks; during periods of shallow water they often completely blocked the river. On meeting such an obstruction, the entire crew piled out of the boat— fortunately the water was warm—and portaged the cargo to navigable water on the lower side of the bar. Then, lifting and heaving, they skidded the boat across. On one grim day they had to fight their way over five such bars. Sometimes their labors did not suffice. When that happened, Lewis sent men out to find farmers with draft horses or oxen capable of pulling the boat over the hump. The owners of the animals, he discovered, "are generally lazy charge extravegently . . . and have no filanthropy or contience." One even demanded the "exorbitant" price of two dollars for his and his animals' services.

Another obstacle was fog. At night, air temperatures dropped into the sixties, but the water, as Lewis determined by frequently dipping in a thermometer, stayed in the low seventies. "When the air becomes most cool," he noted in his journal, "which is about sunrise the fogg is thickest and appears to rise from the face of the water like steem from a boiling kettle," a phenomenon that delayed each morning's start until the mist burned off about eight o'clock.

The "canoe" he had purchased in Pittsburgh turned out to be leaky and unable to carry as much cargo as necessary. On reaching the small riverbank village of Georgetown, he paid eleven dollars for another canoe, probably, like the first, a dugout or small pirogue. That one leaked, too, and the journey turned into a sequence of struggles to keep his goods dry from the river underneath and the sky above, which every now and then dumped deluges onto them.

No one was very happy about the course of things, but the soldiers in the crew had to obey orders or face court-martial. Not so the civilians, additional numbers of whom he had hired for handling the dugouts. The labors irked most of them as much as their attitudes irked Lewis. At the little towns they passed, he fired and hired. Only Shannon and Colter functioned well and so made permanent places for themselves on the expedition.

They spent eight hard days covering the hundred miles to Wheeling. Mercifully the captain decided to lay over there for the better part of two days so that the men could rest, wash their clothes, and trade the flour that had been issued to them for bread already baked by women in the town. He also discovered that the depth of the river had not increased as much as he had hoped. Unable to accommodate in the keelboat the cargo that had come from Pittsburgh by wagon, he bought yet another "canoe." This one was bigger, sounder, and generally more satisfactory than the other two. Though Lewis doesn't describe it, it probably resembled the most common class of pirogues on the river: close to fifty feet long, five feet of beam, and equipped with a mast and sail. It meant another hiring and a reshuffling of assignments for the men. Whether or not Lewis kept one or both of the smaller, leaky vessels does not appear. He had canoes, plural, when he reached the mouth of the Ohio, but they may have been replacements picked up along the way.

The little fleet left Wheeling at three o'clock in the afternoon of September 9 and almost immediately was engulfed in another deluge. Water dashed under and between the boats' oilcloth coverings, and the holds acted like bathtubs. Lewis struggled ahead anyhow—that was his nature, as Attorney General Levi Lincoln had pointed out to Jefferson earlier in the year—and did not land until twilight. Stumbling around with lanterns, they bailed out the boats and readjusted the cargo and coverings. Finally, at midnight, Lewis wrote, "I wrung out my saturated clothes, put on a dry shirt turned into my birth," presumably in the cramped stern cabin of the keelboat.

There were pleasant interludes. On the 11th and again on the 13th, the flotilla ran into numbers of gray squirrels migrating across the river from west to east, swimming lightly and making good speed, Lewis noted. The creatures provided sport for the dog, Seaman, and a treat for Lewis. At his master's bidding the big, black Newfoundland jumped into the water, caught a squirrel, crunched it to death, and brought it back. "They wer fat and I thought them when fryed a pleasant food."

More gravel bars stood in the way, but the voyagers were far enough down the river now to breach them with relative ease. The gravel was small and loose, the current brisk. After the men had dug a small trench through the barrier with spades and paddles, the water swept through, washing out a channel big enough for the boats. Only twice, when the gravel was intermixed with clay and driftwood, did the captain have to call in draft animals to help.

September 7 dawned sunny and warm. Spotting a clean bar ahead, Lewis decided to land and give his cargo its first thorough check. To his dismay he found some of it in bad shape despite nightly bailings of the boats, oilcloth coverings, and stowage in casks and supposedly waterproof bags. Rusty guns, tomahawks, and trade knives had to be oiled. Clothing was spread out to dry. Some "biscuit," probably hardtack, was damaged beyond salvaging.

At sundown the boats were reloaded. The next day Lewis's journal entries ceased and were not resumed until November 11, when the wayfarers were at Fort Massac—a gap of fifty-four days and 694 miles. Possibly he kept his log in another book that was later lost, though the appearance of the one that survives makes this seem unlikely. Or he may simply have grown bored: what point was there in describing again routines that had grown tedious, and in a well-known land whose natural history he had not been instructed to examine? Or, just possibly, the failure of his hard work to keep things spick and span had triggered another of his deep depressions.

A long letter written to Jefferson in Cincinnati on October 3 helps fill the gap in the journal and demonstrates how remarkably well Lewis, building on his own interest in natural history, had absorbed the paleontology lessons given him during his spring training course in Philadelphia.[20] A natural animal trap called the Big Bone Lick lay near the outskirts of Cincinnati. Animals coming there during many centuries to lick salt sometimes became mired. Dying, they left the mud studded with bones, some quite massive. Though the existence of the lick had been known to whites since 1739, its antiquity wasn't realized until a German visitor recognized some of the bones as akin to those of the extinct Siberian mastodon.

The flurry of interest reached as far as the American Philosophical Society. It also prompted a Cincinnati physician, Dr. William Goforth, to dig in the mud, in the spring of 1803, a pit thirty feet square and eleven deep in the hope of finding the complete skeleton of a mammoth. No luck. He did cart home, however, several huge bones plus some teeth and tusks, one of which was twenty-two inches in circumference at the base and upwards of six feet long. Lewis visited Goforth in Cincinnati, looked over the collection, and obtained permission to have other specimens dug up and shipped to Jefferson via New Orleans. Unhappily the freight was lost in a shipwreck. However, the minute descriptions of tusks and teeth that he put on paper did reach and, he hoped, impressed the president.

It is not hard to believe that the long and carefully crafted letter to Jefferson was intended as a form of compensation for his recent failures. Before starting West he had made much of ascending the Missouri for many hundred miles before winter set in. Because of a drunken boatbuilder whom he, the personal representative of the president of the United States, had not been able to handle, that hope was blasted. He had not been able to go down the Ohio without damaging a part of his cargo. But perhaps he could regain stature in Jefferson's eyes by focusing clearly and cogently on a phase of natural history in which Jefferson was deeply interested.

His desire to wash away the stigma of failure emerges still more explicitly in the last paragraph of that long letter. Congress was about to meet to consider the treaties implementing the Louisiana Purchase. And what would those august men think of Lewis's progress so far? To keep them in "good humor" (Lewis's words) "I have concluded to make a tour this winter on horseback of some hundred miles through the most interesting country adjoining my winter establishment; perhaps . . . towards Santafee." And would Jefferson please send him official copies of the treaties; they might induce Spanish officials in St. Louis to give him more information about the Western country than might otherwise be the case.

To anticipate: Jefferson's reply was delayed until the treaties, confirmed by the Senate on October 20, 1803, could be put into print. What he said then was crisp. Lewis should not undertake the proposed excursion. It might be more dangerous than the expedition up the Missouri "& would, by an accident to you, hazard our main object . . . [finding] the direct water communication from sea to sea formed by the bed of the Missouri & perhaps the Oregon." His time would be better spent and his stores conserved if he made his headquarters in American territory near St. Louis and did what he could in that city to learn what awaited in the land ahead.[21]

So much for that rash notion of a long winter trip toward New Mexico, a proposal that confirmed again Levi Lincoln's estimate of Lewis's headstrong nature.

Because of the gap in the 1803 journal we know nothing of how the boats were run down the Falls of the Ohio, a two-mile-long series of cascades formed by water foaming grandly over limestone ledges. The usual route ran close to the north (Indiana) side, where Clarksville lay near the bottom of the turbulence. Louisville stood opposite, in Kentucky. Lewis's fleet arrived at one or the other of the towns on October 14, but just where or under what circumstances the co-captains came together is also unknown, which is a cause for regret.

In some ways they were much alike. Both were over six feet tall and in superb physical condition, except that Clark suffered intermittently and painfully throughout his life from some obscure digestive ailment. Lewis was leaner, Clark more heavily set. Both were fiercely loyal. Army discipline was deeply ingrained in them, yet they were flexible enough to improvise as frontier conditions necessitated.

There were striking differences as well. Lewis had a better formal education, though when he wrote rapidly his spelling was almost as unrestrained as Clark's, and his sentences were even more convoluted. Lewis was moody, intense, and speculative; his nature seemed to require occasional times of solitude. When the occasion arose, he could be charming socially. Unlike Clark, who was accompanied west by a devoted black slave, York, he took no personal servant along on the trip. He frequently sought the company of young women and seemed, especially after his return from the expedition, eager to marry. He never did.

It would be a mistake to assume Lewis was the more intelligent. Clark's bent was simply more practical, given to dealing with things to which he could put his hands. He was bluff, hearty, and gregarious. As far as we know, his eye for girls was not as quick as Lewis's, but shortly after the expedition ended, when he was thirty-five, he married sixteen-year-old Julia (sometimes called Judy) Hancock. He named his first child Meriwether Lewis Clark, a compliment Lewis probably would have returned if circumstances had allowed.

The pause in Clarksville lasted nearly two weeks. Many farewell parties must have held sway there and across the river in Louisville, for the Clarks were a large, prominent, and well-liked family, and the upcoming expedition was one to attract attention. By day there were chores. The larder had to be replenished, the keelboat spruced up. Because the river remained low and there were more men to transport, the captains decided to keep the big pirogue Lewis had purchased in Wheeling. They may also have replaced the small, leaky pair with one or two sounder craft.

Although Clark had interviewed many volunteers while waiting for Lewis, he had selected—and only tentatively—no more than seven: William Bratton, the brothers Joseph and Reuben Field, Charles Floyd, Jr., George Gibson, Nathaniel Pryor, and John Shields. Shields, aged thirty-five, turned out to be the oldest man on the trip. He was married and had at least one child. This ran contrary to Lewis's instructions about signing on only bachelors, but Clark had made an exception because of Shields's known talents as a blacksmith and gunsmith, and Lewis let the enlistment stand.[22] Charles Floyd was an inheritance of sorts. His father had served under George Rogers Clark during the Revolution, and his son was enough like him that the captains later called on him to be one of the group's sergeants. Another sergeant-to-be was Floyd's cousin, Nathaniel Pryor, who, after the expedition was disbanded, would embark on a fruitful and adventurous career in the army and as an Indian trader. The Field brothers seemed to turn up whenever trouble threatened and distinguished themselves in what followed. So Clark had picked well, even though Bratton and Gibson were accorded no special remarks when Lewis summarized the merits of the party's men in a letter to the secretary of war on January 15, 1807.[23] The two were not alone in this; only six of the twenty-nine men Lewis listed drew particular praise. But everyone, the captain said, deserved "warmest approbation and thanks."

The reinforced party left Clarksville on October 26. On November 11, at Fort Massac, Lewis's river journal picks up again as abruptly as it left off. The post, occupied that fall by seventy-three soldiers and three officers, had a reputation as a sickly place. Perhaps this took some of the spirit out of the garrison. Although the post commander, Captain Daniel Bissell, had been ordered by the War Department to recruit volunteers for the Corps of Discovery, as the party had been named by Jefferson, he had managed to sign up only Joseph Whitehouse and John Newman—and the latter would be cashiered later on for insubordination. Another, greater disappointment was the failure of Major McRae to send from South West Point, Tennessee, to Fort Massac the six to eight volunteers he had been instructed to provide.

There was one marked gain—George Drouillard, about twenty-eight, the son of a French-Canadian father and a Shawnee Indian mother. When Bissell recommended him as an expert hunter with a good knowledge of the Indians' character and their "hand talk," Lewis promptly offered him twenty-five dollars a month if he would join the expedition as a civilian interpreter. Drouillard, whose name was consistently given the phonetic spelling Drewyer in the trip journals, hesitated. But he did agree to go to South West Point, about three hundred miles away, to pick up the volunteers there and bring them to St. Louis. For this he drew a thirty-dollar advance. Meanwhile the seven soldiers who had come down the Ohio with Lewis dropped out, to continue to their own destination, Fort Adams. The nine volunteers Lewis and Clark had signed up took their places at the oars.

The captains wound up their work at Massac late in the afternoon on November 13. Though Bissell surely pressed them to stay, enough was enough. After sailing and rowing three miles, they camped on the riverbank. That night Lewis came down with a violent "ague"—what else could be expected of a place like Massac? He dosed himself with some of Rush's thunderbolt pills, probably spent the next day in and out of the boat, and by the time they reached the junction of the Ohio and Mississippi he was able to move about more normally, though "extreemly week."

His sense of duty was still haunting him, and the party spent six days at the confluence, making up chores for themselves. Lewis, still very shaky, passed on some of his recently acquired knowledge of surveying techniques to Clark, who calculated the width of the rivers: the Ohio, 1,274 yards; the Mississippi, 1,435. Below the junction the Mississippi spread out to 2,002 yards, somewhat more than a mile. The junction was a prominent geographic spot, of course, and noting the geography of the expanding nation was one of Lewis's assignments. Still, neither the river statistics nor the sketches they made of bars and islands in the vicinity proved very much, for the rivers were exceptionally low. High-water marks on the banks showed that the Mississippi at times reached an extraordinary fifty-two feet above the point where they stood when measuring it. Lewis must have wondered what would happen if he met water like that when the boats started up the Missouri in the spring.

To add to his sense of usefulness he practiced being an emissary. One way and another—rowing, walking—part of the group visited a few Shawnee and Delaware hunting camps, some on the west bank of the Mississippi. Lewis informed the Indians that the great father of all the tribes now lived in a city bigger than St. Louis, one called Washington. It is unlikely that this talk of distant and unknown rulers impressed the Indians. Lewis's big black dog, Seaman, was far more interesting. One Shawnee offered three beaver skins for him. Lewis shook his head.

At some point along the way, Clark was stricken with one of his stomach disorders. In spite of that he rowed with the others, going along with a small group that traveled down the Mississippi in search of a key fort that William's brother, George Rogers, had built in 1780 and named Jefferson for the then newly inaugurated governor of Virginia. It had stood near the eastern shore atop a bluff on an island called Iron Banks.[24] Not a trace remained in 1803. The disappearance was the sort of thing moody Lewis might well have brooded about; how long did any work of man last?

On November 20, with Clark still ailing, they started up the Mississippi. Concerned for his friend, Lewis went out of his way to kill a grouse and make a broth he hoped Clark could keep in his stomach. It did not help. The invalid was still laid up on the 23d when the boats swung to at the Cape Girardeau landing and Lewis set forth on what can be regarded, in spite of the extemporized visits with the Shawnees and Delawares, as his first official errand in newly acquired Louisiana.

Before Jefferson turned the northern part of the territory into a huge Indian reservation, he needed to know how many whites and, in particular, how many Americans would have to be relocated on the eastern side of the Mississippi. The obvious source of information about the number of those living in the Cape Girardeau region was the man who governed them for the Spanish—a man named Louis Lorimier.

Lewis was not sure how Lorimier would receive him. The fellow, who was George Drouillard's uncle, had fought for the British in the Ohio country during the Revolution. This had made him fair game for a detachment of George Rogers Clark's men. They fell on his trading post, just missed capturing Lorimier himself, and then looted his establishment of two hundred packhorse-loads of goods. What they couldn't carry they burned; losses were estimated at twenty thousand dollars. Disliking the American jurisdiction that spread over the trans-Allegheny region after the war, he moved to Cape Girardeau about 1793 and somehow managed to be appointed its commander by the lieutenant governor in St. Louis. He had continued in that post under France and would continue to hold it until the territory was formally transferred to the United States. He might not relish hearing of the change from an associate of William Clark.[25]

Lewis need not have worried. He reached Lorimier's settlement at the close of a horse-racing celebration during which the winners took possession of the losers' animals. It was a wild scene—yelling, drinking, fighting, cavorting. The frontier Americans, who were in the majority, struck the somewhat supercilious emissary from the United States as "dissolute and abandoned . . . of desperate fortunes [with] but little to loose either character or property." Though Lorimier had lost four horses during the meet, he greeted Lewis cheerfully and invited him to dinner with his family, away from the disorders.

Two things about the man struck the explorer. One was Lorimier's hair. He wore it in a queue that reached down his back as low as his knees and was held in place by a broad belt. (He was about five feet eight inches tall.) When he unbraided it, it touched the ground. There was not a gray strand in it, though Lewis guessed him to be sixty years old. (Actually he was fifty-five.) The other notable attraction was his daughter, "much the most descent looking feemale I have seen since I left the settlement in Kentuckey a little below Louisville." In addition to thoroughly enjoying the family gathering, he picked up useful census figures from "a young man," probably Lorimier's son; the *comandante* himself could neither read nor write. The district, which had been in existence for only ten years, already held 1,111 souls. During 1802 and the first ten months of 1803, 406 persons had arrived, some of them Americans. This headlong immigration, coupled with a high birthrate, was likely to increase the figure rapidly. Could so many people be readily uprooted and moved out of the country for the sake of the Indians? Was it his business to make suggestions after collecting more data?

Clark's health improved, and as the cold, weary miles of bucking the current dragged past, Lewis's restlessness increased. He disliked being cramped in a boat under the best of circumstances. As the number of settlements on both banks of the river increased, he could no longer contain himself. Surely he could find a horse and cover ground that way much faster than by following the winding river in a cranky vessel. Clark's army experiences had involved boats; he could manage the flotilla better than Lewis could. So why not ride ahead, check in at Fort Kaskaskia about personnel and an extra boat for carrying supplies to the upper Missouri, as authorized by the War Department, and afterwards continue to St. Louis to confront the region's lieutenant governor, Carlos Dehault Delassus?

Delassus. It was not a Spanish name. But as Lewis knew by then, many enterprising French had entered Spanish service during the closing decades of the past century. Delassus was one. He might try to end his tenure at St. Louis by being resistant. As far as Lewis knew, no copies of the treaties had reached Missouri, and anyway the Spanish were vociferously insisting the sale of Louisiana to the United States had no legal standing. Lewis did not even have a Spanish passport to use for gaining entrance to St. Louis in the event Delassus chose to keep him out.

It could be a serious block. None of the maps he had studied in Washington had been based on the knowledge of people who had actually been in most of the country he and Clark proposed to enter. If such maps existed, they would be in St. Louis. If traders who knew the upper Missouri River could be run down, it would be in St. Louis. He had to determine, by drawing on the wisdom of such people, how many men he would need and then enlist them; he was already sure the roster would exceed the fifteen for whom he had bought guns and shirts in the East. He would need to recalculate and then buy and package the additional supplies he would need for his own party and as Indian gifts to be used as he urged the tribes to shift their allegiance from old friends to new. Those tedious shopping chores could be completed only in St. Louis and vicinity. Finally, he hoped desperately he could establish winter quarters along the lowest reaches of the Missouri, not just for convenience, but for face saving. It would be humiliating, after a year's work on the project, to have to admit to the world that he had not even crossed the old boundary into the new acquisition. The sooner he confronted Delassus the better.

At 8:00 A.M. on November 28 he wrote in his journal that he was turning the boat over to Captain Clark.[26] Handing the journal to his partner, who would keep it until the site of the wintering was reached, he departed. The separation would last intermittently for the next five and a half months.

FIVE

Facing Reality

His first stop on the way north was Fort Kaskaskia, Illinois. Two companies of infantry were stationed there, one under Captain Richard Bissell, brother of Daniel Bissell of Fort Massac, and the other under Captain Amos Stoddard. Though the latter was twelve years older than Meriwether Lewis, they were either already fast friends or soon would be.

Times had been dull for Stoddard. When the Jefferson administration had been preparing for war in 1802, he had been ordered to take his company to the ancient French town of Cahokia, across the Mississippi and four miles downstream from St. Louis, and build a fort there. Before he could start work another message had been rushed to him: Louisiana now belonged to the United States and the fort was no longer needed. Instead he should sit tight at Kaskaskia, ready to receive, as America's representative, Upper Louisiana from the lieutenant governor in St. Louis. Both Stoddard and Bissell welcomed Lewis expansively, hoping he had more recent news than they did. But he had been hoping the same of them.

Bissell, heedful of his orders from the War Department, made no trouble about lending a supply boat, a corporal, and six privates to help the expedition partway up the Missouri during the ensuing summer. The men would report for duty as soon as Lewis knew where his winter quarters would be, a determination that depended on whether or not Lieutenant Governor Delassus would let the Americans enter the Missouri. In any event, Bissell wanted his soldiers back before Christmas, 1804.

How many hands, he may well have asked, did Lewis and Clark have for continuing from the Missouri's headwaters to the Pacific? Meriwether counted them out—the two he had picked up at the start of his trip, the seven Clark had recruited at Louisville, two more from Fort Massac, and eight from South West Point, assuming Drouillard returned with that many acceptable volunteers. Nineteen all told, more than the twelve authorized by Secretary of War Dearborn, more than the fifteen Lewis had bought guns and shirts for at Harpers Ferry. Evidently he had some unrecorded understanding with his superiors about signing on as many permanent recruits as he felt he needed. Or maybe, though it seems reckless even for him, he had the understanding with himself. Anyway, the count at the moment was nineteen, plus himself, Clark, the slave York, and Drouillard, if the interpreter consented to continue with the party. Hardened men all—enough, he thought, to turn back possible Indian attacks, yet not too many to find food for during the final push. And speaking of food, he had his winter camp to consider. Would Captain Bissell be so kind as to introduce him to the contractor who was already supplying Fort Kaskaskia with staples?[1]

He also asked about an interpreter, for he spoke no French and he had learned Delassus understood no English. The man recommended to him, John Hay, was postmaster of Cahokia and part-owner of a prosperous American trading firm doing business along the upper Mississippi. He turned out to be a jewel—thirty-four years old, nimble, loyal, intelligent, and well acquainted in St. Louis. He had entered the North West Company of Canada at the age of fourteen and had traded extensively for furs on the Assiniboine and Red rivers, west and northwest of the headwaters of the Mississippi.[2] He had listened intently to the tales of men who had risked the upper Missouri's snag-filled currents and collapsing banks, and had obtained sketch maps from some of them. He had a broad knowledge of Indian ways and of such unsung but essential arts as the proper loading of keelboats and pirogues.

Accompanied by this redoubtable volunteer and a fellow trader named Nicholas Jarrot, Meriwether Lewis crossed the Mississippi on December 8 to call on Carlos Delassus. From the water the city presented a deceptively fine appearance. Three streets, each about a mile long, ran parallel to the river along the top of a low bluff of yellowish limestone—an important bluff since it resisted erosion by the Mississippi and collected at its base a sandbar on which keelboats could be loaded and unloaded. About two hundred houses, together with their outbuildings, were scattered along the streets. Most were constructed of squared logs eight feet tall set on end and chinked with mud, French fashion, rather than laid horizontally as American log cabins were. The larger dwellings, often built of stone and two stories high, were shaded on two or more sides by wide galleries; kitchen gardens and fruit trees occupied the cluttered areas in the rear. Nearly all buildings, large or small, gleamed with whitewash.

Long years since, the inhabitants had hewn steep troughs into the bluff so that carts and wagons could reach the sandbar. One of the streets, called Tour, continued across the parallel thoroughfares to the top of a second bluff, on which stood a round stone fort built in 1780 to repel a British attack that never came. In 1803 it housed St. Louis's small contingent of troops. The other street, called Bonhomme, led Lewis and his companions up to the Rue Principale, later called Main Street. The government house, where Delassus lived and worked, stood there.

Delassus's round, balding pate was fringed with curly white hair. He had a wide mouth in a round face. Behind his small, wire-rimmed spectacles his eyes, too, looked round. He wore a starched, stand-up collar decorated with a bow tie. Beneath the cherubic appearance lurked a quick temper. According to Lewis, writing Jefferson on December 28, 1803, the lieutenant governor frequently popped some of the wealthiest of his citizens into the "Carrabose" for the slightest of offenses. "This has produced a general dread of him among all classes of people."[3]

After looking at the identifications Lewis offered, the governor asked testily, through the interpreters, why the American did not have a passport from the Spanish minister in Washington. Lewis was prepared for that. Inasmuch as Spain had sold Louisiana to France some time since, he said suavely, he had expected to find French officials installed in St. Louis; therefore he had supposed his French passport would suffice. Moreover, he added, he had been informed while on his way West that the United States had purchased the territory from Napoleon.

Delassus granted that those things might be so. (Word of the Louisiana Purchase had, in fact, reached St. Louis the preceding August.) But since no instructions had come to him from Spanish sources, he could not allow undocumented foreigners to enter the interior provinces. He promised, however, to write his superiors in New Orleans. Meanwhile, Lewis should return to Cahokia and wait there (if he persisted in going ahead) until a reply arrived.[4]

Lewis would rather have pressed a short distance up the Missouri, but this was not a time to stand on his rights, especially since he hoped to spend much of the winter interviewing knowledgeable sources in St. Louis. Amiably he said that of course his party would stay east of the Mississippi—not at Cahokia, though he might make his own headquarters there, but at a place already recommended by Mr. Hay. This was the mouth of the small Rivière du Bois (Americanized to Wood River) which ran into the Mississippi directly across from the mouth of the Missouri. The site lay eighteen miles above St. Louis, far enough so that his recruits would not be distracted by the temptations of the town. There they could be drilled and disciplined for what lay ahead.

Delassus, who was interested in protecting his own flanks from attack when administrations changed, agreed to the quid pro quo and even invited the visitors to spend the evening at his home. The next day the trio returned to Cahokia. Clark was waiting there, the keelboat and the two pirogues showing signs of the violent wind and rains they had encountered on the way upstream.[5] The captains swapped accounts of their experiences and talked late into the night, reviewing plans.

The division of responsibilities they worked out was all but preordained by their natures. Clark, the frontiersman, would build the winter camp at Wood River, collect and pack the supplies that came in, train the men, and ready the boats for a spring start. Lewis, the more socially and politically trained of the two, would seek out men who could give him the kinds of information about Upper Louisiana that Jefferson needed for executing his Indian removal plan and that the expedition would require for carrying out its multitude of assignments. The pattern was not rigid, however. Now and then during the coming months the captains would exchange places, Lewis going to the camp and Clark to St. Louis, so that each could become familiar with the entire scene.

Delassus kept his part of the bargain. When Antoine Soulard, the surveyor general of Upper Louisiana, declined, out of fear of the governor, to let Lewis copy the maps and census figures in his office, Delassus cleared the way with a note of permission.[6] Later, after Lewis had won the cooperation of the town's leading merchants and traders, René Auguste Chouteau and his younger half-brother, Jean Pierre Chouteau, the influx of material swelled to a flood.

Lewis sifted it first for information relevant to Jefferson's plan of resettling Upper Louisiana's non-Indian residents somewhere in the East, in order to turn the West into a vast Indian reservation. To this end he collected statistics about the region's handful of Spanish, the deeply entrenched French, the inpouring Americans, and the numerous blacks, both free and enslaved. He sent questionnaires to leading residents about land holding and land use patterns, about the underpinnings of the economy, and about exploitable natural resources.

Did he really believe that a population he estimated at 10,000 including 2,000 slaves and 5,500 American frontiersmen could be shuffled around at will—to say nothing of the Indians? He assured Jefferson that he did. Yet he also seemed to think the process would take a long time, for he suggested that during the radical change-over Upper Louisiana should be divided into three counties and attached to Indiana Territory for the sake of orderly government.

(In the end neither plan was adopted. What eventually happened was the herding, against their will, of Eastern and Southern Indians far enough west not to be a burden, at least for a while, to white settlers. Very few whites were ever relocated during this cruel offspring of Jefferson's original plan.)

While gathering these statistics, Lewis stayed alert to his own needs. The moment the whites took over the territory, it would become his and Clark's duty to impress awareness of the change on as many Indian and foreign traders as they could reach during their ascent of the Missouri River. They had to know what to expect. Exactly where and how did the Missouri turn and twist on its way from the mountains? What sequence of tribes lived along its banks? What alliances existed among them? What enmities? By what routes did traders bring merchandise to them, and how did the Indians respond to those traders? Could they develop a program for turning the Indians away from their old purveyors toward the traders of the United States?

Lewis's probings brought him maps, journals, and gossip from many sources—from President Jefferson and Governor Harrison of Indiana Territory, who mailed him material they had picked up from sources of their own; from Surveyor General Antoine Soulard; from John Hay and the Chouteau brothers; from the dean of the Missouri River traders, James Mackay; and from no one knows how many now-anonymous, semiliterate but shrewdly informed rivermen.[7]

James Mackay soon came to embody, in their minds, the essence of these diffuse sources. The trader visited the Wood River camp on January 10, 1804, and personally handed Clark a packet of documents the captains later carried up the river. Almost as valuable as the papers was a flood of oral data that Clark did not record in his journal, but that he certainly recorded in his orderly mind. Lewis, too, might have met Mackay. An opportunity to do so came late in February or early in March when Clark and he rode with Pierre Chouteau and other influential residents of St. Louis to the St. Charles district beside the lower Missouri, where Mackay lived. There the visitors halted a Kickapoo war party bent on attacking an Osage village farther upstream.[8] From this experience in wilderness diplomacy and from stories of other adventures Mackay may well have told both at Wood River and St. Charles, the captains learned much about the sort of problems they were likely to face along the river—a river not nearly as unknown in the West as they had supposed.[9]

The difficulties of which their informants made much had begun in the fall of 1792, eleven years before, when a naturalized Spanish subject, Jacques D'Église (the Spaniards called him Santiago Leglise), arrived in town with a small, gaunt crew, a meager invoice of pelts, and a cargo of tales that astounded and alarmed Delassus's predecessor, Lieutenant Governor Zenon Trudeau. The trader said he had discovered, far up the Missouri, two related tribes of Indians hitherto unknown to the Spanish. They were the Hidatsas and the Mandans. About five thousand of them, by his estimate, lived in eight or so villages of dome-shaped, earth-covered houses scattered for nearly a dozen miles along the Missouri, both above and below the point where the Knife River flooded into it, in what is now the west-central part of North Dakota.

This was Spanish territory. Nevertheless, an old Canadian, Pierre Ménard, lived in one of the earthen towns, as thoroughgoing an Indian in his ways as the Mandans. Other Canadians on occasion came south from their posts beside the Assiniboine and Red rivers (in today's Manitoba) to trade for horses, corn, buffalo robes, wolf skins, and beaver pelts. Moreover, D'Église added, many of the horses in the Indian villages bore Spanish brands, and he had seen Spanish bridles in some of the lodges. Clearly they had come from New Mexico. What then was to prevent English soldiers from following British-Canadian traders to the earthen villages and afterwards continuing along the trail of the Spanish traders to the silver mines of Mexico?

Actually, D'Église had touched on a more complex system of barter than he or Trudeau realized. The Mandan-Hidatsa contact with distant New Mexico was not direct but through a chain of tribes that ranged across the central and southern section of the Great Plains. Those tribes acquired many horses but little armament from the New Mexicans, who did not want European weapons in the hands of the Indians. By contrast, the tribes of the northern plains were fairly well equipped with armament brought them in canoes by British-Canadian traders, who seldom used horses. Northern guns for southern horses and vice versa: it was a trade flow that the Mandans and Hidatsas were well fitted by geography for expediting as middlemen. This far-flung exchange was what D'Église had glimpsed without comprehending it.

D'Église asked for a trading monopoly among the Indians he had "discovered." When it was refused, he found a partner with a little capital, Joseph Garreau, filled two pirogues with goods, and toiled dreadfully back upstream. This time he was blocked by Arikaras (or perhaps Sioux; records are not clear) in what is now the north-central part of South Dakota. They roughed him up a bit, took some of his goods, and paid miserly amounts for more to use in their own dealings. What little was left, Garreau, "inspired by a troublesome and wanton spirit, used . . . for other purposes than those for which they were intended." That is, he had found one or more young women with whom he wished to exchange pleasures. Or so his senior partner reported when he returned to St. Louis in quest of more merchandise and, he hoped, favorable reconsideration of his request for a monopoly.

He simply did not pack enough weight. Lieutenant Governor Trudeau had already written his superior in New Orleans, Baron Francisco Carondolet, that the best hope of keeping the British away from Mexico was to grant the monopoly to a trading company capable of stringing a series of forts along the Missouri and on to the Pacific. The forts would not be primarily for garrisoning soldiers but for housing traders whose goods and good will would wean the Indians from the British merchants and thus cool their desire to move on south. Governor Carondolet not only approved the plan but in addition promised a prize of two thousand pesos to whoever brought back from one of the Russian posts on the distant coast a letter, written in Russian, that said the crossing had been completed. Later he raised the prize to three thousand pesos, which apparently was all the public money Spain was able to afford for a wilderness riposte against the hated British.

The monopoly that resulted was called La Compagne de Commerce pour la Decouverte des Nations du haut du Missouri, generally clipped in everyday usage to the Missouri Company. As field manager the investors hired Jean Baptiste Truteau. He may have been a relative of Governor Trudeau who, for some reason, spelled the last part of his surname with a *t* instead of a *d*. For the time and place he was well educated. He had been St. Louis's first schoolteacher, and he had also traded with the Indians along the Des Moines River in Iowa.

In June 1794, Truteau started up the Missouri in two pirogues loaded with goods that cost the company 46,747 pesos. His instructions were explicit. If necessary, he could use half his merchandise to bribe his way past any piratical tribe that tried to stop him; this would be "onerous, but it is proper to make some sacrifice to attain success." On reaching Mandan territory, he was to build, as his headquarters, an English-style log cabin (horizontal logs rather than upright ones) and try to learn, while conducting his trade, the geographic truths about the Rocky Mountains, the Indians that lived on their far side, and the rivers that flowed westward. Above all he should dilute British influence among the Mandans by telling them about the great chief of the Spaniards, "the protector and friend of all red men, who loves the beautiful land, free roads [that is, an open river], and the serene sky."[10] Reinforcements whose duty would be to push on to the Pacific would follow him upstream the next year, 1795.

Alas for plans. The Sioux delayed Truteau so long he could not possibly reach the Mandans before the river froze. To escape his tormentors, he slipped back downstream to an uninhabited stretch of the river valley, where he built a crude winter hut. The Mahas, or Omahas, led by their villainous chief, Parajo Negro (Blackbird), discovered him there and heaped on more indignities. He survived and spent another year roaming the edges of the plains without ever reaching the Mandans. During those wanderings he kept a journal describing the country and people he saw. He bewailed the second-rate goods that had been given him, the high prices he was supposed to charge, and the low esteem in which Spaniards were held because of the violence and licentiousness of their voyageurs, most of whom were French-Canadians. He declared wisely that exploration and commerce did not fit well together, a point that must have interested Lewis and Clark when his journal fell into their hands at about the time Mackay was telling these stories.

In May 1795, while Truteau was still being bullied by Blackbird, his first reinforcement party started up the Missouri with goods worth 96,779 pesos. Their leader is known now simply as Lécuyer. His orders were to join Truteau at the Mandan villages and then continue to the Pacific. In the event, he bogged down among the Poncas in northeastern Nebraska—a total fiasco. The Missouri and its Indians, Lewis and Clark were soberly realizing, were an enormous obstacle.

Before word of Lécuyer's collapse reached St. Louis, the stockholders in the Missouri Company prepared, for launching in August 1795, what was to be the culminating thrust of their westward drive. They loaded four pirogues with a reputed two hundred thousand pesos' worth of merchandise. One pirogue carried placating gifts for the Sioux, "whom it is necessary to flatter in order not to risk being beheaded," one for the Arikaras, one for the Mandans, and the fourth for the still unknown tribes of the Rockies and on beyond to the Pacific.

The commander of the expedition, James Mackay, was carefully chosen. He had emigrated from Scotland to Canada at about the time of the American Revolution and had found employment with the North West Company. For a time he was stationed at Fort Espérance near the junction, in today's Saskatchewan, of the Qu'Appelle and Assiniboine rivers. In 1787 he took a few men and a dab of merchandise due south to the Mandan towns. The arrival of white men was still a novelty then, and the Indians, in their excitement, hoisted the visitors onto buffalo robes and paraded them into the village. They stayed ten days. What Mackay collected other than bits of information is unknown.

It is not known, either, why he left Canada for St. Louis and became a naturalized subject of Spain. The reputation he achieved there as a trader was such that the Missouri Company not only agreed to pay him four hundred pesos a year to lead this climactic expedition, but also granted him a share of the profits.

The man Mackay employed as his second-in-command is next to unbelievable. He was John Thomas Evans, aged twenty-five, recently arrived in St. Louis from Wales in quest of a lost group of

Welshmen. Pure fable. A standard item of Welsh lore declared that a certain Prince Madoc had led ten shiploads of colonists to America in 1170. They had vanished into the interior. Perhaps they had maintained themselves through the centuries as Christians, or they had lapsed into savagery, though still white of skin. Whatever the truth, they clearly needed redeeming. Given a pittance of seed money by a group of true believers in Wales, Evans made his way west, supporting himself with such jobs as turned up. In St. Louis his hopes leaped when he heard that the Mandans were unusually light-skinned. The lost Welshmen! He also learned that a band of traders under James Mackay was preparing to visit them. Evans promptly asked to go along as one of the thirty-three hands.

Mackay was reasonably sure that no Welsh blood flowed in the veins of any Mandan he had seen, but Evans was husky and, of greater importance, powerfully motivated. He signed him on not as an ordinary voyageur, but as a first mate of sorts. Inasmuch as there was no possibility of reaching the Mandan towns ahead of winter—not with an August start—Mackay halted in northeastern Nebraska, several miles above the mouth of the Platte, close to Blackbird's Omahas; there he built a post he named Fort Charles, after King Carlos IV of Spain.

It was a strategic spot. So that those who followed him could make the most of it he set about establishing sound working relations with the local tribes, which meant outfacing Blackbird. He also wanted reports on the land ahead. To that end he sent young John Evans up the frozen river with a small group of chosen hands. The explorers departed in February 1796. If they were lucky, they were mounted on horses obtained from either the Omahas or the Otos, who resided a little farther south. Horses were expensive, however, and they may well have walked, with only a packhorse or two along for carrying their gear. Whatever the means, they covered some eighty leagues and had reached the mouth of the White River, near today's Chamberlain, South Dakota, when a party of Sioux Indians discovered them. Cat-and-mouse for four days. Then a blizzard whooped across the plains. The whites escaped under its cover and hurried back to Fort Charles. Those Sioux had made it clear that they did not want St. Louis traders cutting in on the commerce they had developed with British interests to the northeast. If Mackay's group hoped to navigate the upper river, they'd better start smoothing the way now—one more item for Lewis and Clark to remember.

Mackay had not yet completed all he wanted to do in the Fort Charles area. Moreover, according to Blackbird, British goods were reaching the river not only through Indian middlemen but directly. British traders with packhorses, so the chief said, had gone up the Platte the year before, and more merchants were gathering on the St. Peters (Minnesota) River for a push south-westward toward the Sioux and Arikara. If true, and Evans's experience made it seem so, this was a serious trespass on Spanish territory. For the sake of the company's trade Mackay wanted to turn it back. This meant that Evans, for whom Mackay had developed considerable respect, would have to press on upriver with a few men, get in touch with Truteau at the Mandan towns, and work out means of continuing to the Western ocean.

Indian messengers invited the principal Sioux chiefs to the Omaha villages for a conference. Mackay greased palms, swore undying brotherhood, and argued that in due time his company would be better able than the British to send them whatever items they most desired. They thought it over. Mackay had an impressive assortment of merchandise on display in Fort Charles and he himself was clearly a cut above the other St. Louis traders they had seen. Very well. They would let a small party carrying a few bundles of goods go through. With that Evans loaded a pirogue and on June 8 started upstream. Quite probably some of his men, including his interpreter, had visited the Mandans with James Mackay in 1787 and then, like him, had chosen to leave Canada for Louisiana.[11]

The party spent two months covering the seven hundred miles to the Arikara villages.[12] They had to live off the country as they went, and undoubtedly they stopped to give a sales talk to every Indian band that showed the least signs of friendliness. Evans, moreover, was making a detailed map of the river that he anticipated would be useful not only for the Missouri Company but also for his countrymen when they followed him West to rescue the Welsh Indians. The Arikaras delayed him for six weeks, but after that progress quickened, and he reached the Mandan towns on September 23, 1796. By that time his map covered seven separate, long sheets. There is no evidence that he ever saw Jean Baptiste Truteau, who may have dropped in on the Arikaras earlier that summer but who had then grown discouraged and returned to St. Louis.

What Evans did find, between a Hidatsa and a Mandan village

and about three miles below the mouth of the Knife River, was a "small fort and a hut." Unoccupied at the time, the buildings had been erected two years earlier by a party led to the site by René Jessaume, a rascally trader associated with the North West Company. Appropriating the habitation, Evans ran up a Spanish flag. The act of defiance helped soothe his bitter disappointment: there was nothing about the Mandan Indians to make him suppose they had ever been related to Prince Madoc's legendary Welsh colonists.[13]

No Truteau was around to help point him toward the Pacific. Working on his own, he found the width of the Missouri to be a hefty thirty-two hundred feet and decided its source must be much farther west than had hitherto been imagined. He heard, possibly from old Pierre Ménard, a far wanderer, of the Yellowstone River and of the Missouri's Great Falls, a little west of the central part of today's Montana. Most surprising was the glimmer that came to him about the Rockies. Apparently they were made up not of one ridge, as shown on Arrowsmith's map, but of four or five parallel chains. The Missouri, his informant indicated, headed among them far to the south and then ran north between two of the ridges before breaking out of the mountains, perhaps at the Great Falls.[14] There is no indication that he pictured those ridges as being anything more than normal hills such as he had seen when traveling through Pennsylvania on his way to St. Louis.

He estimated by dead reckoning how far west he had come from the Missouri city, whose longitude he knew. From this he deduced that the Mandan villages were located at 107°48' west of Greenwich, England. (Mackay, basing his estimates on his 1787 trip, had come up with 110°–111°.) Actually the Mandan villages lay at 101°27'. Since degrees of longitude are separated, at that latitude, by about 41 miles, Evans placed the towns roughly 260 miles (and Mackay 370 miles) too far west. These figures led Evans to believe he was closer to the Pacific than was actually the case.

He was never able to test the theory. René Jessaume, the fort builder, showed up with a party of Canadian traders. Evans brusquely ordered them off: this was Spanish land. Angered but not wishing to embroil their principals in an international incident, they withdrew. After a few stiffly polite letters had been carried back and forth by Indian messengers, Jessaume reappeared. According to Evans, the Canadian tried to hire a few Mandans to violate the tribe's deeply felt laws of hospitality by killing their guest. The chiefs, discovering the plot, "shuddered at the thought of such a horrid Design and came and informed me of the whole." Jessaume then decided to do the work himself and "came to my house with a number of his Men, and seizing the moment that my Back was turned to him, tried to discharge a Pistol at my head loaded with Deer Shot but my interpreter having perceived his design hindered the Execution—the Indians immediately dragged him out of my house and would have killed him, had not I prevented them."[15]

Pyrrhic victory. The Canadian companies decided that no one really knew which side of the international boundary the villages were on and that they could drive Evans away with a flood of cheap goods. This they proceeded to do. Later that year, the North West Company sent its great astronomer, David Thompson, to the Missouri to determine the exact location of the towns.* They were indeed in Spanish territory, but by then the point was moot. Evans had given up and had gone back down the river. At Fort Charles he discovered that Mackay too had decided that carrying out the Missouri Company's plans was not worth the risk and labor involved, and had gone to St. Louis to tell the investors so. He had arrived there in May 1797; Evans followed in July.

Thus Lewis and Clark learned, with more than a little somberness, that Spain's only determined effort to reach the Pacific, with an expedition larger than and as well financed as theirs, had ended in failure. Could they do any better?

When collated, the maps, journals, and oral accounts obtained in St. Louis and at Camp Wood gave the trail blazers a remarkably full directory of the many tribes that inhabited the banks of the Missouri as far north as the Mandan and Hidatsa towns.[16] They knew which groups were powerful enough to require special attention, which might be helpful, and which dangerous. From this emerged a more comprehensive understanding of the preparations that would have to be completed before the corps's departure in the spring. The physical side of the task fell to William Clark under circumstances that were, to state it mildly, taxing.

Immediately after reaching the mouth of the Wood River on December 12, 1803, he had put his men to work clearing a site for

---

*See page 33.

the camp on the south bank of the little stream.[17] That done, they had chopped down trees and cut them into logs for eight or nine cabins, including one for Clark. The men also hauled the unwieldy keelboat partway up the bank and stabilized it with wedges against the fluctuations of the rivers. More heavy ax work was required to break a road about a mile and a half long through the timbered bottomland to an adjacent prairie so that supplies could be brought in by wagon from nearby farms and from Cahokia, for floating ice in the Mississippi would make the river route unusable much of the time. Fat turkeys, grouse, opossums, rabbits, and occasional deer furnished the basis of the meals turned out by soldiers assigned to do the camp cooking.

Though formal drilling is almost never mentioned in the records, Clark, as a seasoned professional, may well have believed that routine parade-ground maneuvers were necessary for knitting the group into a team. Periodic breaches of discipline—drunkenness, insubordination, absence without leave, and fighting whether for sheer joy or for proving one's manhood—were often followed by courts-martial, their members chosen from the ranks by Clark, that at times decreed floggings for the culprits. At other times Clark was more ingenious: when privates John Potts and William Werner got into a bloody fistfight, he had them work off their excess energy by building a cabin for a local woman who had offered to serve as the camp laundress.[18] On the positive side he rewarded good shooting and commendable actions during duty with extra rations of grog. He also put up prize money, generally a dollar, for the winners of shooting matches with local "countrymen," as he called their civilian neighbors. The troopers generally won.

On December 16 George Drouillard arrived with the eight men he had been directed to bring in from South West Point, Tennessee. It had been a fast trip and since he was not an army man he had controlled his charges with the strength of his character and, on occasion perhaps, with his bare knuckles. They were not a choice bunch. Lewis, disappointed that none was a hunter, interviewed them carefully, found only four suitable, and asked Clark to check the decisions. Clark concurred entirely. Meanwhile they again urged Drouillard, who had been on temporary assignment while shepherding the men, to join the expedition as hunter and interpreter for the standard pay of twenty-five dollars a month. After wavering for a time he agreed, provided he was given time to straighten out his personal affairs. The request granted, he disappeared from the records until the following May. He and York were the only nonmilitary persons to travel the entire distance from St. Louis to the Pacific and back.

On January 9, while hiking through snow squalls to examine a nearby Indian mound, Clark broke through the ice of a slough. On returning to camp he found his feet frozen into his shoes, "which rendered precautions necessary to prevent frost bite." By the next day—the day he welcomed James Mackay to the camp—he was very ill. He blamed the indisposition on his wetting and the "excessive cold." Probably, though, it was a flare-up of his familiar digestive disorders, for he kept complaining about being sick for a month and eventually tried to cure himself with pills made from walnut bark, an ancient folk remedy. Throughout much of this time the thermometer never rose above freezing. Yet Clark could write on January 25 in his field notes, "a verry Clear mone Shiney night . . . Trees and small groth ar Gilded with ice from the frost of last night, which affords one of the most magnificent appearances in nature, the river began smoking at 8 o'Clock and the thermometer stood at 2° below 0."[19]

He kept himself busy practicing with the astronomical instruments Lewis had left with him, and recording meteorological data —wind, snowfall, ice conditions in the river, temperatures, and so on. He also worked hard at things he could do inside his cabin. He drew plans for reconstructing the keelboat and began making a map of the lower Missouri, using material gleaned from Mackay and, presumably, from notes sent him by Lewis. He also tried to read the future. How much time would reaching the Pacific require? How many men; how many boats?

On January 20 he began estimating distances. Using Evans's and Mackay's charts and perhaps their notes as well, he came within six percent of accuracy in gauging the miles from Camp Wood to the Mandan villages—fifteen hundred miles instead of the correct sixteen hundred. But as a guideline for the stretch from the villages to the ocean he used the King and Arrowsmith maps he and Lewis had brought with them. One reason for the choice may be that he felt sure David Thompson's instrument readings for the Mandans' location, as shown on the Arrowsmith-King charts, were reliable, whereas the Evans dead-reckoning estimates contained too much room for error. On top of that was the force of tradition. The King map showed the main branch of the Missouri running almost due west from the villages; Evans's map, by contrast, showed a long dip to the south, and theoretical geography allowed for no such aberration. The Missouri, as shown by King, also allowed for a direct, short portage to a presumed south fork of the Columbia. That Clark was thinking, in his estimates, of a very short, traditional portage across the "Rock Mountains," as he called them, is indicated by his failure to allow extra time for surmounting the divide.[20]

Using a distance of 41 miles between parallels of longitude and allowing generously for windings in the rivers, he came up with 1,550 miles from the Mandan towns to the Pacific. (The actual distance the expedition traveled turned out to be, for that stretch, 2,550 miles.) On the basis of these estimates, he figured that if the party left Camp Wood on May 1 and traveled 12 miles a day, it would reach the foot of the mountains about September 5. A rate of 10 miles a day, which took into consideration pauses for Indian councils, would bring the expedition to the Rockies late in September. In either event, the explorers would camp at the headwaters of the Missouri throughout the winter. Then they would cross the Rock Mountains on Indian horses if possible, make new dugouts, and triumphantly gain the ocean by early summer, 1805.

His concept of the party's size wavered between twenty-five and fifty men. "Those numbers will Depend on the probabillity of an oppisition from roving parties of Bad Indians, which it is probable may be in the [name blotted] R." One suspects the "R" he was thinking of was the Bad River in central South Dakota, where the most belligerent band of the Sioux tribe often sought to assert their dominance over any trade moving along the Missouri. If the number of men needed to challenge them rose, so would the number of craft needed for transportation—perhaps as many as three: the keelboat and two pirogues. Clearly the idea of a dozen men skimping along on the twenty-five hundred dollars authorized by Congress had long since been abandoned.

Dissatisfied with the keelboat, he planned to reconstruct it, beginning with a single new mast thirty-two feet tall and jointed at the bottom so it could be lowered. He decided on twenty oars, ten to a side.[21] The rowers would occupy cramped quarters, each pair sitting elbow to elbow on benches three feet wide. Between them and the sides of the boats he would construct lockers 2 ½ feet wide and 1 ½ feet deep. Their hinged tops could be raised in case of attack by Bad Indians. When the lids were lowered, they would form *passe-avants* from which the men could set their poles when propelling the craft by thrusting hard against the river bottom. About ten feet of the bow would be decked over to protect goods and perhaps a few beds from the weather. The high cabin in the stern, clearly shown in his working sketches, contained more lockers and was an inheritance from the original builder in Pittsburgh. A final bit of ingenuity was pure Clark: an awning held by three removable, fork-topped poles to protect the rowers from the sun.

The support boats were pirogues. One had six oars and was called the white; the other, of seven oars, was called the red. Whoever sat in the stern of the red pirogue would manipulate the seventh oar as a rudder. The boats may have been the ones Lewis had purchased in Pittsburgh and Wheeling to lighten his load while descending the Ohio. Or one may have come from Fort Kaskaskia. Or both may have been purchased in St. Louis. There is no way of telling, though several people have tried.

At the end of January 1804, Lewis put in his first appearance at the camp, accompanied by John Hay and one of Hay's employees, to talk over developments. Realizing quickly that Clark needed a rest, Lewis suggested they change places for a few weeks, and on February 9 or thereabouts, the older of the two leaders went downriver to St. Louis. He walked into a highly pleasant situation created by Lewis with the adroit cooperation of the town's social leaders René Auguste Chouteau, then fifty-five, and his half-brother, Jean Pierre Chouteau, nine years younger.

Though René Auguste had helped found the city in 1764, when he was fourteen, and Pierre had begun trading with the Osage Indians in the 1780s, they were not pioneers in the American sense, but were urban gentlemen of grace and polish. Like the other prominent French inhabitants of the town, they lived in imposing stone houses with polished wooden floors, elegantly crafted furniture, fine china and silverware. They sent their children to Montreal or Quebec or sometimes to France for a few years of schooling. Their dinners, Captain Amos Stoddard wrote, were "sumptuous . . . almost every sort of food dressed in all manner of ways . . . the best wines and other liquors." The women were pretty and danced well, although, in Stoddard's opinion, somewhat theatrically.[22]

As handlers of most of the furs brought out of the interior and as owners of prosperous farms, a gristmill, and a distillery, the Chouteaus were the dominant economic, political, and social figures of St. Louis. Wary even before the Louisiana Purchase of the bumptious Americans who were elbowing across the Mississippi, they were profoundly shocked when word arrived from Governor Harrison of Indiana Territory that the United States had acquired the trans-Mississippi region. But they, and most of the other leading traders of the city, were too intelligent simply to withdraw and sulk. Eager to maintain their positions under the new government, they had welcomed Lewis effusively and they were equally considerate of Clark. Quite naturally but not very diplomatically, the American officers responded with a favoritism for the Chouteaus that created cankering jealousies among their rival traders.

Clark stayed busy while his health mended. With Chouteau's help, he distributed a long questionnaire designed to elicit detailed information about the characteristics of the Western Indians: their traditions, warfare, hunting and farming practices, medicines, morals, amusements, and so on—a list originally drawn up the year before for Lewis by Dr. Benjamin Rush and his other tutors in Philadelphia.[23] And Clark, apparently, was the one who opened negotiations with Pierre Chouteau about escorting a delegation of Osage chiefs to Washington to visit the president.

Punctilious about outward forms, however much he might contrive in private, Jefferson had refrained from meddling with the Indians of Louisiana until the physical transfer of the territories was completed in both New Orleans and St. Louis. As soon as he learned by special courier that the New Orleans formalities were ended and that those in St. Louis would soon begin, he rushed word to Lewis to start advising the Western Indians of the change of sovereignty and to discuss with them the establishment of government trading posts in their country. Implicit in the letter was a charge given Lewis in the first set of instructions handed him shortly before his departure from Washington: "If a few of their influential chiefs, within practicable distance, wish to visit us, arrange such a visit . . . at the public expense. . . . If any of them should wish to have some of their young people brought up with us, & taught such arts as may be useful to them, we will receive, instruct, and take care of them."[24]

The practice of taking Indians to the seat of government so they would be impressed with the might of the whites was almost as old as the New World. In 1804 the long-tested strategy seemed particularly important in dealing with the Indians of Louisiana. Most of them had scarcely heard of the United States. Many a chief considered himself more powerful than the cowering Spaniards who came to his people begging for trade; the only rivals they worried about were other natives desirous of contending with them for control of the commerce that trickled up the rivers and across the plains. Jefferson mentioned the Sioux as a nation on which he hoped the explorers would make an especially strong and friendly impression, a directive that would have, as we shall see, almost fatal consequences.[24]

For the time being, however, the Sioux were out of reach. Closer by were the Osages, about five thousand of them, most of them living in what is now southwestern Missouri and northeastern Oklahoma. The Chouteaus exerted a persuasive influence over the tribe, and when the American captains suggested that certain chiefs be selected for a pilgrimage to Washington, Pierre jumped at the chance—provided his role was kept secret lest this new evidence of partiality make his St. Louis rivals more jealous than they already were.[25]

Before the Washington visit could be arranged, a new excitement arose—the ceremonies transferring Upper Louisiana to the United States. By means of a letter dated New Orleans, January 12, 1804, Napoleon's representative in charge of the transfers, Pierre Clement de Laussat, had written Captain Amos Stoddard at Fort Kaskaskia, appointing him the French representative to receive the territory from Governor Delassus. Laussat also named Meriwether Lewis, Antoine Soulard, the surveyor general, and the trader Charles Gratiot, a brother-in-law of the Chouteaus, to witness the correctness of the ceremonies. Stoddard in turn wrote both Delassus and Lewis from Fort Kaskaskia on February 18, saying he would shortly dispatch a contingent of troops under Lieutenant Stephen Worrell upstream to Cahokia by boat and that he would cross the river on or about the 24th to confer with Delassus about details.

The letter prompted Lewis to make arrangements for leaving Camp Wood. He placed command in the hands of John Ordway, who had been a sergeant at the time he volunteered to join the expedition. He named twenty-year-old Charles Floyd, son of a friend of the Clark family and, in Lewis's words, "a young man of merit," to be Ordway's assistant. To give Floyd weight in the eyes of the somewhat older and considerably more obstreperous troopers, he raised the young man to a sergeant's rank.

By the 24th of February, both Lewis and Stoddard were in St.

Louis. Delassus, completely gracious now, entertained them, along with Clark and many of the town's leading socialites, at a regal banquet in Government House. On the 29th, the American troops necessary for lending stature to the occasion landed at Cahokia. And there they stayed, immobilized by clots of ice along the Illinois shore.

Nervous about affairs at Camp Wood, Lewis hurried back. (How he crossed the river that chained Stoddard's troops does not appear.) He found his sergeants frantic with frustration. Reuben Field had refused to stand guard when his turn came, and John Shields had backed the insubordination. John Colter, John Boley, John Robertson, and Peter Wiser had visited a local grogshop in defiance of orders.

A grim Lewis ordered the entire contingent to attention in the camp compound while he excoriated the delinquents for failing to measure up to the opportunity that was being presented to them. He outlined the importance of the expedition, said that there would be times when neither Clark nor he could be in camp, and warned that on such occasions the directives of duly appointed sergeants had the same authority as the captains'. He then confined the offenders to the camp area for the next ten days.[26] On March 3, after keeping the kind of eye on affairs that made the troopers squirm, he returned to St. Louis to attend to his duties there.

Gradually the ice that had immobilized the soldiers at Cahokia began to thin. Allowing a safe margin of time for further improvement, the men in charge of the two-day ceremony scheduled the first event, the transfer of the territory from Spain to France, for noon, March 9, 1804. On the dot of the hour, the dignitaries who had taken position in Government House stepped outside, resplendent in dress uniforms or impeccable black civilian garb—Delassus, Soulard, Gratiot; Stoddard, Lewis, and Lieutenant Stephen Worrell. If Worrell's soldiers were in St. Louis at all, they kept a low profile; tomorrow would be their day. And nothing is said anywhere about Clark, though he was certainly in attendance.

A Spanish soldier stationed on the Government House second-floor veranda leaned out and waved his hat as a signal to a sentry watching from the tower-fort at the top end of Rue Tour. Orders rang out, drums rolled, and Spanish infantrymen in parade dress with knapsacks on their backs marched double time down the street. Silence fell on the close-pressed crowd of French Creoles, many in tears, on lounging American newcomers, on staring Indians, on roughly clad rivermen and field hands, and on the numerous blacks, who, being slaves, were the lowliest of all. The Spanish sergeant barked his men into line and snapped for shoulder arms. The officers drew their swords. Drums rolled again, then stopped. The governor made a farewell speech in French and Spanish. Gratiot translated it into English. Stoddard, acting for the moment as an agent for Napoleonic France, answered formally, and again Gratiot interpreted. Papers changed hands; the Spanish flag slowly sank from the staff in front of Government House. As Stoddard received it, the battery in the stone fort on the hill fired eleven salutes. The dignitaries vanished inside the house, and the crowd slowly dispersed, uncertain of their own emotions.[27]

That night Delassus was host at a lavish public dinner and ball in Government House. The next morning, March 10, the same crowd gathered for the symbolic ceremony transferring French Louisiana to the United States. Worrell's troops landed below the bluff and marched up Bonhomme Street (now Walnut) to stand at attention where the Spanish soldiers had stood the day before. At 10:00 A.M. the same officials, with Clark added this time, stepped outside, Stoddard carrying the Stars and Stripes. Meriwether Lewis and his fellow witnesses stepped forward to testify to the actuality of the transfer, and the little cannon up on the hill boomed out another series of salutes.

Upper Louisiana was now legally American. As soon as travel was possible, the Corps of Discovery, its status long anomalous, could openly enter the lands of the West. Both Lewis, who was sometimes a prey to his emotions, and the more placid Clark must have keenly felt the impact of the moment. From now on every move they made would be imbued with the full majesty of their nation. With that must have come a new sense of dignity and a heightened determination not to fail. Yet neither of them, as far as is known, ever left a written word about their reactions to that magic moment.

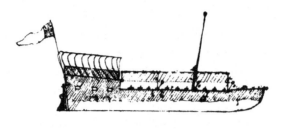

SIX

Smoky Water

The same thinning of the ice that let Captain Amos Stoddard's troops reach St. Louis for the ceremonial transfer of Louisiana to the United States also opened the rivers to more distant travel. As expectancy swelled, Lewis and Clark set a departure date, April 18, that would let them tackle the lower part of the Missouri between the peak of high water that came with the melting of snow in the central Midwest and the later surge of runoff from the distant Rockies.[1]

Let's go! Carpenters began whipsawing logs into planks for the lockers and seats in the keelboat. Blacksmiths set up a forge and hammered out hasps, hinges, and other pieces of ironwork. Supplies of all sorts moved in from St. Louis and nearby farms and were segregated, itemized, boxed, and baled. Bushels of corn were parched so that it would keep well, and accounts were settled with the contractors. The final list of permanent crew members was drawn up—twenty-five all told. The men were divided into three squads, each under one of the sergeants, Charles Floyd, John Ordway, and Nathaniel Pryor.[2] Each squad was further divided into two messes. Camp utensils were allocated and sleeping quarters adjusted so the new groups could get used to living together. Soldiers, handpicked for manning one of the two support pirogues, were put under the charge of Corporal Richard Warfington. Experienced French rivermen were hired to handle the second, larger dugout, called the red pirogue from its bright new coat of red paint. Not all of the exuberance was constructive. Most of March 29 was taken up with a court-martial involving John Shields, John Colter, and Robert Frazer.

While Clark oversaw the work at Camp Wood, Meriwether Lewis, helped by Stoddard, who had taken over the reins as military governor of Missouri, confronted the Indian problem. Scores of Native Americans from both sides of the Mississippi were pouring into St. Louis, hoping to discover clues about the future. Every day for several days, the cannon in the stone fort on the bluff boomed out shots to announce to the skeptical that the Spaniards were indeed gone but, in Stoddard's words, "You will be protected and sustained by your new father, the head chief of the United States." As an earnest of the promise, he passed out presents and sips of whiskey and gave medals to the more prominent visitors. If this were not done, he told Lewis, the disgruntled Indians might commit depredations, and enough of them were around for such outbreaks to develop into a serious matter.[3]

For his part, Lewis concentrated on putting onto paper long speeches that would be delivered by surrogates to Indian groups he could not meet in person. The talk, filled with the grandiloquent language favored by whites in formal meetings with Indians, was addressed to the Sauks and Foxes, an alliance of defiant, British-oriented tribes who were drifting, under pressure of the advancing frontier, across the Mississippi to wilderness lands south of the Des Moines River. The oration advised the natives of the agreement whereby the chief of the seventeen nations of America (he meant the seventeen states that made up the Union) replaced the old fathers of the Indians. This great, new father, called president, as powerful as he was wise and benevolent, hereby adopted the Sauks and Foxes as his children. Like any concerned parent, he wanted them to live in peace and behave with discretion.[4]

A Sauk who happened to be in St. Louis at the time carried the message to a gathering of his people. It was read aloud by an English trader who twisted the wording so it was "not much to the advantage of the United States." When information about the happening reached Amos Stoddard, he dispatched a special interpreter to the tribes to rectify matters.[5]

Lewis in the meantime had dispatched a second oration to the Iowas and Sioux. Despite his faith in the power of solemn words, he must have wondered how much impact the messages were really having. (It turned out to be practically nil.) What he wanted was to be able to talk in person, albeit through an interpreter, to the leaders of every Indian nation bordering on the Missouri. The conferences completed, he would urge the men to travel to Washington under military protection, meet Jefferson, and see for themselves the might of the United States. His first real opportunity would be with representatives of the Osage tribe already being sounded out by Pierre Chouteau. Success would please Jefferson, for, as the president said, "they are the great nation South of the Missouri . . . as the Sioux are great North of that river. With these two powerful nations we must stand well, because in this quarter we are miserably weak."[6] Nervously Lewis kept his fingers crossed, hoping the delegation would arrive before the date scheduled for the expedition's departure. It was a contradictory business sometimes, trying to be both an explorer and an ambassador to the Indians.

On April 7, 1804, the two captains, attended by York and an unnamed aide, met in St. Louis to buy last-minute supplies and complete last-minute errands. Not by chance their work coincided with a banquet and ball given by Amos Stoddard as repayment for courtesies extended him earlier by the townspeople. The affair cost $622.75 and he firmly believed the United States government should reimburse him. The participants would have testified it was worth every penny. The gaiety did not end until nine o'clock Sunday morning. "No business to day," Clark noted, heavy-eyed, in his journal.[7]

They spent Monday through Wednesday shopping and packing. The purchases were loaded into a barge belonging to Nathan Rumsey, agent for military procurement in St. Louis, and rowed upstream to Camp Wood. Lewis stayed behind, waiting for Chouteau's Indians. At the camp Clark issued the men lead and powder for the trip, began the final packing, and, yielding to the electric anticipation, passed out an extra ration of whiskey to everyone. Later he may have wished he hadn't. Wanting still more liquor, several troopers visited one of the blind pigs the officers had not been able to keep away from the vicinity, and on April 16 he had to confine them for their derelictions.

Lewis did not appear until the 18th, the day scheduled for departure. He was downcast. Chouteau had not arrived and the start would have to be postponed. The river, Clark noticed, was falling that day—just as they had hoped. And there they sat.

Although neither man speculated about the delay, in the docu-

ments that still survive, its cause can be deduced. The transfer of
sovereignty had upset the Indians, who were inherently conservative. When a Chouteau trader took word of the change to a band
of Osages on the distant Arkansas River, they called the paper a
lie and burned it: the Americans had *not* taken their country. And
when one boatload started down the Missouri to learn what was
afoot, they were surprised by Sauk warriors who killed some and
made prisoners of the others. Those Sauks! "They certainly do not
pay that respect to the United States which is entertained by other
Indians," Stoddard complained to Secretary of War Dearborn.
Chouteau was going to be hard put to calm the confusion.[8]

He managed well. On April 21, a cannon boomed on the Missouri. As the men in Camp Wood ran to the bank of the Mississippi
to watch, a bargeful of Osages—twenty-two of them, plus Chouteau and his voyageurs—swung over to the landing place. Adrena-
lin flowing again, Lewis and Clark ordered a pirogue manned and,
leaving Ordway in charge at the camp, dashed downstream with
the delegation.

The cats were away—and, besides, the letdown brought on by
the delay had hurt morale. In defiance of Ordway's angry orders,
the men played rambunctiously. When Clark returned on the 25th,
he had to deal with more than the ordinary amount of insolence
and drunkenness. To restore order he dredged up chores. He had
the keelboat heeled over on its side and made doubly sure every
crack in the bottom was watertight. Trader John Hay came up
from Cahokia to look over the lading, disliked what he saw, and
spent several days directing a systematic rearranging of the bales
and barrels to make unpacking and repacking easier at the points
where the material would be needed. Then, as the shamefaced men
began showing repentance, Clark ordered target practice, which
they enjoyed, and fostered more shooting matches with the nearby
countrymen. On May 8, he loaded the spick-and-span keelboat,
manned it with twenty oars, and rowed it several miles up the
Mississippi. The trial went smoothly and spirits lifted.[9] Another
boost was Drouillard's arrival on May 11 with engagés who had
been hired earlier for handling the big, seven-oared, red pirogue
and then, following the postponement, had been released to live
with their families to save government money. Surely their reappearance meant something was about to happen.

On the 13th, so Clark wrote in his journal, a courier arrived with
letters from Lewis, who was still struggling to organize the Osage

delegation and get it started toward Washington. Letters. No further remarks. The omission showed remarkable self-control, for one of the communications contained bitter news. The preceding February Lewis had written Secretary of War Dearborn, asking why the captain's commission he had promised Clark had not yet arrived in St. Louis. Delays could affect his friend's seniority. Dearborn received that letter on March 20. On examining the list of openings, he saw the only appointment available was that of second lieutenant in the Corps of Artillerists. He gave it to Clark and, following standard procedures, passed it on to Jefferson. Incomprehensibly (unless he had private reasons for not overriding Dearborn), the president made no objection and, in violation of his promise to Lewis, sent the belittling appointment to the Senate for confirmation.

Lewis was furious, yet, like the president, he did not remonstrate. Why? Perhaps because he knew no rectification could reach the Corps of Discovery until its return from the Pacific. Or perhaps he felt there was no use bucking the system at that point. "It is not such as I wished or had reason to expect," he wrote Clark, "but such it is. . . . I think it will be best to let none of the party or any other persons know any thing about the grade, you will observe that the grade has no effect upon your compensation, which by G—d, shall be equal to my own."[10] An easy oath, since Dearborn had already promised Clark a captain's pay.

Years later, Clark told Nicholas Biddle, who was editing a narrative of the expedition for publication, "My feelings on this Occasion was as might be expected. I wished the expedition sucksess, and from the assurance of Capt. Lewis that in every respect my situation Command &c, &c, should be equal to his own . . . I proceeded. I do not wish that any thing relative to this Comsn. or appointment should be inserted in my Book, or made known . . . and I do assure you that I have never related as much on this subject to any person before."[11] Certainly he said nothing at Camp Wood that would lower him in the men's estimation. But the hurt may well have lain behind his sudden decision to cross the Mississippi and start up the Missouri toward his appointed rendezvous with Lewis on May 14, a day earlier than they had agreed on. Purposeful activity might keep him from brooding.

Arms were checked—the fifteen short-barreled .54-caliber rifles Lewis had procured at Harpers Ferry and the .44-caliber Kentucky long rifles that the volunteer soldiers they had picked up later had brought with them. Clark gave experimental twists to the swivel guns that had been mounted on all three boats—a small-bore cannon and two blunderbusses on the keelboat, and a single blunderbuss on each of the pirogues.[12] The weapons could be loaded with whatever was handy—musket balls, buckshot, scrap iron, or even stones—and could be devastating at close range. There was a frantic scurrying around as the soldiers struck their tents (heat had caused them to move out of their huts a week or so earlier), packed their personal gear, and scoured the area for mislaid objects. The news of the impending departure spread rapidly through the neighborhood, and although rain fell intermittently throughout the day, a small crowd of country people gathered to cheer the Corps of Discovery on its way.

It is not possible to determine exactly how many men left Camp Wood that dismal spring afternoon—or for that matter how many continued up the river to the Mandan villages. Clark gave one set of figures for those in the keelboat; sergeants Ordway, Floyd, and Pryor, who had been ordered to keep journals to increase the likelihood that some record would survive in the event of catastrophe, gave variants. (Two or three privates also volunteered to keep diaries but only Joseph Whitehouse's has survived.) The following totals are not far askew, however: twenty-five, including York, in the keelboat; nine Frenchmen under their *patron*, Baptiste Deschamps, in the red pirogue, and seven soldiers, including Corporal Warfington, in the smaller, white-painted pirogue.

At 4:00 P.M., according to Clark (Ordway made it 3:00 P.M.), the cannon of the keelboat roared bravely, the watchers on shore whooped, and the little flotilla started for the Pacific, its members optimistically expecting to be back by the end of the following summer. That first day they traveled four miles and camped at the upper end of the first island in the Missouri at the beginning of a deluge so strong it later doused the cook fires and put everyone to bed with cold suppers and wet blankets.

As they breasted the current the next day, they began to get an inkling of what lay ahead. The river was high, the current punishing. The banks, composed largely of fine, alluvial soil, were covered with fallen and standing trees, many of them huge and all interlaced with grapevines. Occasionally an undercut section collapsed into the river with a sound like distant cannonading. Cave-ins along two thousand miles of stream had given the water the color of coffee laced with condensed milk, in the eyes of one observer. Another, seeing the river under a different light or with a different sense of color, said it was a thick yellow-green, a hue borrowed from thousands of shifting sandbars. Indians called the stream Smoky Water; Americans, the Big Muddy.

Clark was astonished by the quantities of driftwood, some of it driving at the boats like lances. Frequently these floating logs caught in the branches of toppled trees. Thick silt coated them, more driftwood collected, and gradually the tangled mass, called an *embarras* by French voyageurs, thrust far out into the river. Or the earth-laden roots of a lone tree might catch on the river bottom; its leafless top, pointing downstream, waited just above the water like a hungry fang. Sawyers were even more worrisome. The North West Company's great explorer, David Thompson, described them thus: "The sawyer is generally a Tree of large dimention broken about the middle of its length, it's roots are in the mud. . . . the strong current bends the tree as much as the play of the roots will permit, the strain of which causes a reaction, and the tree rises with a spring upwards above the water and with such force as will damage or destroy any vessel.[12]

Another hazard was logs so saturated they had lost buoyancy and drifted along under the surface, out of view in the opaque water. During the expedition's first full day on the Missouri, the keelboat banged into three such logs. Timely warnings. The stern of the vessel was loaded too heavily, so that on impact the light bow tended to ride up the obstruction in such a way that any one of the episodes might have torn out the bottom. The men would have to shift more weight forward when they reached the village of St. Charles, where Clark expected to meet Meriwether Lewis.

Drawing on his own army experiences, on talks with boatmen in St. Louis, on the vessel's trial run on the Mississippi, and on his initial contact with the Missouri, Clark worked out a navigational pattern—Lewis reviewed it and signed it on May 26—that would hold as far as the Mandan villages with only temporary adaptations to fit special circumstances. He put one of the sergeants at the bow, a second in the middle, and a third in the stern. The positions rotated regularly.[13]

The sergeant in the bow was to inform the man in charge of the keelboat of anything unusual he saw—obstructions, approaching river craft, Indians lurking on the bank. He would use prearranged signals to communicate with the corps's shore parties and was provided with a setting pole to help the regular bowman ward off floating debris.

The sergeant in the center managed the square sail, which was seldom used because the river kept twisting away from the wind, and saw to it the rowers kept pace with each other. He was the one who decided when halts should be called to rest the men, and how long each pause should last. He posted a sentinel whenever the boat halted. Accompanied by the guard for the day, he reconnoitered for a hundred and fifty yards around each camping place. At night he made sure all three boats were properly beached, and appointed sentinels to watch them until morning.

The sergeant at the rear of the boat managed the big, long-handled rudder that curved down over the stern. He made sure no loose impedimenta obstructed passage on the quarterdeck or along the *passe-avants* formed by the locker tops. He kept an eye on the compass in order to assist Clark, who was making a detailed map of the river as they traveled, a job that on the first stretches consisted mostly of checking his observations against those of earlier chart makers.

No matter which position Sergeant Ordway held for the day, he was the one who issued rations, in a prescribed order, to supplement whatever game the hunters brought in—salt pork and flour, salt pork and Indian meal, lyed corn (hominy) and grease. No pork was issued when freshly killed wild meat was available.

A little after noon on May 16, the fleet hove to opposite the little string town of St. Charles. Its population, numbering about 450, was almost entirely French; their houses, fields, and small businesses stretched for about a mile along the south bank. Clark fired a cannon salute, and as a crowd came running to the principal dock, he had himself rowed over for conversations. He quickly learned that Lewis had not yet reached town and no one knew when he might.

Preparing the Osages for their trip into what was, to them, as mysterious a region as the River Styx was the primary cause of the captain's delay. The government, worried about runaway costs, had limited to twelve the number of Indians from any one tribe who would be given a free trip to Washington. This meant cutting the group Pierre Chouteau had brought to St. Louis almost in half, outfitting them in proper style, and at the same time softening, with appropriate gifts, the disappointment of those left behind. Considerable mind changing by the Indians slowed the process, but the final delegation was impressive—"the most gigantic men," Jefferson later wrote to Gallatin, "we have ever seen." Two boys accompanied the party, in accord with the president's desire that youngsters be sent East, if possible, for instruction in civilized ways. No women were included.[14]

The head of the Osage delegation was Cheveux Blancs, or White Hairs. Legend says he got the name when he snatched a gray wig off the head of an American with whom he was grappling during an early battle. Ever afterwards he wore the trophy on special occasions. It was said, too, that White Hairs was the creature of Pierre Chouteau, who had helped him usurp the rights of the Osages' legitimate head chief.[15] Pierre Chouteau, opportunist *extraordinaire*. His firm provided the delegation with supplies that cost the United States $4,749.79. He received another $2,858.50 "on account of public service"—all formally authorized by Meriwether Lewis.[16]

(The Chouteaus, it might be added, also provided the bulk of $3,879.72 worth of Indian gifts Lewis and Clark bought in St. Louis to supplement the meager $669.50 worth Lewis had purchased in the East before starting west. The favoritism so aroused two of Chouteau's rivals in St. Louis, Manuel Lisa and Manuel's fur-trade partner, Francis Benoit, that they threw every block they could in the expedition's way. Lewis, in some respects a very naive young man, grew outraged in his turn. "Damn Manuel and triple damn Mr. B," he exploded by letter to Clark. "I have come to an open rupture with them; I think them both great scoundrels." As for Chouteau, after sizing him up while the delegation was in Washington, Albert Gallatin, the secretary of the treasury, told Jefferson, "What he wants is power and money," more specifically total control of the Indian trade of Louisiana which, incidentally, he did not get. All in all, the fur trade, as carried on by both whites and Indians, was more viciously competitive and far more complex than either Lewis or Clark fully realized throughout their time in the wilderness.)[17]

During the delay caused by readying the delegation for the trip, Lewis found time to turn to other of the numerous duties Jefferson had assigned him. In March, he had forwarded to the president cuttings and lengthy descriptions of two characteristic, fruit-bearing shrubs of western Missouri and adjacent regions—the Osage plum and the Osage orange. Now he added to the list specimens of lead and silver ore, a rubberlike ball of hair taken from the stomach of a buffalo, and a horned toad. He wrote a long account of salines in the Osage country and sent a sample of salt with the letter, for the availability of good, readily obtainable salt was an important consideration to pioneer settlers. He also sent along a map of the lower Missouri, the first of many maps he and Clark prepared. That done, he appointed Amos Stoddard his agent in St. Louis and at last was ready to join the Missouri fleet.[18] Accompanied by an escort of army officers and influential civilians, he rode overland, through heavy rain, to St. Charles on Sunday, May 20, 1804.

During the five days of waiting among the limited but tempting fleshpots of St. Charles, Clark had maintained firm control of the men. The first breach of discipline had drawn a quick court-martial followed by an order of the day that bluntly stated he would move camp out of the reach of town if the men did not show a "true respect for their own dignity." They hadn't even grumbled much when he had set them to reloading the boats in order to put more weight in the bows. And they had welcomed with considerable interest two professional Creole voyageurs, Pierre Cruzatte and François Labiche, who had enlisted as army privates in order to see what the other side of the continent was like.[19] They were the only true rivermen in the permanent detachment—except George Drouillard, and he was not a soldier.

River wisdom was only part of what the pair brought the expedition. Both had spent several winters trading as far up the Missouri, on occasion, as the Platte River. Both spoke at least bits of several Indian tongues, Labiche rather the more, and both were acquainted with sign language, with Cruzatte holding ascendancy in that field. Cruzatte's mother was from the Omaha tribe; Labiche, like most Creole rivermen, probably had Indian blood in his veins, too, but the details have been lost. Because of their experience both were given crucial assignments in the keelboat. Cruzatte became bowman. Labiche handled the front oar on the port side; the other rowers would key their strokes to his. Cruzatte's peculiarities have left him better remembered than Labiche. He was small, wiry, an exuberant fiddle player, and blind in one eye. His remaining eye is said to have been nearsighted, but a bowman needed to be farsighted and the oft-repeated tale of his myopia may have risen, mythlike, out of his greatest claim to immortality: during the return trip he accidentally shot Meriwether Lewis in the behind.[20]

The trip did not begin auspiciously. Though the captains had hoped to be under way shortly after noon on May 21, the festivities being staged in their honor by the excited townspeople held them until after four. They had scarcely started when another blustery spring rainstorm pelted them head on. They fought it and the current for three miles, gave up, and made a wet camp on one of the river's many islands. They were still in sight of settlements on either bank.[21]

The next day the wind favored and they covered eighteen miles. If the easy progress bred smugness, it was dashed by Cruzatte or Labiche or Drouillard or the Frenchmen in the red pirogue, most of whom had traveled this section before. Wait for the Devil's Race Ground! But before they got there Lewis himself almost created catastrophe. It was May 23. Sandstone cliffs three hundred feet high crowded close to the water along this stretch of the southern bank. At their base gaped a huge cave one hundred and twenty feet wide, forty feet deep, and twenty high. Many names decorated the walls inside, some carved into the stone and some written on it with charred sticks. The place was called the Tavern, perhaps because it really had served as a rest stop for travelers in the forgotten past.

The top of the cliff, its outer edge weathered into points Clark called "peninsulers," overhung the water.[22] The challenge was too much for Lewis. While Clark was adding his name to the register inside the cavern, Meriwether found a break in the precipice, ascended it, and began working his way along the edge. A foothold crumbled. He slid and bounced downward about twenty feet. Just short of disaster, Clark wrote in his journal, "He saved himself by the assistance of his knife," driving it wildly, one assumes, into some crevice that held. Just how he extricated himself from his dizzy perch does not appear.

No mention of the incident appears in the narrative of the expedition that Lewis was preparing at the time of his death in 1809 and that was finished by editors with whom Clark worked closely. Why was it omitted? Irrelevance? The fact that it made Lewis appear foolhardy? Or because it might trigger speculation? What would have happened to the Corps of Discovery if Jefferson's handpicked leader had died from an unnecessary fall within sight of the settlements along the Missouri? Would Clark, the mapmaker, the estimator of distances, the old Indian hand, the degraded second lieutenant of artillerists who had been pressed into service to handle just such contingencies—would he have been allowed to continue with what history would then have remembered as the Clark Expedition? Would he have consented? Under what terms?

The Missouri is a much swifter river than the Mississippi, for obvious reasons. The latter falls only 1,478 feet between its source in the Minnesota hills and the Gulf of Mexico, 2,552 miles away —an average drop of a little more than half a foot a mile. By contrast the Missouri, 2,950 miles long, falls 6,560 feet between its beginning in southwestern Montana and its junction with the Mississippi—an average drop of about two and a quarter feet per mile, almost four times the fall of the Mississippi.

Rather than buck such currents head-on, Missouri River boatmen tried to pick up eddies created when the curving streambanks deflected fast water from one side of the sinuous river to the other. A strong back eddy would sometimes carry a keelboat several hundred yards upstream with no effort on the part of the crew. (Some eddies were hard to break out of, too.) One hallmark of a good bowman—Cruzatte, for instance—was his ability to spot the right place for cutting across the river in order to pick up a usable eddy.

There were other tricks. Occasionally a boat could creep along in slack water close to the bank. While the men on the water side used their oars, those next to the bank seized branches and bushes and pulled the boat forward. If the bottom was solid and the water not too deep, a line of men on the *passe-avant* could put the padded ends of setting poles in their armpits and shove the boat ahead, walking as they pushed until they reached the end of the line and then ran back to their original places to repeat the maneuver. But the main reliance, when the force of twenty long-sweep oars proved insufficient, was the tow rope.

It was several hundred feet long. One end was tied to the very tip of the bow. The crew carried the other end onto the bank. Separated from each other by short intervals, they floundered ahead, pulling as they went, through brush, nettles, grapevines, prickly wild roses, and boggy spots, over downed logs and boulders, along the steep sides of gravelly banks, pausing now and then to cut a leaning tree out of the way. Using a long rope reduced the tendency of the bow to nose in against the bank. Even so, the bowman and his helper had to be constantly using their poles to keep the boat clear.

A device for reducing entanglements was the cordelle, wherein the tow rope was tied high up the mast and then run through a ring attached to an auxiliary rope affixed to the bow. The cordelle lifted the tow rope above some of the obstructions along the way and reduced still further the thrust of the bow toward the shore. There is no direct evidence in the journals that the Corps of Discovery resorted to cordelles—but, then, the diary writers seldom wasted words describing processes that were, to them, everyday occurrences.[23]

Even less is said about the handling of the two pirogues. (No one in them was required to keep a diary.) Pirogues in general were paddled as often as they were rowed, and that may explain why Lewis so often referred to pirogues as canoes. The journals, however, regularly speak of oars and it is necessary to assume them. (Oars do provide more force than paddles.) The pirogues were big enough and stable enough for crewmen to stand in them and pole forward. But eventually, when the river grew really boisterous, the tow rope was their ultimate resort, too.

The day after Lewis's fall they reached the Devil's Race Ground, hissing water rushing down a narrow chute between an island and bank-crowding rocks. Some of the men were put ashore to heave on the tow rope while the rest set their young strength against the oars. At times the boat seemed to hang motionless; occasionally it slipped backward. The captains yelled encouragement; the men quite probably took to shouting, in unison, the beat of the oar strokes. Slowly they pulled past the projecting rocks and thought they were clear.

Up ahead, the bank formed a concave bend, its upper part curving to the right. Part of the current that had plagued them in the Devil's Race Ground slammed across the river into the curve. Even as they watched, great chunks of undermined earth collapsed into the flood. The men with the tow rope scrambled for safety, meanwhile casting horrified glances backward as the bank peeled off toward the keelboat. Clark bawled for the helmsman to steer for the island. Frying pan into fire: the boat ran into a sandbar and stuck fast. The towers tried to heave her free, but the rope broke and the craft swung broadside to the current.

As it heeled over, everyone aboard "high-sided." They threw their weight against the upper rim, and when that did not suffice, they went over into the water, bending like hairpins as they clutched the gunwale with their hands and braced their feet against the precariously tilted side of the boat. The current toyed with them. It washed the sand out from under the vessel, which slowly came back to even keel. No rowers were aboard to hold it in place, however. It wheeled end for end downstream, hung up broadside again, listed, washed free, and wheeled once more. Swimmers—York, as powerful in the water as on land, was probably one of them—carried a rope to the men on shore, and they managed to drag the errant craft to safety. By that time the collapsing bank that had driven them into this trouble had stabilized, and they toiled up beside it in perfect safety. Clark was still dry-mouthed when they found shelter for the night in an abandoned cabin. "The worst I ever saw," he told his diary. But he hadn't reached the Pacific yet.

Nearly every day brought fresh difficulties: dragging the tow rope through the jungle growth on the banks; struggling with the oars against water hammering around the point of an *embarras*; breaking the mast against a leaning tree; hanging up on a snag while "immens large trees were Drifting down and we lay immediately in their Course"; riding out squalls that dashed waves clear over the boat. And, more blessedly, being pinned down by the wind for an enforced rest. Joseph Whitehouse got lost while exploring a cave. Drouillard and Shields, who were bringing up four horses for the hunters to use, failed to make contact with the river group for a week and emerged from their trek as gaunt as dry cornstalks.

Rain gave way to such stifling heat that the men, sweating copiously, had to take off their heavy shirts. (Clark blamed the excessive perspiration on the peculiarities of the Missouri's turbid water. As an experiment they let a pint of it stand overnight; half a wineglass of sand settled out.) Mosquitos drove them wild. Searching for a repellent, they bought three hundred pounds of animal grease from a trader bound downstream and smeared it on their bloody skins. They developed suppurating boils, the result, they thought, of that muddy river water coming into contact with the numerous cuts and scratches they all had. There were occasional disciplinary problems. While standing guard one night at the mouth of the Kansas River, John Collins tapped the whiskey barrel, became thoroughly soused, and encouraged Hugh Hall to join him. Both were found guilty by a court-martial of their peers and painfully flogged, as was Alexander Willard for falling asleep while on guard duty. These were not beatings with leather whips, but stinging—and humiliating—lashes from ramrods or willow branches; after all, the captains could not afford to have good oarsmen incapacitated.

There were compensations amid the toil. Some stroke of foresight had led Meriwether Lewis to purchase mosquito netting, which made sleep possible. Venison was so plentiful some of the excess was jerked so that when the meat was thoroughly dry it could be pounded with parched corn, mixed with bear oil, and boiled into a savory stew. A carefully measured ration of whiskey was issued each evening, and doubled if the day had been particularly trying. Cruzatte's fiddle was a godsend and often stirred the men to dancing reels with each other around the campfire. Undoubtedly there was a good deal of horseplay and storytelling, and constant speculation about the Indian women they hoped they would soon be meeting. And always there was the lush beauty of the untouched wilderness. Phrases like "butifull beyond description," "delightful prospect," "rich and well timbered," "one of the most beautiful places I ever saw in my life" (Ordway) keep popping up in the diaries. These men were of pioneer farming stock and were looking at the kind of fertile land that was a major component of the American dream of their era.[24] They knew the significance of their errand, and it kept them enthralled. Clark remarked more than once in his journal about their general good health, high spirits, and quick responses to whatever demands were put on them. "I can say with Confidence that our party is not inferior to any that was ever on the waters of the Missoppie," the last word being an extraordinary orthographic mix even for him.[25]

Lewis was out of the boat more often than in, examining the growth in the bottomlands, especially the huge cottonwood trees, and hiking or riding one of the hunting horses up the bluffs for more distant views. He collected, in Clark's words, "many curious Plants and Srubs," but not, for the first few hundred miles, any that were new to science. (Still, it was useful to extend the known range of familiar species.) Signs of changing biotic environments were appearing, however. The thick forests on the uplands were thinning out. Prairies broader than those of Illinois and Kentucky stretched between the groves, hints of the Great Plains, of which he had read without yet grasping their overwhelming magnitude. When the hunters returned to camp at day's end, he always asked them for descriptions of the soil and vegetation they had seen and about the navigability of the side streams.

If he kept a journal on this leg of the trip, it has been lost, though some rough notes have turned up. It is hard to believe he did not heed Jefferson's adjurations about records—and yet other lapses occurred, notably during Lewis's descent of the Ohio, which we have already noted, and again from August 27 through December, 1805, with two minor exceptions. The blanks are unfortunate, for Lewis's handling of the technical information they gathered was superior to Clark's. Also, we have, at many critical junctures, only Clark's observations to go on, plus the bare-bones accounts kept by a few untrained enlisted personnel, and different men do see things differently.[26]

Clark, being the better riverman, generally stayed close to the keelboat. He kept a compass reading for every shift in the stream's direction and made eyeball guesses of the distances between prominent points and curves. From these fragments he calculated the length of each day's travel and kept a running total of those sums.[27] His eyes were good. When the expedition reached the mouth of the Platte, he announced they had come 600 miles from the mouth of the Missouri. Instrument measures made several years later gave a total of 611. Distances were only part of the geographic study. They determined the latitude and longitude of every prominent river junction and hill, even when they had to chop trees out of the way to get a sighting on the polestar, as happened at the mouth of the Osage.

The sergeants soon caught on to the dead-reckoning process, and Clark occasionally turned the work over to them in order to go hunting with Lewis or Drouillard, or even by himself. On June 23, exactly one month after Lewis's misadventure on the Tavern cliffs, he suffered an embarrassment of his own. He had a good day with his gun—one fat bear and two deer, which he left where they fell. Drouillard would pick them up with his packhorse and take them to the river, skin them, and hang the carcasses where the boatmen would find them. Clark wandered on and at evening dropped down to the river. A high wind had sprung up. The keelboat, he sensed correctly, would be pinned to the bank and he would have to bivouac until morning, when it could move again.

He peeled bark off a tree and spread it on the damp ground as a mattress. He gathered punky wood to create a smoke to drive away mosquitos. He was hungry and there might be game on a nearby, brushy island. He waded out, mired down in bottomless muck, and with a little stab of fear actually wondered, as he heaved on one leg and then the other, whether he was going to pull free. When he did, he was layered with mud from head to foot. He scraped it off, stripped down, and, blackened by mosquitos, washed himself and his clothes. Hunting relief, he crouched for awhile in the smudge he had built and then fired his gun to let anyone in hearing know where he was. Shortly Drouillard appeared. He had picked up Clark's game and was searching for the captain when the gunshot gave him guidance.

To keep the fresh meat away from predators, they hung it to a low branch that reached out over the water—so low that the hindquarters of the carcasses dangled just above the surface. During the moonlit night, Clark awoke and saw a huge snake rising like a small Loch Ness monster out of the water toward one of the hanging deer. It was a doe, its udder tight with milk. Its orphaned fawn was probably wandering lost somewhere in the hills—unfortunate, but there were forty-six men on the boats to be fed. Clark assumed the snake was after the milk in its udder. Not wanting to wake Drouillard, he threw sticks to drive the serpent away. When it persisted, he killed it. He doesn't say how. One likes to imagine a gunshot that brought Drouillard out from under the saddle blanket that covered him like a cork from a bottle. Indians!—though they had not yet seen a trace of a wild Indian.

A night in the life of a hunter. Clark summarized it in his field notes, but omitted the mudhole from the "official" journal he put together later, during the winter.[28] As with Lewis on the Tavern cliffs, there was no use reminding posterity of every foolish misstep.

They ushered in the Fourth of July by firing one of the swivel guns on the keelboat. Joseph Field added to the excitement by being bitten on the heel by still another snake. Lewis did not see the creature. Uncertain whether it was poisonous, he slapped on a poultice made of Peruvian bark mixed with gunpowder. A few days later he relieved Robert Frazer's sunstroke with saltpeter, a known diuretic. A Creole riverman was treated for a venereal complaint, details unrecorded, and nearly always someone had a thundering headache brought on by the heat or a painful boil that needed the pus squeezed out before a poultice of elm bark or Indian meal could be applied.

Again there were compensations. Wild grapes, plums, berries, and sand cherries were ripening. The men poured heaping handfuls of the latter into the whiskey barrels, though whether they were flavoring the fruit or the liquor remains unsaid. They began catching big catfish and whitefish, pleasing variants for their meals. (As was true with the fur brigades, the cooks, who were relieved of other camp duties, prepared only one big meal a day, in the evening; leftovers did for breakfast and lunch. Time was too important to be wasted among pots and pans.)

Bits of excitement enlivened the toil. The Field brothers brought in a young wolf they hoped to tame—this happened near the Kansas River—but three nights later the animal chewed through the rope that held it and escaped. One man who had gone out hunting claimed he had seen a buffalo. Elk became numerous. Lewis's big Newfoundland dog dived into a beaver house and chased its terrified inhabitants out.

One major element was missing, however—Indians. Jefferson had insisted that as many tribes as possible be contacted, studied, informed of the change in Louisiana's sovereignty, and told what America was expecting of the land's natives and what they could expect from the Americans. The captains had worked hard in St. Louis and at Camp Wood to familiarize themselves with what lay ahead, and they conscientiously gathered more information from each boatload of traders—at least eight—they encountered bound downstream with their winter harvests of fur, deerskins, and animal fat. Regis Loisel, head of the frequently reorganized Missouri River Fur Company, for which James Mackay and John Evans had worked, was particularly accommodating, at least on the face of things.[29] In addition to data he gave them, Clark said, "letters"— presumably introductions to employees who were stationed among different tribes along the river.

One of Loisel's hired hands, Pierre Dorion, was floating downstream a few days behind his employer. A shrewd, hard-twisted, semiliterate half-breed, Dorion had lived intermittently with the Yankton band of Sioux for twenty years. After several hours of earnest talk, the captains persuaded him to leave his party for theirs and act as their guide and interpreter as far as the Sioux country, where they hoped to enlist another delegation to visit Washington. Dorion exacted a high price: the Americans would not only pay him an interpreter's salary but would also buy supplies and Indian gifts from him.[30]

Like Loisel before him, Dorion told gruesome tales about a smallpox epidemic that in 1802 had decimated the earth-lodge villages of the once-powerful Missouris, Otos, Poncas, Pawnees, and Omahas, or Mahars, as the captains pronounced the last word. Almost as terrifying to the Indians as the plague were new fears of the Sioux. Being nomads, those Indians had not suffered as much from the epidemic as had the river tribes, who lived in densely packed villages. Their raids could now devastate the tribes. As a safety measure, Dorion speculated, the weakened river people were probably combining into new units capable of fighting off their ancient enemies.

The Sioux. That was the tribe, made up of many far-ranging bands, that Jefferson most wanted to pull into the American orbit. It would not be easy. Except for the Yankton Sioux, whom Dorion had helped woo toward Spanish St. Louis, the tribes were oriented toward the British posts on tributaries of the Red River of the North, which led to Hudson Bay, and tributaries of the upper Mississippi, outlets to Montreal. Consequently, the Sioux, as principal carriers for the Missouri River and High Plains trade, would want to keep the commerce flowing eastward. Because of the epidemic, their dominance over the river tribes might be harder than ever to break—unless the river peoples' amalgamations were restoring their strength. More than ever, therefore, it was important to contact all the tribes along the Missouri, assay their vitality, promise peace and protection, and then try to win the cooperation of the Sioux.[31]

Eager to hold their first Indian council, the Corps of Discovery pressed on as fast as wind and water allowed. On July 21, 1804, while rain squalls hissed along the surface of the Missouri, they came to the mouth of the Platte. It was a many-braided stream, freckled with islands and sandbars, swift flowing and thick with silt. Tantalizing promises clung to it, for it was believed to head far west in high mountains near legendary Santa Fe. Many tribes lived and hunted along its banks, the nearest of them being the remnants of the Otos and Missouris and perhaps one or two bands of Pawnees. Supposedly those tribes could not be visited by water, but that was another bit of campfire gossip the captains were determined to test.

They made the effort in the red pirogue, manned by its experienced French voyageurs. They turned the boat into what seemed to be the Platte's main channel and were straightway buffeted by a current that Clark, overawed, estimated at eight miles an hour. The water was pallid with loads of fine white sand in suspension. Obstructed, the mass would build quickly into a tremulous dam, then break loose and rush on, giving a boiling, rolling look to the surface. Channels kept intertwining. After little more than a mile of strenuous effort, the captains gave up and let the pirogue drift back. Gossip was right. If the tribes of the lower Platte were to see the American offerings and hear their harangues, they would have to be lured to the Missouri by emissaries traveling overland.[32]

Searching for a suitable camping place, the expedition moved ten miles up the Missouri to a place named White Catfish Camp for an albino catfish one of the men caught there. George Drouillard and Pierre Cruzatte, equipped with sausage-shaped bundles of twisted tobacco called carrots, rode off west to find whatever Indians they could. While waiting for the messengers' return, the rest of the crew continued their perpetual hunting—forty-odd empty bellies to fill every day—made new oars and setting poles, dried provisions that had become wet during the struggle with the Platte, raised a flagstaff, and checked their arms. Lewis worked on his field notes and Clark on a map to send to Jefferson when the soldiers in Corporal Warfington's squad went back to Kaskaskia at the end of the summer. Gusts of wind rolled the boat so heavily they could not accomplish much in the cramped cabin, and yet if they went outside they were attacked by mosquitos "about the sise," Clark declared, "of house flais [flies]."[33]

On July 25, Drouillard and Cruzatte returned. They had found the Otos' principal village and had seen fresh tracks, but had not located a single person. Having planted their corn and squash, the villagers evidently had moved en masse onto the plains on their annual buffalo hunt.

Considerably deflated, the explorers crept on—into luck. On the 28th Drouillard came in with a Missouri Indian he had found skinning an elk with two Otos. The fellow said that about twenty lodges—perhaps a hundred men, women, and children—were camped about four miles away. Off at some distance was the habitation of a French trader who had lived with the Otos long enough to win their trust. What now?

The decision was to gain a little time by sailing up the Missouri for two more days while a voyageur called La Liberté, who knew the Oto language, traveled overland with Drouillard's Missouri Indian as guide, to lure the French trader and as many warriors as possible to a meeting. Forty miles above White Catfish Camp, on the west bank of the river, the boat people found a delectable, easily reached spot. They named it, in anticipation, Council Bluff. (Later, after Fort Atkinson had been built on the site, the name spread to the entire region, including the city of Council Bluffs, Iowa, about fifteen miles downstream from the scheduled meeting place.) Tiers of prairies and bluffs led Lewis and Clark, who climbed the rise together, to a stupendous view of "one Continued Plain as fur as Can be seen"—the heart of prairie America. Below them the Missouri meandered through lush groves of willow, cottonwood, elm, sycamore, hickory, walnut "& Oake in addition." All about, Clark wrote, were fruits, berries, nuts, and "a great Variety of Plants and flowers not common to the United States. What a field for a Botents [botanist] and natiriless [naturalist]."[34]

August 1 was a day of mixed emotions. Clark busied himself for a time preparing what he called a "verry flashey peace pipe" for the Indian conference. Then, because it was his thirty-fourth birthday, the camp was treated to a special feast of fat venison, elk, and beavertail, finished off with a medley of fruits and, probably, a dram of grog. Joseph Field killed a new animal, a badger, and then, while out hunting deer with his brother, Reuben, got lost, settled down for the night in a rough bivouac—and awoke to find that the expedition's two horses, essential for packing meat, had strayed. Meanwhile neither the Indians nor La Liberté had appeared. "we fear," Clark wrote, "Something amiss."[35]

The suspense ended the next day. Drouillard and Colter found the horses, and at sunset the trader, whose name Clark rendered as Fairfong, arrived with fourteen male Indians, six of them minor chiefs. All, probably, were on horseback. There was no sign of La Liberté, though the Indians said he had left their camp a day ahead of them.

The captains sent food and presents to the visitors and suggested they gather the next morning under an awning made from the keelboat's sail. Lewis, with Clark at his elbow, stayed up late that night, writing out what they hoped would be an epochal speech, forerunner of many more to come. The soldiers unpacked and brushed off their uniforms for a dress parade. At the assigned time the two groups came together, each with totally different expectations of what was going to emerge from the encounter.

SEVEN

Emphasis on Indians

"Children," began Meriwether Lewis, looking over the Indians seated in front of him. Every paragraph he spoke to them opened with that word. "Children." It breathed authority and had been used for generations by the representatives of different governments contesting for the allegiance of the Native Americans. It assumed the right of the speaker to give instructions; it implied the duty of the listeners to heed or risk condign punishment.

"Children." The American flag rippled overhead. Uniformed soldiers, rifles held at ease, stood to one side. He continued: the great chief of the seventeen great nations of the United States—the chief who was also the father—now controlled the Western rivers. Only vessels that acknowledged American authority could bring merchandise to the interior. If the father's children displeased him, he would cut off trade, and the families of the Otos and Missouris would suffer want. But if all went well and if the Missouri River became a true road of peace for both red men and white, commerce would flourish and in time the great father would establish trading posts at convenient spots among the tribes. So that the Indians could understand the power and beneficence of the new sovereign, let them choose representatives to visit him at his lodge in the East and see for themselves his cities, "as numerous as the stars in the heavens" and the source of gifts munificent beyond their imagining.[1]

The next part of the ritual was a process called "making chiefs." As required by tradition, the captains had brought with them many hollow silver medals of different sizes, each hung on a loop of colored ribbon. Each bore on one side a likeness of President Jefferson and on the other a symbol of hands clasped in friendship. The medals varied in size and were handed out according to the tribal standing of the recipients.[2]

Though there were no principal chiefs at the Oto council, the captains went grandly ahead with those that were available. Having selected the person who seemed to be held in the most esteem by his fellows, Lewis gestured for him to step forward. A second-degree medal was placed around his neck; his hand was shaken. His lieutenants, as determined by the captains' observations, then received their accolades—in some cases parchment certificates that attested to the good character of the Indian named on the face of the document. A distribution of gifts completed the formal part of the ceremony. Again status counted. Leaders received more and better military coats, leggings, hats, gunpowder, and so on than did the rank and file, who were content with beads, fishhooks, small mirrors, and the like.

Lest easy giving be mistaken for weakness, the whites added implicit warnings by demonstrating their technological superiority. Magnets, compass needles that returned to their original resting position no matter how they were shaken, and magnifying glasses that focused the rays of the sun tightly enough to start fires were always impressive. To the list Lewis added a demonstration of his airgun. Take aim, pull the trigger . . . pop. No smoke, no roar, and therefore no ball. Yet when the watchers ran out to examine the target that had been blazed earlier on a tree trunk, they saw, with cries of amazement, dents in the wood that could have been deadly in flesh. All that, and then a sealing of the new bonds with "white man's milk"—a bottle of whiskey that was given to one of the chiefs to pass out sip by sip according to his own discretion. No responsible treaty maker or trader liked the mischief inherent in liquor, which many Indians craved insatiably, but if one didn't use it, the competition would, and gain advantage thereby.

The Indians at that first meeting, excited by the prospect of a more dependable and, they hoped, cheaper supply of merchandise than they had been accustomed to, responded genially. They probably would have been equally amiable toward any trader who made promises as big as those of Meriwether Lewis, and that wasn't the kind of unswerving loyalty the expedition was trying to create. Yet why should the Indians be loyal to an unseen chief of seventeen nations that were said to exist somewhere off toward the rising sun? What the Americans needed was a gesture that would apply directly to the listeners.

The seed for such a gesture existed. The captains had learned, probably from Fairfong, that the Otos were at war with the Omahas, or Mahas, who lived several miles farther up the Missouri. The visiting Otos said they would like to see the conflict ended.[3] Such a peace would also help establish the American hegemony over Louisiana that Jefferson wanted. Eagerly the captains proposed to act as mediators if some of the group under the awning would go with them into Omaha territory to attest to the validity of the request for peace.

Not a man agreed. They were afraid of being killed, they admitted, a reaction that spoke volumes about their opinion of the expedition's ability to protect them, even though it possessed a magic airgun and was the largest and most heavily armed party that had yet appeared on the river. With no principal chiefs on hand to get things rolling, the disappointed captains gave up the idea.

The council broke up early in the afternoon of August 3. Anxious as always to make the hours count (the Mandan villages were still nearly a thousand miles away) the boatmen resumed the upstream push at once. They had not gone far when one of the soldiers, Moses Reed, exclaimed he had left his knife at camp and asked permission to retrieve it. He would overtake the flotilla as it wound slowly along. When two days passed with no sign of him, his sergeant examined his knapsack, discovered that his extra clothes and ammunition were not there, and reported he had probably deserted. No such breach of discipline could be countenanced —and besides, the captains thought, here might be a chance to get a peace movement underway. Reed had almost surely made for the Oto town. Let a dependable posse go there and pick him up dead or alive—La Liberté with him. By then Little Thief, principal chief of the Otos, and Big Horse, chief of the Missouris, might have returned from their buffalo hunt. If so, the search party should try, with Fairfong's help, to persuade the men to hurry after the flotilla and join the American captains in council near the Omahas' village.

George Drouillard, two tough privates, Reuben Field and William Bratton, and the Oto-speaking voyageur, François Labiche, made up the search party. Though the assignment left the expedition short-handed by six men, counting the two deserters, a blessed south wind took their place on the 9th, filled the sails, and scooted their boats along for fourteen easy miles. By the 11th they had reached the foot of a steep knoll about three hundred feet high. A post was visible on its top. Blackbird's grave, Dorion said, and added that the Omaha town over which the notorious chief had once ruled—the town where the captains hoped the peace council could be held—was only eight miles away.

The captains looked at each other. Why not visit Blackbird's tomb? They had time enough, thanks to the wind. Besides, hadn't Benjamin Rush and President Jefferson suggested funeral customs as an item to look into while learning the culture of the Western Indians? Up the two captains went with ten men, talking meanwhile about what was known of the old villain.

The Omahas had been a powerful tribe not long since and had exacted heavy tribute from traders traveling along the river. Leader in the rascality was Blackbird. Whenever he wished to eliminate an Indian rival he invited him to a feast laced with arsenic he had obtained from some unscrupulous riverman. His own agonies came in 1802, the year smallpox swept through the village, creating such a frenzy of fear that the men not only burned their moundlike houses but also, Clark heard, "put *their* wives & children to *Death* with a view of their all going together to some better country."[4]

When Blackbird caught the disease, he asked his followers to bury him on the knoll, eight miles away, that had been his favorite lookout. (Hilltop burial was an Omaha custom.) From its summit he had been able to survey miles of the curling river, spot travelers, and have his warriors ready when the visitors reached the vicinity of the town. Legend says his tribesmen sat his corpse upright on his slain horse, held both erect while they packed sod around them, and crowned the mound with an eight-foot pole embellished with the chief's pipe, his fringed tobacco pouch, and his shield decorated with eagle feathers and scalps taken in war. To this collection Lewis and Clark added a pennant, perhaps to win favor from the Omahas who, they noted, still placed food on the hilltop as sustenance for the slain chief's spirit.[5]

The captains spent August 12 doing more work on their maps and reports. On the thirteenth they sent a mission under Sergeant Ordway to the Omaha village to prepare for the council. The scouts returned the following day to report the village deserted.

Evidently the Indians were still out hunting buffalo. "A great misfortune," Clark scribbled in his field notes.[6]

More time to kill. On August 15 Clark and ten men made a brush seine and, after dragging it up the sluggish mouth of a tributary creek, caught 318 catfish, pike, bass, perch, and a species they mistakenly called salmon. The next day Lewis repeated with twelve men and caught about 800. During that time his co-captain and the carpenters of the group made and set a new mast in the keelboat.[7]

Late in the afternoon of the 17th Labiche appeared and reported the search party was on its way with Reed—La Liberté had escaped—and with nine mounted Indians, including Little Thief and Big Horse, intent on making peace. But no one was around to make it with. Cursing wryly over the irony, the captains had some of their men climb out of the river bottom and start a prairie fire, a standard signal for summoning Indians. Black smoke billowed high, but no Omahas appeared. All in all, the 18th, which would mark Lewis's thirtieth birthday, was not going to go far toward redeeming the shortcomings of the first council.

Moses Reed, quickly found guilty after his return, was sentenced to run four times through a gauntlet made up of the entire body of enlisted men, each armed with nine willow switches. Immediate objections came from Little Thief and Big Horse, who had been traveling for some days with the prisoner and considered him an integral member of the tribe of whites. Indians would not inflict such an indignity on a band member. The captains explained its necessity, to the Indians' satisfaction they hoped, and the soldiers laid on with a will because, Ordway wrote, anyone showing leniency would have to run a gauntlet himself. The culprit was then read out of the expedition and assigned as a laborer to the French pirogue in La Liberté's place.[8]

The evening was merrier. An extra gill of whiskey was issued so the men could toast Lewis's birthday. Cruzatte tuned his fiddle, and the young soldiers worked off the energy that had been building in them during the days of inactivity by dancing jigs and reels until midnight. The Indians saw nothing strange in an all-male dance. That was the way they went at it, too, and perhaps they demonstrated.

Somberness returned with dawn. Sergeant Charles Floyd, Jr., son of one of Clark's friends, was stricken with what the captains diagnosed as bilious colic. Probably one of them bled him. They may also have dosed him with Rush's thunderbolts, for indiscriminate purgings were the common way, in those days, of ridding the body of unhealthful substances. Nothing could have been worse, for the nature of Floyd's symptoms has led modern doctors to suspect peritonitis from a ruptured appendix.

If the sufferer's moans were heard at the next day's awning-shaded council, they were a fitting accompaniment. There was another speech by Lewis to the great father's children, another making of chiefs and a handing out of gifts. But there was no meeting of minds. Little Thief declared the Otos didn't care with whom they traded as long as quality and price were right. Big Horse drew a stern rebuke from the white diplomats by offering to keep his young men from going to war if he was given whiskey to distribute among them. There were hurt feelings among those who felt their medals and certificates weren't true measures of their status. In spite of the general sullenness, however, Little Thief did accept Lewis's invitation to visit Washington the following summer. The council broke up with neither side satisfied with what had been achieved.[9]

William Clark spent that night sitting beside Floyd, doing what he could to bring comfort. In the morning some of the soldiers carried the patient onto the keelboat. Toward noon they halted to prepare a warm bath for him, but before it was ready he whispered to Clark, "I'm going away. I want you to write a letter." The next moment he was dead. His companions wrapped him in a blanket and carried him to the top of a knoll shaped much like Blackbird's but on the other side of the river and upstream, within the present limits of Sioux City, Iowa. He was buried with military honors, Lewis reading the service. A nearby stream was named Floyd's River. Two days later the men elected Patrick Gass to fill his place as sergeant. In the midst of death, life goes on.

The day of the election must have brought with it another tug of alarm. Lewis fell violently ill, and Clark thought he knew the reason. In spite of high winds that filled the air with sand, Meriwether had insisted on prowling around a bluff that showed streaks of what Ordway called "ore." Clark guessed the stuff was a mix of alum, copperas, cobalt, and pyrites. Guesses weren't enough for Lewis. He pounded chunks of the "ore" into powder, sniffed its sulfurous smell, and took several experimental tastes. Shortly thereafter his stomach knotted, and Clark added arsenic to his list of suspected ingredients. Avoiding thunderbolts, Lewis dosed himself with "salts" as a purge.[10]

Either the treatment or his own healthy constitution sufficed. The next day, sand still blowing in such clouds as to interfere with Clark's sightings for his map making, Meriwether felt well enough to walk out with ten or twelve men to see a buffalo Joseph Field had shot—the expedition's first. The labors of everyone who went to view the huge beast were needed to cut up the carcass and lug the meat to the boat.

There was, indeed, no end to curiosities. During yarn-telling time at the last Oto council, an Indian had described a race of little men, eighteen inches tall and equipped with murderously effective bows and arrows. The midgets reputedly slew all humans who came close to the conical hill on—or in—which they lived. Skeptical, the captains sailed the fleet on past the creek the Indian had said would take them to the wonder. Then curiosity and conscience got the best of them. Just suppose such creatures did exist and they left the discovery to someone else?

Choosing nine dependable men, they boarded the white pirogue and dropped back to the disembarking place. For three hours they walked through crushing heat toward a symmetrical hill rising out of the level, treeless plain. Lewis's heavily furred dog, Seaman, collapsed. Lewis, still debilitated by his "poisoning," almost did. The usual high wind was blowing, and when they sought shelter from it on the lee side of the hill, they discovered that innumerable insects had preceded them, as had clouds of swallows drawn by the flying feast. This surprising swirl of life, they concluded, was the basis of the Indian legend.[11] The hill, incidentally, is now called Spirit Mound; it rises in the southeastern tip of South Dakota near the town of Vermillion.

The next day they overtook the keelboat, which had been going slowly upriver in charge of Sergeant Nathaniel Pryor. Anticipation rose. They were nearing the mouth of the James River, a geographically and, in 1804, a politically significant tributary of the Missouri, for it opened a way to far-flung British canoe routes. One led down the Red River of the North to, eventually, Hudson Bay. The other wound via the French-pioneered Great Lakes traverses to British fur companies in Montreal. The powerful Sioux nation sat astride both routes, receiving manufactured goods both for themselves and, as middlemen, for customers farther west.

That British orientation Thomas Jefferson wanted to break for the commercial future of American merchants emigrating into Upper Louisiana.

Sioux. The word sounded like a hiss and probably was meant to. It derived from the Ojibway (Chippewa) sneer *nadowe-is-iw*. To the Ojibway, a *nadowe* was a big snake and hence, metaphorically, an enemy, in this case the Iroquois. The diminuitive form, *nadowe-is-iw*, sometimes written *Nadowesseis* or *Nadowesi* by early explorers, meant "little snakes," Sioux for short. The Sioux, however, called themselves *Dah-kota*, modernized to Dakota, which means "allies." There were seven main bands of them, and those bands were further divided into many subbands.[12]

For decade upon decade, in olden times, Dakota and Ojibway had fought strenuously for control of the wild-rice lakes of Minnesota, a principal source of food. On at least obtaining guns from the French traders of Montreal, the Ojibway had been able to drive the "little snakes" west across the Mississippi into, roughly, the southern quarter of present-day Minnesota and the adjacent fringes of Iowa and South Dakota. There were buffalo in the new homeland to make up for the loss of wild rice, but as population increased hunting grew poorer, and some of the main Dakota bands resumed their migrations westward. The two that could be readily contacted from the Missouri, and hence were of prime importance to Lewis and Clark, were the Yanktons, who ranged from the southwestern tip of the Minnesota along the James to its mouth, and the aggressive Tetons, who utilized a broad strip of woodland and prairies west from the James across the Missouri to . . . well, no one knew how far.

Sioux. "On that nation," Jefferson had written his ex-secretary in St. Louis on January 22, 1804, "we wish most particularly to make a friendly impression because of their immense power." To this Lewis no doubt added wryly the specific Indian information Jefferson had directed him to learn in the instructions that had been handed him in Washington on June 20, 1803. The explorers were to collect data on the strength, trade patterns, territorial claims, dispositions, languages, tools, clothing, customs, medical skills, laws, living patterns, propensities toward war, and the alliances of every tribe they could reach.[13] It was a monumental task, with scant time allowed for completing a survey of any one tribe the flotilla passed. But at least the captains were beginning their

Dakota confrontation with the amiable Yanktons. Moreover, they had with them an interpreter, Pierre Dorion, who had lived with the Yanktons for many years. His son still resided there.

On reaching the James, the traveling diplomats set the usual prairie fire to attract Indians. Anticlimax followed. The first person to appear the next morning was George Drouillard, weary from an all-night hike. The previous afternoon he and young George Shannon had killed an elk. While they were butchering it so they could load the edible parts on their horses, the animals had strayed. During the search for them, the hunters had lost track of each other, and Drouillard had not been able to find either his companion or the two horses—the only pack stock the expedition had.

Shannon, the youngest member of the group, lost with two horses in Indian country! Besides, in Clark's opinion, Shannon was a poor woodsman. So, though Dorion insisted the Yanktons were friendly and might themselves bring the lad back if they found him, the captains sent John Shields and Joseph Field out to look for him.[14]

At about the same time, three young Indians swam across the stream with word that a mobile village of Yankton Sioux was located nine miles up the James. Because the explorers wanted the Indians to be impressed by their strength and the tempting lading they carried, they chose not to visit the town but instead invited the Indians to a council at Calumet Bluff, twenty miles farther up the Missouri. The invitation was delivered by old Dorion, Sergeant Nathaniel Pryor, and one of the French voyageurs.

Deprived of the inflow of the James, the shoaling Missouri shrank still more. The keelboat grounded several times, and on August 28, with Calumet Bluff in sight, the French pirogue (the one that had been painted red back at Camp Wood) ran into a snag that punched a big hole in its hull. Fortunately Clark was nearby with the keelboat. He ordered it alongside, and nearly everyone jumped overboard to help. They got the craft unloaded, dragged onto the beach, and overturned for repairs. Of necessity that spot, opposite the side of the river on which the Yanktons were located, became the council site. Making camp, they set up a flagpole and contemplated their situation.

Shannon was one problem. The searchers had discovered tracks that showed he had found the stray horses and was riding upstream at a good clip, unaware of the halt at Calumet Bluff. John Colter was given a load of provisions and told to run him down. Meanwhile the carpenters in the group, led by Sergeant Gass, went to work on the red pirogue. If it didn't prove serviceable for upstream navigation afterwards, it would be sent back to St. Louis with the reports and maps Lewis and Clark had been working on whenever they could find free time. The soldiers in the white pirogue would continue, as agreed, until ice became a threat, and then they too would retreat.

About sunset on August 29, the emissaries to the Yanktons appeared on the far bank with sixty or seventy Indians. The natives spent the night there, making their own preparations for the coming affair. After a heavy fog had burned off the next morning, the white pirogue was pressed into service as a ferry. As it returned, packed tight with Indians, the swivel gun on the bow of the keelboat banged out two salutes. The reply by the Yanktons was livelier. Four men, their naked bodies painted in different colors, leaped from the prow of the pirogue, shaking rattles and singing. Each carried a barbaric shield of buffalo hide covered with antelope skin ornamented with feathers and quills. More feathers, porcupine quills, and paint, along with ornate moccasins, high leggings, and buffalo robes painted different colors on the inside bedecked the warriors who followed. "The squars," Clark added, "wore Peticoats [probably made of thin, beautifully tanned deerskin caught at the shoulder with string] & a white buffalow roab with the black hair turned over thar necks and sholders."[15]

Lewis gave his Children speech, which Dorion translated. A making of five chiefs of different degrees followed; the usual presents were passed out. The recipients retired behind some bushes to divide the booty with their fellows. They would give their replies in the morning, a delay that was a standard Indian custom.

The intervening evening was spent watching a fire-lit dance put on by warriors who had painted their faces and breasts with streaks and patches of white. Music came from rattles, from "little instruments" (Private Whitehouse called them jew's harps; if they were, some earlier trader had passed them around) and from a drum whose taut leather head was a gift from Meriwether Lewis. Every now and then one of the warriors let out a whoop and sang about his brave deeds. The American soldiers kept the merriment rolling by tossing out pieces of tobacco and small gifts.

The next morning the principal chief, Weuche, appeared, resplendent in his gift from the explorers, a richly laced, red artillery officer's coat and cocked military hat decorated with a plume. Ornamented peace pipes passed back and forth. The chiefs made their harangues. They were poor; they needed trade; if the visitors did not provide it from their richly laden boats, Weuche hinted, the Yanktons might have to stop the next craft that appeared and requisition what they needed.

Behind the Yankton's protestations of poverty lay a complexity that Lewis and Clark did not fully grasp. The Indians wanted manufactured goods not only for themselves but for resale at a big annual Sioux trading fair held each summer on the upper James River. The Yanktons could get some of the things they carried to the fair from contacts on the Des Moines River in Iowa. More came from British traders who operated out of tiny posts on the upper Mississippi and the St. Peter's (now the Minnesota) River. The demand for white-made merchandise was voracious, especially on the part of the Teton Sioux, who carried what they acquired at the fair west for trade with the tribes along the Missouri and still farther west. The Yanktons were eager to fill the Tetons' demand, but Loisel's overly extended Missouri Fur Company could not provide it. Perhaps these Americans could. So they made their pitch feverishly, threatening, through Chief Weuche, to hijack boats if that was the only way they could get what they wanted.

The Americans tried to explain. They were not traders but explorers, opening a road from St. Louis for professional merchants to follow. To achieve that goal they would need the goods in their boats as gifts to tribes living farther up the river. Then, in the days that followed, everyone would be well supplied.

Easy talk. But how could the Indians be sure the whites were speaking with straight tongues?

Make peace with the tribes around you, the captains urged, and go with Dorion to St. Louis and Washington, to see for yourselves the power and richness of America.

After prolonged dickering Weuche agreed, and in high spirits the captains rounded out the day collecting Sioux vocabularies, learning the names and territories of the tribe's many bands, and, for Jefferson's sake, gathering other bits of ethnographic lore about beliefs, weapons, dress, and so on.

The only sour note was sounded by a lesser chief, Half Man.

Though the Yanktons had listened to the visitors, "those nations above," he said, "will not open their ears." In other words, don't get overconfident. The captains, in their euphoria, paid no heed. They even left Dorion behind as they started on, thinking it more important for him to nail down the Yanktons than to continue with the boats as interpreter, though they had no other person fluent in Sioux with them.

The distance from the mouth of the James River to the mouth of the Bad, where the Corps of Discovery expected to encounter the Teton Sioux, was, by Clark's calculation, about 250 miles. In that relatively short traverse to the northwest—from about the ninety-eighth meridian to the far side of the hundredth—the explorers left the humid setting familiar to most Americans of their day and entered a region of wind, sun, and treeless space whose very aridity demanded new life forms and new ways of living.

In the bottom of the Missouri's broad trench the change was not immediately noticeable. The river's islands and flood plains were still cloaked with groves of many kinds of trees among which grapes, plums, chokecherries, and other fruits grew riotously. Occasional meadows and sandbars provided delectable camping places. But a short climb above the flood plain brought a foretaste of a radically different environment.

First the hikers reached treeless terraces that were a mile wide in places. After crossing the terraces, they encountered steep hills whose gullies sheltered patches of dry-land junipers and stunted oaks. The crests of the hills, sometimes called breaks, were high enough—up to six hundred feet above the flood plain—and rough enough that Clark called the country mountainous. That was a deceptive view, however, for beyond the breaks the land leveled off to a treeless, gently undulating plateau that stretched out through air of brilliant clarity to a horizon as sharp as a knife blade.

These High Plains, as they came to be called, were matted with short, curly, appropriately named buffalo grass studded with clumps of prickly pear cactus. Magnificent hawks sailed overhead; lovely black-and-white magpies made pests of themselves around the camp, snatching food almost from a man's fingers. Buffalo abounded. Soon everyone, including York (who, as a slave, was not legally entitled to carry a gun) was firing away at the massive beasts, killing them on the plains and river terraces, on the islands and even in the water. Big, black-tailed deer became common; Lewis named them mule deer because of the size of their ears. Another far-bounding creature defined by its oversized ears was a large hare called jackass rabbit, or jackrabbit for short, though strictly speaking it was not a rabbit at all. Big wolves were another everyday sight—and their howling an every-night sound. So, too, with smaller, elusive, yipping creatures the captains called foxes until they were able to kill one for study. It was not a fox, they decided, but a "small wolf"; today we know the species as coyotes.

Two more biologically inappropriate names came from early French voyageurs. One was attached to those soft-furred, yellow-gray little rodents, relatives of the ground squirrel, that lived in immense colonies throughout the High Plains. *Petit chiens,* the amused viewers said—little dogs of the prairie, or prairie dogs. The other misnamed animal was smaller than a deer, with a light brown back, white underparts, white throat stripes, and a white rump. The French called it *cabril,* or goat. After Clark finally succeeded in killing a male, he dissected it and arrived at the conclusion that it was "more like the Antilope or gazelle of Africa than any other species of Goat." The creature lacked a beard. Its horns were soft and hollow, and were shed annually—nothing like a goat. It was a pronghorn, a species found only in western North America. Now it is commonly known as antelope, which is as erroneous as calling a bison a buffalo. Change is unlikely, however.[16]

Because prairie dogs were small, Lewis and Clark decided to capture one alive, cage it, and send it to Jefferson when the red pirogue turned back downstream. A colony sighted, most of the crew advanced on it with shovels. The little animals rushed about like a mass of disturbed ants, each to the low mound of earth that ringed its burrow. For a moment they sat ramrod-straight on the mounds, barking shrilly—or whistling, as the captains sometimes wrote, though they also used the term "barking squirrels." Then, as the invaders neared, each *chien* dived out of sight into its steeply pitching tunnel.

After trenching fruitlessly to a depth of six feet, the frustrated hunters switched to water. They filled five barrels with liquid lugged up from the river in kettles, poured the contents into another burrow, and flushed out one miserable specimen, which they took alive. Water was indeed a strange substance to the little animals. As Lewis correctly deduced from the huge colonies they later examined many miles from any stream or pond, prairie dogs never drank but subsisted by metabolizing minute amounts of moisture from the vegetation they ate.[17]

The captains also wanted to send Jefferson the skins, horns, and bones of both male and female pronghorns. After Clark had prepared the male he had shot, Lewis set out, on September 17, with two flankers to obtain a female. The hunt is remarkable mostly because the account of it is one of the very few passages in his hand about the long push up the Missouri. A sense of release and exuberance suffuses his tale. After wending their way through a mile-wide colony of barking squirrels, the three hunters climbed to the top of the breaks and confronted the vastness beyond. The exhilaration arising from those infinite miles was heightened by the "immense herds of buffalo, deer, elk, and antelopes we saw in every direction." Surely they would get what they wanted. But no. Though they painstakingly stalked several groups of pronghorns, they never crept close enough for a shot. There was recompense, however—a vivid memory of the animals' extraordinary fleetness, "equal if not superior to that of the finest blooded courser." A few years later the comparison became, in Biddle's version of the journals, "a speed equal to that of the most distinguished racehorse."[18] Faster, probably. The advent of automobiles has allowed the clocking of fleeing antelope at sixty miles an hour. (Later on, incidentally, the explorers did bag a female to send East with the male. Another anticlimax. The Osage Indians who had visited Washington earlier that summer at Pierre Chouteau's and Lewis's instigation had already showed Jefferson a well-tanned skin, its sex unrecorded.)

The abundance of game was of no help to the expedition's lost hunter, young George Shannon. Believing the boats were still ahead of him, he kept going upstream through the tangled woods of the flood plain as fast as the state of the two horses he had recovered permitted. That formidable outdoorsman, John Colter, could not overtake him, partly because of Colter's own irrepressible trigger finger. Whenever an edible animal crossed his path, he killed it, cut the meat into strips, and placed them on wooden racks to dry. On September 6 he turned back, flagged down the boats, and as they toiled along pointed the way to the jerky he had prepared.

Cold rains and high winds swept the river. A mast snapped off and had to be replaced. The river level stayed low in spite of the erratic storms. Shoals and sandbars grew more numerous. The keelboat kept grounding. Unable to make much headway with either poles or oars, the men had to tumble out and resort to the device they hated most, the tow rope.

On September 11, Shannon amazed them by materializing out of a clump of trees, hungry and with only a single horse. A few days after starting his ill-judged pursuit of the boats he had expended the last of the little ammunition he was carrying. By whittling substitute bullets out of wood he had managed to knock down a rabbit, but when that morsel was gone he had only grapes and wild plums to eat. Once a buffalo plodded by within thirty feet of him, but he had only been able to stare at it in frustration. When one of the horses played out, he left it to die uneaten, at least by him. He kept haunting the riverbanks, hoping some trader's boat would come along, but none did—not that late in the season, so far up the river. Clark greeted him with combined relief and anger, the reaction many parents exhibit when errant children return unharmed. Imagine starving in a land of plenty, he wrote scornfully, forgetting that after Shannon had expended his ammunition, he could do nothing other than survive on grapes.[19]

The next day, September 12, the keelboat hung up on a sandbar and nearly overturned. Though they straightened it out after a struggle, the current along that stretch was so fast they made only four miles between breakfast and supper. Meanwhile wind-driven rain was seeping through the tarpaulins of all three boats and wetting the ladings. When the 16th dawned clear, the captains decided to halt, dry out the merchandise, and reload in such a way as to lighten the keelboat.

Most of the excess cargo went into the red pirogue. Because its new load and the lading of the white pirogue would be needed during the winter among the Mandan Indians, the crews of both boats, the captains announced, would have to keep on rowing the full distance. That meant wintering among the Indians, because if the pirogues turned back after finally reaching the villages, their crews would risk being icebound. The decision was a blow for everyone. Lewis and Clark were violating promises they had made to the men in St. Louis—promises that may have led voyageurs and soldiers alike to make winter plans of their own. And Jefferson would not receive until the following summer the specimens, maps, and reports over which Lewis and Clark had worked so assiduously.[20]

Did anyone complain? The journals don't say. As far as the captains were concerned, the order was the result of military necessity and hence not subject to discussion.

The adjustment in lading helped. On September 20, aided by favoring winds, the flotilla covered twenty-seven miles of what was called, variously, the Great Detour and the Grand Detour. At that spot, about thirty-five direct miles southeast of present-day Pierre, South Dakota, the river bulges northward in a big, inverted, lopsided, tight-mouthed topographic U. Wanting his map of the curiosity to be accurate, Clark left the boats and stepped off the distance across the bottom of the bulge. Two thousand yards, he found. Dropping into the river trough, he rejoined the boats and picked up the observations that had been made along the course of the detour. It turned out that the river wandered thirty miles through the bulge while advancing a meager 2,000 yards down country.

Camp that night was on a sandbar whose perpendicular sides rose several feet above the level of the river. It was an almost disastrous choice of sites. As usual, a few of the men slept on the boats. Most spread their blankets on the ground near the edge of the bar. Between one and two o'clock in the morning, a sudden rocking of the keelboat and a shout of alarm from the guard awakened Clark. Along with the rest of the party he reared up into a frightening scene silvered by the light of a full moon.

On either side of the three boats undercut banks were caving into the water—a peeling off of tons of earth that was closing in on the camp like the jaws of an agitated vise. The captains shouted the men into place and they escaped just ahead of a roaring cataract of sand and clay. The pirogues at least, and possibly the keelboat, would have been sunk if they had been caught. As for the campground where many had been sleeping, it vanished.

That afternoon they received a portent of more trouble, an abandoned island trading post constructed the year before by Regis Loisel, head of the reorganized Missouri Company. He had built well, there on Cedar Island, where he planned to trade with some of the Teton bands of the Dakota nation. Pickets thirteen and a half feet high formed a square some sixty or seventy feet to a side. Bastions at diagonally opposite corners allowed armed men inside the projecting boxes to rake attackers with an enfilading fire. Inside the stockade was a log building that housed a trading room and counter, a storage room for merchandise and pelts, and living quarters for the traders. But from what Loisel and Dorion had said, it was clear the Teton Sioux, correctly sensing the timidity of the traders' underpaid voyageurs, had not been fazed by the mere appearance of strength.

We have the story of the unhappy winter from one of Loisel's principal clerks, Pierre Antoine Tabeau of Montreal (*Tabeau's Narrative of Loisel's Expedition to the Upper Missouri,* translated and edited by Annie Heloise Abel in 1939). Lewis and Clark must have already heard parts of the tale from Loisel and Dorion, and it was not reassuring.

The most malicious of the traders' antagonists had been a chief called the Partisan, for unknown reasons. His band was a division of the Tetons called the Bois Brulés because, one suggestion runs, of their unusually dark complexions. The Partisan's bullies had concentrated particularly on Pierre Dorion, blowing out the half-blood's candles, walking off with his pipes, and in general humiliating him in front of both the voyageurs and the mocking Indians. The Partisan rewarded his swaggering "soldiers" by giving them blankets he pilfered openly from the stocks in the store. The gang had once closed the post to trade until they had been bought off with a barrel of brandy. But the worst was a notion that had grown up among the Bois Brulés that if an Indian could lay hold of, and keep hold of, a pirogue's mooring rope, the boat became a prize of war. That had happened to Loisel, and he had recovered a portion of his goods only by pleading his case in front of a council attended by a few of the band's less hostile chiefs. Trade at the island fort was so unprofitable, indeed, that when spring came Loisel had sent Pierre Antoine Tabeau and seven men upstream to try their luck among the Arikaras.

The Partisan's harassments were intended to benefit not only his Indians but also his friends the British, whose support he coveted in his rivalries with the other Bois Brulé chiefs. "He intrigues," Tabeau sputtered in ink, "he agitates, he incites, he inveighs against against our meanness, forbids dealing with us, and encourages reserving the pelts for [the Canadians at] the River St. Peter's."[21] How could Lewis and Clark, struggling to replace the British with American traders, cope with such a man in one short meeting?

Pushing the worry aside, they pressed on upstream. With Pierre Cruzatte doing his poor best as interpreter, they learned from some Indian boys they met that two villages of the Bois Brulé lay ahead, one beside the Missouri and the other a short distance up the Bad River, whose mouth was not far away. Good, the captains answered; tell your people we want to hold a council with them.

A little farther on, they overtook John Colter, who had been hunting with the single horse the expedition still possessed. He had shot an elk and while the disjointed carcass was being put aboard one of the pirogues, the horse disappeared. Stolen, Colter was sure. On encountering five mounted Indians a mile or so upstream, the captains jumped to the conclusion they were the thieves. Through Cruzatte, with François Labiche perhaps chiming in, the captains demanded the animal's return.

The Indians, surprisingly agreeable, said they knew nothing of the horse. If anyone from their village had taken it, they added, it would be returned. Accepting the statement, the captains gave the five some tobacco and let one of them sleep on the keelboat that night. The five were still with them the next day when they reached their stopping place, an island in the mouth of the Bad River, which they renamed the Teton, perhaps in the hope of flattering the tribe. (The name was later changed back to the Bad and remains that today.) For safety's sake, they anchored the boats well out in the Missouri. Except for the cooks, who did their work on the sandy beach of the island under the protection of a few guards, everyone slept on board.

In the morning—it was September 25—they erected the usual awning of sailcloth and raised a flag. Most of the soldiers then donned dress uniforms—cocked hats, white belts crisscrossing on their jacket fronts. The captains buckled on swords; the troopers saw to their rifles. Toward midmorning, sixty or so Indians drifted in from their villages two miles up the Bad. They were a colorful group, their moccasins decorated with porcupine quills and the insides of their buffalo robes garishly painted. Warriors who had won the right to do so wore eagle feathers in manes of hair that crested their scalps. There were women and children with the men, which was reassuring. After thirty or so chiefs and warriors had found seats in the shade under the awning, each side offered the other generous gifts of food. A pipe passed around, and when the last puffs of smoke had threaded away into the autumn air, the talks began.

EIGHT

Into Winter

Although Pierre Cruzatte did his best with hand talk and the few Sioux phrases he and Labiche knew, he could not convey to the listening Indians the full meaning of Lewis's speech. Sensing this, Meriwether shifted, with Clark's help, to tableaus designed to show American strength as typified by disciplined soldiers—something the Tetons had never seen.[1]

Wearing their dress uniforms, which by then were inevitably rumpled, the entire force, less those assigned to stand watch over the boats, lined up on the loose sand. There must have been at least twenty of them. A wind-whipped Stars and Stripes snapped overhead. They slogged and wheeled to the sergeants' barks: "By the right flank, march! Company halt! Present arms!"

The Indians watched stony-faced. The lack of enthusiasm continued as the captains passed on as grandly as they could to the next part of the routine, the making of three chiefs: Black Buffalo, the Partisan, and Buffalo Medicine, all of the Bois Brulé band. A few warriors let parchment certificates be pressed into their hands. The impassiveness broke only with the distribution of gifts, and in a totally unexpected way. The Indians sneered. Such stingy offerings would not serve as passports to the upper river. Either the Americans stayed with the Bois Brulé Tetons and traded with them alone, or the explorers would have to surrender one of their pirogues and its cargo as tribute.

This was public humiliation—yet Jefferson had said to deal with all Indians in a conciliatory manner. Swallowing their pride, the captains shifted to a tried and true diversion. Lewis fired his air-gun. Always before it had drawn exclamations, but this time the Brulés watched unmoved. Expansively then the captains invited the chiefs and some of their leading warriors aboard the keelboat. It was a mistake. After demonstrating a few of the boat's novelties, Lewis and Clark let each visitor swallow a quarter of a glass of whiskey. The drinkers immediately pretended intoxication, reeling and shoving.

With difficulty the whites herded their obnoxious guests aboard the pirogue, manned by three or four Frenchmen, that was being used as a ferry. As its prow ran up onto the sand, one warrior put his arms around the mast. Others who were waiting on shore seized its "cable," probably the mooring rope. In just such fashion one of the Missouri Company's pirogues had been made a prize of war at Loisel's Cedar Island trading post several miles downstream.

Clark jumped ashore, with Cruzatte and Labiche as interpreters. The chief called the Partisan reeled up against him and said again, straight in his face, the Americans had traveled as far upriver as they were going to. Furious, Clark jerked his sword from its scabbard and signaled Lewis, who stuffed musket balls and buckshot into the keelboat's two swivel guns. As the black mouths swung toward the group several Indians strung their bows and reached for their arrows. At that point Black Buffalo broke in, perhaps to forestall a cannonade that would take down women and children as well as combatants—or perhaps to show the Partisan who was the number-one chief. He ordered the men holding the cable and the one hugging the mast to back off. It was no gesture of friendship. Grasping the mooring rope himself, he repeated that the river was closed. Clark retorted, so he wrote in his journal, "in verry positive terms."

During the jostling that followed, Black Buffalo lost his hold on the rope. At a gesture from Clark, the rowers on the pirogue dug water to the keelboat and took aboard twelve soldiers, rifles ready. Meanwhile Black Buffalo and Clark engaged in something of a small-boy shouting match, while the interpreters, sweating with apprehension, relayed what they could of the exchange. Clark: "We're not squaws!" Black Buffalo: "If you try to go ahead, our warriors will follow and pick your men off one by one." Clark: "We've enough medicine on board to wipe out twenty nations like you." Meaning what? The Corps did have a small supply of smallpox vaccine with it, and perhaps he thought it could be used to infect an enemy. Otherwise the boast has to be taken as pure bluff.

The altercation gave the soldiers in the pirogue time to land. The Indians, conscious of both the rifles and the swivel guns, let their arrows drop back into their quivers and drifted cautiously away. The three chiefs withdrew for a consultation. Clark waited a few moments and then decided to salvage the council if he could. Walking over to the trio, he offered his hand.

They spurned him. Wheeling back to the pirogue, he ordered the rowers toward the keelboat. Behind him Black Buffalo and Buffalo Medicine—but not the Partisan—experienced a change of heart or else devised a new strategy. Accompanied by two warriors, they waded into the water, offered convoluted apologies, and begged the Americans to take them to the village upstream, where their women and children could see the boats and the wonderful things they contained.

Open the river to American trade, Jefferson had said. The captains had to test every possibility. So they took the four aboard and had the boat rowed upriver a little more than a mile to a willow-covered island. There, as twilight folded down, they went into camp. A heavy guard was posted, and there was little sleep that night in spite of the hostages they had with them.

The next morning a four-mile pull against the current brought the three boats abreast of an impressive village of eighty conical tepees, by Sergeant Patrick Gass's count. The habitations, each made of fifteen to eighteen dressed and painted buffalo hides circling a frame of inward-leaning poles, were arranged in a neat ring around a big ceremonial lodge, also made of hides. The keelboat dropped anchor well out in the stream. The pirogues shuttled back and forth. Presumably women and children took turns viewing the boat while Lewis and a small bodyguard of soldiers looked over the town.

It was the beginning of two days of inquisitive poking around by both sides, of formal talks whose contents were butchered by the interpreters, of feasting and entertainment. The Corps never let its guard down. Only a handful of soldiers was given leave at any one time; the rest stayed under arms on the boats. The captains, too, took turns ashore, until it was felt that both should attend, as a matter of protocol, a meeting with the village chiefs and leading warriors in the big central lodge.

Seated around a ceremonial fire, they ate roasted dog and cakes of pemmican, the latter compounded of pulverized dried meat mixed with congealed buffalo fat and pounded chokecherries. For a side dish they were presented with a kind of bread made from the flour of the prairie turnip, a large white root that grew prolifically on the High Plains. They listened to speeches. The purport of the talks, as raveled out by the interpreters, was that the Sioux wanted and needed the expedition's trade more than the upstream Arikaras and Mandans did. In response the captains repeated what they had said before: they were preparing the way for the rich American trade that would follow if the red children of the great father opened their arms to him and to all other tribes.

The male Indians began the evening's entertainment by dancing to the beat of tambourines and drums and the jingle of tiny antelope hoofs affixed by cords to the ends of long sticks. The exhibition was like the one the Yanktons had performed for the explorers downstream near Calumet Bluff. The women's dance was sharply different—a rejoicing, with a strain of ferocity beneath. It was a celebration of war. Equipped with scalps and other booty taken in battle by their menfolk, the women formed into two lines. Stirred by the thump of the drums, each line advanced toward the other, withdrew, and repeated. Every now and then a male chanter broke in to proclaim, in a high singsong, the victories the tribe had won. Occasionally his tribesmen, seated in rows on the lodge floor, added their resonant voices to the singer's.

The performance must have served, in Clark's mind, as a sobering reprise to an ugly experience he'd had while walking through the village earlier in the day, jotting down ethnographic data in his notebook. Several "retched and Dejected looking" women and children of the Omaha tribe caught his attention. Less than two weeks before, he learned, a Sioux war party had fallen on their town, its defenses shredded by the smallpox epidemic of two years earlier. During the raid, the Sioux had killed seventy-five males, had captured forty-eight women and children, and had burned practically every lodge in the town.

To show sympathy Clark sent Pierre Cruzatte among the captives with awls, needles, and other useful trinkets. Both Lewis and he asked the Bois Brulé chiefs to turn the prisoners over to Dorion, downstream among the Yanktons. Dorion would do what he could to put the shattered people in touch with their relatives. In that way a confrontation between the Bois Brulé and the revengeful Omahas would be avoided. The matter was important, for revenge was a prime cause of guerrilla warfare among all tribes.

The Bois Brulé chiefs agreed, but the captains must have wondered how long the promise would be remembered after the Corps's boats had departed—if, in fact, the Sioux intended to let the whites continue their journey. The whole Indian situation was discouraging. Raids, war dances, threats: and opposed to that their thin talk of peace. War was part of the continuous present of Indian life. The major struggles were economic, to control food resources or trade channels, but within that broad cultural context were powerful, perhaps ineradicable, social pressures. Dances like the women's scalp ceremony were designed to heat the courage of the males. A young man attained recognition by receiving a hallucinatory vision of battle, telling his peers about it, and leading them on a successful horse-stealing, battle-related exploit. Retaliation, especially to affronts from the outside, was part of a warrior's view of his own wholeness. Yet Jefferson expected that a few words in passing, delivered from a superior moral position, as the whites regarded it, would be enough to change a culture.

Curiously, the journals never questioned the feasibility of the stance. Perhaps that was the way the military mind worked: do as you are told. Or perhaps a government emissary does not raise critical questions when reporting on the outcome of an assignment; for, of course, the Lewis and Clark journals were reports and not debates about policy. Evaluation would, or at least should, come later on the basis of their findings.

They stayed in the village a second day, still loyally trying to win the Sioux to the American plan. Another high moral stance may have helped defeat them without their knowing it. Each evening as the captains wearily left the ceremonial lodge, they were offered young women as bed partners. This standard form of Indian hospitality was quite outside their experience, and they rejected it. Their abstinence—after all, they were vigorous young men long removed from feminine companionship—was probably compounded out of several inhibitions: a cultural reluctance toward such liaisons; a wariness of becoming beholden in any way to their pugnacious hosts; and fear of the rampant venereal diseases that white traders had first brought to the tribes and that had spread as swiftly as smallpox across plains and mountains. Pride may have been involved; they just did not want any sniggering among their less restrained men.

The Indians were mystified. The husbands among them had lenient views of sexual diversions as long as the carryings-on had their permission. The offer of a wife—many had more than one—was a sign of hospitality. There was also the notion of power transference. During various of their rituals the young men would expect old men to impart, through the sexual act, some of their acquired qualities of wisdom to the young wives, who would then transfer the gain to their husbands in the same manner. In the minds of many Indians of the day the whites' scientific and technological skills were also evidences of desirable qualities of power. Those qualities, too, could perhaps be transmitted through sexual union. Finally, there was always the probability the whites would give valuable trinkets to the women who pleased them, and, be it said, who were simultaneously pleased by the encounters.[2]

In spite of the captains' breach of manners, the Partisan and one of his warriors were allowed, at the close of the second night's ceremonies, to go with Clark to the keelboat, which remained anchored in midstream as a precautionary measure. Lewis, a few troopers, and several Indians remained on the shore, gossiping. Unfortunately the helmsman misjudged the current. Its force caught the pirogue in such a way that it swung in an arc with its own prow as a pivot and slammed broadside against the keelboat. The larger craft tipped violently and probably would have gone clear over if the anchor cable had not snapped. With a great splashing the craft righted itself—loose in the current. The pirogue meanwhile was having its own troubles staying upright.

Clark bawled for all hands on all three boats to get to their oars. Answering shouts rang out. Lewis and his companions ran and stumbled along the dark shore in pursuit of the wayward craft. The villagers, most of them still in or around the ceremonial lodge, immediately supposed a war party of the Omahas and their allies were attacking in revenge for their earlier defeat. Whooping and firing their guns to awaken any sleepers in town, the men ran across the terrace to the water's edge. Their intent was to defend the boats and their valuable cargo from the enemy—or so the Corps's three sergeants believed.

Both Lewis and Clark had a different explanation. They believed the rapacious Sioux were trying to take advantage of the confusion. The notion was reinforced after the boats had been brought to and then moored beside a high bank. Pierre Cruzatte came to them with a rumor whispered to him during the uproar by one of the Omaha prisoners: in spite of the friendly meetings of the past two days, the Sioux intended to maintain their control of the river, by force if necessary.

If that was their intention, the boats tied up at the foot of an overlooking bank were in a precarious spot. Quietly, so as not to precipitate an attack by letting the milling Indians know of the forewarning, they put the entire party on alert, rifles and swivels ready.

Nothing happened. The next morning the men moved the anchorless keelboat to a more defensible position beside a relatively open shore. They were determined to go ahead that day, but they wanted to be able to keep the keelboat in midstream in case the Sioux followed. But the turbid Missouri was against them. Though they probed diligently with boat hooks and setting poles and dragged the bottom with a weighted cord stretched between the two pirogues, they could not find the anchor under the sand that had collected around it. There was nothing for it but to break clear and later on gather heavy stones as substitutes.

All this while the Sioux were prowling the bank. "Some," Ordway wrote, "had fire arms. Some had Spears. Some had a kind of cutlashes, and all the rest had Bows and steel or Iron pointed arrows." Chiefs and favorite warriors crowded aboard the keelboat and both pirogues.

What followed could hardly have been wholly fortuitous, although the journals say nothing of prior planning. Clark went into the keelboat's cabin with Black Buffalo, the head and most amiable chief. At that point Lewis ordered all Indians off the boats and told one of the American soldiers to cast off. To prevent him, several warriors seized the rope. Fearing to be caught in the fire if shooting started, the Indians aboard scrambled for land.

The uproar brought Clark and Black Buffalo out of the cabin. If carnage developed, the chief's blood might well flow at the first shot. So there were no shots. But the warriors holding the rope continued to hang on. Lewis drew his sword to cut the mooring rope and free the keelboat. Clark seized a firing taper, ready to touch off the nearest swivel. "Give them tobacco!" Black Buffalo cried, for tobacco was a ceremonial tribute and would help the Partisan and his followers back down without losing face. The captains complied in as insulting a way as they could, and then managed to break loose, but not free, for Indians and fear followed them for days up the river.[3]

They had one advantage. Not far from the Sioux encampment they picked up Buffalo Medicine, whom they had ranked as third most important chief during the opening rituals, and they already had Black Buffalo with them. Yet even with hostages aboard, travel was little better than a moving siege. Messengers raced after them, urging them to turn back; new groups had arrived and wanted to council with the whites. The whites refused. Mounted bands yammered at them from the shore. Black Buffalo heaved out a bundle of tobacco, but the boats did not stop. The Partisan showed up, promising women for entertainment. No deal there, either.

To the captains' disappointment the chiefs did not linger with them. Buffalo Medicine dropped off on September 29. The next day Black Buffalo, who had been planning to visit the Arikara towns farther upstream, gave way to panic. During an afternoon of raging wind, the keelboat smacked into a log. The blow threw it into a trough in the waves. Loose objects flew to the floor of the cabin, rattling and clanging. Working quickly, the crew adjusted the sail and let the wind right the craft and carry it plunging into safer water. It did not seem safe to Black Buffalo, however. He demanded to be put ashore. Reluctantly the captains gave him a blanket and a knife, had a last smoke with him, and let him go.

Grim times. The weather was cold, wind unremitting, food short. They had no horse—there is no indication they tried to get their strayed or stolen animal back from the Sioux, and even if they had succeeded, the captains were unwilling to ask anyone to ride along the bank looking for game. Nor did hunters risk going out afoot. So they fell back on some corn the Sioux had given them during the pleasant days and on such staples as they had brought from St. Louis for emergency use.

On October 1, they reached the mouth of the Cheyenne River, which drained out of the Black Hills in the western part of today's South Dakota. Ten years earlier, as they had learned from reading the journal of Jean Baptiste Truteau and from talking to James Mackay at Camp Wood, the area around the river junction had been spotted with several fortified villages of Arikara Indians. The Corps of Discovery however, found only ruins.[4]

Fortunately, they also found, at the Cheyenne, one of Regis

Loisel's traders, Jean Vallé, and his two helpers, one a boy. During a talk of several hours' duration, Vallé gave that indefatigable geographer, William Clark, dollops of data about the sources of the Cheyenne and the Black Hills, wintering ground for innumerable antelope, bighorn sheep, and grizzly bears. Of more immediate import, he fortified the bits of knowledge about the Arikaras the captains already possessed. (Modern readers have the further advantage of being able to draw on exhaustive archeological studies conducted in the area during the 1960s.)[5]

Once the Arikaras had dwelled in three dozen or so villages, each made up of about thirty circular, dome-shaped, earth-covered lodges. They perched their towns on the lips of the terraces in the river's broad trench, as near water as possible but above the reach of floods. After the spring spates had subsided, they planted corn, beans, squash, and sunflowers, producers of edible seeds, on the flood plains, harvested the mature vegetables, dried them, and stored them in deep, jug-shaped caches in the floors of their houses.

In spite of the seeming permanence of their towns, the Arikaras were, necessarily, a footloose people. Their corn soon depleted the fertility of their fields. Their houses, the defensive stockades they built around the clusters, and their household fires devoured nearby timber. Every so often the shortages forced them to move to new locations, where once again they erected building frames, covered the timbers with layers of willows, grass, and earth, and cleared away patches of the river's thick riparian growth for new fields. Most of this heavy work was done by the women, who also owned the houses and fields and therefore were not quite the abject slaves early white visitors, including Lewis and Clark, thought them to be.

The grisly smallpox epidemic of 1780–81 wiped out an estimated seventy-five percent of their population. The remnants of the bands coalesced into new groups, not without acrimony, for the original villages had been wholly autonomous and the remnants of each wanted to retain power in the new settlements. The trader Jean Baptiste Truteau counted nine towns scattered out in the vicinity of the Cheyenne in 1795. (The Corps of Discovery, toiling nervously upstream in early October 1805, noted the remains of five of those nine.) In 1797, two years after Truteau's visit, a flare-up of trouble with the Sioux sent the whole Arikara tribe migrating up the Missouri in the hope of making an alliance with the Mandans. It didn't work. According to the Mandans, the Arikaras started the trouble, just as they had in times past, and about the turn of the century the whole group dragged south again. This time they halted a little above the mouth of the Grand River, just south of the present boundary between North and South Dakota. They were not well settled when smallpox again scoured the Missouri trench. The Arikaras who survived coalesced into three villages—three out of what had been more than thirty less than a quarter of a century earlier.

Whatever else they lost, they retained their skills as traders. A main item was horses. A small but steady inflow of the animals had been reaching them for about half a century. The original source of the animals was, of course, Spanish ranches in Texas and Spanish haciendas and Indian pueblos in New Mexico. An interlocked chain of horse thieves—Comanches, Utes, then Kiowas and Cheyennes—relayed the booty along to the tribes of the plains and the Missouri. According to trader Vallé, the Cheyennes picked up as many of the mounts as they could afford —or steal—during an annual monthlong trip south from the Black Hills.[6] (To an Indian warrior nothing else was quite as honorable as stealing a good horse, especially if it was under guard at the time of the theft.)

The Cheyennes passed their surplus stock on to the Arikaras, who were not good raiders. The Arikaras, in their turn, were the chief suppliers of the Teton Sioux, principally the Oglala and Bois Brulé bands. The nomads bought the mounts, totally essential by then to their new life-ways, in exchange for manufactured goods they had picked up at the great Dakota rendezvous on the James River. The Tetons also offered the Arikaras dried meat, buffalo robes, and soft, wondrously prepared antelope-skin clothing in exchange for the dried vegetables they needed as supplemental food for their growing population during winters.

Most of the Sioux-Arikara swaps took place during the Arikaras' bustling harvest fairs held at the Grand River villages late each summer—fairs attended also by Cheyennes, Arapahos, Kiowas, and occasional Crows. An ironclad truce prevailed at the rendezvous. At other times the Sioux, yielding to impulse, occasionally raided the cornfields, stole horses, and beat up little parties of Arikaras they caught away from the stockaded villages. This apparent hostility led early white visitors, Lewis and Clark among them, to call the Arikaras the slaves of the Sioux. No doubt the town dwellers did fear the nomads; such apprehensions are as old as history. But in the case of the Sioux and the Arikaras, at least, profit was a more powerful motive than terrorism in keeping the bonds between the two from splintering.[7]

By the time Lewis and Clark reached the mouth of the Cheyenne, the fair was over and groups of Sioux were drifting south to join their fellow tribesmen beside the Bad before moving onto the plains for their prewinter hunt for fat buffalo. Vallé hoped that by intercepting them he could catch late bargains. He told the officers of the Corps that he expected a large party to drop by almost any time.

The unwelcome news kept the hunters away from the shore. As a consequence, the crewmen went without the meat they craved until October 5, when four antelope swimming in the river fell to their guns. "Verry sweet good meat," Sergeant Ordway wrote happily, and that wasn't the end. Later the same day Clark bagged a deer while walking across a large island covered with ryegrass.

The men needed a boost. The mornings were frosty, the ropes stiff to handle. The opaque river had spread out nearly a mile wide, and the main channel was hard to find as it wound through a peppering of islands and sandbars. Twice the explorers crawled so far up subsidiary channels that they dragged the boats across the sand to the next opening rather than go all the way back and try again.

On October 8, they reached the lowest of the Arikaras' remaining three villages.[8] It stood near the center of an island that was three miles long and almost solidly cultivated, the different family plots separated from each other by brush fences. A stockade of earth-banked, man-tall pickets ringed sixty or so houses. The lower wall of each dwelling rose fairly straight for about five feet and then rounded off to a smoke hole in the apex. The slopes of the earth-covered roofs were gentle enough for the inhabitants to loll about on them, taking the sun, the men chipping arrowheads or working on their medicine bundles, the women weaving baskets or stringing ears of corn. Entrance was by means of a protruding tunnel. In the view of one trader whom they found living in the lodge of an Arikara war chief, Pierre Antoine Tabeau (not to be confused with Jean Baptiste Truteau), the huts were fit only for

"Ricaras, dogs and bears."⁹ Cheerless Tabeau: he had been well educated in Montreal for a different sort of living, and he had a jaundiced opinion of everything Arikara.

As the whites' three boats passed up the sixty-yard-wide channel that separated the town from the mainland, a crowd ran out to watch. Men in buffalo robes and high, everyday leggings made from old tepee coverings; women in girdled dresses of fringed antelope skin; children, some of them, in nothing at all. The mixture boded well. But the captains had read in the journals of earlier travelers about the tribe's truculence; moreover, they had no way of knowing, as yet, what messages the Sioux may have sent upstream about them. So the Corps stayed alert. One pirogue nosed against the bank just long enough to pick up a bearded French trader, Joseph Gravelines, of Loisel's company. Then on the flotilla rowed, past the tip of the island to a fine sandbar. There they settled in with "all things arranged," Clark wrote, "for Peace or War."

Just why Private Robert Frazer chose this particular moment to leave the soldier crew in the white pirogue and enlist in the Pacific-bound permanent detachment remains unsaid. But he did, filling the place of the discharged would-be deserter, Moses Reed. So life with the Corps of Discovery could not have been wholly intolerable in spite of its labors, discomforts, and dangers; and Frazer must have been a good man to have been accepted.¹⁰

Joseph Gravelines turned out to be a marvelous acquisition—"honest, discrete, and an excellent boatman," in Lewis's words. He was a mainstay of Regis Loisel's Missouri Fur Company, of which his friend and associate, Antoine Tabeau, was the field manager, so to speak, and he knew the Arikaras and their language well. After going with him to the lower village for an introductory smoke with the chiefs there, Lewis's optimism soared. Though the Arikaras were somewhat reluctant allies of the Sioux, they were clearly less hostile, at the moment at least, than the Tetons had been.

Problems, to be sure, did develop. Windblown sand delayed the council for a day. (Lewis needed calm weather for his airgun demonstration.) When the meeting finally got underway, the chiefs of the two upper villages, located on the western bank of the river and not on the island, delayed coming down out of jealousy. They feared, correctly, that the whites would recognize Kakawissassa, head man of the island village, as principal chief of all Arikaras, though he had no authority in the upper towns. And they slid around suggestions that they break off relations with the Sioux. It was a curious situation. The chiefs said they feared to visit Washington lest the Tetons catch and kill them, and the Americans had great trouble enlisting a single delegate to go down the river on Gravelines's trading boat the next spring. Yet the tribes kept right on "gardening" for their oppressors, to use Clark's term. So how far, the captains began to wonder, could the Arikaras really be depended on? Finally, quite apart from the Indian problem, there was the matter of Private John Newman. He flatly refused to obey an order and accompanied the insubordination with foulmouthed, mutinous language. It wouldn't do to punish him in sight of the villagers, yet for the good of the expedition he had to be dealt with.

Gains offset the troubles. Gifts were exchanged with undisguised pleasure on both sides. The captains added to their store of data about languages, tribal hunting grounds, geography, and natural history, much of it gleaned from Antoine Tabeau after he joined them. Then came a promise by Kakawissassa that the Arikaras would never close the river to Americans, as the Sioux had tried to do. This was followed by a lesser chief's agreeing to go upriver to the Mandans with the explorers and try to bring an end to the guerrilla warfare the tribes had been waging for several years. Both developments helped salve the wound left by the Tetons. An Arikara-Mandan alliance, if it could be brought about, would help isolate that truculent group, lessen their power, and create a favorable climate for American commerce.[11]

The enlisted men meanwhile were cementing relations in their own way. For the first time in almost a year there were plenty of women around with whom they could satisfy pent-up sexual energies without restraint. Male relatives raised few objections, token payments sufficed, and the women, according to both Clark and Ordway, were for the most part handsome, clean, lively, and lecherous. York, fat, tall, and enormously strong, was a favorite. The Arikaras, who had never before seen a black, were not sure he was wholly human. He made the most of the notion. Through the amused interpreters he told the Indians he had been born wild and had lived off the flesh of children until Captain Clark had caught and tamed him. With a roar he would turn on the crowds of young ones who followed him around and send them flying—"more turribal than we wished him," Clark wrote. They put an end to that, but not to his unflagging sexual prowess.[12]

Having hired Gravelines as interpreter, the expedition bade the Arikaras farewell with fiddles and bugles. Later, Newman's court-martial and punishment stilled the gaiety for a time. He was given seventy-five lashes, to the distress of the Arikara chief who was going along to make peace with the Mandans. The whipping completed, he was transferred to the French pirogue as a common laborer, as Moses Reed had been. Otherwise, the autumn journey turned, despite discomforts, into something of an idyll.[13]

True, the nights were cold. Snow fell on October 21. Winds were high, yet suitable at times for sailing. Mosquitos vanished. Though colored leaves were being whipped from the trees, the bottomlands contained thicker timber than they had seen for miles. Game was everywhere, providing not only the feasts the crew had sorely missed after leaving the Sioux but also skins they could use for making winter clothing and moccasins.[14] In addition, George Drouillard and those of the crew who had brought traps along began catching beaver, always a source of extra money.

Along the way they came across several hunting camps, Arikaras at first and Mandans later on. On October 16, they watched an extraordinary slaughter of pronghorns. Indians lying in wait at a ford across the river caught, in the water, a herd migrating to winter range in the Black Hills. The hunters killed several with arrows, clubbed others to death as they floundered in the stream, and then dragged upwards of fifty corpses ashore, a goodly haul for a people who passed much of their lives at the edges of starvation.[15] (Just the year before a flood had destroyed much of the Arikaras' crops, and many had perished before a new harvest was ready.)

Whenever opportunity allowed, whites and Indians, several women among the latter, visited back and forth. While Lewis and Clark and the Arikara emissary smoked peacefully with the Mandan elders in the camps, the young people sang, danced, and made merry all night. The women, Clark admitted in his journal, were "verry fond of carressing our men &c." There is no indication that either Lewis or he joined the frolics. And they did have quieter pleasures. While the weary crew toiled up the shoaling river with tow ropes and oars, the officers hiked easily through the country-side with Gravelines and the Arikara chief, gathering material about soil conditions—it was increasingly alkaline in spots, and the side creeks were bitterly purgative—and about flora and fauna —Lewis discovered that at least one species of bird, the whippoorwill, actually hibernates—and they listened to many Indian myths and much lore that Clark, in an unusual lapse, considered too absurd to record.

In the vicinity of present Bismarck, North Dakota, they passed several abandoned Mandan villages, for that tribe, too, had been harrassed by epidemics and Sioux, and had migrated sixty miles farther north to the area where the Knife River flows into the Missouri. As the expedition approached the new site, scores of Mandans galloped or ran out on foot to greet them. The Indians were afire with excitement. Except for visits from Jacques D'Église and, afterwards, from John Evans in the 1790s (see pages 77–84), no whites had reached them by way of the river, and those meagerly equipped predecessors had not prepared them for a fleet as large as this one. Surely the newcomers carried an enormous quantity of trade goods with them!

The Americans, too, were excited. During the past 164 days they had covered 1,610 miles. One man had died of natural causes; one, La Liberté, had deserted from the French boat; two had been read out of the army for disciplinary reasons. But the Corps had spread the word Jefferson wanted spread. It had gone farther into the interior of the continent than any other Americans yet had, and in the process had gained more information than could be assimilated for a long time. Now their first goal was in sight, and they deserved—needed—a chance to pause, collect their thoughts, and prepare for the next, climactic stage of their journey. How well they succeeded here would probably determine, in large measure, how well the remainder of the great experiment would fare.

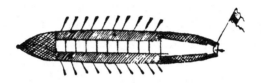

NINE

The Grand Plan

The first Mandan village they sighted contained, within its stockade of short pickets, about forty big, dome-shaped, earth-covered habitations, almost exactly like those used by the Arikaras. It stood atop a bluff about fifty feet high, the Missouri curling at its base. To land at the narrow beach below the town would give the villagers, if they turned hostile, a strategic advantage no army officer would consider. Nor did the captains want to expose their whole group by advancing in a body. So they moored the boats half a mile downstream. Clark, suffering from rheumatism, stayed with part of the men at the landing place. Several Mandans stayed there also, watching intently as the white cooks set up a little steel mill and ground parched corn into meal for corn pones—a great improvement, certainly, over rolling, as the Indians did, a round stone back and forth over a flat rock, with the kernels in between.

Lewis, meanwhile, accompanied by interpreters George Drouillard and Joseph Gravelines and a squad of riflemen, hiked with a crowd of Mandan men, women, and children to the village. Its name, as Clark later spelled the word phonetically, was Matootonha. (Today's archeologists call the site Mitutanka.) Its principal chief was Sheheke. Because Sheheke was fat and of light complexion, the handful of French-Canadian traders who either lived in the area or visited occasionally from the British posts to the the northeast called him Le Gros Blanc, or Big White in English.

Big White and several other of Matootonha's leading men

smoked cordially with the visitors—tobacco was an essential prelude to any important meeting—and Lewis returned to the boats in high spirits. The Corps should have no trouble setting up a council for all five of the neighborhood towns, only two of them Mandan. After that they could settle in for the winter. High time, too, to judge from the flights of geese, swans, cormorants, and ducks passing overhead, the wavering Vs of each southbound flock outlined sharply against the pale sky.

The next morning both captains visited Matootonha. This time they picked up René Jessaume, a free trader who had been living with the Mandans and their neighbors, the Hidatsas, for the past fifteen years. English traders who knew Jessaume considered him devoid of morals. When John Evans, working for the Spanish in 1796, had ordered him to leave the Missouri and return to Canada, Jessaume had tried to kill him, or so Evans charged. After talking with Jessaume for a time, Clark wrote him down as "cunnin, artful, and insonce [insolent]." But the Canadian could speak the Indians' language and understood the power hierarchies in the different villages, attributes that would stand the captains in good stead when the moment came to hand out medals and red coats to the chiefs they formally recognized.[1]

With Jessaume in one of the boats the whites rowed up the sweeping meanders of the Missouri past a second Mandan village. Clark, struggling with the heavy sounds of an unfamiliar tongue, called the village Rooptahee. (Today's archeologists call it Nuptadi.) Not quite as populous as Matootonha, Rooptahee lay on the opposite, or northeastern, bank, surrounded on three sides by the coiling river. Upstream from the town, where the brush of the flood plain had some years since been cleared away for gardens, the Corps made camp. Nearby they raised a flagpole to mark the site for the big council they had scheduled for the following day, October 28. They had already told the Mandans about the meeting. Now they hired three young Indian runners to carry the word, along with carrots of tobacco, to the three Hidatsa villages that dotted the lower mile and a half of the Knife River, where it ran almost parallel to the Missouri.

(A note on nomenclature, which can be skipped if desired. The first white travelers to visit the five riverside villages in what is now central North Dakota lumped them together as the Mandan towns. The Mandans lived only in the lower two, however. The next village above them—the domed huts stood on a west-side bluff overlooking the confluence of the Knife and Missouri rivers—was the home of a group that the Mandans, and hence Lewis and Clark, called the Wattasons or sometimes the Ahaharways. Though the Wattasons spoke their own dialect, they were related to the tribe that lived in two villages of earth-covered lodges farther up the Knife—villages called Metaharte and Big Hidatsa. The latter was by far the largest town in the area. The Mandans, and hence Lewis and Clark, called the dwellers in those upper two towns the Minitaris. Jessaume and his fellow French-Canadians added other names: Souliers (Shoes) for the Wattasons and Gros Ventres (Big Bellies) for the Minitaris. Today the surviving Knife River people call themselves Hidatsa, after the now-vanished village of that name.[2] This account will also use Hidatsa for the tribe, though it means differing from Lewis and Clark's usage.)

Odd similarities marked the Mandan-Hidatsa council and the one the captains had recently concluded with the Arikaras. In both instances clouds of sand stirred up by strong winds forced a postponement. Influential representatives from the upper towns of both neighborhoods failed to appear because of deep-seated jealousies. The upriver Arikara had not wanted a downriver Indian made head chief over every village. The Hidatsas, on their part, feared the Mandans might take precedence in whatever trading arrangements these strangers from the far-off mouth of the river might establish.

There were also profound differences, the main one being that the residents of the three Arikara towns belonged to the same tribe. The Hidatsas and Mandans were different tribes. The Hidatsas were the more bellicose; their war parties regularly rode far west to attack the Indians who lived in the Rocky Mountains—a matter of importance to the captains, who needed to refine their understanding of the lands between the Missouri and the sea. The Mandans, by contrast, stayed close to their fields and only fought, they said, to stave off guerrilla strikes by the Sioux and Arikara.

Winds howled again on October 29, but Lewis and Clark did not want to ask for another postponement lest the volatile groups grow impatient and disperse. Accordingly they had the enlisted men set up a canvas enclosure topped with a canvas awning. The swivel guns boomed; the enlisted men paraded. To the tune of the flutterings and cracklings of the canvas, and with Jessaume interpreting,

Lewis gave a long speech "Similer," Clark wrote, "to what we had Delivered to the nations below." Bored by it, one aged Hidatsa stirred restlessly and would have left the gathering if some of the others hadn't rebuked him for his rudeness.[3]

The usual making of chiefs followed. A head man was named for each village and a grand chief for each tribe. Black Cat of Rooptahee was declared principal chief of all Mandans; Kakoaksis of Big Hidatsa—he was Le Borgne to the French because of his single eye—was put over the Hidatsas. The ceremony of recognition was something of a rump session, for Le Borgne was off with a war party, and Big White, named chief of Matootonha town, had been unable to cross the wind-swept river in his frail boat of buffalo hide and willows. The presents intended for the two had to be entrusted to messengers, and so some of the impact was gone.

At the captains' urging, those chiefs who were in attendance consented to smoke with the Arikara peace delegate whom the Corps had brought upstream as part of Lewis and Clark's slowly evolving strategy of opening the river by isolating the obstreperous Sioux. Hidatsas, Mandans, and Arikaras against the Tetons . . . if old bonds could be turned upside down. The Arikara representative played his part so well that Clark rewarded him with a U.S. silver dollar as a medal. The Mandans were more restrained. Though Big White agreed with Black Cat of Rooptahee that peace was wonderful and there might be some advantage in visiting Washington, he added sourly that whenever violence occurred, it was the fault of either the Arikaras or the Sioux or of both acting together. In the battles that followed, he said, the Mandans slew the enemy as easily as if they were little birds. His people might as well make peace as coast along that way. All in all, it was a lukewarm denouement to a council that had begun with cannon fire and parades. But at least the program had been laid before the Indians, and the captains had the rest of the winter in which to improve its luster.

A related problem concerned their handling of foreign traders. One of the people who had come to the riverbank to stare at the flotilla as it hove into sight below the villages had been Hugh McCracken, an illiterate Scot recently arrived from a North West Company post on the Assiniboine River, a hundred and fifty miles to the northeast. His first reaction must have been astonishment: Americans, here where none had ever been before! Louisiana Purchase? He probably had heard nothing about it. On being told, he must have wondered what it meant to him. Would the Americans insist, as the Spanish had tried to do, that British fur men would not be allowed to ply their commerce south of the still unmarked border?

The captains themselves weren't sure. Under the terms of Jay's Treaty, signed by the United States and Great Britain in 1794, traders of each nation were allowed to work in the other's territory *if* they subscribed to regulations applied by the host nation. In the United States this meant that every trader, American or British, had to purchase, for a small fee, a government license. But did the generous fur-trade provisos of Jay's Treaty extend to Louisiana, which had been acquired *after* the signing of that document? As Lewis and Clark surely knew, many St. Louis merchants, hoping to keep British competitors out of the huge area, were arguing that the treaty did not apply and therefore the western reaches of the border remained closed, as in Spanish times, to foreign traders. At the time of the Corps's departure from St. Louis no governmental decision had been reached.

Yet how could Lewis and Clark ask the Indians to acknowledge American jurisdiction without demanding the same recognition from the foreigners who dealt with Indians? (The word "foreigners" of course included such resident French-Canadians as René Jessaume, who lived in the villages with their Indian wives and exerted varying degrees of influence over their red neighbors.) So, granted the dilemma, what stance should the captains take, and under what authority?

They decided, in spite of Lewis's ingrained prejudice against all Britons, to be conciliatory. (One senses Clark's calming hand.) When McCracken told them, shortly after the Indian councils ended and he had learned their tenor, that he was about to ride back to his post, they prevailed on him to carry a letter to his superior, Charles Chaboillez. In the letter they stated they had been dispatched by their government to explore the Missouri and the western part of North America "with a view to the promotion of general science." As proof of the "literary" nature of the project, they enclosed a copy of the passport the British ambassador in Washington had granted Lewis at Jefferson's request. The Corps expected, Lewis and Clark continued, to remain in the neighborhood of the Mandans throughout the winter. There need be no frictions. As individuals "we feel every disposition to cultivate the friendship of all well-disposed persons."

"Well-disposed." They used the term again when stating it was the policy of the United States to allow "free egress and regress [Lewis's words, surely] to all citizens and subjects of foreign powers with which she is in amity." And would Mr. Chaboillez kindly have those of his men who came to the villages pass on such information as they possessed about the country's geography and natural history?[4]

It was an adroit letter, not wholly candid. It said nothing about license requirements or the possibility of a complete interdiction of British trade with Indians who lived in American territory. It did establish a precedent of sorts by inviting the Canadians to come on down, an unauthorized step American fur men might well decry. But its very cordiality, Lewis and Clark hoped, might dissuade the British, to whom the Indians were accustomed, from stirring up anti-American acts that would jeopardize the expedition's future. Furthermore, the letter put Chaboillez under an obligation to repay courtesy with courtesy by directing his "well-disposed" traders to tell the American captains what they knew about the Western country and its native inhabitants.

On November 2, the captains, freed of their diplomatic chores, selected a site for the fort that would have to shelter and protect about forty-five people during the winter that loomed ahead. The spot they chose lay approximately six river miles below the confluence of the Knife and the Missouri and half that distance below the closest village, Matootonha, but on the opposite (left) bank. A few score yards back from the site, a bluff rising steeply out of the trees of the bottomland marked the edge of a grassy terrace. Beyond the terrace the bordering hills of the river's broad valley sloped upward to a height of five hundred feet or so. The fort would be built in the shape of a triangle, its apex pointing toward the bluff and its open front facing the Missouri, close to the beach where the keelboat and the two pirogues were moored.

Decisions about personnel accompanied the decisions about the fort. A French-Canadian, Jean Baptiste Lepage, who said he had ventured as far into the wilderness as the Black Hills, was hired to replace the discharged John Newman. Newman, desperately regretting his mutinous flare-up, wanted to be taken back into the Corps. No chance. If the other enlisted men thought discipline was not ironclad, so the captains reasoned, a general unraveling might take place that would jeopardize the entire project. Newman and

Moses Reed could stay out the winter at the fort, but their positions would remain those of common laborers.

Though Newman and Reed remained with the group, the French crew of the red pirogue did not. To save the cost of their wages and to reduce the number of mouths that would have to be fed during the winter, the captains discharged them shortly after the boats reached the Indian villages. Nor were they allowed to try to race the ice downstream in the red pirogue they had labored with for the past five months; Lewis and Clark had decided it and the white pirogue would be needed when the upstream journey was resumed in the spring. So there the Frenchmen were, totally on their own. That was the way employment was handled in those days: pay and transportation ended with the job, as the boatmen had understood when signing up. What they did from then on was up to them.

The Arikara peace delegate set an example. He and a few lesser Mandans and Hidatsas started downstream for the Arikara towns in either a boat of buffalo hide or a dugout hewn from a cottonwood tree—no journal mentions the craft. Their intent was to seal the recent truces during a ceremonial smoke with the villagers. Gravelines would follow them in a day or two to guide the arrangements, and an indeterminate number of the French crew decided to accompany him in one or more hurriedly created dugouts. Since Gravelines is known to have reached the Arikara towns (Lewis had employed him to escort some Washington-bound chiefs to St. Louis the following spring), the Frenchmen presumably also reached the villages. If they did not stay there—no records exist—they ran the risk of being caught by either ice or the Sioux.

Those of the French group who did not depart with Gravelines decided to build a small hut near the fort-to-be and winter among the Mandans, trapping beaver and enjoying the favors of the complaisant Mandan girls. When spring came—well, they would worry then.[5] Perhaps they hoped they would be allowed to catch rides back to St. Louis aboard the keelboat. Because it was too big for use on the upper river, it would be sent downstream after the ice had broken with specimens and reports for President Jefferson. The craft would be manned on its descent by Corporal Warfington's soldiers, erstwhile crewmen of the white pirogue. Newman and Reed would also return in the keelboat. Until it left all of them would have plenty of winter work to keep them occupied.

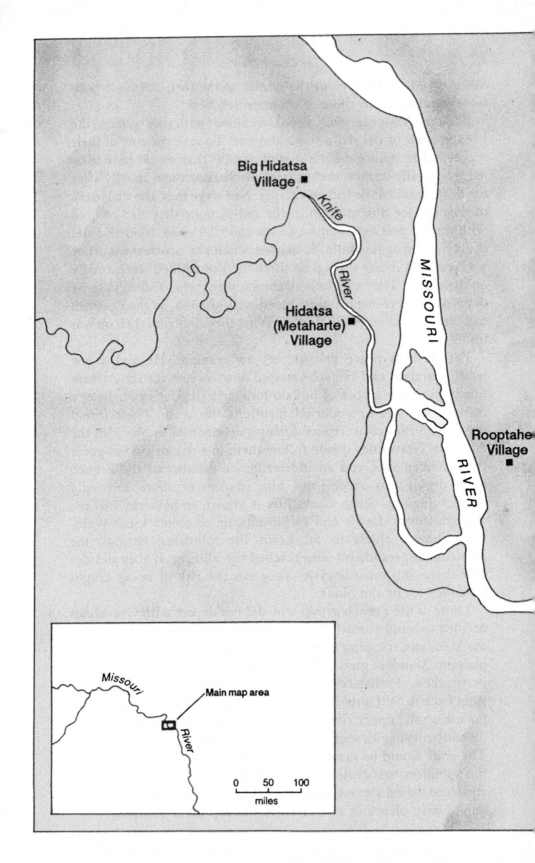

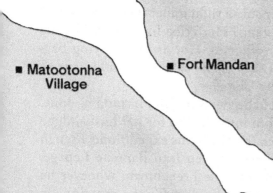

Winter Camp at Fort Mandan
1804-1805

```
0               1               2
|_____|_____|_____|_____|
            miles
```

■ Matootonha
   Village

■ Fort Mandan

Still another decision involved interpreters. René Jessaume and his wife and child moved into a tepee beside the site of the fort the day construction started, to be on hand whenever interpreting was needed. The family was followed within twenty-four hours by another resident trader, Toussaint Charbonneau, known today to more Americans than any other man of the party except Meriwether Lewis and William Clark. The reason, it hardly need be said, was his then noticeably pregnant fourteen- or fifteen-year-old Indian wife, Sacagawea. She, along with another of Charbonneau's women, accompanied him to the embryonic fort. Her name has other spellings: Sacajawea and Sakakawea. The hard *g* or the second *k* is generally preferred to the *j*. Pronunciation is important, according to Sacagawea aficionados, because the name spelled with a *g* or *k* and accented on the second syllable is Hidatsa and means "Bird Woman." A soft *j* makes it Shoshoni "Boat Launcher."[6]

By birth Sacagawea was a Shoshoni. In 1800, aged ten, she had been captured by a Hidatsa war party while trying to flee across the Missouri River at a distant place later called Three Forks. When she turned nubile, Charbonneau either bought her or won her from her captor in a gambling game—take your choice, as with the spelling of her name.

When the Corps of Discovery reached the Mandan towns, Charbonneau was away on a hunting trip. Learning somehow of the council and of the explorers' destination, he realized he owned a profitable bit of merchandise. He hurried to the fort, showed off his wares, and asked for a job as an interpreter. The captains demurred. Jessaume was interpreter enough; besides, he spoke some English, while Charbonneau did not. The trader spluttered back through whoever was translating for him. Listen! This girl —he may well have pushed her ahead right under their noses—was a Shoshoni. Shoshoni, understand? Her tribe lived in the Rocky Mountains. They owned many horses. Horses for carrying baggage across the Continental Divide. The captains would have to have someone who knew their language.

Translation, to be sure, would be awkward. But it could be done. Sacagawea would turn Shoshoni into Hidatsa for her husband; he would transform it into French for one of the expedition's French half-breeds, Cruzatte, or Labiche, or even Jean Baptiste Lepage, whom the captains had just hired. The Frenchman, whoever he was, could then put the words into English for the captains. So

Charbonneau was hired. He would receive the pay; Sacagawea would do the work. Curiously the journals mention no hesitation over the fact that the teenager would be carrying a newborn infant at least as far as the Rockies.

The final decision about personnel had to do with the laying in of food for the first part of the winter—food enough for more than forty people, together with the neighboring Indians, who would expect the whites to share what they had, just as the Mandans shared when hunger pinched. It has been estimated that on a single day the crew and associated people could devour an entire buffalo or, in its place, four deer, or one deer and an elk.[7] George Drouillard and six selected but unnamed men were ordered to go downstream in one of the pirogues and bring back as much meat as they could carry. Until they returned, the construction workers would have to depend on whatever corn, dried squash, buffalo steaks, and buffalo tripe the Mandans brought them, either as gifts or for barter.

The builders pitched tents for shelter and then, racing the cold, set about clearing the area the fort would occupy. The green cottonwoods were heavy—full of water, Clark said.[8] Lugging and levering those felled in and close to the clearing was hard enough. The effort grew as distance increased. It took at least four men to bring back one big, trimmed log. The quartet would first roll the timber onto a pair of crosspieces, one near either end. Heaving the cradle and its burden upward, the workers toted it ahead, often chanting to the rhythm of their steps. For help in boosting the log onto the rising walls, they rented a horse from the Mandans and rigged up a rope pulley.

Each arm of the V-shaped structure was to contain four rooms, each fourteen feet square, seven feet high, and designed to hold a stone fireplace that was used for cooking as well as warmth. The point of the V did not quite close; an opening was left that would let armed men squeeze into a rounded bastion whose loopholes commanded a view of the outer walls of the triangle's sides, each fifty-six feet long. The walls of this bastion were made of contiguous pickets about seven feet tall. In time the enclosure would be roofed in order to provide space for storage.

The ceilings of the eight rooms were made of puncheons, which are logs adzed flat on one side. The flat sides, facing up and covered with grass and clay, would form lofts that would be used mostly as dormitories. The outer walls of the lofts projected a little beyond the outside walls of the lower apartments, an overhang designed to add space while discouraging attempts to scale the edifice. The base of the triangular fort, which fronted on the river, eventually was closed off by massive pickets eighteen feet tall and set deep in the ground.

The roofs of the structure sloped toward an inner court. In that limited space the men would often show off their jigs and reels to visiting Indians. A sentry regularly paced the walkways on the roof—after all, this was a military establishment, designed in part to impress the land's native inhabitants. After the chinks between the often crooked cottonwood logs had been daubed with clay and sticks, the place became not only draft-proof but "almost Cannon Ball Proof," to borrow the words of a Canadian who visited it late in November. It was named Fort Mandan in honor of the neighboring tribe.

It was a lively place. The days during the first part of November stayed above freezing; construction went apace. Many Mandans (but few Hidatsas) rode by on their way to their hunting camps, or just appeared with their families to see what kind of dwellings white people lived in. They let their horses graze on the good grass in the bottomland while they smoked, ate, and talked as best they could with the always busy whites.

On November 12 and again on the 13th, daytime temperatures slipped to fourteen degrees above zero—"naught," as the captains put the figure on their weather charts.[9] Chunks of ice floated down the river; thin lenses of ice rippled along the shoreline. Hastily the men filled one of the storehouses in the bastion with supplies unloaded from the boats. Lewis and a crew then rowed an empty pirogue up the river to gather stones suitable for chimneys. On the way back, the overloaded craft stuck on a sandbar. Over the gunwales the men went, into icy water, to work the boat free. Cold air on wet feet during the rest of the journey resulted in frostbite for some. But, wrote Sergeant Ordway, "it hapned they had Some whiskey with them to revive their Spirits."

Dwindling food supplies were another worry. Not having heard from Drouillard's hunters for two weeks, the captains sent a "frenchman" (Baptiste Lepage?) downstream to look for the missing men. The next day, just as the cooks were dipping into their reserves of salt pork, the searcher reappeared with Drouillard and word the hunters were stalled thirty miles below. Drift ice had damaged the prow of the pirogue and rowing was almost impossible. The captains responded by sending back a tow rope and enough tin to sheathe the boat's prow. On November 19 the pirogue returned, laden with the dressed carcasses of thirty-two deer, eleven elk, and five buffalo. Considering the rate at which the party consumed meat, the supply would last about three weeks, yet they cooked up enough the next day to provide a feast for several Indians who heard the good news and appeared with grins of anticipation. They also sent Sergeant Pryor to Matootonha to swap trade goods for corn that could be used to stretch out the supply.[10]

On the day the ice started flowing in the Missouri, Black Cat, head man of Rooptahee, brought an Assiniboin chief and seven "men of note" to the fort to meet the captains. Mindful that the Assiniboin tribe ranged mostly on British soil, Clark refrained from giving the chief an American medal or an American flag but substituted a length of gold braid plucked from the storehouse's supply of ribbons—or perhaps from his or Lewis's dress uniform. The gift pleased the fellow, Clark wrote afterward—but, he added, the group as a whole was a surly lot, as was to be expected, since they were related to the Sioux.[11]

For a few days following the Assiniboin visit, not a Mandan appeared at the fort. On the 18th, Black Cat arrived with an explanation. The time had been filled with a huge festival to cement trade relations among the Mandans, Hidatsas, seventy lodges of visiting Assiniboins, and a few of their associates, the Crees. During the celebration the Assiniboins had publicly mocked the Mandans for their friendliness with the Americans. Did the Missouri River Indians suppose they could really get merchandise from southern sources? Hadn't another white man, John Evans, made similar promises eight years ago, only to leave and never return? Stick with us, the Assiniboins said. We and the Crees will buy your vegetables and your horses with our dried meat and leather and with guns and brass kettles and cloth we obtain from the traders in the north. Stay with us, your best suppliers. Or take the consequences.

The high-pressure salesmanship upset the Mandans so much that they held council to discuss alternatives. Should they retain their Assiniboin connections by turning their backs on the Americans? Or should they risk Assiniboin retaliation by opening their ears to the promises of these energetic men from the south?

Though no consensus had been reached at the meetings, it was clear the American program was in trouble.[12] If bullying from nomadic tribes made all the village Indians cower—and how reminiscent of the Sioux-Arikara situation this was!—the river might end up not only being closed to American trade but also to American use as a main section of the route to the Pacific.

What to do? Lamely the captains told Black Cat his people certainly could believe the American promise of bringing a rich trade to the Mandans. Developing the necessary procedures would take time, but if the Indians were loyal, so would the Great Father be.

The talk placated Black Cat, who was friendly already. But what of the Hidatsas, with whom the Corps had had very little contact during the push to complete the fort and provision it with meat? Those chores were finished now except for building a stockade across the open end of the stronghold, and the explorers could return to the murky waters of diplomacy.

Treating with the Hidatsas fell to Lewis. Off he went on November 25, with Charbonneau and Jessaume as interpreters and six riflemen under Sergeant Ordway as a guard. Somehow—journal details are often exasperatingly sparse—they got a pirogue across the ice-choked river. Somewhere Lewis and the interpreters obtained horses for riding along the snowy, wind-swept terraces to the Knife River communities. Ordways's detail walked; horses were expensive even to rent, and with the long journey to the Pacific looming ahead, the captains were reluctant to expend the trade goods that were their only currency.

Results of the errand were mixed.[13] The party was able to find shelter at the middle Hidatsa village, Metaharte, partly because that was where Charbonneau and Sacagawea had lived before moving to Fort Mandan. Lewis held productive talks there with Black Moccasin, the man Clark and he had recognized a month earlier as the head man of the town. He counciled with chiefs in the other two towns, some of whom seemed reluctant to take his gifts, and he won a bland promise from certain influential warriors not to go to war any more with their accustomed quarry, the Shoshoni of the mountains.

As the weather turned stormy on the 26th and 27th, so did negotiations. One chief, the Horned Weasel, declined to see the Americans. And there is no record that Lewis tried to contact Le Borgne and other principal men of Big Hidatsa village. What really jarred him were rumors of Mandan duplicity. Their conniving was based on tales brought to the villages by Indian travelers: the Sioux planned an attack on the Hidatsas for having entered into an alliance with the Arikaras. The Americans, the account went on, planned to join the war on the side of the Sioux. Why else had they built so strong a fort while talking so earnestly of peace? Why else had Jessaume and Charbonneau and their families, one-time residents among the Hidatsa, moved into the stronghold, if not for the sake of being safe when the battles erupted? And what of that other long-term trader with the Hidatsas, Baptiste La France? He had just arrived on the Missouri with a small party of North West Company men and was popping off with scurrilous remarks about the Americans, each time adding that the Britons were the Hidatsas' only true friends. Why would he say such things?

The reasons seemed clear to Lewis's interpreters. The Mandan villages, located farther down the Missouri than the Hidatsas', were in a good geographic position to capture whatever trade began moving up the river from the south. If the Hidatsas became enemies of the Americans, the Mandans' chances of taking over the role of middlemen for the new commerce improved in direct proportion. Baptiste La France, having sniffed out the way the wind was blowing, was trying to improve the North West Company's standing with the Hidatsas by joining the anti-American chorus.

Lewis countered vigorously. He prevailed on two, perhaps more, important Hidatsa chiefs and several warriors to return with him through the snow to the fort and with their own eyes and ears measure its friendliness toward all the villages, Hidatsa and Mandan. (He did not know that at that very moment a small group of Hidatsas were at Fort Mandan, unable to talk to Clark because, ironically, the interpreters were with Lewis.)[14] And Lewis had a chance to speak his mind directly to the Nor'Westers. While riding between towns, he bumped first into the clerk, or second-in-command, of the small party, Charles McKenzie. What they talked about is not of record, but Lewis's stiffness may account for McKenzie's later remark in his journal that the captain was prejudiced against the British. Next Lewis encountered, at Black Cat's village, the head man himself, François-Antoine Laroque. Well educated and affable, Laroque was only twenty. (His birthday was August 18, one day ahead of Lewis's, who was then thirty-one.) He had not yet heard of the Louisiana Purchase. At the time of his departure from his base on the Assiniboine River, Hugh

McCracken had not yet arrived with Lewis and Clark's carefully polite letter to the district manager, Charles Chaboillez. Even so, Laroque was prepared to be cooperative. He was eager that this, his first major assignment, go well—a hope that depended in part on enlisting Charbonneau as interpreter. But Charbonneau, he had learned on reaching the Missouri, was with the Americans, though not actually with Lewis right then, for apparently the interpreter had ridden on to the fort while the captain paused to talk to Black Cat. It was in the chief's lodge that the Canadian asked to "borrow" Charbonneau until his commerce was launched. Lewis agreed and invited the young man to dine at the fort with Clark, the Hidatsa chiefs, and him the next evening, November 28. His prejudices, if any, obviously did not blind him to the advantages of amiability.

Laroque missed the date. He waited in Black Cat's lodge for Charbonneau to show up, but it was snowing hard and the interpreter did not appear. So the next day Laroque rode down to the fort to collar the fellow. There he walked into a chill that matched the weather's. From some unnamed source the captains had heard that the North West people carried British flags and medals for distribution among the Missouri River Indians. Crisply Lewis and Clark told the Canadian to refrain while he was on American soil. The Indians, they added, had been warned to reject any and all tokens of British sovereignty.

The nonplussed trader said his party had neither medals nor flags with them and hence no intentions of handing any out. His earnestness restored accord, and he was allowed to borrow Charbonneau, as arranged earlier, whenever the man's services were not needed by the Americans. With this proviso: the interpreter was not to be asked to translate remarks in any way derogatory to the new owners of Louisiana Territory. And then the captains explained what their aims on the upper Missouri were. Science and the finding of a usable route to the Pacific, yes. But there was more—an alliance of the Mandans, Hidatsas, and Arikaras against the Sioux that would benefit everyone's trade. For of course British subjects had a treaty right to trade south of the border if they obeyed the same regulations under which Americans operated— no liquor, no following the Indians out to their hunting camps, and so on. In the future, moreover, the United States government might extend its own trading houses up the river in order to make sure the Indians were not gouged by grasping traders from any nation.

Laroque's observations, if any, were not recorded. They would have been interesting, for though he was young he was not naive. After the conversations, he wrote dryly in his journal, "During the time I was there a very grand plan was schemed, but its being realized is more than I can tell, although the Captains say they are well assured it will."[15]

As Laroque and his clerk, Charles McKenzie, would soon learn, there was reason to be skeptical about the plan. The Hidatsas were not as convinced that joining a U.S.-sponsored alliance would be useful. What seemed to them Lewis and Clark's excessive boasting about the power of the distant Great Father had turned them off. Several chiefs, fearing that there might be harmful medicine in the medals and certificates that were presented to them, had given the symbols away. They felt, too, that the visitors were incompetent, except for the blacksmith and the mender of guns. They wondered why the Americans, who talked about great riches, had not brought more gifts, trade goods, and ammunition with them in their big boats. And if the Americans thought that young Hidatsa warriors would abandon the fighting through which they gained recognition, they were ill informed indeed.

One development turned out to be more than gossip. A little after sunrise on November 30, a Mandan from Matootonha yelled across the river that he had news for the Americans. After a pirogue had battled through the ice to reach him, he apologized; the river by the village was frozen solid and he had supposed it would be frozen here as well. Anyway, he had been sent to tell the captains that a roaming party of Sioux and Arikaras—there was no mistaking the emphasis on *Arikara*—had surprised five Mandans hunting buffalo on the plains eight leagues to the southwest. The attackers had killed one hunter, wounded two, and made off with nine horses.

Here, the captains thought, was a chance to replace words with action. Let a party of volunteers march to Matootonha, consult with Big White and the other chiefs there, and if hostile attack seemed imminent, join with warriors from all the villages and engage the Sioux—those damnable Sioux. Though the strategy seems fitted to Lewis's impulsive nature, Clark apparently was its originator.[16] And because Lewis had only recently returned from the long, snowy, exhausting ride to the Knife River villages, Clark led this foray.

Within an hour twenty-three men, including both Charbonneau and Jessaume, had been ferried to the timbered bottomland on the far side of the river. There Clark spread the men out in skirmish formation and advanced, with a good deal of floundering, through thick brush and foot-deep snow toward the terrace bluff. After scrambling up that, they swung across open ground toward the town. The sudden appearance of so large a group in military formation alarmed the Indians. To calm the excited people, Big White and a delegation of other chiefs wrapped themselves in buffalo robes and walked out to discover what was afoot. Clark explained. They wanted to help the Mandans chastise the Sioux "for taking the blood of our dutifull children."

Big White said the matter needed discussion and invited the soldiers to divide into small groups and make themselves at home in different lodges, resting and eating while the leaders talked. To Clark, what followed was total anticlimax. The chiefs insisted the murderers could not be overtaken on the snowy plains; vengeance would have to wait for spring. Recriminations erupted next. A chief called Big Man blamed the Americans for the tragedy by saying that the injured party, believing peace had been achieved, had gone onto the plains with a recklessly small group and had paid the price. The Arikaras might talk peace, but in reality they had always been liars and aggressors.

To keep Lewis's and his grand plan from crumbling then and there, Clark drew on all the persuasiveness he possessed. The snowstorm was unfortunate, he said, for the Americans wanted to show tribes everywhere what would happen to those who were foolish enough to harm the Great Father's allies. Also, it was wrong to blame all Arikaras for the actions of a few. Those few clearly had felt they must follow the Sioux's bad advice in order to get firearms and ammunition from them. Mandans should understand that kind of pressure. Didn't they have to stay on good terms with the Assiniboins and Crees to obtain what those middlemen brought them? But as soon as American goods were flowing up the river and the villagers lived under American protection, the Mandans and the Hidatsas could become independent people at last.[17]

Had he made his point? He hoped so. The Mandans fed the soldiers liberally and expressed polite thanks for the Americans' concern. Taking as much satisfaction from that as he could, Clark gathered his detachment together, paraded them through the village plaza, and then crossed the ice to the other shore. As the cold descended—that night the Corps's thermometer dropped below zero for the first time—they slogged back through brush and drifted snow to the fort. "Verry fatigueing," Clark summed up the experience after passing out extra measures of cheap rum to the men.

Fatiguing—and worrisome. Hoping to learn what was really going on down the river, the captains found a messenger who was willing to ride to the Arikara villages with a letter for Tableau. What *was* the situation there—and would the trader please do all he could to hold the grand alliance together?

On the personal level there was more warmth. Three days after the fiasco, the father and brother of the man the Sioux had slain appeared at the fort with gifts of dried pumpkin and pemmican. The village chiefs might believe privately that the American offer to lead a winter pursuit of the murderers was stupid, but in the minds of the those most concerned, the interest had "produced a grateful respect . . . which pleased us very much."[18]

And on that note the Corps settled down to the arduous tasks of surviving the present while preparing for the future.

TEN

Forty Below—and Far to Go

On forty different sunrises during December, January, and February (plus two more in March), temperature readings at Fort Mandan sank below zero. The most frigid day, though not by much, was December 17: 45°F below at sunrise and 28° below at 4:00 P.M. All sunrise temperatures from January 5, 1805, through January 15 were −10° or lower; −48°, −38°, −36°. The average for the three-month period was four degrees above zero. For comparison: during the thirty-year span from 1951 through 1980, the average temperature for the same months in the same general area was 12.3° above zero—roughly twenty degrees below freezing. Even granting the likelihood that the Corps's thermometers were less precise than modern ones, the winter at Fort Mandan was remarkably chilly.[1]

Double suns shone in the southern sky. One night the moon wore halos and bars. Moisture in the air occasionally froze into a floating murk that resembled fog. When breezes were gentle—not often—frost collected in deep rinds on the barren limbs of the trees. Then a rising wind would shake the boughs and the frost crystals would fall like snow from a bright blue sky. Sometimes one of the cottonwoods Clark had described as full of water would explode with a boom like a cannon shot. Gales roared with discouraging frequency, sweeping the plains bare except for ridges of drifted snow that lay like welts across the earth.

On December 7, Big White galloped to the fort, shouting and pointing. Shaggy buffalo, seeking relief from the chill of a violent northwest wind, were streaming off the plains and down the slopes of the river trench into the timber-filled bottomlands. Village hunters were gathering for the kill, but would hold back until the whites joined them.

During the next bitter week Lewis and Clark took turns leading detachments of the Corps into the numbing cold to join the slaughter. Afoot, they watched enviously as mounted Indians armed with bows and arrows surrounded a number of buffalo and eased them out of the trees onto the terraces or into clearings where their excited horses could maneuver. Each rider chose a quarry, ran his horse up beside the ponderously galloping beast, and with his powerful bow drove an arrow all but out of sight into its flesh. The Mandans killed about twenty that first day, twice as many as the whites, hunting among the trees, brought down with their rifles. Three that members of the Corps felled were shot within sight of the fort. One of the trio, a cow, leaped off the bank onto the ice, broke through, and died in the "vacancy" as Clark expressed it. Somehow the men got a rope braided out of elk hide around the animal, dragged her to the boat landing, and butchered her there. She was pregnant. Cutting the fetus free, the whites gave it to the wives of the interpreters who cooked and ate it with zest.[2]

Of the ten buffalo the whites killed, they were able to butcher and lug back to the fort only five before darkness fell. Wolves and Indians claimed the other five. To increase the speed of retrieval —the buffalo were drifting farther away from the fort—the captains bought one packhorse and rented three from the Mandans. Even so, they did not recover nearly as many animals as the hunters killed. The below-zero cold made quick butchering impossible, and predators devoured whatever was left unattended for long. To protect some of the spoils Meriwether Lewis and then William Clark, on separate occasions and accompanied by a few men, shivered out the darkness beside the inert mounds of flesh.

Casualties among the enlisted men were high—frosted feet, hands, faces, and in York's case a nipped penis, presumably incurred while he was relieving himself. But there was no telling when buffalo would come as close again, and so the Corps stayed stubbornly with the hunt until December 12, when the sunrise temperature was −38°F. The hunters still out were called back, and for the next few days the men ventured away from the fort only to gather firewood on their hand-drawn sleds. Their great dislike was sentry duty on the rooftop, even though turns were limited to half an hour each during the coldest weather.

As temperatures rose, the buffalo drifted back to their grazing on the high plains. The men resumed cutting timber and building a wall of massive pickets across what had been the open end of the fort. Crowds of Mandans came by to visit, often making nuisances of themselves by pilfering small articles and importuning the captains to exchange trade goods for corn. This presented Lewis and Clark with a dilemma. The merchandise in the storerooms had to be used as good-will offerings for Indians as far away as the Pacific. Yet if the buffalo stayed away the Corps would need the Mandans' dried vegetables as a source of food. How could they get the provisions without jeopardizing their own future?

An unnamed entrepreneur devised a solution. Why not let William Bratton and Alexander Willard, who knew something of blacksmithing, and John Shields, who was both a blacksmith and an expert gunsmith, offer to repair and/or sharpen the relatively few metal objects the Mandans had collected from British traders over the years—hoes, skinning knives, kettles, and occasional firearms—in exchange for agreed-on measures of corn and dried vegetables? The idea took hold. Sergeant Gass supervised the building of a covered pit in which wood could be reduced to charcoal; on the day before Christmas the blacksmiths set up the forge and bellows, which until then had been seldom used.[3] The Indians thronged around open-mouthed. Magic!

Work did not begin on Christmas, however. The Mandans were asked to stay their distance, since that was a great "medicine day" for the whites, though if any religious activity did take place, that fact, too, goes unrecorded. (There is no indication that any group worship of any kind was ever held during the course of the expedition.) Shortly before sunrise, the enlisted men and the discharged French who were living in a nearby hut woke the captains with volleys of rifle shots. A flag was raised, the swivels boomed, and Clark passed out rum that was gulped down before breakfast. There was a special feast—bread baked from a limited supply of flour, pies made of dried apples, pepper for spicing the steaks, and more rum. One of the rooms was cleared for dancing, Cruzatte tuned his fiddle, and the frolic began. Bored after a time, a few of the men went hunting. By nine in the evening everyone was ready for bed, as tired as if they had been working all day.[4]

On New Year's Day, 1805, there was another celebration. At the request of the chiefs of Matootonha and with the captains' permission, Ordway and Charbonneau led sixteen men across the river ice to the Indian village. They took with them "a fiddle & a Tambereen & a Sounden Horn"—a bugle. They fired a rifle salute outside the village, were invited in, and fired another volley in the plaza. The townspeople were enthralled by their dancing, as were all Indians they met. One of the Frenchmen jigged while standing on his hands.

Not wanting to put a damper on the fun, the captains stayed at the fort, but when word arrived of an altercation, Clark went up with York, Jessaume, and an unnamed soldier. Whatever the problem, it was over when he arrived, and the merriment was going strong. York added to it with a solo performance that drew resounding applause. At sunset the whites returned to the fort except six who asked for and were granted permission to stay the night. Those six learned, among other things, that during cold weather each Mandan family stabled its best horses in its lodge, in stalls prepared to the left of the tunnellike entrance. For food the animals gnawed the bark off cottonwood limbs that were thrown to them.

Black Cat, who had spent the day with Lewis and the other half of the expedition at the fort, thought it would be fine if his people at Rooptahee could see the whites perform. Lewis agreed, and the remainder of the enlisted men enjoyed their boisterous turn on January 2.[5]

Shortly after New Year's, the Mandans of Matootonha held a celebration of their own. The whites referred to it as the Buffalo Calling Dance. To the Indians it was the Red Stick Ceremony.[6] Like most Indian rituals, the Red Stick gathering was designed to fill a need, in this case the luring back of the buffalo that had wandered far away, leaving the Indians short of food.

Basically the performance was a symbolic dramatization of a myth too involved to be summarized here. First, twelve old men esteemed for their wisdom carried twelve red boards, representing buffalo, into the lodge of a man who, prompted by dreams, had volunteered to hold the ritual and provide the necessary foods. The boards were arranged like pickets in a straight line from the central fireplace to the rear wall. Criers went through the village announcing that the four-day ritual was about to begin. Old men came to the lodge and seated themselves inside, at the left of the entrance. Several young men and their wives gathered to the right.

The wives were clad only in buffalo robes draped loosely around their bodies. The idea was to lure the old men to have intercourse with them. Clark, who obtained his information from Corps members who participated in the ceremony, felt the affair had been designed by the ancient ones for their own benefit. The Indians' intent was different. They believed wisdom and power could be transmitted from old men to young through the medium of women.

After such preliminaries as feasting and smoking had been completed, one of the ancients simulated intercourse with a small doll dressed like a female. The act launched the ceremony. Each young husband said to his wife, "Help me become fortunate. Walk with my father," by which he meant an elder of a different clan from his. If the ancient one chosen by the youth was agreeable, the pair went outside, the woman clutching the elder's medicine bundle for strength. Apparently the coupling took place in the open air, in the dead of winter, with the woman's robe as a bed.

If the elder turned out to be impotent, the young people felt disgraced. The embarrassment could be remedied, but only to an extent, by a simulation of the essential act—or by choosing a substitute. The Corps's enlisted men were eagerly sought, for all whites, at that time and place, were considered to possess great wisdom, for how else could they create such wonders as guns, magnifying glasses, cloth, and shimmering blue beads? "We sent a man to this Medisen dance last night," Clark wrote on January 5, "they gave him 4 girls all this to cause the buffalow to Come near." His observation skipped a step, however. The buffalo came because the red-stick symbols, having certified the ceremony, transmitted the message to the herd: let them approach so one more necessary cycle of life could be completed, an honor to the sacrificial buffalo as well as to the people the animals saved by nourishing them.

Four days after the conclusion of the ceremony, the buffalo did indeed return. Temperatures skidded fearfully. Laroque, writing letters in a lodge in one of the Hidatsa villages, reported, "The ink freezes in my pen, though I sit so close to the fire as I can without burning my leg." The sunrise reading at Fort Mandan on January 10 was forty below.[7] Again a high wind roared out of the northwest, and again herds of gaunt buffalo, this time accompanied by many elk, streamed into the bottomlands.

Whites and Indians poured out for the hunt. And again there were casualties. Shortly after sunrise on the day the thermometer dropped to forty below, a Mandan boy aged about thirteen—actually he had been taken prisoner during a battle and then adopted by a Mandan family—appeared at the fort's new gate. He had been out hunting with his adoptive father the day before. Seeing how the cold was getting to the lad, the older man told him to seek the shelter of the fort. Dark caught him trudging through the snow. Breaking off some branches and scraping together some dead leaves, he lay down on them, protected only by his small buffalo robe, light leggings of antelope skin, and moccasins.

When he limped into the fort the next day, his feet were frozen. The captains thawed them in cold water, but soon it was obvious the toes could not be saved. First "they" (Lewis probably, since he was generally regarded as the camp doctor) plucked off the dead tissue. When the infection spread, they "sawed" off the members, perhaps stanching the flow of blood with a hot iron. There was no anesthetic, of course, and inasmuch as the expedition's inventory mentions no surgical saw, one doesn't like to think what sort of instrument was used. "Our captains," Ordway reported, "took the greatest care of him possible." But recovery was slow and he had to stay at the fort until February 23, when his father arrived with a sleigh to take him home.[8]

As a contrast: another Indian who spent the same forty-below night in the bottomlands without shelter reached the fort uninjured, prompting Clark to write, "Customs & the habits of these people has anured [them] to bare more Cold than I thought it possible for man to endure." Equally impressive, he thought, was the solicitude of the entire village for the two temporarily lost people. The boy had not been born into the tribe and the man was a person of no distinction, yet all Matootonha was anxious about their safety.[9]

The poor meat picked up during the January hunts, most of it lean elk fortified by an occasional thin deer, did little to replenish the Corps's larder. Fortunately the Indians' desire for ironware remained insatiable. The blacksmiths cut into four-inch squares an old sheet-iron stove the expeditions' cooks had burned out during the trip upriver, and exchanged each piece for seven or eight gallons of corn; the buyer then fashioned his acquisition into iron arrow points or hide scrapers, infinitely better than similar implements made of stone. Another fast-selling item was iron war hatchets fashioned for the buyers out of iron obtained—the journals don't say where. In any event, the Corps stayed mostly on a vegetarian diet while entertaining the first Hidatsa chiefs to visit the fort. During the same period the captains refused Laroque's request to accompany the party to the Pacific—why should a U.S. expedition help a Canadian fur company scout out the resources of the land? And, most arduously, the crew tried to chop the three boats free from ice that had encased them to the gunwales and was threatening to crush them.[10]

Vegetarianism did not suit for long men who were expending great amounts of energy in a bitter climate. Accordingly Clark set out on February 4 to find enough buffalo to quiet the grumblings of their stomachs. He took with him, according to Lewis, who was to attend to the journal during Clark's absence, sixteen members of the Corps and two of the Frenchmen who were living in the hut near the fort. The group traveled down the valley with their equipment in two homemade sleighs, each pulled by a horse. Overflow was loaded on a third animal. One of the horses was a gray mare followed by a young colt; another had been borrowed from Laroque's clerk, Charles McKenzie.[11]

Hard going. In places the river had, on occasion, thawed enough to send a sheet of water across the ice downstream. The surface had then frozen again, creating a trap of sorts. Clark broke through once, soaked his moccasins and leggings, and afterwards blistered his feet walking on ice that held him, just barely, but was rough and uneven, demanding great care to prevent slipping. During the first forty-four miles of travel the crew killed enough buffalo so that after the carcasses had been boned and the fat meat cut away from the lean, they were able to send the three horses laden with food to the fort and still keep enough to provision themselves.

On they went, pulling the sleighs by hand. Having no way to transport the meat they obtained during the rest of the journey, they put it, after butchering, into log cribs tight enough to fend off wolves, ravens, and magpies. The last cache they built was hidden in the trees near the mouth of the Heart River, where Bismarck, North Dakota, stands today. Wearily then they turned around, planning, once they reached their destination, to send a fresh party after the cached beef. On the last day, February 12, they walked thirty miles, sometimes on rippling ice and sometimes short-cutting across timbered points where the snow lay nearly knee-deep. They arrived, Clark said, "fatigued."

On the 14th, Drouillard, recently recovered from being bled and purged for pleurisy, headed downstream with the two sleighs, the three horses, and the frisky colt. Three men went with him, Robert Frazer, Silas Goodrich, and the discharged John Newman, who was working hard to be reinstated as a member of the Corps of Discovery. Toward evening, after they had traveled some two dozen miles, a hundred and six Sioux (literally) came yammering down on them. A few of the attackers cut the two horses out of the sleighs and dashed away with them. (McKenzie's would have to be paid for, adding that mite to the total cost of the expedition.) The whites grimly held onto the frightened, plunging mare. The attackers also stripped the Americans of two knives and a tomahawk, but then, apparently fearing that the whites were about to shoot, returned the tomahawk.

A strange standoff. The Americans wisely held their fire, perhaps at Drouillard's barked advice, and it was not the Indians' way to risk lives unnecessarily no matter how the odds favored them. They'd added to their reputation by taking two horses from these whites who were continually bragging about their country's power; they could count that coup dramatically for years to come. Enough! Away they raced, whooping triumphantly. Unwilling to expose themselves in a forlorn camp, the whites, the mare, and the colt trudged back through the darkness to the fort, which they reached at two in the morning.

Those damnable Sioux! Lewis sent messengers to Matootonha: come help us pursue our mutual enemy. Big White and a lesser chief responded immediately with a few men, "Some [armed] with Bows and arrows," Clark wrote, "Some with Spears & Battle axes, 2 with fuzees"—outdated muskets; hunters were out on the plains with the good guns, Big White explained. About twenty volunteers from the fort joined in. The rest stayed behind to keep an eye on the Assiniboins who were roving about the neighborhood, to gather firewood, and chip away at the icebound boats.

The only trace of the Sioux the avengers found were some cast-off moccasins, horse tracks, and the galling remnants of one of Clark's caches, which the brigands had rifled of meat and burned. But the Sioux had missed the lowest one, which Lewis found intact. Realizing at last that there was no chance of overtaking the quarry, he cooled off and turned his party to hunting. After they had bagged thirty-six deer and fourteen elk they hitched the gray mare to a sleigh loaded with six hundred pounds of meat. They piled a ton more, poor quality, winter-lean stuff, on the other, and, with sixteen men pulling on its ropes, returned to Fort Mandan. They arrived about dark on February 21.

Ten days before that, the makings of one of the West's better-known legends received a major boost toward immortality. Sacagawea, Charbonneau's child-wife, went into labor. The husband was off with the hunters, and René Jessaume's spouse, aided conversationally by René, was acting as midwife. As the pains grew more excruciating (Indian women don't always drop babies as easily as buffalo drop calves), either the midwife or Jessaume offered the suggestion that powdered rattles from a rattlesnake, swallowed with water, would hurry things along. Indeed? And how did one obtain rattlesnake rattles in the dead of winter? Captain Lewis, perhaps: he was always collecting natural history specimens.

Sure enough, Lewis did have snake rattles. He handed Jessaume two "rings." Ten minutes after the dose was administered, the baby was born and given, on the father's return, perhaps the most common of French-Canadian Christian names, Jean Baptiste.[12] (A supposition, offered without firm evidence: what if Charbonneau, recalling the Catholic rituals of his boyhood, had asked Clark to be the infant's godfather? Would that help explain Clark's warm regard for the family and his wish to raise Jean Baptiste "as my own child"? Lewis, by contrast, considered Charbonneau of no worth except as an interpreter; Lewis was also indifferent toward the child.)[13]

The last days of February were marked by a run of fine weather: the sunrise temperature on the 22d was eight degrees above zero, and from then until well into March, afternoon readings were thirty-two degrees or higher. The men put their clothes and bedding out to air, and as the mercury rose, so did the pace of preparations for the coming summer.

For more than a month the crew had been struggling intermittently and fruitlessly to free the two pirogues and the keelboat from the ice. Initially the captains had feared the accumulation would crush them. The ice was three feet thick, with lenses of water caught between the layers that frustrated both chopping and picking. Later, as warming days turned the surface of the ice soggy, apprehension shifted. When the spring breakup occurred, immense floes would sweep down the river, battering the boats to pieces on their way.

Efforts redoubled, beginning February 22. Using iron-pointed levers and ropes of elk hide, the crew managed to crack both pirogues free. After smoothing out a road for log rollers, they hauled the pair ashore and up beside the pickets of the fort. The keelboat proved more stubborn. While Indians crowded about to watch, the straining workers broke the rope again and again, until at last they doubled the cord, dug in, and succeeded.[14]

Even before the boats had been brought ashore, the captains had revised their transportation logistics. As a result of their experiences with the shoaling Missouri the previous fall and of talks with the Indians, they decided the keelboat would be a handicap on the upper river. Consequently they determined to send it downstream. Corporal Richard Warfington's soldiers, who had wrestled the white pirogue upstream, would act as crew and fight off the Sioux if that proved necessary. Those of the red pirogue's erstwhile French boatmen who remained in the vicinity would go along as passengers, as would the discharged and disgraced Reed and Newman; though Lewis recognized Newman's efforts at rehabilitation, he sternly refused to reinstate him. The returning craft would also carry two dozen crates of specimens and a bundle of reports for Jefferson.

The two pirogues, both more maneuverable and of shallower draft than the keelboat, would be used for completing the ascent of the Missouri. They were not roomy enough, however, to hold the thirty-three persons and the one dog of what would become known as the permanent party, plus, of course, their baggage. At the end of the month, accordingly, part of the fort's garrison was sent upstream to find cottonwood trees big enough for making dugouts—six long, narrow affairs, unstable but capable of being sailed when the wind was right. The trees the scouts found were awkwardly located some six miles up the Missouri and another mile and a half from its banks.[15] Carrying the finished dugouts to the stream would be difficult, but no matter. Pushing to the Pacific was the consuming thought right then.

Concurrently with the tree hunters' departure, Joseph Gravelines, two Frenchmen, and two Arikara Indians arrived at the fort. From them Lewis and Clark learned, with renewed anger, that the Sioux who had attacked Drouillard and his meat gatherers two weeks earlier—one hundred and six of them by Gravelines's count —had stopped at the Arikara towns on their way downstream and had boasted of their deeds. This annoyed the Rees, as the Arikaras were often called, who were out of sorts with the Sioux, anyway. For stories had reached the river Indians that Murdock Cameron, a British trader on the St. Peter's, was selling guns to the belligerent tribe. Cameron had supposed the buyers would use the weapons against their old enemy, the Chippewa, who had recently killed three of his men. But the feeling of power brought by the guns had led several bands of the Sioux to vow an attack on the Arikaras for entering into an alliance with the Mandans. During the battling the Corps of Discovery was to be annihilated for engineering the disruption. Only Black Buffalo, who had helped restrain the Bois Brulé Tetons during the September confrontation with the explorers, was refusing to join the projected assault.[16]

This information was counterbalanced, in the captains' estimation, by a letter from Antoine Tabeau that Gravelines delivered. Frightened by the Sioux threat, the trader wrote, the Arikaras wanted to cement their tentative alliance with the Mandans and Hidatsas by moving north to live close to the upper river Indians. Would the Mandans and Hidatsas be agreeable?

Delighted, Lewis and Clark conveyed the message to both tribes. With some reserve the Mandan and Hidatsa chiefs suggested that a proper Arikara delegation be sent up the Missouri to talk things over. Still, it looked as though the Grand Plan for breaking the Sioux's grip on the river was going to work. Using the Frenchmen who had arrived with Gravelines as couriers, the captains sent a letter back to Tabeau, urging him to press for the conference. As for Gravelines, he stayed at Fort Mandan. The captains, who considered the trader to be, in Lewis's words, "an honest discrete man and an excellent boat-man," had hired him to pilot the keelboat down the Missouri, picking up as many Arikara chiefs along the way as would consent to come aboard. He would also collect whatever Yankton Sioux, Omahas, Otos, and Missouris Pierre Dorion had managed to gather during the winter. (No Mandans or Hidatsas would agree to join the excursion for fear of the Tetons.) After landing in St. Louis, Gravelines would help escort the red dignitaries to Washington.

Washington! Although Lewis and Clark's thoughts kept veering toward the Pacific, they could not leave until they had finished putting into orderly shape for Jefferson's eyes the staggering number of specimens, maps, and detailed reports they had been working over since their departure from Camp Wood ten months before.

They had collected enough objects to equip a small museum—sixty-seven specimens of soil, salts, and minerals; sixty examples of plants, including one supposed to be a sovereign remedy for the bites of rattlesnakes and rabid wolves; the hides of many animals, some stuffed and several unknown to Americans of the time; four live magpies, a live sharp-tailed grouse, and a live prairie dog, probably the one they had driven from its burrow farther downstream with kegs of water; a variety of embalmed insects; and many Indian curiosities. All this had to be annotated, packaged, and labeled.[17]

The annotations were essentially rewritten field notes about materials collected under severe limitation. Neither man was a trained scientist. Lewis's crash courses prior to his departure from Washington had taught him how to focus his inquiries in different disciplines, but not much else. Both, however, were conscientious observers, each with a particular talent. Clark was more adept at eliciting information from Indians and at illustrating his written descriptions with rough-hewn but accurate drawings. Lewis had an unusually sharp eye for the details of flora and fauna, and a trenchant pen for conveying the essence of his studies.

To the physical objects they sent downstream on the keelboat they added voluminous reports on the climate, topography, river drainage systems, soil fertility, and Indian cultures of all Upper Louisiana Territory. Because they had been locked inside the Missouri River trench, except for climbs to occasional viewpoints, they'd had to extend their observations by questioning Indians through interpreters and by interviewing such knowledgeable traders as Antoine Tabeau and Hugh Heney of the North West Company, the latter of whom had joined Laroque at the Hidatsa villages in December.

The geographic material they had collected they organized into two documents with similar titles. One, a discourse prepared by Lewis, described the streams that discharged into the Missouri—their length, navigability, sources, and the appearance of the lands through which they flowed. He called his compilation "A Summary View of Rivers and Creeks." Clark supplemented that essay with four arithmetic tables that gave the distances from one stream mouth to the next one upstream, an estimate of each tributary's length, and a record of latitudes taken here and there by the captains during the upriver journey. He called these tables "A Summary View of Rivers, Creeks, and Remarkable Places," the last term referring, in the main, to large islands and the site of both deserted and occupied Indian villages. Both summaries ended with guesswork, based on Indian information, about the country that lay west of the Missouri.[18]

Their data on the territory's native inhabitants were contained in what Lewis and Clark entitled "Estimate of Eastern Indians," eastern because it dealt with tribes living on the inland side of the Continental Divide. When including the "Estimate" in a special message to Congress on February 19, 1806, Jefferson retitled it "A Statistical View of the Indian Nations Inhabiting the Territory of Louisiana and the Countries Adjacent to its Northern and Western Boundaries." The "Estimate," like the "Summaries," was based largely on hearsay, as the captains frankly admitted. Even so, it contained more information about Upper Louisiana than anyone else in the United States could muster, and it would give would-be traders a basis for planning.

The last point was important. Although Jefferson had told Lewis to hunt out knowledge for its own sake, the president had not overlooked pragmatic goals. The dichotomy is clearly revealed in the captains' handling of Indian studies. Before leaving Washington, Lewis had been advised to collect information about such things as Indian pulse rates, menstrual cycles, funeral customs, medical practices, and religious observances. At the same time he was to record anything that might be helpful in establishing and maintaining commercial contacts. Quickly realizing the impossibility of ferreting out extensive anthropological detail during the limited time they could spend with most tribes, Lewis and Clark had concentrated their search on matters that would primarily interest traders—language, the home territories of the different tribes, the peoples with whom they were at peace or war, the potential value of their commerce, and, for the government, the possibility of relocating important tribes near federal trading posts in the event the Indian Bureau decided such interference with private enterprise was advisable.

For example, consider the Hidatsas, who were called Minitaris in the "Estimate." According to Lewis and Clark, the tribe often left their domed houses to range along both banks of the Missouri up to and beyond the mouth of the Yellowstone. The area abounded in beaver. The Hidatsas did not hunt the valuable fur-bearing animals, however, because the chase was difficult and they could get the supplies they needed by bartering horses and vegetables with the Assiniboins, Crows, Cheyennes—and from the Canadians. Private traders would like to know such things. And the government would like to know that the Hidatsas probably could be prevailed on to relocate their villages near the mouth of the Yellowstone if a federal trading post were established there. Such a move might be necessary, for Lewis and Clark had heard, through Charbonneau, rumors to the effect that the North West Company was planning to build a post at the mouth of the Knife.

And the Sioux. Their many bands, named and located in the "Estimate," roamed a huge area. Of these bands the Tetons were "the vilest miscreants of the savage race," a remark that overlooked Black Buffalo's perhaps temporary coolness toward joining the projected war against the Mandans and the Americans. The Tetons' trade, the captains said, might be of value if those Indians were reduced to order by armed intervention. And that, too, was something every trader in St. Louis would read with interest.

An inevitable question arises: How did Lewis and Clark themselves evaluate this territorial acquisition about which they had written so much? In his journal Clark had noted such unfavorable factors as growing alkalinity in certain creeks and bordering ground. Both had read in the diaries of their predecessors' remarks about sterility and semiaridity. They had experienced the harsh, desiccating winds that blew almost constantly across the High Plains. They had endured the crushing cold of a plains winter. But were they pessimistic about the area's adaptability to white settlement? The answer has to be a firm negative.

A recurrent phrase in Clark's upriver journal is "butifull prospect," which is not a term he would have applied to views that struck him as unfavorable to human occupation. Lewis is more specific. In a letter he wrote his mother just before leaving Fort Mandan, he grows almost ecstatic.[19] The Missouri, "so far as we have yet ascended, waters one of the fairest portions of the globe." He had heard the area was "barren, steril, and sandy." Not so. A fertile soil of loam sustained a luxuriant growth of grass on which game abounded. The only lack was timber, and that was not the result of adverse climate or inadequate soil, but of raging grass fires the Indians kindled either carelessly at their camps or set deliberately, partly for excitement and partly to control the movement of game. For that matter, the Corps had started some towering blazes, too, to attract the attention of tribes they wanted to contact, a matter the letter did not mention.

(Lewis's challenging remark about the treeless nature of the plains, incidentally, has stout defenders. In spite of relatively light precipitation trees can be grown there, as many a farmer has discovered. The Nebraska National Forest in the western sandhills of that state, which was planted as a calculated experiment, flourished as soon as grass fires were controlled.[20] No major lumber company has sought to exploit the area, however.)

At this late date it is hard to know to what extent Lewis saw the plains through preconditioned eyes. The American West was supposed to be fertile. America's advancing frontier, and hence a great part of the young nation's strength, depended on that axiom.[21] Jefferson knew of the treeless expanses in the continent's interior, but, less aware than Lewis of fire's ravages, he suggested that the soil out there was not too poor, but *too rich* for trees, thus turning the average pioneer's conventional wisdom upside down. Both Meriwether Lewis and William Clark, children of agriculturists, had absorbed the faith of an expansive agrarian society without question. The multitudes of grass-eating animals the Corps subsisted on proved that nutritious growth existed, and the herds were said to become more numerous as one pressed on west from the Mandan-Hidatsa villages—settlements which were, after all, based on agriculture. Though the captains had not yet laid eyes on the valley of the Yellowstone River, it, too, was reputed to be another terrestrial paradise. Why doubt? The best was yet to be.

The key that locked these data together was a map of a highly conjectural West that Clark drew during the long nights at Fort Mandan. Its base was the King-Arrowsmith chart he had studied at Camp Wood when first estimating distances and potential routes to the Pacific. On that foundation he superimposed such new information and corrections as Lewis and he had gleaned from talks with Indians and with every trader they had met during their upstream journey.

First, Clark filled in the largely blank areas between the upper Mississippi and the Missouri, drawing his facts from Hugh Heney, once a partner of Regis Loisel's but more recently an employee of the North West Company of Canada. That done, Clark turned his attention to the lower and middle Missouri's major tributaries—the Osage, Kansas, Platte, Niobrara, and Cheyenne rivers. In all cases he showed the streams heading too far west. Most were represented as rising in the Black Hills of present South Dakota, a range that Clark showed as extending much farther north and south than is the case. Contributing to his errors was Lewis's miscalculation of the longitude of the Mandan villages—99°24′45″. The correct position is 101°27′. David Thompson of the North West Company had been roughly ninety miles closer to the truth half a dozen years earlier, although the captains, convinced of the superiority of their methods, boasted to Laroque that they had corrected his colleague's figures.[22]

Lewis and Clark's primary challenge, of course, was learning as much as possible about the country they—and after them the pioneer merchants of the United States—would need to know in order to reach the Orient-facing harbors of the Pacific Coast. In this instance their informants were the Mandans and Hidatsas. Fortunately the early hostility of the latter tribe thawed; for the Hidatsas, the captors of Sacagawea, were accustomed to range as far west as the Continental Divide during their horse-stealing raids against the Snake Indians. There is no evidence, incidentally, that the young Snake woman, Sacagawea, contributed in any way to the production of the map.

The obstacles to accurate mapping were prodigious.[23] The Indians had no compasses. They indicated directions by pointing more or less along the lines followed by the sun at different seasons of the year. This resulted in a certain fuzziness for a geographer hoping to move from one distant point to another along a zigzagging course. The Indians, moreover, did not measure distances in miles, but in "sleeps" or "suns." The ground they covered during one "sun" depended on the pace of their horses. The Corps, however, hoped to journey as far as the Missouri's headwaters by boat. Correlating the two standards was tentatively done, to say the least. In addition, the Indians had scant notions of navigability, so that their descriptions of streams as they appeared to a man on horseback were hardly definitive for boats. Plus this: on their war excursions against the Snakes, the Hidatsas avoided the rough breaks south of the Missouri and struck directly across the plains. As a result they had not even seen the river for long distances. Finally, there were the usual frustrations of grasping information that passed through several mouths—a Hidatsa warrior to Charbonneau, Charbonneau to Drouillard or Cruzatte, and thence to the interrogator.

The Indians could draw rough maps, however, either on hide or on smoothed patches of earth, using an awl or a twig to scratch out river courses and adding little heaps of sand to indicate mountains.

Directions as well as topography emerged with fair accuracy on such charts (if communication came through accurately), but distances remained elusive. Perhaps the best way to show the differences between what the captains anticipated and what they found will be to outline the expectations portrayed on the map and then let reality emerge in the narrative as it progresses.

First, the *Yellowstone River.* Lewis and Clark had picked up glimmerings of the stream from the journals and cartographic speculations of their predecessors, Jean Baptiste Truteau, James Mackay, and John Evans. During their talks with the Mandan chief Big White and with various Hidatsas, the Yellowstone and its major tributaries, such as the Bighorn, emerged with fair correctness. But somehow they got the notion that the river rose in the Rockies near the spot where "the Spaniards reside." Hardly, especially when one considers the nature of the lofty peaks that intervene between the Yellowstone's farthest headwaters and those of the "Spanish" streams, presumably the Platte, Rio Grande, and Colorado. However, awareness of the Yellowstone did enable the captains to get rid of the Lesser Missisourie of the King-Arrowsmith chart (it became today's relatively insignificant Little Missouri), and with that out of the way they were able to accommodate a main Missouri bending far to the south in western Montana.

They also visualized the Yellowstone as boiling down out of rough, heavily timbered country into "one of the fairest portions of Louisiana, a country not yet hunted and abounding in animals of the fur kind." Now, that was information that would cause a stir in St. Louis. (It also stirred young François Laroque, who, after being denied permission to accompany the Corps to the Pacific, set out with a party of Crow Indians to look over the Yellowstone region for the North West Company. On the trip Laroque did hear of the Great Falls of the Yellowstone, but he did not reach as high as today's Yellowstone National Park.) Inasmuch as Jefferson had advised Lewis to keep an eye on the Missouri's southern tributaries—he had been thinking of ways to reach Spanish New Mexico—Lewis promised him, when writing in April 1806, that the Corps would explore the Yellowstone on its return from the Pacific. This is significant, for it shows they had already learned that a short trip east from Three Forks over what is now Bozeman Pass would bring them into the lovely valleys of the upper Yellowstone near today's Livingston. Fur traders would relish that knowledge, too.[24]

The White Earth River. The stream, its name a translation of the

Indian *Ok-hah, Ah-zhah,* was said to debouch into the Missouri from the north, three miles below and opposite to the mouth of the Yellowstone. Supposedly the source of the White Earth lay far to the north, near the south fork of the Saskatchewan. If so and if Louisiana Territory was held to embrace every tributary of the Missouri, this would thrust a barrier across Canadian expansion to the west and, as Lewis wrote triumphantly, would give American fur traders a good run at the fabled beaver regions of Athabasca.

The Milk River. The Indians called it *Ah-mah-tah, ru-shush-sher,* or "The River that Scolds at All Others." Lewis and Clark believed that it, too, might give access to the Saskatchewan. According to their understanding of Indian information, it was the last major northern tributary of the Missouri. Encountering it would mean they were well on their way to the thunderous Great Falls of the Missouri, a natural phenomenon that both awed and fascinated their Indian informants.

The Great Falls. The roar of this "most tremendious cataract" reputedly could be heard for miles. The river rushed so fast, Lewis reported in his "Summary View of Rivers and Creeks," that on reaching the brink of the precipice it shot out so far that there was space, at the bottom, "for several persons to pass abrest underneath the torrent, from bank to bank, without wetting their feet." Passing around the cataract was no problem. A half-mile portage along the level plain on the north side of the river would bring the Corps to the spot where the Missouri "assumes it's usual appearance, being perfectle navigable."

The Sun River. The Indians called this stream the Medicine. It enters the Missouri from the west, and according to the Indians (insofar as the captains understood them) it rose in the Rocky Mountains opposite to a west-flowing stream that presumably was a tributary of the Columbia. But the Medicine was reported to be too swift and shallow to be navigated. Besides, the captains had been ordered to explore the Missouri to its headwaters. Accordingly they spent little time trying to unravel the confusing details that clustered around the natives' descriptions of the small stream.

Three Forks. Before the captains reached the Great Falls they would notice that the trough of the Missouri bent from its westward course to the southwest. It would maintain that direction through several parallel ridges. A little more than a hundred miles beyond the Great Falls, as the explorers computed the distance, the stream would divide into three forks. The western one would lead to a fifteen-mile portage across the Continental Divide.

The *Continental Divide* looked on Clark's map much as it looked on the King-Arrowsmith—the westernmost of four north-south ridges that rose rather mildly out of gentle valleys or perhaps out of a slightly elevated plain. Clark even retained the mythological names of some of the divide's peaks—the King, the Heart, and so on. The western base of this easily crossed divide, the Indians asserted, was washed by a large river that ran from south to north. Farther than that the Hidatsas had never been. The captains were confident, however, that this river was the hypothecated south fork of the Columbia. After flowing through plains almost as level as those bordering most of the Missouri, the fork would enter the main Columbia. The journey from the divide to the Pacific should be little more than three hundred miles. With that notion firmly in mind, Lewis assured Jefferson that the Corps could easily reach the ocean and return to the headwaters of the Missouri or perhaps even to the Mandan towns before winter set in.[25]

By March 20, 1805, the six pirogues designed to take the place of the keelboat had been completed. Clark took enough men upstream to lug the new craft a mile and a half to the river and then float them amid chunks of broken ice to the fort, where they were carefully caulked. During their labors the explorers were amazed by a kind of Indian hunting totally new to them. Buffalo trying to cross the stream at breakup time were often marooned on big cakes of floating ice. Seeing one approach, a hunter or two would take off to intercept it, jumping dexterously from floe to floe until they reached the cake the buffalo occupied. Rendered harmless by its insecure footing, the shaggy beast received its death wound almost without a struggle. The hunters then paddled the icy hearse ashore.

Charles McKenzie's journal supplies an additional item. During the winter many buffalo had died upstream. They, too, floated down, on the floes or among them. Young Indians skipped from cake to cake with ropes to haul the nauseating creatures ashore, for when "the flesh is a greenish hue . . . and so ripe, so tender, that very little boiling is necessary—the stench is intolerable—yet the soup they make from it . . . is reckoned delicious."[26]

By April 6 the river was clear of ice, and the boats were ready to start both upstream and down to their separate destinations. The men, Lewis wrote, were "in good health [except for the usual venereal complaints] and excellent sperits, zealously attached to the enterprise, and anxious to proceed."[27] But there was a last-minute delay. A messenger crossed the river, probably in an Indian bullboat, and reported that the entire Arikara nation, or so the captains understood, was coming north to build new towns nearby.

Promptly Lewis and Clark dispatched an interpreter over to meet the throng. It turned out there were ten Arikaras, the delegation the Mandans and Hidatsas had requested to come upstream to smoke in amity while discussing the proposed relocation of the Arikara towns. The interpreter also passed on a letter from Tabeau that stated that three Sioux chiefs (probably not Tetons) and some Arikaras had listened to his blandishments and would board the keelboat when it passed the villages on its way to St. Louis. Tabeau asked permission to join the party with four hands and three thousand pounds of fur.[28]

Good omens. The captains' diplomacy was showing firm signs of moving ahead, and the keelboat would be well protected if any band of truculent Sioux tried to interfere. In high spirits the little fleet of two pirogues and six small "canoes" pushed off at 4:00 P.M. on April 7. Lewis, who by then was definitely keeping a journal, eyed the procession proudly. "This little fleet altho' not quite so rispectable as those of Columbus or Capt. Cook, were still viewed by us with as much pleasure as those deservedly famous adventurers beheld their's." Clark, less given to introspection, used his journal to call the roll of those aboard (not counting himself and Lewis): Sergeants Nathaniel Pryor, John Ordway, and Patrick Gass. Privates William Bratton, John Collins, John Colter, Pierre Cruzatte, Joseph Field, Reuben Field, Robert Frazer, George Gibson, Silas Goodrich, Hugh Hall, Thomas Howard, François Labiche, Baptiste Lepage, Hugh McNeal, John Potts, George Shannon, John Shields, John Thompson, William Werner, Joseph Whitehouse, Alexander Willard, Richard Windsor, Peter Wiser. Interpreters George Drouillard and Toussaint Charbonneau. York, Sacagawea, and her two-month-old infant, Baptiste. And Clark should have added the dog Seaman, who ate as much as any one of the men.

A mixed bag and far to go. But by that time all who were capable of looking ahead had been thoroughly tested both individually and as a unit, except for Charbonneau and Lepage, both added at Fort Mandan. Probably the others would have echoed Lewis's statement to Jefferson, "With such men I have every thing to hope and but little to fear." Most of the crew (there's no telling about Sacagawea) might even have agreed with Lewis's statement in his journal, "I could but esteem this moment of departure among the most happy of my life," though whether or not they would return "was for experiment yet to determine."[29]

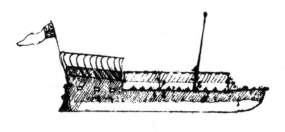

ELEVEN

Hazards by Water

The white pirogue, smaller but more stable than the red, was the queen of the little fleet. In her lockers the captains stored their astronomical instruments, several casks of gunpowder, medicines, their best trade goods, their journals, and other valuable papers. For safety's sake, the three privates of the expedition who could not swim were assigned as oarsmen to this "flagship." (The boat's full complement of rowers was six.) Also riding in the white pirogue were Sacagawea and her two-month-old baby, her husband, Toussaint Charbonneau, the hunter-interpreter George Drouillard, and captains Meriwether Lewis and William Clark.[1]

The close association continued at night, when the captains sought shelter with Drouillard, Charbonneau, and his family in a movable leather tepee. It was made of several expertly tanned buffalo hides sewed together in such fashion that they formed a tall cone when draped around a dozen ten-foot-long lodge poles.[2] Presumably the poles were also carried in the boat, for suitable slim, straight timbers were not always easy to find along the river's edge.

Generally speaking, Indian women set up their families' lodges after each move, but it would have been unduly time-consuming for Sacagawea to have struggled alone with the awkward tent each morning and evening. Since it is difficult to imagine Charbonneau losing face, in his own estimation, by lending her a hand, conjecture veers to York. The black slave (Clark always referred to him as "my servant") was enormously strong, fat, amiable, and trained by long experience in the ways of wilderness housekeeping. Probably York and Sacagawea also cooked for the occupants of the tepee. Charbonneau, who was an expert at making *boudins,* a sausage encased in somewhat cleansed buffalo intestines, may have helped prepare other dishes as well.

During the first week of travel, the expedition traversed the crinkled, miles-long curve called the Great Bend of the Missouri. There the Mississippi-bound river gave up its eastern course and struck south. For the boatmen, passing the Great Bend meant they were at last heading due west toward the setting sun, the Pacific. Spirits were high, and the spring weather smiled in accord. Gray disintegrating heaps of ice, pushed onto the banks and sandbars during the breakup, were the only remaining signs of winter. The trees in the bottomlands were beginning to bud; flowers spangled the greening plains, where flocks of geese fed on the new grass. Their square sails raised whenever the winds favored, the two pirogues and the six cranky new dugouts covered the ninety-three miles to the mouth of the Little Missouri in slightly more than four days.[3]

Paradise did have flaws. Riverside bluffs were occasionally obscured by mephitic smoke rising from seams of lignite coal set to smoldering years before either by spontaneous combustion or by grass fires—the source, probably, of tales told by French-Canadians of volcanoes in the mysterious West. (Years later, the surveyor Ferdinand Hayden declared, "The sulphurous smell which issues from these fires is exceedingly offensive.") Other disagreeable odors rose from scattered piles of decaying buffalo carcasses; the animals had drowned when the spring-softened ice gave way under them, and afterwards had been deposited on exposed shores by the high water of spring. A more familiar discomfort appeared on April 9, the year's first "musquetor." By the next day the pests were troublesome, and would stay that way for months to come.

Food was limited, at first, to parched corn and jerky. The men craved fresh meat, but Hidatsa and Assiniboin hunters had frightened the game out of the river valley within two or three days' ride of the villages. The animals the Corps finally did see were too winter-lean to be acceptable, except for their tongues. Another substitute was the flesh of the beaver they shot or trapped; a single long, flat tail provided, when broiled, a feast for two hungry persons. They killed geese now and then, and also helped themselves to the eggs in whatever nests they found. To their surprise, most of the goose nests they spotted were high in lofty cottonwood trees. Sacagawea showed them how to find caches of unfamiliar but edible roots that gophers stored near piles of driftwood. Meanwhile, buffalo calves were growing and were fat, even if their mothers weren't. So buffalo veal became, for a time, a mainstay of the thirty-two adult travelers and of Lewis's big, black Newfoundland dog.

As the days passed, the violence of the north and northwest winds increased. Sudden squalls added to the problem. Early in the afternoon of April 13, while Toussaint Charbonneau was at the tiller of the white pirogue and the boat was bounding easily over high, opaque waves where the river was several hundred yards wide, an unexpected gust lashed obliquely across the water. The boat listed dangerously. Charbonneau froze. Lewis yelled for Drouillard to take the tiller and for the other crew members to drop the sails. The boat staggered upright, undamaged. "This accedent," Lewis admitted in his journal, "was very near costing us dear." But he did not shift any of the pirogue's valuable cargo to other boats or make any changes in the crew's assignments.

Perhaps he thought there would be no use in doing so. The six long, narrow dugouts, invariably called "canoes" in the journals, were particularly vulnerable to the unremitting force of the wind. This was especially true when the fleet had to turn some long, exposed point. Slapped hard by the waves, the unstable craft and, more than once, the pirogues shipped water. If the wetting was serious, the cargo had to be unloaded and spread out to dry.

Sometimes the travelers could buck adverse winds by breaking out the tow ropes and dragging the craft ahead. At other times, perhaps for a few hours and on occasions for an entire day, they could not move at all. At such times they tried to find a cove where they could tie the dugouts to the shore and anchor the pirogues in front of them as breakwaters. The gales blew sand off the bars in streamers like smoke. "We are compelled to eat, drink, and breath it very freely," Lewis wrote, to which Clark added, "The party complain much of the Sand in their eyes." In time the inflammations grew serious enough that Lewis dug into the medicine chest and concocted an eyewash of white vitriol and sugar of lead (zinc sulphate and lead acetate). Meanwhile Clark fretted that "the winds of this country . . . have become a serious obstruction to our progress onward."[4]

Wind or not, the captains never forgot that one of their main assignments was to learn what they could of the land and its wildlife. Lewis was the one who spent the most time afoot on this assignment. Head bent against the gales, he wandered along the broad trails the buffalo had trampled into the earth and noted admiringly the exactness with which the shaggy beasts had worked out the most efficient routes from one point to another. He climbed the bluffs on both sides of the river to learn how plants, birds, and animals had adapted to the varied environments. He detected the difference in the habitats preferred by mule deer and white-tailed deer. He marveled at the way wolves would cut one antelope out of a herd and then spell each other as they ran the fleet-footed prey to exhaustion. He listened intently to bird calls so that he could render the sounds phonetically on paper. When he came across unfamiliar plants he tested them with his tongue, nose, and fingertips in order to be able to convey the most accurate description possible—descriptions often hundreds of words long and composed by the dwindling light of the evening's campfire. Unfortunately he never published a scientific paper on his findings and so later naturalists, acting in full honesty, often received credit for bringing to the world's attention bits of lore that Meriwether Lewis had first portrayed.[5]

Clark contributed fully. Sometimes he left spare accounts of things he had seen. More often he told Lewis about the discoveries he had made during one of his own strenuous hikes and let his friend handle the paperwork. Clark's main job was cartography. As he had done on the way up the Missouri to the Mandan villages, he kept careful compass records of the river's many turnings and of mileages between prominent points, as computed by dead reckoning. He then transferred the data onto separate sheets of paper, as he had done the previous year. Limited though the strip maps were to the river's immediate environs, they nevertheless could be used to check, in part, the accuracy of the big, conjectural map of the West he had drawn at Fort Mandan during the winter, relying mainly on information collected from the Indians and then transferred to the basic King-Arrowsmith map they were carrying with them.[6]

Results excited the captains. The Little Missouri came in from the south and the White Earth River from the north, as the Indians had said they would. The Indians had also said, or so the captains had understood, that the White Earth was navigable almost as far north as Canada's South Saskatchewan River, as portrayed on their King-Arrowsmith chart. If so, the White Earth could be used for tapping the great fur country of the Canadian Northwest. Buoyed by that hope, they walked beside the tributary for about four miles. It should not have struck them as prepossessing. Its low, steep banks were stained white with patches of alkali; its bed, Lewis wrote, "seems composed of mud altogether." Swollen by spring runoff, it was about sixty yards wide. Later settlers, seeing the stream at a drier season, would name it Little Muddy Creek. But Lewis and Clark wanted it as a highway for American commerce, and they wrote about it with the ink of hope, a strange aberration for two normally competent observers.[7]

Three or four miles above the mouth of the White Earth, another tributary of special interest to Lewis and Clark entered the Missouri. This one came from the south and was truly majestic. The Hidatsas called it Mee, Ah-zhah. As noted earlier, it was not unknown to white men. French-Canadian voyageurs and traders of the original Missouri Fur Company had been calling it Roche Jaune for more than a decade. Roche Jaune, the River of Yellow Rock, or Yellowstone. The name is inexplicable, for there is no indication that any of the whites who wrote about it had yet heard of, let alone seen, the vivid yellow walls of the river's upper canyon. Nevertheless, the stream, labeled Yellowstone through some strange coincidence, appears strongly on Clark's conjectural map, where it reaches much too far south across lands barely rippled by mountains..

Such a stream merited actual examination, not guesswork. During their winter with the Mandans, the captains had laid plans to explore it on their return journey to the States. Before then, however, they wanted to determine the geographic coordinates of its mouth for the sake of Clark's strip maps. When contrary winds pinned the fleet against the banks of the Missouri, Lewis decided to speed matters by going ahead on foot, accompanied by Drouillard, Ordway, and the brothers Joseph and Reuben Field. After taking his readings, he would wait for the boats to follow when they could.

The quartet climbed to the top of the Missouri's southern bluffs and struck overland toward what they assumed would be the junction—if Indian descriptions were correct. Elation filled them. There it was, strong and beautiful, curling lazily through a wide, fertile plain streaked with magnificent stands of trees, their new leaves glistening in the sunlight. Then and there Lewis decided, with the sense of wonder that is one of his most appealing charac-

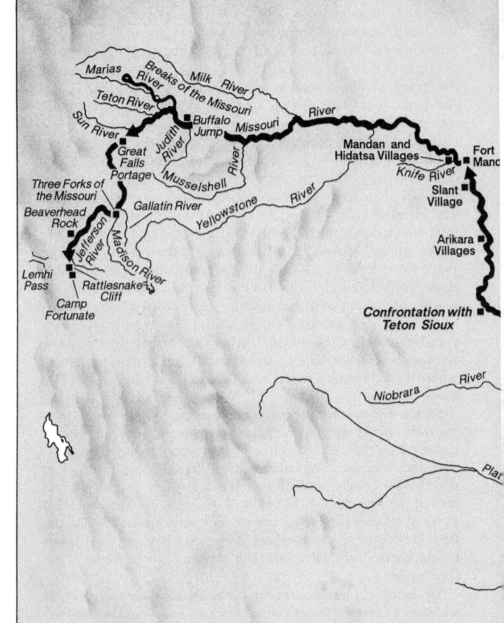

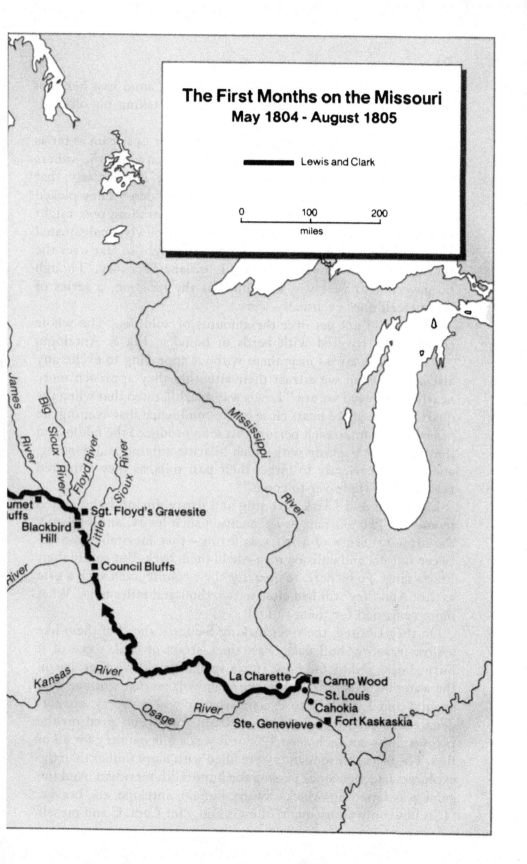

The First Months on the Missouri
May 1804 - August 1805

━━━━━ Lewis and Clark

```
0          100         200
           miles
```

James River

Big Sioux River

Floyd River

Little Sioux River

Mississippi River

urnet luffs

Sgt. Floyd's Gravesite

Blackbird Hill

Council Bluffs

River

Kansas River

Osage River

La Charette

Camp Wood

St. Louis

Cahokia

Ste. Genevieve

Fort Kaskaskia

teristics, to camp on the Yellowstone's banks, amid vast herds of wildlife, and enjoy the pristine scene before taking his observations.

The next day Joseph Field explored the river upstream as far as he could walk and return before dark. Meanwhile the others roamed the area around the junction, thinking, inaccurately, that no other white men had seen this unspoiled Eden.[8] They picked out a site where a United States government trading post might be located in competition to the British, if the newly amalgamated Hudson's Bay and North West companies sought to take over the fur business of this lovely section of Louisiana Territory. (Though no government post was ever built at the junction, a series of commercial ones eventually were.)

They could not get over the amounts of wildlife. "The whole country was covered with herds of buffaloe, Elk & Antelopes . . . so gentle we pass near them without appearing to excite any alarm, and when we attract their attention they approach more nearly to see what we are." Lewis was so exhilarated that when the quartet rejoined the boats close to the confluence that evening, he ordered "a dram to each person; this soon produced the fiddle, and they spent the evening with much hilarity, singing and dancing, and seemed perfectly to forget their past toils, as they appeared regardless of those yet to come."[9]

Did Lewis and Clark ever sing and dance during lighthearted moments? The journals never mention such levity, and probably the captains' sense of what was fitting—that inevitable gap between officers and enlisted men—held them back. But surely their hearts sang. To be here, to open for their countrymen such a gate as this! And they still had close to two thousand miles to go. What more remained for them to find!

On they labored, the river making S-curves ahead of them like a slow-traveling bullsnake. Past thick strata of coal, some of it burned dark red by old fires. Into a spell of frigid weather: ice on the water buckets, a dervish dance of snowflakes that whitened the ground and led Clark to exclaim that it was a "verry extraordenarey climate, to behold trees Green & flowers spred on the plain & Snow an inch deep."[10] But it was a fine country for all of that. The broad bottomlands were filled with more timber than the explorers had seen since passing the hundredth meridian. And the game was fattening—ducks, swans, buffalo, antelope, elk, beaver. "It is now only amusement," Lewis said, "for Capt. C and myself to kill as much meat as the party can consum." But except for grizzly bears they killed no more than they needed, and they restrained the men as well. Their superiors in Washington would read such remarks with interest, for any army detachment ordered to penetrate the West would have to live off the land.[11]

On May 8 they reached, sooner than they had expected, a large tributary flowing into the Missouri from the north. Since the Indians had said there was only one such stream beyond the White Earth River (or so the captains had understood), this must be it. Not liking the Indian name, which translated as "The River That Scolds at All Others," they rechristened it Milk because it was "about the colour of a cup of tea with the admixture of a table-spoonful of milk." The persistence of hope: if the White Earth did not "furnish a predictable and advantageous communication with the Saskashiwan river," this one might.

On and on, into adventures the captains, to whom safety was a prime requisite, probably would have been glad to skip—their feud with grizzly bears and, simultaneously, additional mishaps with the white pirogue.

Bears! The trader Jean Vallé, whom the Corps of Discovery had met far downstream, below the Arikaras, had spoken of the huge beasts with almost tremulous awe. The Mandans and Hidatsas were frankly terrified. Before hunting a grizzly, the Indians painted their bodies as if they were going to war. If a kill resulted, they cherished the creature's curved black talons, each more than four inches long, as fully as they did an enemy's scalp.

Lewis was supercilious about the tales. After all, the natives had nothing better to hunt with than bows, arrows, and notoriously wretched trade muskets. A skilled white, equipped with one of the new Harpers Ferry rifles, should have no trouble. The fact that the bears were carrion eaters, leaving their huge tracks in profusion around the heaps of drowned, decaying buffalo corpses, may have added to his scorn without his being aware of it.

His first encounter did little to change his mind. While walking along the shore early in the morning of April 29, a companion and he ran across "two brown or yellow bears." (At first the explorers called the bears white, as their informants had. A strange error. The massive beasts are not white. However, the tips of their yellowish, reddish, or even almost black hair are lighter than the basic strands, so that in certain lights they do appear grizzled. Lewis later spoke of "grisly bears," Clark of "Grisley bears." Grizzly

... or perhaps "grisly," in the sense of "terrifying, ghastly"?)[12] The two hunters each picked a target that April morning and each accurately fired the single ball in his rifle. One bear fled. The other performed as the Indians had predicted; it charged. It was badly hurt, however, and the hunters were able to reload and bring it down. It was half-grown, a mere three hundred pounds, Lewis estimated. He admitted that it had been much more "furious" than an ordinary black or brown bear would have been, but he still believed that grizzlies "are by no means as formidable or dangerous as they have been represented."

A week later, Clark and Drouillard spotted a full-grown one, "turrible looking," standing in the water. Probably it was fishing; the stroke of a grizzly's front paw is lightning fast. Taking careful aim, each man fired, reloaded, fired again for a total of ten shots. Perhaps because the animal did not sense from which direction the attack was coming, it did not charge but swam with a tremendous roaring half the distance across the river to a sandbar. There it died. Some of the party dragged the body back with a boat. It measured eight feet seven and a half inches from the tip of its nose to the extremity of its hind feet. Clark thought it might weigh five hundred pounds; Lewis, six hundred. An autopsy showed that five balls had gone through its lungs; five more had lodged in other parts of its body. Its heart was as large as that of a large ox; its maw, ten times the size of an ordinary black bear's, was filled with flesh and fish. Its fat, rendered out for future use in cooking, as was that of most bears killed later on, yielded a small cask of oil.

The experience, Lewis said, left half the party content to live and let live. "Others however seem keen for action." One of the unconverted was William Bratton. He was suffering with boils— that scourge had broken out again—and was given permission to seek relief by turning his oar over to someone else and walking along the shore. Late in the afternoon he "came running up to the boats with loud cries and every symptom of terror and distress." While alone, he had shot a grizzly dead center, whereupon the enraged beast had pursued him half a mile, but, slowed by its wound, had not quite overtaken him.

No bear could get away with *that*. Lewis and seven men tracked the animal by its blood and found it had dug itself a kind of nest two feet deep, into which it had curled. They poured a volley into it. By the time it had expired, Lewis was converted. "I . . . had rather fight two Indians than one bear." A figure of speech: he had never fought an Indian. But he had seen grizzlies die, and their fierce farewell to life, he confessed, "intimidated" him.

Nor was that the end of the Corps's education in the ways of bears. On May 14, the six men oaring the two rear dugouts spotted a grizzly snoozing in an open spot and decided to bag it. They crept up behind a little mound until they were within forty paces. Four fired; two held off, in case of emergency. The bear charged and two more shots banged out. One bullet broke the animal's shoulder but scarcely slowed it. The terrified men scattered, hunting cover where they could reload. This did not mean just levering another shell into the firing chamber. As National Park Ranger Dan Murphy, who knows muzzleloaders, has put it, "Get out powder, measure, and pour into barrel. Get out greased patch and ball, put patch on barrel. Put ball on top of it. Draw rammer, ram ball home. Return rammer. Open frizzen. Get out powder again, pour small amount into frizzen pan. Close frizzen. Fire. Repeat."[13]

Each shot seemed simply to direct the bear toward the shooter. Two men, hotly pursued, flung guns and shot pouches aside, and jumped over a twenty-foot bank into the river. The bear jumped after them and was about to close on one when a man on top of the bluff shot the grizzly (grisly?) and killed it. Thoroughly subdued, the sextet made their way to camp and there found that their act had been topped, unbelievable though it seems, by another of Toussaint Charbonneau's misadventures with the white pirogue.

Both Lewis and Clark had gone ashore that afternoon, leaving the boat and its irreplaceable cargo in charge of Pierre Cruzatte. A shift in the wind was favorable; up went the sails. Distracted by something, Cruzatte turned the helm over to Charbonneau. History repeated. A squall jerked the brace of the square sail out of the hands of the man attending it. Charbonneau lost his grip on the tiller. The boat rolled onto its side and would have turned full turtle if its motion had not been checked by an awning that had been erected earlier to shield the boatmen from the sun. While Charbonneau was "crying aloud to his god for mercy," Lewis, watching aghast from the shore, tore off his coat before realizing he would almost surely drown if he tried to swim to the rescue through three hundred yards of high waves.

Brandishing his rifle and howling like the squall itself, Cruzatte brought Charbonneau to his senses. The men in the boat threw their weight against the high tide. The pirogue ponderously righted, filled with water to within an inch of its gunwales. Bailing and rowing frantically, the crew got it ashore. All this while Sacagawea, sitting up to her waist in water and presumably holding her child in one arm, reached out and with "fortitude and resolution caught and preserved most of the light articles which were washed overboard" (Lewis's words).[14]

Two narrow escapes in a single day. The bear might well have killed one or more men. The loss of the white pirogue could have ended the expedition altogether. As the soldiers put up a makeshift camp before spreading the baggage out to dry, the captains decided "to console ourselves and cheer the sperits of our men and accordingly took a drink of grog and gave each man a gill." As a more permanent memento they named the little side creek near the site "Brown Bear Defeated Creek."

They spent two increasingly precious days drying out the pirogue's cargo. The main losses turned out to be a disturbing amount of medicine, some gunpowder, and several cooking utensils. On the 17th they took off again, hauling the boats against the wind by tow lines. As usual, they went to bed that night without extinguishing their campfires. Long after those in the leather tepee had fallen asleep, the guard roused them. A big dead tree had caught fire and was about to topple onto the lodge. Hastily its occupants moved the tepee about fifty yards away, whereupon the tree crashed. "A few minutes later we should have been crushed to attoms" (Lewis). But they had not escaped entirely. Wind-dashed sparks severely damaged the leather lodge and set piles of driftwood afire, which "much harassed" the party and resulted in naming the nearby side stream, on Clark's strip map, "Burnt Lodge Creek."

One more naming. May 29. All but the sentry were asleep. A huge buffalo bull swam across the river, bumped into the white pirogue, and heaved itself over the stern. From there the heavy-shouldered beast charged into the camp, its big hooves thundering within inches of some of the sleeping men. Alarmed by the yells of the sentry, the bull swerved directly toward the hard-used tepee. The dog Seaman's furious barking drove it aside and shortly the pandemonium subsided. At daylight the Corps discovered that the bull had broken, during its climb across the pirogue, the stock of one of the swivel guns, part of the rudder's mechanism, and York's rifle. "it appears," Lewis wrote, "that the white perogue, which contains our most valuable stores is attended by some evil gennii." The closest creek was named "Bull Creek."

And a postscript. May 30. Not long after leaving Bull Creek, the fleet passed the mangled, horribly odorous remnants of at least a hundred buffalo that the men decided had recently been stampeded over the cliffs above by Indians. Lewis expatiated on the procedure. A fleet-footed decoy disguised in a buffalo hide placed himself between a herd and "a precipice proper for the purpose"—a phrase to remember. Other Indians who had quietly surrounded the herd on all but the cliff side suddenly leaped upright and frightened the animals into flight. The decoy guided them to the brink of the precipice, then stepped nimbly aside and over the animals went, a waterfall of flesh.

Though buffalo *pishkins* (a Blackfoot word) certainly occurred, modern archeologists who have clambered about the site described by Lewis and mapped by Clark doubt that those particular precipices were "proper for the purpose." They can be approached only across a long span of steep, ragged ground not conducive to a headlong stampede. According to the doubters, the putrid heap on the bank was composed of animals that had perished by falling through the spring-weakened ice and had later been deposited by high water, as had other collections of dead buffalo the Corps had noticed farther downstream. Maybe so. But at least one documented killing took place there, among the enormous number of overfed wolves that had collected around the corpses. They paid so little attention to Clark as he walked among them that he was able to step up beside one and, as an experiment, thrust his espontoon (more generally spelled "spontoon," which is a short pike equipped with a steel point) through its rib cage into its heart. With these many items in mind, the captains named the next stream they came to "Slaughter Creek," a designation settlers later changed to Arrow Creek.[15]

During the latter part of this month of namings, the land grew markedly more arid. The sides of the river trench were more broken, and the Missouri itself, murderous with sawyers, grew still more crooked. Most side channels were either dry or contained trickles of water so impregnated with alkali as to be scarcely potable. Springs of the sort common in the eastern United States were rare, and dews almost never occurred. A snow flurry early in May and a shower on May 18 were the only precipitation the Corps encountered during seven weeks after leaving the Mandan towns.

Except for a few scraggly pines and patches of low, ground-hugging juniper that appeared near the tops of the steep bluffs north of the river, the principal growth on the hillsides consisted of different varieties of sagebrush, saltbush, and prickly pear cactus, all of them typical of arid lands. A useless country, Clark implied: "[It] may with propriety I think be termed the Deserts of America for I do not think it can ever be settled." Even that persistent romantic, Meriwether Lewis, spoke of "a desert, barren country," and rejoiced in the cottonwoods of the bottomlands, whose "appearances were quite reviving after the drairy country through which we have been passing."[16]

The Musselshell River, whose mouth they visited on May 20, aroused no particular comment. The name came via translation from the Indians, who long before had noticed the huge number of fossilized mollusc shells in the vicinity. The circumstance suggested an ancient inland sea, as that amateur paleontologist, Thomas Jefferson, and some of his friends in the American Philosophical Society might have realized. But Lewis and Clark, pressed for time, did not pause to look for fossils.

What really interested them right then were the distant, isolated ranges of high, snow-streaked mountains that rose out of the plains both north and south of the river. A puzzle. According to the captains' calculations, based on their well-worn King-Arrowsmith map as amended according to Indian information, they were still far from the Rocky Mountains. The Indians, moreover, had not mentioned these islands in the sky, or at least neither Lewis nor Clark had picked up any such statements. In an effort to explain the solitary massifs, the captains decided the mysterious peaks had to be a northward extension of the Black Hills, whose length they had already greatly exaggerated. This new conjecture was also wrong, but it was comforting, for it put an otherwise inexplicable phenomenon into context.[17]

Another surprise (for it, too, had not been mentioned during the winter's interviews with the Hidatsas) was a clear, handsome stream that entered the Missouri about two and a half miles above Slaughter Creek. After hiking up it for several miles, Clark "thought proper to call it Judieth's River," after Julia (Judy) Hancock. Julia was then a child of thirteen and one hesitates to think that Clark was already contemplating marrying her, as he did when she was sixteen, or that Lewis supposed he would. Nevertheless this gesture toward the fair sex, the first of its kind among scores of namings, impressed Lewis's romantic bent, as we shall shortly see.

By the latter part of May the Corps was traversing, with infinite labor, a wildly beautiful stretch of the river known today as the Breaks of the Missouri and still a fantasyland in spite of being partially mutilated by the huge Fort Peck Reservoir. In a section the explorers called the Stone Walls, the multihued bluffs were banded with a thick stratum of almost horizontal white sandstone. In places this band was seamed perpendicularly by intrusive dikes of dark brown volcanic porphyry. Erosion of the softer material around the dikes had left the jointed rock standing as trim as walls, only a few feet thick and often scores of feet tall, of "workmanship so perfect . . . that I should have thought that Nature had attempted to rival the human art of masonry" (Lewis). Elsewhere water draining off the land back of the steep bluffs had worn the white sandstone "into a thousand grotesque figures . . . collumns of various sculptures both grooved and plain . . . some collumns standing and almost entire with their pedestels and capitals . . . some lying prostrate and broken." Pyramids, organ pipes, spires, niches, alcoves—scores of scenes of "visionary inchantment."

Fittingly enough, this entrancing region was inhabited by large numbers of Rocky Mountain bighorn sheep. As early as April 29, some members of the Corps had glimpsed a few of the creatures skipping gracefully over rocky hillsides that looked too precipitous for any hoofed animal to cross. At that time the explorers had been unable to obtain specimens. In the Breaks, however, the sheep became common, and on May 25 three members of the party shot three animals. Lewis described them and their massive, circular, laminated horns in admirable, even practical detail: "I have no doubt of [the horns'] elegance and usefullness in hair combs, and [they] might probably answer as maney valuable purposes to civilized man, as [they do] to the native Indians, who form their water cups, spoons, and platters of it," as well as fancy, transparent, and elastic bows. The animals were perhaps too lovely for their own good; the Audubon subspecies of the bighorn, which was the one Lewis described, became much sought after by hunters and is now extinct.[18]

The Corps worked their way past these visionary enchantments at heavy physical cost. Although the Missouri was about as wide as ever, it had grown shallower and swifter. Near the mouths of side streams were jumbles of rocks that had been washed into the main river by occasional flash floods. The only way to surmount the dancing rapids that resulted—and also to buck the wind with its flying clouds of powdery sand—was to tow the boats. Sometimes the men struggled ahead in icy water up to their chests. Sometimes they hobbled, in their homemade leather moccasins, through cactus and over sharp stones fallen from the cliffs. The year's first sustained rain, which fell on May 29 and 30, made matters worse by turning the clay soil into a slippery goo so tenacious they had to fight their way ahead on bare feet.

If an elk-hide rope stretched out and broke in the swift water, the boat involved was apt to swing sideways to the current and drift downstream. If it then struck a rock, it was likely to overturn unless salvaged first by the nimble work of the pursuing boatmen. In bad places, accordingly, the human draft horses observed great caution. In spite of that, the only hemp rope in the outfit, and the one reserved for the white pirogue, snapped. Heeling around, the craft barely touched a boulder and almost upset before crewmen could leap aboard and put it to rights. Lewis was disgusted: "I fear her evil gennii will play so many pranks with her that she will go to the bottom one of these days."

In his mind her days were already numbered. Risks were growing so great he planned to transfer her cargo to the collapsible iron boat he had designed in Washington and had ordered specially built at Harpers Ferry. With that in mind, he killed six elk on June 2, intending to use their skins for covering his invention. That same day a grizzly pursued Charbonneau, who managed to dive into a dense copse and hide while Drouillard killed the beast with a shot in the head. So there was much to think about on June 2, but at twilight all was driven from the explorers' minds by what looked like a shocking geographic betrayal.

Up ahead, where the bluffs on the south lost some of their height and the bottomlands widened, the river split into two branches of approximately equal size. Impossible. The only major northern tributary the Hidatsas had told Lewis and Clark about was The River That Scolds at All Others. The Corps had passed that stream, after renaming it the Milk, nearly four weeks before. Moreover: the sole tributary the Indians had mentioned as entering the main river from the south was the Musselshell. They had not talked of the Judith. Only of the Musselshell, which was unmistakably behind them. Yet here were two streams. One had to be the Missouri. One had to be a branch, perhaps the Missouri's north fork, as shown on the King-Arrowsmith map. Which was which? Why hadn't the Indians warned them?

It was essential they learn immediately. For if they chose wrong and ended up stranded far from the Columbia's headwaters, there would not be time to come back and try again, even if the discouraged soldiers were willing to make a second effort. Choose now. Choose right. Or the Corps of Discovery was finished.

The next morning they moved camp directly below the junction, on the north side of the main river. While canoe and land parties made preliminary investigations of both streams, the captains scrambled to the top of the wedge of land separating the branches. This led to the discovery that a pretty little creek sliced through the wedge to enter the north fork a few miles above the junction. Because of that creek's bordering hills, they could not get a view of the course the north branch followed. But they did have a magnificent panorama of what lay to the south and southwest. First came the looming, snow-streaked peaks known today as the Highwoods. Beyond and somewhat to the west of the isolated Highwoods another stretch of peaks extended dimly a little west of north until their snowy summits disappeared beneath the horizon. The first ridge of the Rockies at last! Or so Lewis and Clark supposed.

With the supposition came, like a flash of sunlight, a possible solution to the problem of identities. The Hidatsas had said that after issuing from the easternmost ridge of the Rockies, the Missouri flowed northeast a hundred or more miles, passing a thunderous waterfall before veering fully east to pick up the Musselshell, The River That Scolds, and the Yellowstone.[19] The windings of the south fork and the gentle undulations of the land rolling out from the skirts of the peaks prevented the captains from tracing the course of the river far enough to know beyond doubt that it was the stream of which the Hidatsas had spoken—the Missouri, whose headwaters they had been ordered to find as a prelude to reaching the Pacific. Yet what else could it be?

Well, there was that troublesome junction, that extra stream, just behind their heels. Why hadn't the Indians mentioned it? What was it?

Probably Clark offered the explanation. During the spring, after talking about geography with the Hidatsas (also known as the Big Bellies), he had drawn on his conjectural map of the West a dotted line labeled "The War Path of the Big Bellies." This was the route the Hidatsa warriors used in reaching the horse-rich Snake and Flathead Indians of the Rockies. The fast-traveling raiders disdained the labor and slowness of boats. Instead, they rode directly across the plains, well south of the Missouri, until they intersected the river at the awesome landmark Clark had labeled "Falls" on his map. The worrisome river junction lay well north of the war path. Quite possibly the Hidatsas had neither seen nor heard of the junction. So of course they had said nothing about it.[20]

Back to camp Lewis and Clark went, satisfied with their conjectures. And there they found that the enlisted men had developed a contrary logic of their own. For well over two thousand miles they had been following a notoriously turbid river whose bottom was thick with silt and whose surface had a heavy, undulant motion. The northern branch retained those characteristics. The southern was so transparent it was possible to see flat stones and gravel in its bottom. Its surface was swift, sleek, and sparkly. How could a stream that looked like crystal be the famed Big Muddy?

This was a military expedition and the captains could have ordered, without explanation, the contingent to go where the officers chose. But to start the men along a route they clearly believed might be disastrous would destroy the high morale that had been a major element in the expedition's success so far. Consequently, Lewis and Clark replied patiently to the demurrers, pointing out that streams recently emerged from the mountains—and that description certainly *seemed* to fit the south fork—retained their clear, dancing appearance for several miles. By contrast, the north fork, which by measurement had turned out to be smaller than the south, was so laden with silt that it must have flowed a long distance through the plains. Perhaps it did not reach as far west as the mountains at all. If that were true, how could the expedition reach the Columbia by following it? Besides, what of all the things the Indians had said?

The men weren't satisfied by these arguments. Nor were the scouts who had been sent out that morning any help. The depth of both the south and north river troughs and the rolling nature of the plains had kept them from developing any firm information about the rivers' distant courses. Clearly a broader reconnaisance was needed.

In the end it was arranged that Clark, Sergeant Gass, Shannon, the Field brothers, and York would follow the south fork until they were sure of its trend. Meanwhile Lewis would go up the north fork with Sergeant Pryor, Shields, Windsor, Cruzatte, Drouillard, and Lepage. The seventeen men who stayed in camp under Sergeant Ordway would hunt, both for food and for deer and elk hides the Corps could sew into clothing and use for covering the iron boat frame. In particular, they all needed moccasins for feet torn and bruised by towing the boats barefooted over miles of stones and thorns. And all of them were still cheerful. No, it would not have done to shake morale such as that by arbitrarily ignoring the men's opinions.

The new reconnaisance was conducted during a miserable period of mixed rain and snow.[21] Clark's party was the luckier in that they were able to stay dry in an abandoned Indian tepee during their first night out. There was probably considerable kidding of Joseph Field, who escaped a grizzly's charge by the thinnest of margins. The next day the scouts got even, in their own minds, by slaying three huge bears and dining on part of one. And all the while the river trench kept pulling them southwest. The Missouri for sure, Clark announced, though the others still had reservations. Turning around the next day, the little party made a forced march back to the junction, carrying with them, as raw material for more clothing, the hides of seven deer they killed along the way.

Lewis's trip was more arduous. At times thirst and wind-whipped rain drove his group off the plains into the bottom of the north fork. Not for long, however. The valley was narrow; in many places steep ridges dropped into the water. To get around such places they would either angle across the faces of the bluffs or clamber back to the plains. At night they sought shelter in thickets of riverbank willows. The brush broke the wind but did little to turn the rain.

By June 6 (the day Clark returned to the junction), Lewis felt confident the fork he was following angled too far north of west to strike the landmarks the Hidatsa had said lay along the true Missouri. To make doubly sure, he sent Pryor and Windsor ahead to a distant hill to take additional sightings. While waiting for them, he and the others constructed two small rafts. Floating down the river would be easier than walking either along its banks or atop the wind-swept, ravine-creased plains. Or so they assumed. When Pryor and Windsor returned about noon with word that the river continued north of west, they loaded their rafts for the return journey. The flimsy contraptions bucked and tilted. After soaking the elkskins they were taking to camp and almost losing their guns, they abandoned the effort, to spend another "disagreeable and wrestless night" without shelter.

The next day they tried to negotiate the faces of bluffs they had crossed readily on the way upstream. This time, however, the soaked ground was as slippery as bear oil. One pass turned out to be especially dangerous. (By "pass" Lewis meant a narrow, horizontal ledge and not a low saddle between hills.) When he tried to walk along it, his feet flew out from under him "and but for a quick and fortunated recovery by means of my espontoon I should been precipitated into the river down a craggy pricipice about ninety feet." (Shades of the knife thrust that had saved him from a disastrous fall near the Tavern, a short time after the expedition had started up the Missouri!) Behind him Windsor landed belly down on the same slippery ledge, his right arm and right leg dangling into space. Calmly Lewis coaxed the frightened soldier ahead to safety and then ordered the others to backtrack, descend the bluff, and wade around its base in ice-cold water breast deep. Lewis and Windsor soon joined them, and they walked dourly through mud, water, and wet brush until, like Clark's party, they found shelter in an old Indian lodge.

At about ten o'clock the next morning, June 8, the sun broke through the clouds. Listening to the songs of an almost incredible number of birds, Lewis felt his spirits soaring. He had found a new river, and it needed a name. Clark had used Judith for a river he fancied, so Lewis decided to lay claim to this one and call it Maria's River in honor of Maria Wood, a cousin of his. Its turbulent and muddy water, he admitted, "illy comported with the pure celestial virtues and amiable qualifications of that lovely fair one." It was a noble river, nevertheless, passing through a rich, picturesque landscape where magnificent animals abounded. More important, it opened the way to a valuable fur country (that fantasy again!). Maria. Maria. But Meriwether Lewis, unlike William Clark with his Judy, never did marry her or anyone else.

Having compared notes, the captains announced their decision for the shallow, swift-flowing south fork. To gain manpower for handling the boats in the difficult current, they decided to leave the red pirogue hidden in a stand of thick cottonwood timber on an island near the junction. Part of its cargo, together with the heaviest material in the white pirogue and in the dugouts, would be cached in a slender-necked, deep, bulbous pit dug into a dry spot well back from the river. Whatever essentials the red boat had carried would be distributed as evenly as possible among the remaining craft.

Lewis carefully explained to a meeting of the men the evidence prompting the choice. The soldiers agreed to go wherever they were taken, but they were still not satisfied. With Cruzatte, the best riverman in the group, acting as their spokesman, they politely listed once more their reasons for favoring the familiar-looking north fork. To placate them once again, the captains agreed that Lewis and a small group of scouts would go up the south fork ahead of the main party to determine whether the Great Falls of the Missouri did indeed lie up that branch. If they did not find the cataract within a reasonable distance, they would return and halt the boats before the error became irremediable.

That weight off their minds, the soldiers, most of whom had spent the day dressing skins for clothing, "passed the evening dancing singing &c and were extreemly cheerful." Lewis, though, was feeling unwell. Nervous stomach? Possibly. He seldom suffered from such an ailment, but this day the expedition was standing on the threshhold of what could be its most serious crisis to date. Anyway, he purged himself with a dose of salts and told his diary that the action brought him relief.

His was not the only ailment. Sacagawea, normally active and helpful, awoke wan and listless in the leather tent the morning after Lewis's purge. It was not a good time to drag. Both captains were absorbed in trying to bring order to the major adjustments facing the party. Rain-wet baggage had to be spread out and dried. The earth from the six-foot-deep cache had been placed on skins, lugged away, and scattered where it would not be noticed by passing Indians. Now the cache itself had to be lined with sticks and grass so the materials placed in it would stay dry. Items to be stored were segregated from those that would go. The former included bundles of furs, kegs of pork, hulled corn, powder and lead for bullets, traps, and all but the most essential tools—altogether about half a ton of material, Sergeant Gass estimated.[22]

Because the blacksmiths worked up to the last minute putting the necessary tools into shape and repairing firearms, including Lewis's airgun, a second, smaller cache had to be prepared for the forge and bellows. A duplicate store of powder and lead also went into the second pit, so that if Indians found and rifled one cache, the other might remain to fortify the explorers on their return journey. Meanwhile the big red pirogue had to be inched into its island hiding place and covered with boughs.

At some point during the hurly-burly, Clark noticed that Sacagawea was suffering from more than an ordinary indisposition. Severe pains in the lower abdomen. Lips dry and feverish. Opening his razor-sharp lancet, he slit into a vein on the inside of her elbow. After letting as much blood flow as he deemed wise, he applied a tourniquet. The process probably terrified the young mother, even though she must have heard about and perhaps have seen the operation performed on male members of the expedition. But she had complete confidence in Clark, which may be why he rather than Lewis did the bloodletting.[23]

All the principals in the performance were in the leather tepee that night, June 10. As Lewis listened to Sacagawea stir when the baby whimpered, he must have thought, before dropping asleep, how deeply they would depend on her when they met some of her horse-owning tribespeople up the river, as surely they would. As surely they *had* to. But he was too tired to worry for long. After all, didn't the nation's best physicians consider bleeding a sovereign remedy?

The next morning, after a concerned glance at the pallid young woman, he shouldered his pack and started up the south fork with Drouillard, Gibson, Goodrich, and Joseph Field to prove in fact what he already knew from logic: here was the Missouri.

TWELVE

The Great Portage

Eager though Lewis was to locate the falls, he had to call a halt after nine miles of walking because of another intestinal flare-up accompanied by a high fever. He had neither salts nor thunderbolt pills in his pack, a good thing probably. Recalling his mother's herbal remedies, he directed his men—he could hardly stand erect himself—to strip the leaves off a quantity of chokecherry twigs, cut the twigs into small pieces, and boil them until the water was black and bitter. While his companions feasted on the marrowbones of a fresh-killed elk, he drank a pint of the astringent fluid for supper and another pint an hour later. By ten o'clock the pain had left his bowels and he was sweating gently, preludes to a sound sleep.[1]

Another pint of the black brew sufficed to get him going in the morning. Shouldering their packs again, the five men climbed to the flat country atop the bluffs that bordered the river on the north. Walking there let them avoid the bends in the river gorge and circle around the heads of the narrow drainage ravines that sliced down through the side walls. By midmorning, however, thirst engendered by the day's suffocating heat drove them back to the water and, as events turned out, to a sportsman's breakfast. In a grove of cottonwood trees they killed two grizzly bears with their first fire, "a circumstance which I believe has never happened [before]." Then up the sides of the gorge onto the plains again, with the usual fantastic numbers of prairie dogs, wolves, antelopes, deer, and buffalo. A slight rise in the ground gave them a stunning view of the Rockies, ridge after snow-covered ridge trending slightly north of northwest, "an august spectacle . . . rendered more formidable by the recollection that we had them to pass." After walking twenty-seven miles Lewis again called an early halt, blaming his weakness on his recent ailment rather than on the hot day's exertion.

The next morning, June 13, Drouillard, Field, and Gibson split off to hunt. Lewis and Goodrich held parallel to but well back from the river. Shortly they glimpsed what looked like tendrils of smoke feathering out on the wind. Soon the unmistakable thunder of a giant cataract reached them. For seven miles they pressed toward the increasing din and billowing spray until at least they came to the brink of the river trough. Two hundred feet almost directly below them the Missouri—for such it most convincingly was— poured over a precipice at least eighty feet high, part sheer drop and part a crashing course from ledge to ragged ledge.

Scrambling down the steep side wall, Lewis found a seat on a point of rocks from which he stared in delight and astonishment at "the grandest sight I ever beheld," a falling mass of water three hundred yards wide that broke, at the bottom of its plunge, "into a perfect white foam which assumes a thousand forms in a moment sometimes flying up in jets of sparkling foam to the height of fifteen or twenty feet," only to be overwhelmed by backwashes of tremendous, rolling, reverberating waves.

He sat for four hours on his rocky grandstand, exalted by this thunderous demonstration of the rightness of his and William Clark's geographic logic—and by the thought that from his pen, however imperfect, would come the world's first knowledge of this American wonder. Then, as the sun turned downward, he decided to camp a short distance from the bottom of the falls, on a small flat shaded by a few trees. He directed the hunters, who had over- taken him, to cut the meat they had obtained into strips for drying on a scaffold they would build. While they were working and Goodrich was fishing, he walked three miles down beside the rock-studded river, looking for a place where the boats could be taken from the water and carried to the top of the bluffs for portag- ing around the falls. No gateway appeared, though the Indians had said that a portage of half a mile would do the job. But he was still too elated to worry about that yet. That night he and his relaxed men ate sumptuously of buffalo hump, tongue, and marrowbones, parched cornmeal, and a new variety of trout Goodrich had caught, a subspecies that came to be called cutthroat trout because of the dashes of red under the jaw.

Before going to bed he wrote Clark a letter headed triumphantly "from the Great Falls of the Missouri." They were on the right path. But . . . and then truth broke in. No short portage would take the Corps past this cataract. In the morning he would scout upstream for the eagle's nest which, according to the Hidatsa horse stealers, was perched in a tall cottonwood growing on a small island at the foot of the uppermost falls. That would give them an inkling of how long the portage would be.

At sunrise the next morning, Joseph Field started downstream with the letter. Lewis went the opposite way. Apparently he expected hard going, for he seems not to have taken his dog with him, an omission he would regret. Since the river in many places filled the bottom of the gorge from bank to bank, he could progress only by climbing to the ragged top of the north rim and working his way past its many transverse ravines. The land beyond the south rim looked as if it might afford easier going, but he could not cross the river to make certain.

During a walk of nearly seven miles, by his estimate, he saw none of the things he wanted to see. No eagle's nest, which, to be sure, was a tenuous thing to last throughout the years. And no break in the walls by which the dugouts could be returned to the water—assuming they ever got away from it.[2] He was on the point of turning back when he detected the distant growl of, and then saw, another cascade. Shaped like a rumpled horseshoe, it was only about twenty feet high. Still no eagle's nest. But as he moved closer, a greater roar came pounding through the noise of the crooked falls, as he already was calling the twenty-foot drop. Scrambling across a point of land, he beheld yet another astounding plunge, known today as Rainbow Falls. Curving ever so gently and stretching a quarter of a mile from wall to wall, the unbroken curtain of water crashed fifty feet into the rocky bottom, "where [it] rises into foaming billows of great height and rapidly glides away, hising flashing and sparkling as it departs." After struggling with comparisons between this and the lowest fall, he decided the upper cataract was *pleasingly beautiful* while the other was *sublimely grand.*"

A quarter of a mile farther on he glimpsed another noisy drop, only six feet high. He could see no eagle's nest there, either, so on he went, rifle slung across his back and his steel-tipped espontoon, which he often used as a walking stick, in one hand. After hiking two and a half more miles he came to another uproarious cataract, twenty-six feet high with a five-foot drop just beyond the main crest. Below the falls, partly shrouded by the swirling mist, was a small island. Perched high in one of the island's cottonwoods was a big, unkempt bundle of sticks that could only be the eagle's nest the Indians had included in their description of the uppermost cascade. Lewis must have let out a whoop then. For he had at last passed all the rapids and cascades that in the aggregate made up the Great Falls of the Missouri. What was more, the walls of the river's trough at last subsided, just above the final cascade, into low mounds across which the Corps's boats could be carried back to the water.

And there *was* a way to get boats out of the lower canyon. Lewis could see, south of where he stood at the upper falls, another range of isolated, snowy peaks, today's Little Belts. A stream must drain from them into the main river. Surely that confluence, which he had not walked far enough downstream the previous evening to see, would form an exit from the river and an entrance to a portage that would have to be at least sixteen miles long—a staggering ordeal.

Puzzlements flooded across him. Why had the Indians said the portage was only half a mile long? Why had they declared a person could cross the river dry-footed by walking along a ledge that ran from bank to bank behind the greatest fall's stupendous curtain of water? Could Lewis and Clark's interpreters have misunderstood the Hidatsas that radically and yet have placed the eagle's nest with absolute accuracy? The questions defy answering, unless the Hidatsas had been pulling the legs of the white men—a wilderness practical joke.

The Hidatsas had also accurately located the mouth of a river they called Medicine (today's Sun River). Lewis could see its bordering belt of cottonwoods only a little southwest of where he stood. Again his pulse quickened, for the sight made the waters of the once-distant Columbia seem all at once as real and as attainable as the eagle's nest. For the Medicine River, the Indians had said, ran northwest through the front range of the Rockies to within an easy horseback ride of a stream that flowed in the opposite direction. That west-flowing stream had to be the one Aaron Arrowsmith and after him Nicholas King and after them William Clark called "The Great Lake River" on their charts. Supposedly this river ran into the Tacoutche Tesse of Alexander Mackenzie, and the Tacoutche Tesse, the captains believed, was another name for the main stem of the Columbia.[3] Furthermore, notations on the maps declared that by following the Great Lake River, traveling Indians reached the sea in eight days.

Eight! That close—and yet the captains did not intend to follow the Medicine to the Great Lake River, for the former, again according to the Indians, was too swift and shallow to be navigated. Besides, the explorers would need horses to carry their supplies across the Continental Divide, and they might not be able to procure the animals at the headwaters of the Medicine. A surer place was the Three Forks of the Missouri, where the party hoped to meet Sacagawea's people, the horse-rich Shoshoni or Snake Indians. With luck, they might meet those equestrians even sooner. So the Missouri was the route to follow. Still, the Medicine offered the first direct connection with waters of the Columbia that Lewis had actually encountered, or so he thought. Romantic that he was, he wanted to dip his fingers in that exhilarating stream, even if the impulse kept him out all night and caused great worry to his soldiers, waiting for him at the camp near the lowest falls.

The presence of buffalo close by solidified the impulse. He could kill a fat cow for supper (a waste, but you can't shoot just part of a buffalo), look over the Medicine while the carcass cooled, then return to butcher as much of the hump as he needed, camp under a nearby tree, and rejoin his party the next day. Picking out a likely animal, he shot it through the lungs. Without reloading his single-shot rifle, he watched the animal sink slowly to the ground, blood streaming from its mouth and nostrils. At that point he saw a grizzly bear walking rapidly toward him. Would his dog Seaman have distracted the beast long enough for Lewis to have reloaded? Who knows? In any event, Lewis started briskly, with his empty gun, toward the tree under which he had planned to camp. The bear's step quickened. Switching directions, Lewis dashed for the river, which was closer to him than the tree. After jumping down its low bank, he splashed ahead until he was waist deep in water. At that depth the bear would be swimming, and its would-be prey might have a chance to fight back. Hooking his rifle across his back by its sling, he grasped his steel-pointed espontoon with both hands and confronted his pursuer. The unexpected aggressiveness apparently startled the bear. Unbelievably, it spun around and vanished at a dead run among the cottonwoods bordering the Medicine.

Lewis reloaded and followed. After looking over the Medicine's lower reaches carefully enough to be able to write an accurate description, he turned back to the dead buffalo. The local wildlife was not yet through with him, however. He snapped a shot at what looked to be some kind of "tyger cat" that appeared ready to spring at him. Next he had to outface three buffalo bulls. Because "it now seemed to me all the beasts of the neighborhood had made a league to distroy me," he vetoed his plan of camping out and, omitting supper, returned through the dark to rejoin his companions, lacerating his feet on the prickly pear cactus that grew thick along the way. All in all, it was the most exciting day he'd spent since the standoff with the Teton Sioux.

On June 12, the day after Lewis and his five men had started walking upstream in search of the Great Falls, Clark set out with the main group by water. High, steep banks topped with stone cliffs confined the river. Islands split the quickening current into shallow channels where clusters of boulders constantly threatened to tip the dugouts onto their sides. "The fatigue," Clark wrote on the fifteenth, "is encretiatable the men in the water from morning untill night hauling the cord & [boosting] the boats walking on sharp rocks and round sliperery stones which alternately cut their feet & throw them down." Snakes abounded. One man, reaching for a bush by which to pull himself ahead, grabbed a rattler by the head, and yet no one was bitten.

All this while Sacagawea, half unconscious and doubled up with pain, huddled with her baby in the sun-blasted bottom of the white pirogue. Her distraught husband babbled about building a dugout and paddling with her back to the Mandan villages, a trip of about nine hundred miles. Clark ordered him to forget the insanity: the journey would be impossible for a sick woman attended by a lone man of no better qualifications than Charbonneau's. Besides, the captain somehow had to restore Sacagawea to health, for her and the baby's sake and for the expedition's, for she might be its chief resource when an opportunity arose to buy horses.

To relieve her distress he erected a sailcloth awning over the rear of the pirogue and moved her into its shade. Repeated bleedings having failed to help her, he prepared a poultice (he called it a cataplasm) of warm water, flour or bran, and "bark"—probably some of the pulverized "Peruvian" bark (cinchona) Lewis had obtained in the East as a specific against malaria. To the moist mass Clark added a dash of laudanum, which is a tincture of opium. Wrapping this in a cloth, he applied it to her "region," a euphemism for her genital area and lower abdomen, almost certainly a service he had not expected to render on the way to the Pacific. Supposedly the cataplasm would relieve pain and draw out of the afflicted parts whatever poisons were causing the trouble. Clark thought it helped the young mother, at least a little bit.[4]

At four o'clock in the afternoon of June 14, Joseph Field reached the camp with the letter Lewis had dated at Great Falls the morning of that same day. So: the Corps was on the right track. But: according to Field, close to twenty miles of rough, fast water lay between the boats and the first, towering falls. Beyond that cataract another seven miles of rapids led to four more roaring drops of varying height. Clearly, not boating water. However: on his way downstream, Field had passed, about five miles below the Great Falls, a side stream breaking into the main river gorge from the south—the stream Lewis had hypothesized as flowing into the Missouri from the isolated mountains to the south, today's Little Belts. That stream might take the Corps to a slope up which they could climb, with their dugouts and baggage, onto a level plain. A walk of sixteen or more miles would then bring them to the next navigable stretch of the river.

It was not a happy prospect, but at least it led toward horses, the Continental Divide, and after that—so they thought—a blessed downhill float to the Pacific. By exerting themselves "as much as possable with the towing lines" (Ordway) and as the noise of the still-invisible falls swelled in their ears, they toiled upward to within a mile of the side stream Fields had told about. At that point they were blocked by a choppy stretch of water over which they could not take the dugouts, let alone the white pirogue, in which Sacagawea still burned with fever.

While two men went ahead to explore the side stream, the others set up camp on a small, shady meadow that contained enough dry wood for cooking fires, a rarity along that section of the Missouri. They were still bustling about when Lewis and his four companions rejoined them, carrying on their backs, in addition to their personal gear, about six hundred pounds of partly dried buffalo meat and several dozen large, dried trout. At about the same time the explorers of the side stream returned with their report. About a mile above the creek's canyoned mouth, a difficult slope did indeed open a way to the plains. Those plains, however, were slit by impassable ravines draining toward the river. It would be better to forget the south and find a way along the north side of the entrenched Missouri.

Lewis and the men who had been with him on the north side shook their heads. True, the meat they had brought to camp showed that goods could be carried along the north side. The route was arduous, however, and the northern plains were also sliced by ravines. More important, a route up there would run along the outside of the curve the Missouri followed between the falls. A trail south of the river would draw a chord across the inside of the arc and hence would be much shorter.

But, said the captains, remembering the impasse at Maria's River, they would not choose blindly. The next day, June 17, Clark and a small party would start upstream on foot. First they would make, for the government, an exact survey of this astounding stretch of cascades. On their return they would search out the best possible portage trail across the plains to the south of the river. If that route proved impossible, then they would have a look at the north. Meanwhile Lewis would supervise preparations for the carry . . . on the south side; he was sure of that, and the Corps could not waste time sitting around waiting for reports. Some of the men would build wagons for carrying the log dugouts; others would unload the boats and rebale the goods into bundles suitable for backpacking; a few would hunt both for food and for the thirty or more elkskins needed to cover Lewis's iron boat frame. For the white pirogue was too heavy to be transported overland and would have to be hidden in a copse, as its red counterpart had been at the mouth of Maria's River. Some of its cargo, including Lewis's desk, would be cached. The rest would be hauled and carried across the portage and reloaded into the iron *Experiment*, a triumphant justification of Meriwether Lewis's foresight in having brought the untested craft across many thousands of miles from Harpers Ferry.

None of the hurrying and scurrying touched Sacagawea. She lay torpid in the shade of a tree, gaunt, feverish, her pulse faint and irregular. Her fingers and the muscles in her arms twitched spasmodically, probably because of dehydration brought on by bleeding, purging, vomiting, and fever. Clark, at his wit's end, gladly turned over the doctoring to Lewis, who decided against further bleeding, perhaps because of its failure to produce results earlier. He did continue the poultices and also prevailed on the young woman to choke down a few doses of water-softened, pulverized bark and laudanum. Taken internally, the opium might help alleviate pain and induce sleep.

While waiting for the medicine to take effect, he directed a couple of men to fetch back, in a dugout, some casks filled with vile-smelling, vile-tasting water from a sulfurous spring he had noticed bubbling up on an elevated terrace opposite the mouth of the portage creek. He knew of a spring like it in Virginia, one reputed to be therapeutic. So poor Sacagawea had to swallow as much of the stuff as she could stomach. Something worked— Peruvian bark, opium, sulfur water that combated her dehydration, the deep concern of her companions, or perhaps just her own tough constitution. By the next day she was nibbling at bits of broiled buffalo meat and buffalo broth laced with a few drops of sulfuric acid.

When Clark's small party started along the river's edge early in the morning of July 17, they took with them a two-pole chain, a device used by surveyors to mark off points one rod (sixteen and a half feet) apart. So far the explorers had made little use of the apparatus; eyeballing distances between landmarks along the river went faster and sufficed for Clark's strip maps. But in the captains' minds the Great Falls would prove to be one of the wonders of the new territory and as such merited accuracy.* So rod by rod the party measured the chasm's length, a process that also provided Clark with base lines to use when calculating, by trigonometry, the elevation of the falls and the total drop of the river along this scenic stretch. The activity was one of the few bits of precise triangulation turned in by the Corps of Discovery.

Thus Clark found that 286 "poles," or rods—nine-tenths of a mile—separated their camp beside the Missouri from the mouth of Portage Creek, as he was already calling the escape creek on his maps. (Today it is Belt Creek.) The full stretch of cascades and rapids came to 4,747 poles, or 14.8 miles. In that distance, Clark computed, the Missouri dropped 360 feet and two inches. The first and biggest waterfall was 87 feet and 3/4 inch high; the next-tallest

---

*Before the century was out, the stretch would be drowned by hydroelectric dams and power plants, and few Americans ever saw the ladder of cascades in their original glory.

(today's Rainbow Falls, which Lewis had estimated at 50 feet) turned out to be 47 feet 8 inches.[5] A bonus was the discovery, a mile or so above Rainbow Falls, of a huge, fan-shaped spring that each day pours, according to later calculations, nearly four hundred thousand gallons of crystal-clear, blue-tinted, ice-cold water over a ragged six-foot ledge into the river. Today that limpid pool, one of the largest natural springs in the United States, is the heart of a charming Great Falls city park.

There were misadventures on the trip. Clark nearly fell into the river at the big falls. The men watched aghast as a huge herd of buffalo began crowding down a narrow trail to drink from the river a little above Rainbow Falls. Impatient animals in the rear crowded scores of the leaders into the water. Those unable to swim across the swift stream were swept by the current over the lip of the cataract, mangled on the rocks below, and carried downriver to become food for vultures, magpies, wolves, and grizzly bears. And an unexpected blast of wind irretrievably tore several sheets of Clark's notes from his hand, an episode not without moment later on, as we shall shortly see.

After climbing beyond the uppermost cataract (today's Black Eagle Falls), the surveyors swung south, passed the mouth of the Medicine River, and came to a cluster of three islands. Deciding this was a suitable location at which to end the portage, Clark set up camp. Hoping to store meat for use during the carry, he and most of the group waded out to the closest island, where many animals grazed. After dropping one beaver, one elk, and eight buffalo, the men began lugging the meat to camp. The local grizzlies did not take kindly to the intrusion. (Earlier Lewis had noted that the huge beasts were "tenatious of their right of soil in this neighborhood.")[6] One came growling along the tracks Clark had left after butchering an animal he had killed. Before overtaking him, it bumped into Alexander Willard, who was returning for another load of meat. It charged. Willard yelled and dashed for camp. The men there frightened the monster away with volleys from their rifles and then followed it, fearing it might vent its wrath on John Colter, still afield butchering another kill. A lucky presentiment. The grizzly had already chased Colter into the water and was about to follow when the hunters again drove it away. By then dark was near and the vengeful men dared not follow their quarry into the thick brush, eager though they were to rid the neighborhood of so dangerous a competitor. Because of the episode they named the three islands the White Bear Islands. Soon the region would become an outright battleground between bears and men.

During the next two days the surveyors lined out and marked with wooden stakes a carrying trail between the White Bear Islands and the mouth of Portage Creek. As measured by pole chain, the way was eighteen and a quarter miles long. By staying two to three miles south of the river, the route headed all but one of the gullies, Willow Run (now Box Elder Creek), that knifed down into the Missouri. Willow Run's steep, brushy sides would cause trouble, but its bottom contained enough room for a camping place, a small creek of good water, and tangles of sweet willow trees whose wood, tougher than cottonwood, might come in handy for repairing the wagons Lewis was building. The hardest part of the route definitely lay between the mouth of Portage Creek and the far (western) side of Willow Run, a distance of roughly six miles.[7]

By the time Clark reached the lower camp, Lewis's men had concealed the white pirogue in the thick, riverside brush. They had dried much of the baggage and had built two wagons, each mounted on four solid wooden wheels about twenty-two inches in diameter that had been hewn from the trunk of the only sizable cottonwood tree in the area. Axles had been cut from the mast of the white pirogue. Since the wheels were small, the wagons were low. The dugouts—six of them, ranging in length from twenty-five to about thirty-five feet—could be mounted, one at a time, on the running gears of a single wagon and used as a sort of crate for holding relatively fragile baggage. Or flat beds could be made by laying poles side by side along the wagon's running gears—the captains' tepee poles, for example. Both wagons were equipped with long tongues, to which several men could be harnessed like draft horses. Additional force could be applied by soldiers tugging on the sides of the mounted dugout or pushing from the rear.

The first load was to consist of pieces of the iron boat frame that Lewis had ordered made at Harpers Ferry and had named the *Experiment*. (The completed craft was to take the place of the abandoned white pirogue.) Tools for assembling and sheathing the vessel with leather, and the baggage of the men who were to work on it under Lewis's supervision—Sergeant Patrick Gass, John Shields, Joseph Field, and Robert Frazer—were added to the cargo. Sergeant John Ordway, Silas Goodrich, York, Charbonneau, and Sacagawea, who had recovered enough to go fishing,

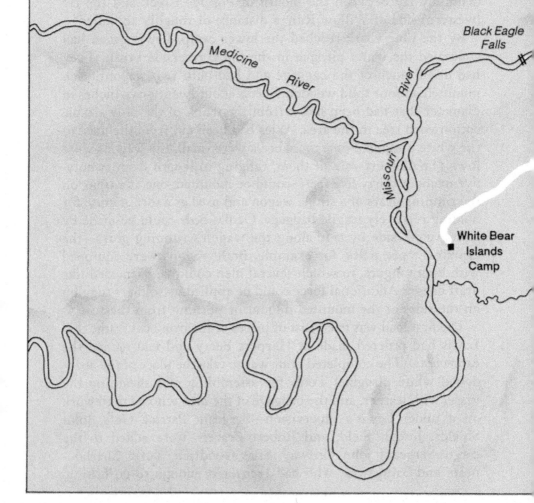

Portage Around the
Missouri's Great Falls
Westbound, June and July 1805
Eastbound, July 1806

——— Wagon portage
▪▪▪▪▪ Hand portage
– – – Shortcuts used by walkers

0   1   2   3   4
miles

Black Eagle
Falls

Medicine

River

River

Missouri

White Bear
Islands
Camp

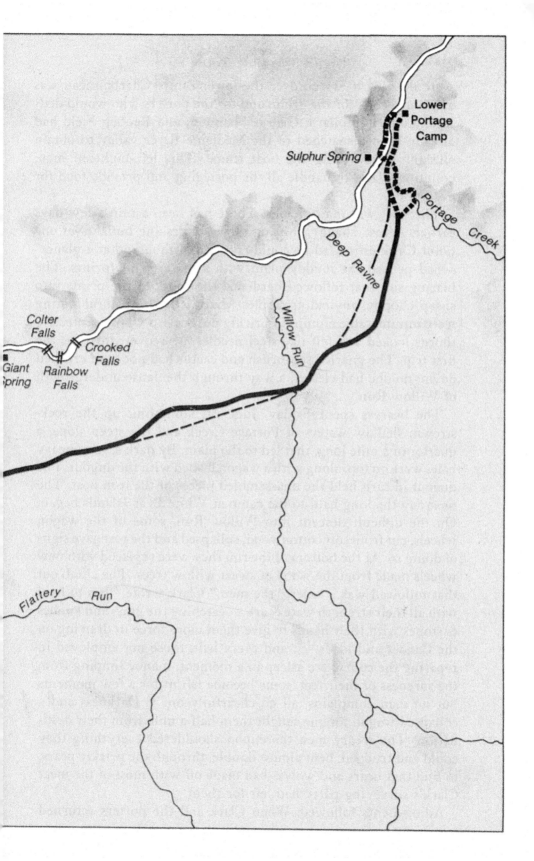

were detailed to watch over the lower camp. Charbonneau was appointed cook for the group and for the porters who would drift in and out. Drouillard, George Shannon, and Reuben Field had already been dispatched to the Medicine River valley to obtain elkskins for covering the boat frame. This left eighteen men, counting Clark, to handle all the portaging and provide food for everyone.

The start was inauspicious. There had been a rain a few days earlier. A vast, shaggy, shifting carpet of grazing buffalo—at one point Clark estimated he could take in ten thousand at a glance[9] —had pocked the muddy plain with a maze of hoofprints. The blazing sun that followed hardened the edges of the prints into sharp, choppy, unyielding ripples. Mixed with this painful footing were innumerable clumps of prickly pear cactus whose protective thorns looked and felt like steel needles. Moreover, this was the first trip. The gnarled sagebrush and cactus had not been crushed down; no one had cleared a way through the dense undergrowth of Willow Run.

The bearers spent Friday, June 21, stumbling up the rock-strewn, shallow waters of Portage Creek and the steep slope, a quarter of a mile long, that led to the plain. By dark several heavy bales were on top, along with a wagon loaded with the dugout. The dugout in turn held the unassembled pieces of the iron boat. The next day the long haul to the camp at White Bear Islands began. On the difficult descent into Willow Run, some of the wagon wheels, cut from soft cottonwood, collapsed and the rest gave signs of doing so. At the bottom of the run they were replaced with new wheels made from the wood of sweet willow trees. The climb out that followed was a killer. "the men," Clark wrote, "has to haul with all their strength wate & art . . . catching the grass and knobes & stones with their hands to give them more force in drawing on the Canoes and loads . . . and every halt, those not employed in reparing the course are asleep in a moment, maney limping from the soreness of their feet, some become fa[i]nt for a few moments but no man complains, all go chearfully on."[10] Darkness and a collapsed wagon tongue caught them half a mile from their destination. The weary men thereupon shouldered everything they could and trudged, bent almost double, through the prickly pears, to find that bears and wolves had made off with most of the meat Clark's surveying party had left for them.

Adjustments followed. When Clark and the porters returned

with the patched wagon to the lower camp for another load, they managed to shorten the route by half a mile, to seventeen and three-quarters miles. At the camp they double-soled their soft elk-skin moccasins with tough buffalo hide. The reinforcement helped the bottoms of their feet but did not keep toes from banging into cementlike obstructions or cactus spines from penetrating ankles. Another discomfort was the swift alternation between suffocating heat and chilling storms. June is a rainy month on the Montana plains. A boil of towering cumulus clouds fills part of the sky, lightning flashes, the wind roars. "it rained amazeingly hard," Whitehouse wrote on the 24th. The shirtless workers (it had been hot moments before) shivered uncontrollably, and the earth turned to a treacherous goo. But there were compensations. If the wind came from the right quarter, the workers could hoist a sail on one of the wagon-borne dugouts and let the enemy push the vehicle ahead for a ways.[11]

Another boost came from Meriwether Lewis. He ignored the prerogatives of his captaincy and made himself cook of the White Bear camp. He cut his own wood, hauled his own water, boiled or roasted enormous quantities of buffalo meat, and at least once "made each man a large suet dumpling by way of a treat." A greater treat, probably, was the sharing. In surmounting the portage, the Corps was welded into physical and spiritual unity. It has even been argued that out of this selflessness came the happiest, most exalted period of Lewis's short life.[12]

On the 29th, when transportation was slowed by wet ground, Clark decided to revisit the Great Falls with York in order to replace statistics he had lost earlier when wind had snatched some of his notes from his hand. Because Charbonneau and Sacagawea had not seen the cataract, he invited them along. Little Jean Baptiste rode, as usual, in a papoose carrier fastened to his mother's back. Clark carried in his hands a rifle and—an astonishing picture —an umbrella, more for protection from sun, probably, than from rain. Attached to his elkskin clothing were a tomahawk, a shot pouch, a powder horn, and a large compass.

While the party was poking around the falls, storm clouds streamed over the canyon rim, accompanied by so fierce a blast of wind that Clark feared they might be blown off the ledge on which they were standing. Accordingly he led Charbonneau and Sacagawea (York was off hunting) into a sheltering ravine just above the falls, close to the spot where he had almost fallen into the river twelve days before. As they crouched under some overhanging rocks, they made themselves more comfortable by setting down their burdens, including the child.

Rain and hail came down like a volley from the heavens (Clark's simile). As a flash flood of mud and boulders pounded down the narrow ravine toward them, Sacagawea swooped up her baby with one hand and extended the other to Charbonneau, who started to pull her up the precipitous slope to safety—and then froze in terror. Clark shoved frantically from behind. The water was clutching at his waist before he was able to pull himself up beside the others, minus the gun and shot pouch he had instinctively grabbed up during the floundering. Tomahawk, umbrella, powder horn, and the compass, the only big one the party had, were also gone.

The cold bit to the marrow. To keep the exposure from harming the baby and his mother, Clark hurried them to the camp at Willow Run, where they could start a fire and get dry clothing from one of the bales. Several porters had also repaired there, bleeding and sorely bruised by hailstones so big that some of the men had actually been knocked off their feet. "I refreshed them [and Sacagawea] with a little grog," Clark wrote, and then the run began to flood and drove them out.

During the next three days the portaging was completed and Clark's compass retrieved by searchers. (They found nothing else he had lost, however.) Concentration shifted to the *Experiment*. As designed by Lewis, it was thirty-six feet long, four feet three inches wide, and twenty-six inches deep.[13] The unfamiliar work of assembling so many pieces—sections of keel, rib, gunwales, and so on— went slowly. Intense hunting had produced only twenty-eight of the thirty-two elkskins needed for encasing the craft; heavier buffalo hides would have to do for the rest. The hair on the elkskins was shaved off; the buffalo hides were singed. Days were spent searching for pliable bark and straight sticks that could be used to support the outer skin of leather, provide crosspieces, and give the oarsmen better footing. Lewis searched the driftwood that littered the shore for pine logs from which he hoped to distill tar for waterproofing the seams between the hides and the eyelets through which thongs were run for fastening the skins to the frame. The kiln he dug into the earth did not work, however—the juices may have dried out of the pine—and he realized uneasily that he was going to have to rely on pulverized charcoal and beeswax mixed into melted buffalo tallow.

The same heat, hail, rain, and wind that plagued the porters interfered with the work of the boatwrights. Whenever the air was still, mosquitoes swarmed unendurably. Grizzly bears padding around the camp at night kept Seaman barking in a frenzy. The monsters were so belligerent that Lewis ordered the men not to leave the camp except in pairs and to sleep with rifles at their sides. When the end of the portaging freed men for a hunt, Clark and twelve soldiers swept the area as if it were a battlefield. The bears had the advantage in the dense brush. Drouillard shot one through the heart—yet it almost nailed him before it died. All told the warriors killed only three by the night of July 3.

The drama of the bears and bison obscures how conscientious Lewis was in heeding Jefferson's behest that he describe as much of the West's flora and fauna as circumstances allowed. Pages of his journals dealing with the Great Falls area are devoted to berries, trout, handsome yellow-fronted meadowlarks, enormous flocks of fledgling blackbirds just learning to fly, thirteen-striped ground squirrels, Rocky Mountain pack rats, prairie rattlesnakes, and the shy, small, lovely Swift foxes that lived in underground colonies like prairie dogs and are now thought to be extinct in Montana. The world was indeed going to know Louisiana Territory when the Corps of Discovery returned to the United States.[14]

On the Fourth, the men who had not seen the falls celebrated by hiking over for a look. That night the cooks turned out a dinner of beef, bacon, beans, and suet dumplings. Afterwards they finished the grog except for a small amount saved for medicinal purposes. Cruzatte brought out his fiddle; the men danced and sang. "We have no just cause," Lewis declared, "to covet the sumptuous feasts of our countrymen on this day."

While everyone else chafed at the slowness, the boat builders carefully applied handfuls of warm, greasy waterproofing to the *Experiment*'s leather sheath. Sergeant Gass, one of the principal builders, was apprehensive, for as soon as the mix dried on the smooth surface of the shaven elkskins, "it cracked and scaled off." But perhaps the rough edges of the seams would hold the goop. When all was ready on July 9, part of the Corps carefully deposited the vessel in a quiet cove of the river. "It lay like a perfect cork," Lewis exulted.

He directed oars to be fitted and seats placed for the rowers. The dugouts were loaded, and the captains were on the point of ordering departure, at long last, from the Great Falls area when a gale descended on them. It "blew so hard that we were obliged to unload the canoes again; a part of the baggages in several of them got wet before it could be taken out." Far worse, the gale finished the *Experiment*. Water oozed through the seams "in such manner that she would not answer" for the rest of the river work.

Hindsight: the tallow stuck tight to the fuzz of hair on the singed buffalo hides. If there had been time to hunt for an additional thirty bison, skin them, and cover the boat once again—but "to make any further experiments in our present situation seemed to me madness." The next day they removed the skins, dismantled the frame, and cached the pieces in a hole in the ground, in case, presumably, the metal skeleton might still come in useful during their return journey. That done, Lewis went off fishing, to compose himself.

As far as the journals show, Clark took the episode matter-of-factly. The *Experiment* had failed, which was unfortunate; now it had to be replaced with dugouts. He went upstream with ten men, looking for cottonwoods of sufficient size. The Missouri flows gently there, looping broadly through lush bottomlands thick with trees. Small trees. The detachment went twenty-three miles by water—eight by land—before they were able to fell two suitable patriarchs. From their knotted trunks, the men hewed, at the cost of several broken ax handles, two dugouts, one twenty-five and the other thirty-three feet long, but only three feet wide. Meanwhile the rest of the crew brought the expedition's baggage up from the White Bear camp in relays, bucking heavy winds along the way. At 10:00 A.M. on July 15, six days after the sinking of the *Experiment*, the Corps of Discovery finally resumed its journey in eight wobbly craft—much to everyone's joy, Lewis wrote. It was a mood that would soon be dispelled by the labors of their travel and the elusiveness of the Shoshoni Indians.

THIRTEEN

The Great Divide

Shortly before breakfast on July 16, as the men were rowing against a gentle current, one of them spotted near the river bank a cluster of about forty empty "booths," or arbors, that had been built of willow boughs as shelters against the sun. Because the bowers were different from other temporary lodgings the captains had seen along the river, they decided, probably after asking Sacagawea her opinion, that the structures had been put together by some of her people, the Snake or Shoshoni Indians. But where were the builders? The captains had been hoping to meet some of the tribe ever since learning they customarily ranged along the headwaters of both the Missouri and Columbia rivers.[1]

A meeting had, in fact, been tantalizingly close. Horse sign around the camp suggested the Indians had departed ten or twelve days earlier. At that time, July 4 to 6, the whites had been gathered at the White Bear Islands, separated from the Indian bowers by approximately forty-five river miles—but only sixteen land miles.[2] White hunters had ranged nearly that far from their base, and Indian food gatherers had probably matched the range. If timing had been right, Shoshoni foragers, armed only with bows, might well have heard the guns of their counterparts. Although the Corps's journalists do not speculate on the matter, it is even possible that the sound of shooting had frightened the Shoshoni into breaking camp.

So very close! Yet there was no use trying to overtake, on foot or in dugout canoes, mounted Indians who had a ten-day start. On the party went, to a buffalo Drouillard had just killed and butchered for their breakfast. There Lewis, experimenting again, ate for the first time "of the small guts of the buffalo cooked over a blazing fire in the Indian stile without preperation of washing or other cleansing and found them very good."

The meal finished, he, Drouillard (who had become Lewis's almost constant companion), and two crewmen started ahead of the dugouts on foot. Their aim was to obtain an astronomical fix on the point, only a few miles ahead, where the Missouri breaks out of the spur of the northern Rockies now known as the Big Belts. It was a pleasant excursion. Lewis liked to walk, and the slopes leading to the gap made by the river were washed with the lemony-gold sheen of blooming cactus and massed sunflowers. He scrambled up a tall pinnacle at the mouth of the canyon and, looking back, marveled at the view of the great herds of buffalo grazing on the plains. Though he did not suspect it, it would be his last sight of those mobile mountains of meat for many, often hungry months to come.

Calculations for latitude made, the four men pushed about five miles into the lower canyon, between walls of hard, black rock some eight hundred feet high. At the foot of a rapid that "roled white over the rocks" (Ordway), Lewis killed an elk for supper. The joy ended after that, for he had forgotten his mosquito netting, and he spent the night flailing at the hordes of insects that attacked him.

The next morning, Clark and the boats overtook the scouts at the foot of the rapid. As a precaution against water damage, the soldiers carried the most vulnerable supplies on their backs to the upper end of the turbulence. The dugouts, double manned, were dragged up with two ropes. The river then became deep, the current slow. Cliffs soared on either side. Tall pines and stunted aspens seemed to rise directly out of the dark, vaulting stone. The constricted bottomlands were choked with sunflowers whose seeds, when mature, could be pounded into flour, currants and serviceberries already "ripe and in great perfection," and gooseberries and chokecherries that soon would be edible. All this Lewis recorded in scientific detail in camp that night, as he did the next morning's sighting of a large herd of bighorn sheep clambering on walls five hundred feet above them, "where we should suppose it impossible for any animal to stand."

About three miles farther on, the fleet came to "a handsome, bold and clear stream, eighty yards wide," which the captains named Dearborn's River, after Jefferson's secretary of war. During the winter, Clark's Hidatsa informants had included the Dearborn's valley with that of the Medicine (Sun) River as furnishing a short way to tributaries of the Columbia. There is no indication in the journals that the captains associated the stream they saw with the one the Indians had told about.[3] Indeed, the whites were growing increasingly baffled by the disparity between what they were seeing and what they had understood the Hidatsas to say during the winter. The river Indians had not mentioned Maria's River, they had been at least partly wrong about the Great Falls, and they had given no forewarning about the profound gorge the Corps was now threading. And so, as Lewis put it, "we are anxious now to meet with the Sosonees or snake Indians . . . in order to obtain information relative to the geography of the country and also if necessary, some horses."

Horses—if necessary. It is a strange qualification. They had been thinking horses ever since Clark had drawn his conjectural map of the West. But their successful traverse of the Grand Portage had, perhaps, inspired them to believe they could cross the Continental Divide in the same manner, without horses, if the carrying place were no longer than the half-day labor the Hidatsas had predicted. But how trustworthy was Hidatsa information?

The Shoshoni could answer the questions—if the explorers could lay hold of some of that tribe. And so Lewis continued in one of his convoluted sentences, "we thought it better for . . . either Capt. Clark or myself to take a small party & proceed on up the river some distance before [i.e., ahead of] the boats, in order to discover them, should they be on the river, before the daily discharge of our guns, which was necessary in procuring subsistence for the party, should allarm and cause them to retreat to the mountains and conceal themselves, supposing us to be their enemies who reach them usually by way of the river."[4]

Clark, Joseph Field, John Potts, and York took the first turn at land travel. It was miserable. Uneven masses of small, sharp fragments of rock covered the ridge tops while blankets of prickly pear covered the lower levels. The second night out, sitting beside their campfire, Clark pulled seventeen thorns out of his cut, bruised feet. Because the others had suffered equally, he decided to drop down to the river the next day and rest until the boats appeared. While waiting, he could hunt game for the dugout crews. Locked in the gorge, they might be having trouble getting enough to eat. And after they arrived he could admit, reluctantly, to Lewis that except for a streak of signal smoke he and his scouts had seen (it had been too far off to investigate) the Indian sign he had noticed was too old to mean much. They were still on a blind path.

Back on the river, the boats moved slowly, pulled against the strong current by tow ropes. Then the canyon grew still narrower. Water filled its bottom from wall to wall, leaving no banks to walk on. Willy-nilly the men had to return to their oars and fight a stream thrust almost as powerful as they were. By Lewis's estimate the walls of the gorge rose twelve hundred feet above their heads. Evergreens cloaked the north-facing slope. The cover on the opposite side was thinner and heavily scarred and pitted by erosion. Unable to land in that gloomy place, the rowers labored on until after dark before finding a flat spot big enough to hold their camp. Searching for a suitable name for so singular a place, Lewis called it, with underlining for emphasis, *"the gates of the rocky mountains."*[5]

The next day the mountains receded. By afternoon the river had split into several channels and was winding through a broad plain bound by parallel ranges. Here Lewis noted the double timberlines characteristic of the high valleys of the northern Rockies: a broad belt of evergreens bordered on top by the gray rocks of the "snowey regions" and on the bottom by the treeless, slowly rising floor of the valley. The spacious land looked fine for grazing, but although the men noticed old buffalo bones and excrement, they detected no living buffalo. As if to help make up for the lack of food, Lewis's dog, Seaman, caught several young geese, their wings not yet feathered enough for them to fly, and brought them to his master. (A few days earlier the dog had dragged a wounded deer from the water, killed it, and added it to the larder.)

On July 22, the swift, shallow water of the narrow channels forced the soldiers to resort again to the tow ropes. At times, when the brush was too thick to crash through, they took up their setting poles. These entailed standing in the wobbly dugouts, jamming one end of the pole onto the smooth, slippery stones of the bottom, and forcing the craft upward with all the strength the boatman could muster. Along this stretch, afternoon temperatures, taken always in the shade, rose into the eighties from the pleasant seventies where the mercury had hovered for several weeks.[6] Even worse was discouragement. At the Gates of the Mountains, to use modern terminology, the river valley had bent not just south but a little east of south, so that their travail was actually taking them *away* from the Pacific.

Into this misery came sudden rejoicing. As the boats were passing a small creek whose banks showed patches of white earth, Sacagawea made her first gesture of recognition. At this place her people collected material for white body paint. Almost surely, she indicated, the expedition would find Shoshoni a little farther on at a place called the Three Forks. Because the Americans had heard of this key spot during their stay among the Mandans, "This peice of information," Lewis wrote, "has cheered the sperits of the party who . . . console themselves with the anticipation of shortly seeing the head of the Missouri yet unknown to the civilized world."

Clark, too, was buoyed by the news when he heard it from the boatmen at his resting place. Any Indians camped at Three Forks or thereabouts, he thought, would be the ones who had set the smoke signals he had seen. Obsessed with the idea of being the first to meet them, he declined to trade places with Lewis. Since only Joseph Field of his original party was fit to continue by land, he enlisted three fresh men—Joseph's brother, Reuben, Robert Frazer, and Charbonneau, who begged to go and might be able to interpret a little. Then off he limped on July 23, covering twenty-three miles in spite of his fatigue and aching feet. He also killed four deer and left them beside the river for the water travelers.

On the 24th he went thirty miles. On the 25th he was even more demanding. That morning he led his men onto a low swell of hills and saw the Three Forks. Left and right and ahead of them a majestic vastness rose to black bands of timber capped by gray, round-topped peaks dappled with snow. Puffs of clouds floated overhead. Below the clouds three streams coiled like dropped pieces of string through sage and grass, willows and rose bushes, but only occasional narrow-leafed cottonwoods. The westernmost stream and the middle one joined first and then drifted on a short distance to pick up the eastern river, where it finished lapping around a gray snout of limestone. He had reached the Three Forks of the Missouri. Beaver sign was everywhere. Otter. Deer. Some antelope. Occasional elk. But no sign of Indians. Whoever had set the smoke signal had vanished. Where?

Clearly the westernmost of the forks reached the high country sooner than the other two did, and so, after impaling a note to

Lewis on a stick and thrusting the stick into the marshy ground, Clark took his men twenty-five miles up the gentle valley, traveling west and southwest. When Charbonneau collapsed, they camped, "all of them much fatigued, their feet blistered and wounded by the prickly pear."[7]

The next morning the interpreter was unable to travel. Leaving one man with him, Clark led the other two on a dry walk through unseasonable heat to the top of a hill twelve miles away. The view was tremendous but revealed no Indians. On the way back the scouts stopped at an icy spring. Clark took what he thought were proper precautions before drinking: he wet his face, hands, and feet in the cold water. The preventative failed him. Almost immediately after gulping copiously, he felt as if he had been slugged. Sore-footed, cramped, and dead tired, he hobbled to the camp where he had left Charbonneau. When Charbonneau said he could walk again, the captain decided to cross the stream they had been following and examine the middle of the Missouri's three forks. They chose as a ford a place where the river was divided by an island. After reaching the island they killed two grizzlies and then waded out into the much deeper water of the second channel. The current was swift and Charbonneau, who could not swim, lost his footing. He might well have drowned if Clark had not dragged him out.

These last exertions almost finished the captain. After forcing himself along for another three miles he caved in, shivering with chills and aching in every muscle. The next morning he staggered on. Arriving at the middle fork, he turned down it, and at three in the afternoon rejoined the main party at the camp Lewis had established near the junction. After he had told Lewis he felt bilious (an old complaint of Clark's) and hadn't had a passage for several days, his friend gave him a dose of Rush's thunderbolt pills and directed some of the men to build a bower where Clark could sleep out of the sun.

Bringing the boats up the river to the forks had been no picnic, either. There were the usual struggles with setting poles and tow ropes. When handling the latter the men often had to leave the brushy banks for the cold, waist-deep water, under a broiling sun. Bearded needle grass added its miseries to the familiar pests of gnats, mosquitoes, and prickly pears. Its barbed seeds, Lewis complained to his diary, "penetrate our mockersons and leather legins and give us great pain until they are removed. My poor dog suffers from them excessively." As for the exhausted men, "I occassionaly encourage them by assisting in the labour of navigating the canoes, and have learned *to push a tolerable good pole* in their fraize [phrase]."

In spite of all this and amid his worries about Indians, he found time, good Jeffersonian that he was, to jot down a continuing run of natural history observations. He described lovely fields of wild flax that he thought could, in time, be profitably cultivated by pioneering farmers. He was less taken by some wild onions he boiled up for one meal—"strong, tough, and disagreeable." As usual he had a sharp eye for new birds such as ruffed grouse and a colorful woodpecker that later ornithologists would name for him *(asyndesmus lewis)*. On seeing several snakes that sought refuge in the water as the boats neared, he helped the men catch some so that he could examine their teeth to learn whether the fangs were hollow and thus capable of releasing stored poison. (They weren't.) On reaching Three Forks he promptly climbed the limestone bluff around which the eastern branch curled and from that vantage point drew a chart of the meandering streams.

Clark's return on the afternoon of July 27 sealed a decision Lewis had already made. In spite of the dangers inherent in additional delay, the boatmen, weakened "from this continual state of violent exertion," had to have rest and time for making new buckskin moccasins and garments to replace clothing ruined by long periods of immersion in water. Clark, too, badly needed a pause. So the word went around: for the next two days they would stay where they were.

They were not idle days.[8] While hunters went after deer for venison and skins, Lewis struggled with a problem of definition. Which of the river's three forks was most worthy of keeping the name Missouri? He ruled out the eastern fork, which was the smallest, but the other two were so nearly equal in size that, in his mind, it would be wrong to give either one the preference. This meant thinking up appropriate new names. Consultations with Clark in his bower resulted in their calling the eastern fork Gallatin, in honor of the secretary of the treasury, Albert Gallatin; the middle fork the Madison, after Secretary of State James Madison; and the western the Jefferson, after "the author of our enterprize."

A poignant Indian drama, they soon learned, was associated with the Jefferson. Five years previously, according to Sacagawea, talking through her husband, her family had been encamped with a mobile village of Shoshoni at exactly the spot where the American explorers were then resting. On being warned by lookouts of an advancing war party of Hidatsas, the mountain Indians had retreated up the Jefferson to a sheltering grove of stunted cottonwoods and brush. The Hidatsas discovered the ruse and attacked. In a running fight they killed four men, four women, and a number of boys. As the defeated Shoshoni warriors fled on horseback from the battleground, the rest of the band scampered for safety as best they could. While Sacagawea was splashing frantically across a shoal place in the river, a mounted Hidatsa had swooped her up and had taken her, probably by way of the Yellowstone, to an enforced new home. But, Lewis wrote, she seemed stirred neither by memories of the abduction nor by anticipation of joining her people again. "If she has enough to eat, and a few trinkets to wear I believe she would be content anywhere."

It was a stoicism the captains were having to match in their own way. Certain shocking geographic truths were dawning on them. From what the Hidatsas had said earlier in the year about the 225-mile *southwestern* course of the Missouri between Great Falls and Three Forks, Clark had estimated the longitude of the latter to be about 117°. To this assumption the captains had attached two known facts: the longitude of the Columbia's mouth was almost 124° and the distance from one meridian of longitude to the next was, in Clark's lexicon, about 41 miles. Seven meridians multiplied by 41 supposedly meant that only 300 or so direct-line miles would separate them, at the forks, from the Pacific.

Matters had not worked out that way, however. Instead of traveling southwest from Great Falls, they had gone a little *east* of south for about 250 miles. As a consequence they were somewhere between meridians 111° and 112°—or about 500, not 300, direct-line miles from the ocean.[9] And of course they could not travel in direct lines. Windings like those they had been following from Great Falls would probably swell the distance ahead of them to more than a thousand miles.

There were other considerations. They could no longer be sure they could cross the divide in half a day, even with horses, as the Hidatsas had said. And once the Corps did reach a navigable stream leading to the Columbia, would they find trees suitable for building dugouts or would the land, like the valley of the upper Missouri, be devoid of timber? In addition, there was the problem of altitude. Although the mountains cupping the Gallatin, Madison, and Jefferson rivers did not seem to rise particularly high above the broad valley floor, the appearance was deceptive. Since leaving St. Louis, the expedition had followed the Missouri for close to twenty-five hundred miles and in that distance must have gained almost a mile in elevation. Winters, for anyone caught in the mountains, would be severe, as snow patches still lingering near the summits late in July attested. "Game," Lewis wrote, "may rationally be expected shortly to become scarce and subsistence precarious."

In spite of this bleak prospect, there is no indication the captains thought of turning back or even sitting where they were on the chance a band of Shoshoni would eventually come long with extra horses they would be willing to barter. The explorers had to advance. The Columbia lay ahead and, Lewis wrote, with just a little posturing for whoever might read his journals in the future, "if any Indians can subsist . . . in these mountains with the means they have of acquiring food we can also subsist."

When the Corps resumed its journey on July 30, Lewis again took up his custom of walking off to the sides of the river—the Jefferson now—to see as much of the local flora and fauna as he could while staying more or less abreast of the boats. This day a maze of beaver dams entangled him. He clambered over the obstructions from pond to pond, waded in mud and water to his waist, fought the dense willow brush, and in spite of his labors missed the boats. No worry. He shot a duck for supper, built a fire, made a bed of willow boughs, "and should have had a comfortable nights lodge but for the musquetoes which infested me."[10]

When the time came to write up his notes, Lewis remarked, as he had at other points along the upper Missouri, on the "vast number of beaver" inhabiting the upper river. He knew fur men would be interested in that and in his recommendation of Three Forks as a site for a trading post (a post would be built there in 1810, but Blackfoot Indians soon put it out of business). What he did not foresee, though the development would not have surprised him, was that at least four of the expedition's men, Peter Wiser, John Potts, John Colter, and George Drouillard, would return to the high, bleak region with parties hunting beaver. Casualties would be high. Indians killed Potts in 1808 and Drouillard in 1810, after horribly mutilating him. Wiser, his tracks befogged by now, found new ways to cross the divide into Idaho, where new bonanzas of fur awaited, only to be killed under circumstances now unknown. Colter escaped a similar fate by outrunning the Blackfeet, who had stripped him stark naked, in a race that became an American legend.[11] As for little Jean Baptiste Charbonneau, Sacagawea's son—but that's another story, for later on.

After the boats picked up Lewis the following day, his sense of the expedition's predicament grew to urgency. All of the men were on the edge of exhaustion in spite of their rest at Three Forks, and there was neither grog nor, on that day, July 31, fresh meat for reviving their morale and strength. The latter shortage led Lewis to one of his rare criticisms of the crew: "when we have a plenty of fresh meat I find it impossible to make the men take any care of it, or use it with the least frugality. tho' I expect that necessity will shortly teach them this art."[12]

A portage like the one at Great Falls would not do after all. The Corps must have horses. The next day (August 1, Clark's birthday) Lewis began a new search for the Shoshoni. As companions he chose, in addition to Drouillard, two men who were not in shape to help with the boats. One was Charbonneau, whose ankles still bothered him. The other was Sergeant Gass, who had wrenched his back in a fall. Lewis himself was discomfited by a combined attack of diarrhea and the operation of the salts he had taken to cure it. The day was hot, and they wasted miles on a mistaken shortcut. Still, there were compensations. Lewis saw and described a noticeable new bird, the pinyon jay. He and Drouillard killed two elk and left most of the meat beside the stream as a birthday present for Clark and his hungry boatmen. Curiously, Lewis seems not to have taken his dog, Seaman, along on these exploratory expeditions, perhaps because of the difficulty of feeding the animal but more probably because of the foot-lacerating needle grass and prickly pear cactus that blanketed the ground away from the stream.

During the next two days they struggled with hot days and cold nights, with foot problems on the dry slopes, and, near the stream, with thickets of brush and with marshes caused by overflow from innumerable beaver dams. On August 4, the splitting of the Jefferson into two nearly equal branches confused them briefly. After carefully examining both banks Lewis decided that the one to the left, as he faced upstream, was the proper choice for the boats. He wanted to make sure, however, by first exploring the right (westerly) fork while at the same time acquiring a little more geographic knowledge. He wrote a note to Clark, advising him to take the flotilla up the Jefferson, as he continued calling the left fork, and said he and his party would rejoin the boats somewhere along its course. Sergeant Gass then cut down a willow pole, fastened the note to the green wood, and set up the message beside the stream where he thought the boatmen would be sure to see it. Then off the scouts went, up the right fork toward the mountains, at whose toes they camped.

The next day neither Gass nor Charbonneau was able to continue. Accordingly Lewis sent them back across country to a timbered hill beside the main fork with orders to wait there for him and for the boats. Accompanied by Drouillard, the captain pushed up the sparkling, swift-flowing, but very shallow right fork into the mountains. Finding that it bent due west and then north, the explorers forsook it to scramble up a high point in the foothills. This gave them an aerial view of the wide valley. No question: the Jefferson was the way. It surely held more water than the unnavigable right fork, and it continued southwest—the direction emphasized by the Hidatsas—to a distant gap in the mountains. True, the Hidatsa geographers had not always been right, but where nothing is known with surety any firm statement is a reed to clutch at.

These conclusions reached, Drouillard and Lewis made their way to the camp Gass and Charbonneau had established, arriving two hours after dark. (One has to assume the two invalids had built a large fire as a beacon.) Because they had no food for breakfast the next morning, Lewis sent Drouillard hunting in the triangle between the forks while he went downstream with Gass and Charbonneau to meet the boats. A lucky decision. From a high point Drouillard caught sight of the dugouts toiling up the wrong branch and hurried over to turn them back.

The days had been brutal for the boatmen.[13] Every two or three hundred yards they encountered rapids so shallow the dugouts grounded and the crew had to go into the water and drag the heavy boats up to the next pool. More immersions came when they were towing the craft and impassable brush on the banks again drove them back into the stream. The constant sliding around on the stony bottom injured their feet and occasionally caused painful falls. The river wound through so many hairpin bends that hours of toil actually advanced them relatively few miles toward their goal. But at least the hunters began getting a little meat, including a bighorn sheep Clark bagged on his birthday out of a herd bounding up a cliff on the far side of the river. Supplemented by trout, a few geese, and an occasional beaver, the sheep meat and small daily rations of venison were spread thinly among the twenty-nine adults of the party and the dog.

On reaching the forks of the Jefferson, Clark found only the stub of the green pole on which Gass had placed Lewis's note. For some reason a beaver, ignoring the masses of willow nearby, had nipped off the lone pole and had carried the note away. After seeing the scouts' tracks going up the west fork, Clark followed. Soon the group was trapped in a braid of channels so narrow that the brush hanging over them united at the top and created hot, green tunnels through which, for one stretch a quarter of a mile long, they had to cut a way with axes and knives. That night they camped on an island so marshy they had to heap up beds of willow boughs to stay out of the mud.

The next morning, August 6, Drouillard turned them back into more trouble. Two dugouts, hanging up on rocks in swift riffles, filled with water washing over the gunwales. A third upset. Another, swinging against a rock, jarred Whitehouse overboard and then floated heavily across him, injuring one of his legs. After meeting Lewis's group at the forks, they crossed to a sunny gravel bar opposite this river of bad luck. There they spread out the baggage to dry. On taking inventory they discovered that so great a quantity of trade goods and equipment had been lost they could abandon one of the dugouts—a bonus, for the action freed more men to hunt the increasingly scarce game they needed.

At noon on the seventh they repacked and moved up the fork Lewis had chosen—the Jefferson. On the morning of the eighth they encountered still another fork, this one coming in from the southeast. Since this new fork and the one where Clark had encountered so much grief were the principal affluents of the Jefferson, the captains decided to name them after what they considered to be two of the president's principal attributes—Wisdom for the lower tributary, Philanthropy for the upper. Not surprisingly, later pioneers renamed the streams after geographic landmarks. The Wisdom has become the Big Hole after the high, handsome valley in which it originates; the Philanthropy is now the Ruby, for the mountain range that is its birthplace. The Jefferson was renamed, above the forks, for Beaverhead Rock, an imposing bluff visible for miles in almost every direction. The Shoshoni were its original christeners, for they fancied they saw in its contours the shape of a swimming beaver.

Sacagawea explained the name as soon as she saw Beaverhead. Unquestionably, she went on, her people would be camped either on the headwaters of the Jefferson/Beaverhead or on another river just beyond the mountains.

The information impelled Lewis to go ahead once again with a small scouting party consisting of John Shields, Hugh McNeal, and, inevitably, George Drouillard. Clark was disappointed. It was his turn to lead the advance party, but he could not because of "the raging fury of a tumer on my anckle muscle." Ominously he added, "three hunters Could kill only two antelopes to day."[14] Because of the shortage, the only food the scouts took with them was a little salt pork and flour purchased more than a year ago in St. Louis, plus a sack of parched corn prepared at the Mandan villages.

Walking briskly, they passed Beaverhead Rock and the Rattlesnake Cliffs, named for the great number of rattlers in the vicinity. On August 10, they stumbled onto a trail that took them through an abrupt little canyon to yet another fork in the river. After deciding that the most recent horse tracks went up the west fork (later named Horse Prairie Creek), Lewis decided to turn that way and put a note on a dry stick advising Clark to wait at the junction until he returned. This was the end of boat travel. But how wonderful to have come so far! "I do not believe," he wrote in his journal, "that the world can furnish an example of a river running to the extent which the Missouri and Jefferson do through such a mountainous country and at the same time so navigable as they are. If the Columbia furnishes another such example, a communication across the continent will be practicable and safe."[15]

It was self-delusion. Passing the Great Falls had hardly been an example of practical travel, and even though the river above that landmark had proved passable, safe limits certainly did not extend beyond Three Forks. He knew, too, that the Columbia dropped to the Pacific in half the distance the Missouri coursed on its way to the Mississippi and would be correspondingly rougher. But he had been directed by his president to find a waterway. Therefore he would disregard whatever ran contrary to his desire.

After camping that night in a wide valley that Lewis called "the handsomest cove I ever saw" (he later named it Shoshoni Cove) the scouts continued up gentle tan slopes and among scattered copses of spruce and fir toward the divide. Losing the Indian trail in thick sagebrush, the quartet spread out at a considerable distance from each other in the hope that one of them would pick it up again. After they had marched about five miles in this fashion, Lewis spotted a human figure, tiny in the distance. Up came his spyglass. A mounted Indian! Making gestures of friendship and finally setting aside his gun so that he could hold out tempting gifts, Lewis advanced toward the now motionless Shoshoni, all the while bellowing "*tab-ba-bone,*" which he thought meant "white man." (He had asked Sacagawea the word for "white man." Since the Shoshoni apparently had no word for such people, she gave him the closest translation she could, *tab-ba-bone,* or "stranger." This did nothing to reassure the horseman.)[16] Meanwhile, one of the privates, John Shields, blundered along in a fashion that alarmed the Shoshoni, who suddenly wheeled around, gave his horse the whip, and disappeared into the brush. "With him," the frustrated Lewis wrote, "disappeared all my hopes of obtaining horses for the preasant."

After chewing out Shields in the best army fashion, the captain calmed down, and they set about trying to track the rider to his camp. A heavy rain ended the effort. The next day, however, they picked up a major trail that led past a collection of huts made of willow brush and on through ground recently disturbed by root diggers. Spirits soared: they were close now. Where the trail crossed a little rivulet, Private McNeal "exultingly stood with a foot on each side . . . and thanked his god that he had lived to bestride the mighty and heretofore deemed endless Missouri."*

Two miles farther on they reached the spring from which the rivulet gushed. Now Lewis exulted. He had reached the very source of "the Mighty Missouri in surch of which we have spent so many toilsome days and wristless nights. Thus far I have accomplished one of those great objects on which my mind has been set for many years, judge then of the pleasure I felt in all[a]ying my thirst with this pure and ice-cold water." Moving on, they topped the dividing ridge, "from which I discovered immence ranges of high mountains still to the West of us with their tops partially

---

*Since Lewis and Clark's time, geographers have decided the true headwater of the Missouri is Red Rock Creek, the fork the Corps did *not* follow to the divide.

covered with snow. I now decended the mountain . . . to a handsome bold running Creek of cold Clear water. here I first tasted the water of the great Columbia river."[17]

He was a proud and excited young man, knowing he had just helped write a new chapter in American history, and it takes the carpings of hindsight to raise questions. Such as:

His statement about his long dream of finding the sources of the Missouri. Such things happen; many young Britons dreamed, before and after Lewis's time, of finding the sources of the Nile. Meriwether Lewis may well have believed he belonged in that sort of company. Not quite, however. This was Thomas Jefferson's project. Lewis had been called on to execute it not because of any dreams he may have had or plans he may have laid, but simply because he had happened to be available when Jefferson decided to expand his original strategies concerning Louisiana. This, of course, does not detract from Lewis's manifold accomplishments during the expedition. But it does make him a first-class manager rather than the innovator he quite naturally viewed himself to be, there on top of Lemhi Pass, 7,373 feet above the level of the sea.

He was also kidding himself about the Columbia. Like all white geographers of the time, none of whom had seen the area, he accepted as an article of faith, not of knowledge, the statement that the headwaters of the Missouri were separated from those of the Columbia by a single, thin dividing ridge.[18] Clark's map, drawn at Fort Mandan and based on that same faith, showed *no* major chain of mountains beyond the last range of the Rockies. So when Lewis surmounted the hills from which the Missouri sprang and saw "immence ranges still to the West," what did he think they were? Perhaps, for all he knew, *those* were the true divide. Perhaps some tributary of the Missouri—the Dearborn, say—took its rise on the western side of Lemhi Pass, flowed north a distance as the Hidatsas had said, and then broke east through the ridge to join the Missouri. If so, his exultations were premature, and the expedition had a lot more work to do.

He declined to face that issue. He had been conditioned to think Columbia and he did think Columbia. Yet even if that faith was right (it was), his and Clark's notion of what lay between the river's headwaters and the ocean—a wide plain like the one the Missouri crossed in the Midwest—was shockingly wrong and chilling times lay ahead. Either way, horses would become more essential than ever.

Finally, a matter of boundaries. Upper Louisiana ended wherever the watershed of the Missouri ended. Lewis and Clark had shown a full awareness of the limitation when considering branches of the Missouri that ran north toward Canada. But no word of political barriers marked the pages of Lewis's journal when he wrote of crossing Lemhi Pass westward into regions where Great Britain's rights were as strong as those of the United States. He intended to exercise the privileges of sovereignty by opening communications with the West Coast, trading and treating with the Indians along the way, and studying the resources of the land as thoroughly as Clark and he had been doing in fully owned Louisiana Territory. He was, in short, an advance agent of American imperialism, and it is hard to believe he wasn't as conscious of his role as Thomas Jefferson was. But you would never know it from what he wrote in his journal as he left the United States and entered what was then no country's land.

They dropped down what may have been Agency Creek toward what they certainly hoped was the south fork of the Columbia. At nightfall they ate the last of their pork, saving a little flour and parched meal until they could find other food. Walking on the next morning, they startled two Shoshoni women and one man into flight. Unable to overtake them, the explorers backtracked the trio toward whatever place they had come from. Along the way they surprised three females, made contact, and calmed their terror with gifts of beads, awls, mirrors, and vermilion. Rejoicing over the miraculous windfall, the women led the strangers toward their band's camp.[19]

Of a sudden sixty mounted warriors, armed primarily with bows, arrows, and bull-hide shields, galloped pell-mell around a bend in the valley toward them. They had reason to charge. Earlier in the year raiders they called Pahkees (Atsinas, allies of the Blackfeet) had killed or captured twenty Shoshoni, had stolen many horses, and had burned all but one of the band's leather tepees. Recently word had arrived that the Pahkees were back; the people responsible for the smoke the Americans had seen had heard gunfire and had assumed Blackfeet.[20] Next, the three Indians who had fled from the explorers that very day had run to the village gasping that Pahkees had actually crossed the divide. So the warriors had dashed out to repel the invasion. They were dazzling horsemen, all of them, even though they rode crude saddles without stirrups and their bridles consisted of no more than a single cord tied around each horse's lower jaw.

Dropping his gun and seizing the American flag Private Hugh McNeal had been carrying, Lewis stepped out to confront the force. The ecstatic women held up the trinkets they had been given, and the warriors reined in. Explanations flowed. Discovering their mistake, the Indians became instantly curious and affable. Dismounting, they took turns embracing the whites and pressing their greased and painted faces against the Americans' cheeks until, Lewis grumbled later, "I was heartily tired of the national hug."

Formal rituals of welcome followed, both at the meeting place and at the nomad's camp in the treeless valley of the yet unnamed Lemhi River. (Curiously, the captains, who named nearly every tributary along the Missouri, did not do as much for the Lemhi, nor did they report the name the Indians used.) On the surface affairs went smoothly. The principal chief of the band, Cameahwait, was an exceptional individual. After meeting him Clark described him as having "Influence sence & easy & reserved manners, appears to possess a great deal of Cincerity."[21] Among his accomplishments was his ability to converse in the sign language familiar to all the tribes of the Great Plains.

The Shoshoni were not a plains people. Their roots lay in the bleak Great Basin country of Nevada and eastern California. About A.D. 1500, archeologists believe, a search for food led some of them across the Rockies into what is now southern Saskatchewan and northern North Dakota. There they began their long feud with the Blackfeet, Crows, and Hidatsas. In those days the battles had been neither bloody nor conclusive, but matters changed in the early 1700s when the Shoshoni acquired horses through the Utes and perhaps the Comanches who lived on the borders of Spanish New Mexico. Astride these terrifying animals, they had been able not only to cow their enemies but to slay all the bison they needed for food and leather. During that period of supremacy, they adopted many plains customs, including sign language.[22]

Not long after the advent of horses, the Indians of the northern plains began picking up guns from the French and British traders of Canada, and the Shoshonis' advantage disappeared. Driven back into the mountain-sheltered valley of the Lemhi, they found the quality of their life deteriorating. From May to September, when salmon came up the river to spawn, they depended mostly on fish for food—but that was uncertain because the migrants arrived in sometimes widely spaced waves and, after laying their eggs, died. Roots, berries, and other plant foods, when mature, staved off starvation, but as the hard months of winter neared, the members of the band had to gather up their courage along with their bows, arrows, and lances (the only three guns Lewis saw in Cameahwait's village were inoperable) and risk going onto the plains for buffalo, whose dried meat might last until the fish returned.

Through Drouillard's sign language Lewis was able to explain something of the Corps's intentions to Cameahwait and his council. After this initial talk they went down to the riverbank to discuss routes. Cameahwait was not encouraging. He said the Lemhi ran north several miles (as the Hidatsas had also said) to join a bigger stream, which then wheeled west through impassable mountains to enter a huge lake where men like the visiting Americans lived. Privately Lewis doubted the information. As far as he knew, no whites had established a settlement at the mouth of the Columbia (assuming that by "lake" Cameahwait meant the ocean). Nor did the land-based Indian appreciate what could be done with boats by skilled rivermen. Cameahwait, he decided, was probably trying to keep the whites from going on so the village could benefit, during the coming winter, from their wondrous technology.[23]

Lewis was not about to bite. But he was worried. The Corps was going to need many horses, not just for bringing baggage across the divide but also for packing it down the Lemhi to some point where trees big enough for boat building could be found—and that was a long distance, again according to Cameahwait. Taking a big party across the divide to meet Clark would involve commissary problems. Lewis's party, armed with rifles, had not killed enough game for subsistence during their own crossing. And he knew the Indians had no backup supply. For when he had chanced to remark, earlier in the day, that he and his men had had nothing to eat for twenty-four hours, the Shoshoni had generously shared the few cakes of dried, pounded chokecherries and serviceberries they had.

Salmon? The run had slacked off. One man had given Lewis a "morsel."[24] It "perfectly convinced me we were on the waters of the Pacific Ocean" (so there had been a thread of doubt about that when he'd viewed the tumbled scene from the top of the pass) but it had also emphasized the problem of scarcity. How willing would the Indians be to go hungry while helping strangers?

They seemed amiable enough that first evening, entertaining their guests with a dance. Lewis went to bed at midnight, "leaving the men to amuse themselves with the Indians." Quite a party. The yelling awoke him several times, but "I . . . was too much fortiegued to be deprived of a tolerable sound night's repose."

The next morning Hugh McNeal divided in half the last of the explorers' flour—one part for breakfast, the rest for evening. He added water and berries to the breakfast portion, cooked it, and distributed the results among the four scouts and Cameahwait. The chief liked the new food and his new friends, but not all his people shared his trust in them. Evidently the rank and file had talked things over during the night and had begun to doubt that the whites were as harmless as they pretended to be. When Lewis harangued them about renting "30 spare horses to transport our baggage," he was met with sullen silence. Did not their implacable enemies, the horse-stealing Pahkees and the Hidatsas, always come at them from the Missouri watershed? How did they know these four alien whites were not trying to lead them into an ambush where their horses would be lost?

After various fruitless arguments, delivered in Drouillard's sign talk, Lewis struck a note that worked. The Shoshoni were cowards. At that Cameahwait swung aboard his horse and delivered another speech that declared his bravery and that of his warriors. Six or eight males thereupon fell in line. The old women of the village promptly began wailing as if the braves were going to certain destruction. Cameahwait's speech had shifted momentum, however. As the cavalcade moved ahead, more men and a number of women joined in.

It was not what Lewis had hoped for. No packhorses—easy prey for raiders—were being led along by the mounted Indians. No riding animals had been provided for Lewis and his men. The suspect whites traveled afoot with their knapsacks on their backs until the captain, by offering compensation, prevailed on four Shoshoni to let the Americans ride double, each clinging to the warrior in front of him. Lewis soon found jogging along without stirrups to be more uncomfortable than walking, and he dropped to the ground while letting the Indian continue toting his pack.

They camped that night in the upper part of the valley called Shoshoni Cove. Lewis himself boiled, in a small amount of water, the whites' last pound of flour and divided it among his men, Cameahwait, and a lesser chief. The next morning no one had anything to eat. Faced with the general discontent, Lewis sent Drouillard and Shields out for game, though they had not been able to produce anything during the past few days. The sight of these two strangers riding with their rifles toward an unannounced destination sent a flutter of alarm through the gathering. More than half the people retreated toward the pass, leaving only twenty-eight men and three women to follow Lewis, who was riding double again, and Cameahwait toward the assigned meeting place with Clark.

Before this remnant was well started, a Shoshoni who had been spying on Drouillard charged up full speed. A deer, fresh killed! A headlong race for breakfast followed. Lewis's Indian companion lashed the horse they were riding at every jump. Unbearably jostled, Lewis demanded a halt, whereupon the Indian jumped off and raced ahead on foot to the feast. By the time Lewis arrived, Drouillard had gutted the kill and had rolled the viscera aside preparatory to cutting up the carcass. Compassion struggling with disgust, Meriwether described a scene that has become infamous in pioneer literature. "each one had a peice of some description and all eating most ravenously. Some were eating the kidnies the melt [spleen] and liver and the blood running from the corners of their mouths, others were in a similar situation with the paunch and guts but the exuding substance in this case from their lips was of a different discription. . . . I really did not untill now think that human nature ever presented itself in a shape so nearly allyed to the brute creation." Actually the episode was not exceptional, except perhaps for the speed of the gulping. Centuries of necessity had conditioned the Shoshoni to devour every bit of a slain animal, down to the soft parts of the hoof. Moreover, as Lewis neglected to point out, the half-starved people did not attempt to seize the meat of the deer's body. They stood aside until Lewis had reserved a quarter for himself and his men and had turned the balance over to Cameahwait to be divided among his people.[25]

As the procession neared the lower end of Shoshoni Cove the Indians took Lewis's cocked military hat from him and in its place draped over his head and shoulders Cameahwait's splendid tippet of one hundred and forty ermine skins.[26] Lewis's men were also adorned with native headpieces. Clearly the additions were to make them look so much like important Shoshoni that if the Blackfeet attacked, the Americans would likely be among the first to be killed. Lewis reacted to the insult (or precaution, depending on the viewpoint) by handing Cameahwait his rifle: You don't trust me. Very well, shoot me if an enemy strikes.

His position, he realized, was growing precarious. If the boats were not at the junction when the cavalcade arrived, the suspicious, taut-strung Indians might well vanish into mountainous areas where he could not find them again. Earnestly he tried, through Drouillard's hand talk (and some of his own, for he had picked up many of the gestures through observation), to arouse enough interest in the boats that the Indians would want to wait for them. Again he told Cameahwait a woman of their band was with the whites. He expatiated on the merchandise that would soon be available for barter. Drouillard sagaciously added that not all the newcomers would be white; among them was an amazing black man with short, curly hair. Lewis then tried to clinch the argument by saying that even if the boats weren't there, a magic message from the approaching whites would be. He sent Drouillard to the junction to fetch it. It was, of course, the note he had left at the junction, telling Clark to wait there for him. Staring at his own handwriting, he declared to the ring of Indians around him that the boats would arrive at the forks on the morrow. Drouillard would return to meet them. To prove he was telling the truth and that no ambush was being prepared, he would give a knife and some beads to any young Indian brave enough to go with the hunter to check on whom he met. Meanwhile Lewis, Shields, and McNeal would stay as hostages with the main body of the Shoshoni.[27]

Reluctantly the Indians agreed to the proposal. There was little sleep for anyone that night. Tossing and turning under his mosquito netting, Lewis tormented himself with fears that Clark had found the Jefferson/Beaverhead unnavigable and had stopped far below the junction, in which case Lewis could never again persuade the Shoshoni he spoke honestly. As for the Indians, most of them secreted themselves in the brush, suspicious still that an attack was coming.

The boats were, in fact, traveling very slowly. The reasons were as they had been for several days—dense brush on the streambanks, gravel bars that grounded the dugouts, treacherous footing, intense daytime heat and cold nights. The stream curved inordinately, so that each day the fleet traveled many miles but went forward very few. Again and again the soldiers begged Clark to let them travel by land, packing their supplies and essential trade goods on their backs as they had done at the Great Falls. Lacking word from Lewis about what lay ahead, he always refused.

As they neared the forks, they heard Drouillard's voice shouting at them. Soon they saw him, dressed like a native and accompanied not by one but by several Indians curious to see the black marvel and the Shoshoni woman they had heard about. At the same time Sacagawea lost the impassivity that Lewis had thought was one of her characteristics. Dancing with the most extravagant joy, she pointed to the Indians and sucked on her finger to indicate they were of her native band. Delighted by the sights, the Indians began singing boisterously.[28]

Then one of the riders drew away from the flotilla and galloped back to the camp in Shoshoni Cove, crying that the *tab-ba-bones*, not the Blackfeet, were on the way. The waiting Indians whooped, Cameahwait hugged Lewis again, and this time Lewis hugged back.

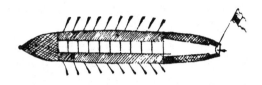

FOURTEEN

Hunger

"every thing," William Clark wrote about the meeting of the boat crews with the horse Indians, "appears to astonish those people. the appearance of the men, their arms, the canoes, the Clothing my black servent & the Segassity of Capt Lewis's Dog." Sagacity? Did Seaman extend a paw to shake hands? Plunge into the river to bring back sticks that had been thrown for him? In any event, as the Shoshoni crowded around, staring, Sacagawea added to the confusion by recognizing a young woman who had been captured with her during the Hidatsa attack at Three Forks. Unlike Charbonneau's wife, that captive had escaped and made her way home —a considerable feat, it would appear from today's viewpoint, for a child ten or twelve years old. The reunion, Nicholas Biddle remarked after hearing Clark's tale, "had in it something peculiarly touching."[1]

As soon as the Shoshoni could lay hold of the newly arrived captain, they led him to one of their easily erected brush wickiups. Long ago, outsiders had taken to defining the builders of those wickiups with a sinuous motion of hand and arm: "people of the woven houses." Or so the theory goes. But the motion might also be taken to represent a serpent's progress. Snake Indians—and, by association, the great Snake River that wound through part of their territory. William Clark's suggestion that the term derived from the Shoshoni's skill in taming serpents is not widely accepted.[2]

Be that as it may, the Indians took him inside and seated him, as a sign of honor, on a white buffalo robe. All those in attendance took off their moccasins. The ceremonial pipe passed back and forth, and Cameahwait decorated the captain's shaggy hair with six pieces of "pearl," or bits of seashell. That indirect evidence of trade routes to the Pacific was exciting.

Because Drouillard was off hunting—there were many people to feed—Sacagawea and Charbonneau were summoned to help translate. It was an awkward procedure. One of the captains spoke in English to the boatman Labiche. He put the remarks into French for Charbonneau, who passed them along in Hidatsa to his wife. She translated them into Shoshoni for Cameahwait. As the talks began, recognition came to her again, this time like a blow. The chief was her brother! Inexpressibly agitated, she threw her blanket over his head (a sign, perhaps, of their sibling bond) and burst into tears. After the two had wept together for a time, the ceremony resumed, "but her new situation seemed to overpower her, and she was frequently interrupted by tears."[3]

This preliminary introduction completed, the whites invited all the Shoshoni in the vicinity to a small-scale replica of the formal councils they had held the preceding year with the tribes they had encountered along the Missouri. Like its predecessors the meeting took place under an awning made from a sail. It may be assumed that Drouillard, back with the other hunters after bagging four deer and an antelope, passed on Lewis's remarks in hand and body language, for he'd had ample practice at other gatherings. Because the Indians' main home was not on American soil—at least not yet —Lewis did not address them as children of the great father. He did, however, point out that the Corps was an official arm of the United States government and was traveling to the Pacific in search of a good route for bringing American merchandise into the interior. Since no commerce could be developed until after the explorers had returned home, it behooved the Indians to speed the explorers along their way by furnishing horses and a guide. The time to start was now, by helping the expedition get its baggage across the divide.

Very interesting, Cameahwait replied, "with his ferce eyes and lank jaws grown meager for the want of food. . . . 'If we had guns, we could then live in the country of buffaloe and eat as our enemies do and not be compelled to hide ourselves in these mountains and live on roots and berries as the bears do.' " But before he could furnish horses, he would have to return to his village and prevail on the people there to help.[4]

It was a risky outlook, but for the time being the Americans had to be satisfied with it. They wound up the meeting by distributing the usual medals and gifts. Lewis fired his airgun—great medicine, that!—and the entire group of Indians at the camp (the number is uncertain; it could have been as low as sixteen) was feasted on hulled corn supplemented by the antelope the hunters had brought in. On their part, the thirty-two expedition members and the dog made short shrift of the four deer.

The talk of trade led to more talk about routes. The Indians the captains questioned agreed with Cameahwait. Men could not pierce the fearful gorges that led toward the sea. If they tried they would starve, for there was no game in those terrible wastes. Though Lewis and Clark remained unconvinced—what of those shells in Clark's hair?—the statements were so positive they agreed they had better look things over before they jumped.

They planned carefully. Clark, whose sore feet and legs had healed, would lead eleven men equipped with boat-building tools down the river until he found trees from which dugouts could be hewn. If timber proved unavailable or if the river really was unnavigable, he would investigate possibilities by land. Charbonneau and Sacagawea would go with him as far as the Shoshoni village. There they would make sure that the Indians, whom Lewis regarded as capricious and undependable, returned promptly with men who, so Cameahwait promised, would be willing to sell horses. In the interim Lewis was to supervise the making of pack saddles and the rearranging of the baggage into parcels suitable for horse transport.[5]

The next morning Meriwether indulged in a bit of aggressive salesmanship. Clark needed a few horses immediately for carrying his party's boat-building tools and enough supplies for an extended stay of construction work, if such developed. Lewis's hunters needed one or two so they could range far to find game enough for those who stayed behind. So after the Indians had collected their mounts, he drew from one of the bales of trade goods a cloth coat, some gay hankerchiefs, a pair of leggings, and a knife, the whole worth, back in St. Louis, about twenty American dollars. How many horses, he asked the watching, yearning riders, would one or more of them give for the collection? After strenuous bargaining, he got three. He turned two over to Clark, the other to Drouillard. Inspired by the success, some of the men (whether of Clark's group or Lewis's is not stated) obtained, for private use, a fourth in exchange for a worn shirt, a pair of old leggings, and a knife. Nor was that all. As Clark's eleven men were hiking toward the pass, the mounted Indians in file beside them, they met a Shoshoni riding one mule and leading another. The fellow was so shocked at seeing the white captain traveling on foot that he promptly gave him one mule and added a Spanish saddle. Clark repaid the generosity with a waistcoat. At lunchtime he also broke into his party's supply of corn and pork to feed the Indians, for they had no food with them, their hunters having failed to find game along the way.[6]

Back at the camp beside the forks of the Jefferson/Beaverhead River, Lewis somberly estimated the number of pack saddles he should have his men make. Twenty, he decided. They produced the necessary boards by sawing off the blades of the dugout oars and by breaking up wooden packing boxes after transferring their contents into specially prepared rawhide sacks. He softened other pieces of leather in water so they could be cut into thongs for taking the place of nails in the construction and into straps for the saddle riggings.

He began his work on August 18, 1805, his thirty-first birthday. It was not a happy occasion for him. As far as the journals show, he had not reminded William Clark, Drouillard, or anyone else of the event. Probably it is not possible now to understand fully why the anniversary triggered Lewis's all-too-easily-induced melancholia. Certain guesses can be offered, however. As an army officer, he could not build up unstrained relationships with enlisted men, and so Clark's departure this particular day may have left him feeling very lonesome, there in the subarctic zones just below the top of the remote Continental Divide. He was, furthermore, very ambitious and hence susceptible to fears of failure. With winter just ahead, if there was no way through the mountains his great enterprise might collapse. Yet when he unburdened himself in his journal—a trip journal, not a personal diary—none of these considerations surfaced. Instead he sounded like a very moody, very introspective, very youthful thirty-one. Which he was.

He had been indolent, he wrote. He had not improved his mind as much as he might have. He had "as yet done but little, very little, indeed, to further the hapiness of the human race or to advance the information of the succeeding generation." In the future, he vowed, he "would live for *mankind* as I have heretofore lived for *myself.*"[7]

Considering what he was doing for country and mankind, the self-flagellation was hardly deserved. Yet it may have helped stir him into filling, during the next several days, page after page of his journal with ethnographic observations about the hitherto unknown Shoshoni, or Snake, tribe. It was the sort of analysis that Jefferson wanted and that more than one "succeeding generation" of anthropologists would find very useful.

The words poured out: family relationships in the tribe, the status of women as he saw it, the characteristics of the people as a whole, foods, dress, weapons, diseases. For the most part his observations were accurate, concise, and objective. At times he added personal reactions. By using nothing more than the sharp tip of a deer or elk horn, he noted, a warrior could chip an arrowhead out of flint "with a quickness and neatness that is really astonishing." A necklace of grizzly bear claws marked its wearer as a celebrity, for first he had to slay the animal, and that deed "with the means they have . . . must really be a serious undertaking."

For practical reasons he was interested in sexual customs. Women and children outnumbered men in the village beyond the divide at least three to one. Most of the women were married—polygamy was acceptable—but, as in other tribes, marital ties did not forbid liaisons with outsiders *if* the husband consented, which, for a trifle, he generally did. Aware of the impossibility of imposing restraint on the Corps's young men, "whom some months abstanence have made very polite to those tawney damsels," Lewis contented himself, for the record, with urging discretion.

He also made inquiry through Charbonneau and Sacagawea as to whether the Shoshoni were subject to venereal complaints. Some were infected, he learned, and the victims often died. The knowledge apparently did not increase his worry about his soldiers or about what they might bring to the Shoshoni. However, it did lead him, as a matter of scientific interest, to speculate that if a tribe as isolated as the Shoshoni suffered from the disorders, sexual diseases were probably endemic to America and not imported from Europe, as was generally believed. He was probably right. Syphilis may well have been carried from the New World to the old by Columbus's sailors.[8]

Twenty pack saddles, Lewis soon realized, were not going to be enough for transporting the Corps's equipment over the hill. Shrunken though his supplies seemed, they would have to be pared still more. Finding a distant place for a cache and making sure the four Indians at camp were not watching, he had some of his men dig a hole. Into it went the natural history specimens he had collected between Great Falls and the divide, as well as every gaudy coat, every carrot of tobacco, and every bar of lead he thought the expedition could spare. The next problem was the dugouts. He did not want the Indians breaking them up for fuel, for they would be needed if the Corps returned this way from the ocean, or from whatever obstacle chanced to turn them back. Accordingly, he filled the boats with rocks and sank them in a pond near the forks.

Shortly thereafter, on August 22, Charbonneau, Sacagawea, and Cameahwait returned with about fifty warriors accompanied by their families and many horses. The sight jarred Lewis. So large a group probably signified that the salmon run had dwindled away and that as soon as other groups of Shoshoni and perhaps some Flatheads arrived to build up their strength, the combined parties would move down the Missouri on their dangerous trek to the buffalo grounds. With them, almost beyond doubt, would go some of the horses he had been counting on.

Hoping that food might keep the Indians amiable while he dickered, Lewis sent Drouillard out with the expedition's lone animal to find as much game as possible. All the hunter got was a single fawn. Breaking into the expedition's reserves, Lewis had the cooks boil up huge kettlefuls of corn and beans. The Indians enjoyed the unfamiliar fare, but it did not incline them to part with horses on the eve of their vital hunt. During a long bargaining session, the captain succeeded in obtaining only five of the twenty or more animals he needed.[9]

The only solution was to go to the village, where horses not required for the hunt should be available. To make the trip he would load the heaviest material on the five head he had purchased, add Drouillard's mount and other animals he could rent, and hire porters to lug along, on foot, whatever the Corps's crewmen, burdened with their personal baggage, could not handle. Unfortunately the porters—women, because the men refused even to listen to such a proposal—would not go unless the entire group they were with also returned to the village.

To keep hunger from upsetting his plans, Lewis had his men prepare a brush drag of the sort that had served the expedition well on some of the tributary streams of the Missouri. With the contraption he and his crew, helped by a few Indians, swept 528 big trout out of the sunny pools below the forks. The Indians' conduct during the operation won Lewis's admiration. They were orderly; they did not crowd or grab. Short of culinary articles of their own, the women borrowed knives and kettles from the whites, and, after the meal, scrupulously returned them.[10]

Geniality did not reduce stubbornness, however. When Lewis sought the next morning, August 23, to start the mixed group toward the divide, Cameahwait balked. More Indians, he said, would soon be passing through on their way to the Missouri and he wanted to talk to them. Reluctantly, for he could do nothing else, Lewis complied, and then turned the delay to his advantage the next day by purchasing three more horses and a mule from the newcomers. Two rented animals and the mount Drouillard had been using brought the total number of available packhorses to twelve. (Charbonneau, using knickknacks Lewis had given him, had bought a riding horse for Sacagawea and her baby, and a friendly Indian, conscious of the needs of dignity, had loaned Lewis a mount, but those animals were not for packing.) Determined to wait no longer, Lewis, at noon on the 24th, pressed ahead with his cavalcade—mounted Indians milling along beside the string of plodding packhorses, porters, and overburdened crew members.[11]

All this put Cameahwait in an untenable position. Government of the Shoshoni, as with most tribes, was by consensus, and he retained his position as principal chief only to the extent that the members of the band respected his judgment. But which way should he lean now? He did not wish to alienate these whites of whom his sister spoke with great favor. They had shared their food with his hungry people. They had promised that if the expedition succeeded, traders would soon bring in firearms and other goods that would enable the Shoshoni to hold up their heads again. Yet Cameahwait understood his band's possessiveness about their horses, the only wealth they had. They had lost many to the Pahkees not long before, and that made them doubly jealous of the rest.

Finally, many of his starving tribesmen were losing patience, saying angrily that it was time they were off on their annual hunt. What obligation commanded that they keep on riding back and forth over the pass for the sake of strangers?

Unutterably badgered, Cameahwait capitulated and secretly sent messengers ahead to the village, asking the people there to catch their horses and ride over the divide, ready for the hunt. Learning of the defection, Sacagawea told Charbonneau of it. Not realizing the seriousness, her husband did not tell Lewis of it until the procession had halted for lunch just short of the divide. The captain was appalled. The moment the villagers arrived, the people he was with would swing around. He would lose the horses he had rented and the services of the women porters. Worse, his hope of acquiring more pack animals for following Clark to whatever trail he had decided on would evaporate.

Summoning Cameahwait and the two lesser chiefs who accompanied him, Lewis upbraided them. Did their promises mean nothing? Did they expect that white men would come to them with trade goods if they did not keep faith and help the expedition reach its goal?

Squirming, the lesser chiefs shifted full blame onto Cameahwait. For a long moment he stood silent. The hunger. His honor. And a chance to get firearms. The latter considerations triumphed and he sent a runner to the village, countermanding his order. But as the group neared the Indian encampment the following day (August 26) he asked Lewis to help him save face by firing a set of volleys. The salute would impress his people and make them aware of the power of guns—a power that his decision about returning would bring to them, if the white men kept *their* promise.[12]

Lewis agreed, of course. He had saved the expedition by maneuvering it through a more critical situation than is generally recognized today. True, he had many horses still to buy, but at least he now had a chance. How important that opportunity had become he learned when he met John Colter in the village with a message from Clark and discovered what lay ahead.

The reader will remember that Clark and his potential boat builders, accompanied by Charbonneau, Sacagawea, and Cameahwait's first group of Indians, had left the American camp near the forks of the Beaverhead early in the morning of August 19. With their heaviest goods carried by a couple of packhorses, they were able to travel fast. According to Sergeant Gass's estimate, they covered thirty-six miles that day, including a crossing of Lemhi Pass. Another few miles brought them to the Indians' main camp, which had been moved a short distance upstream since Lewis's visit. There the whites paused in the band's sole remaining leather tepee for a few hours of ceremony and talk. With Charbonneau, Sacagawea, and an unnamed French boatman acting as conduits for the conversation, Clark cleared off a patch of ground and pressed Cameahwait to draw a specific map of the supposedly impassable river he had talked about only in generalities so far.[13]

After scratching a line in the earth with a knife blade—that was the river, torn by rocks into froth—the chief heaped up mounds of sand to represent mountains dropping steeply into the water, leaving no banks that men or horses could travel. Impassable, he insisted again. For the time being Clark accepted the statement. But what of the seashells and pieces of Spanish horse equipment he had noticed in the camp? Was it possible, he asked, that they came along trails running southwest of the river?

Cameahwait sent for an old man who had once lived several days' travel in that direction. The fellow talked grimly of vast expanses of hostile desert broken only occasionally by canyoned rivers. Scholars now surmise he was talking of the bleak Snake River plains of southern Idaho, but Clark, unfamiliar with the Southwest and confused by fuzzy translations, supposed the fellow was trying to tell him of the approaches to the Gulf of California. For an expedition seeking the mouth of the Columbia, that route would not do.

Next Clark asked about trails northwest of the supposedly impassable river. He'd heard of one, Cameahwait replied. It was said Pierced Nose Indians—the Nez Percé—used it to reach the buffalo. But it was a very bad trail, without game, broken and rocky and heavily timbered. If snow came early, it would be fatal.

Clark was elated. If Indians could get through with women and children, the expedition could. Yet a string of packhorses could be troublesome: rounding the animals up every morning, packing and unpacking them every day, risking sore feet and accidents at critical times. Perhaps he had better evaluate the river, after all. Like Lewis, he still did not believe that Indians unaccustomed to boats knew how to estimate fast water.

When he asked about a guide, Cameahwait produced a man the explorers took to calling Old Toby, a designation belied by the

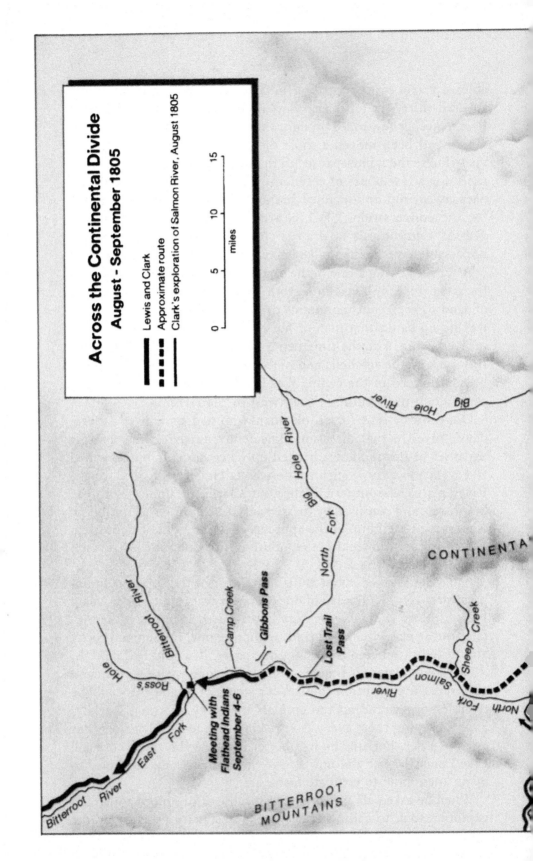

Across the Continental Divide
August - September 1805

Lewis and Clark
Approximate route
Clark's exploration of Salmon River, August 1805

miles
0   5   10   15

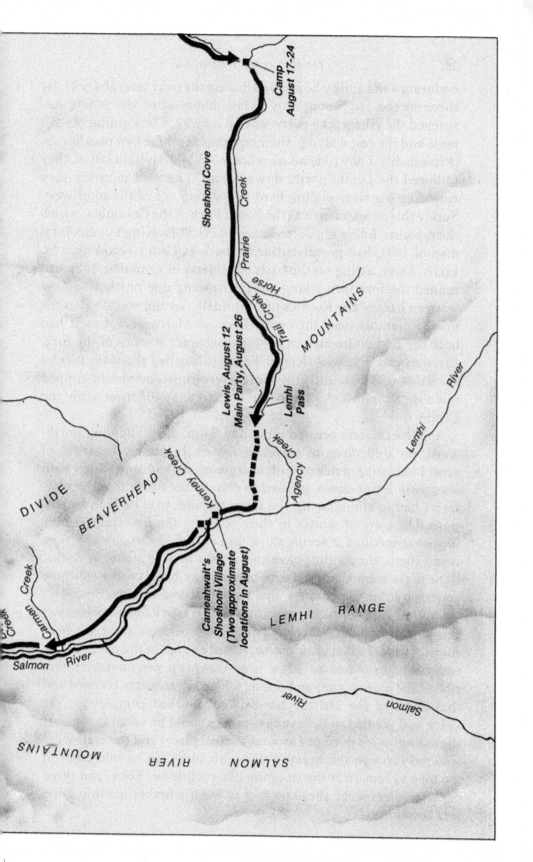

Camp August 17-24

Shoshoni Cove

Prairie Creek

Horse Creek

MOUNTAINS

Trail Creek

Lewis, August 12
Main Party, August 26

Lemhi Pass

Agency Creek

Lemhi River

DIVIDE

BEAVERHEAD

Kenney Creek

Cameahwait's
Shoshoni Village
(Two approximate
locations in August)

LEMHI RANGE

Carmen Creek

Creek

Salmon River

SALMON RIVER MOUNTAINS

Salmon River

endurance and agility he showed during the next several weeks. By three in the afternoon, only a few hours after the scouts had reached the village, the party was on its way, Clark riding his gift mule and the rest walking, their equipment on the two packhorses. (Presumably Toby rode his own horse.) While daylight lasted, they followed the Lemhi north, downstream. The next morning they reached a big river gliding hard and strong out of the southwest. Surely this new stream was the South Fork of the Columbia, which the captains, following dotted lines on Nicholas King's conjectural map of 1803, had postulated as far back as Camp Wood near St. Louis. Later, acting on the basis of Hidatsa information, they had refined the fork into a long stream running due north along the western base of the Rockies until it finally swung west to join the main Columbia near the coast. Because Meriwether Lewis had been the first white man to see the headwater streams of the fork, Clark named it Lewis's River. Today it is called the main fork of the Salmon. The beautifully located, river-girt, mountain-cupped town of Salmon now stands at the stream's junction with the Lemhi.

As the explorers pressed down the Salmon, still flowing northward, the difficulties of travel increased. In places the knees of great mountains, patched with evergreens high up and scaled with sagebrush lower down, pressed so close to the water that the wayfarers had to climb far up the steep hillsides to skirt the obstructions. Unaware of whites in their country, the few Indians they met were terrified at seeing them, but after Toby's voice had reassured them, they either gave the whites or sold them, at trifles, some of the salmon and cakes of berries they had. It was a welcome generosity, for the country was indeed devoid of game.

On the 22d, after passing a tributary that Clark did not name but that is now called the North Fork of the Salmon, the river bent sharply west. Travel grew worse. Again and again the men and the two packhorses had to labor over the steep promontories that ribbed the narrow canyon bottom, where white water boomed and thrashed. On the 23d the horses were blocked completely. Yet Clark still wanted to believe that canoes could be taken through if the ladings were portaged around the bad places and the craft were lowered through the heavy water with cords. So he told eight of the men to remain at the stopping place while he, Toby, and three of the soldiers went ahead on foot to learn whether his thin hope was tenable.

The going was rough—teetering slabs of talus at the base of the cliffs, strong currents slamming against the far walls of the tight bends, water "foaming & roreing thro the rocks in every direction." To complete the whites' education, Toby led them along an Indian path that climbed six miles up a side stream (today's Squaw Creek) to a stupendous view of "the hollers [hollows] of the river for 20 miles." From that vantage point, as Clark put matters dryly, Toby "pointed out the dificulties."

Back they went to the place where the others were camped. There Clark tore a page out of his notebook and wrote a letter to Lewis. He was willing to make a stab at the river under certain conditions: let half the party follow the stream while the other half hunted on the mountains above, coming down now and then to help and change places with the river crews. But the ferocity of the river was such that perhaps the Corps ought to risk the starvation trail used by the Pierced Nose Indians. Old Toby had been there as a youth and believed he could find it again.

This note, and a horse, Clark entrusted to John Colter for delivery to Lewis at the main Shoshoni village. Toby went with Colter so that Lewis could talk to him through interpreters, for Clark of course had been relying on sign language, which he knew only imperfectly from observing Drouillard at work. The others followed slowly, depending for food on the Indians and camping finally beside the Lemhi, a few miles above its junction with the Salmon. No use going farther, for the main party would soon be coming down the tributary. Wishing they had a little red meat to eat, the men began making pack saddles for the horses they supposed Lewis was buying.

After brief talks with Colter and Toby, Lewis agreed they should take the Nez Percé trail. This meant, ideally, a riding horse for each of the thirty-one adults in the party plus another two dozen or so for packing, some of which could be used for food in case of an emergency. Since Clark and he, traveling separately, had brought only fifteen or so across Lemhi Pass to the village, Lewis was going to have to steel himself for a lot of drawn-out dickering. Accordingly he asked Clark, by messenger, for help. Leaving his party's baggage downstream with two men to guard it, Clark and the rest of his group responded promptly.

Realizing their bargaining strength, those Shoshoni who were willing to sell jacked prices higher and higher, and then happily gambled away their profits, "content," in Ordway's words, "to let the world go as it may." Soon the Indians were asking for guns and ammunition as well as for knives and clothing. At that the whites balked. The twenty-nine horses they now owned—good animals but sore-backed because of the Shoshonis' crude saddles—would have to do. The captains, Sacagawea, and a few others could ride, but most would have to walk, yanking the stubborn pack animals along by their improvised halters. At least hunting had improved, and the Corps was able to start out with a little venison to supplement their diet of fish.[14]

The morning of August 30 was a time of swirling color and confusion, the whites loading their fractious animals to go north, the Indians readying their gear for the Missouri hunt. At that point Sacagawea definitely cast her lot with the Americans. Perhaps she did not even question her obligation to stay with the husband who had purchased her and who had no intention of leaving the expedition. It is likely, too, that she preferred the ways of the whites and the security they provided. Clark quite possibly was already calling her "Janey" and her son "Pomp," as he did later on.[15] (His use of the nicknames is not to be taken as evidence of the secret, unrequited grand passion between soldier and Indian maid that aficionados of the latter like to dwell dreamily on. But it does indicate an easygoing relationship that could have appealed to the girl-mother who previously had known little but abuse.)

No journal keeper mentions her decision. Clark was absorbed in the turmoil of departure, to which the private affairs of the interpreter and his wife were peripheral indeed. As for Lewis, he had ceased making, on August 26, journal entries of any sort. Melancholia again? Or, as is more probable, did he fall silent in order to lighten his load of duties? Jefferson, to be sure, had asked that both captains (and other expedition members) keep diaries. But the president was not after different viewpoints; he simply wanted to increase the odds that at least one diary would survive. To those in the field, the duplication must have been onerous at times. Ordway and Whitehouse often copied each other word for word. And was it really necessary, the captains perhaps asked each other, for both to stay up to all hours writing under dim candlelight about the same things? Couldn't they take turns?

That in effect is what they did. Though Lewis continued with his voluminous field notes, he made no more journal entries, except for three short periods when Clark was away on various errands, until January 1, 1806. At that time Lewis resumed his diary—and Clark ceased his. And so, for the period to January 1, we must rely on Clark for a record of each day's traverse, and on Sergeants Gass and Ordway and Private Joseph Whitehouse.

These tell us that after picking up Clark's baggage the cavalcade continued down the right bank of the Salmon, across talus piles that bruised the horses' feet and ankles and then up today's Boyle Creek to a bit of flat land big enough to hold a night's camp and provide grazing for the horses. There the men ate their last sparse ration of venison and topped off the meal with locally grown berries. This shortage of food may be what prompted the six Indians who had accompanied them this far to turn back, so that Old Toby and one of his sons were the only Shoshoni who remained. Having fewer mouths to feed could not have displeased either the captains or the hunters.

Toby was leading them over a shortcut of sorts, scrambling up steep hills, dipping into creek valleys, and threading increasing amounts of timber as elevation increased. That evening, September 1, they camped on the North Fork of the Salmon, six miles above its confluence with the main river—close enough that three men were able to hike down to an Indian camp Clark's party had passed during their exploratory venture and return with twenty-five pounds of dried salmon.

Real trouble began the next day. They had to cut passage through thickets of evergreens, both standing and fallen. They dragged their reluctant horses through deep bogs the men named the Dismal Swamp. While they were clambering up rocky hillsides to escape the narrowing defile through which the creek poured, several horses slipped and fell. Some tumbled down the slope and, burdened by their packs, could not regain their feet. The men had to slide down to them, remove the loads, urge them back onto the trail, and then carry the baggage up for repacking. One animal gave out so completely they had to abandon it and its load. Except for a few "pheasants" (grouse), the hunters brought in nothing fresh to eat. Ravenous, the crew wanted to kill a horse. The captains turned instead to their shrinking supply of pork. Live animals were precious.[16]

September 3 was the worst day. Two men took the horse Lewis had been riding back to rescue the animal that had been left behind. They salvaged it by putting its load on Lewis's stallion and letting it limp back behind them. Then more uphill, more downhill, more trail cutting, more horses falling—"horrid bad going," said Whitehouse, to which Clark added his amen: "some of the worst roads that a horse ever passed." Gloomily he went on, "we met with a great misfortune, in haveing our last Themometer broken, by accident." If the instrument had been sound, it would have set a new low for the season. A rain that had been falling most of the afternoon turned, after dark, to snow. Later the skies cleared, the stars leaped out like a spray of icy points, and everything that was wet froze hard. "Slept wet and hungry and cold," Whitehouse complained. But at least the discoverers had crossed the humpbacked ridge, seven thousand feet in elevation, that divides the waters of Lewis's River from those of the stream Lewis later named Clark's River. It is the Bitterroot today.

After working their way down Camp Creek, the Corps came into a lovely vale holding thirty-three tepees—about four hundred men, women, and children. They were Flatheads, short, stocky, light-hued members of the widespread Salish people. Since Flatheads did not deform their children's skulls, as the coastal Indians did, the reason for the name is unknown, although various theories have been offered.[17] Lewis and Clark had first heard of them from the Hidatsas, who said they dwelt beside a big stream flowing north along the western base of the Rockies, and Clark had located them in that position on his 1805 map. But here, on the scene, a bit of geography suddenly straightened itself out. There was not one north-flowing river at the base of the mountains, as they had thought the Hidatsas had said, but two, separated by the divide they had just crossed—Lewis's River, which they'd seen bend west toward the Pacific, and Clark's River. Whether Clark's River (the Bitterroot) also reached the ocean, no one on the spot could tell them.

The Flatheads were anxious to climb the hill the Americans had just descended. That way they could strike east across the Continental Divide at what is now Gibbon Pass and follow the Wisdom (Big Hole) River to the forks of the Jefferson, where Clark's dugouts had run into trouble a month earlier. The Corps, on its part, was just as anxious to reach the trail of the Pierced Nose Indians. Nevertheless, the prospect of profitable horse trading kept the groups together for a day and a half. In that time the captains purchased at least eleven sound, clean-limbed animals (or perhaps thirteen; accounts aren't clear) and traded off seven of their injured mounts for the same number of healthy ones. Three of the acquisitions were mares followed by unweaned colts.

When the explorers continued through cold rains down the Bitterroot Valley, they had approximately forty good horses in their remuda. Though hunger still pinched them much of the time, they were feeling more confident about the future than they had for several days past. Perhaps Lewis was feeling better about himself, too, for he had taken advantage of slow spells in the bargaining to make notes on some of the new tribe's salient characteristics and to compile a partial vocabulary for Jefferson to use in his studies of comparative languages.

The Lolo Trail, the name later given to the Nez Percé Trail, followed a creek that ran sparkling out of the mountains to join the Bitterroot. The captains halted there to give Lewis time to take celestial observations, for the hunters to gather meat—they did not have much luck—and for the other men to repair their moccasins. While most of the horses grazed, Clark and Toby rode down Clark's River to its East Fork (today's Missoula) to look over the country. More geography fell into place. According to Toby, travelers could veer up the East Fork's left-hand branch to an easy pass over the Continental Divide. The pass opened onto an east-flowing stream the captains had already named Dearborn; it entered the Missouri close to the Gates of the Mountain. The traverse took four days, Toby declared.[18] The Corps had been on the road fifty-two days.

The Hidatsas had told them about this crossing and about a similar one from the head of the Medicine. The captains had not understood the talk clearly. Besides, they had needed horses and the only place they could be sure of finding them (it had been said) was among Sacagawea's people near the headwaters of the Missouri. So they had followed the long hairpin curve—south, southwest, and north—that at the time had seemed the most dependable way. On their return journey, they could check this amazing shortcut, for they seem never to have doubted that they would return home by land—and not by sea, as Jefferson had said they might.

They started up the Lolo Trail in midafternoon, September 11. Straightway they ran into portents. Fresh, unseasonable snow cloaked the high peaks of the Bitterroot Mountains. A hard frost whitened the grass when they awoke on the morning of the twelfth. Later that same day they encountered pine trees from which starving Indians had peeled the bark in order, Sacagawea said, to be able to eat the moist fibers of the bark's inner layers.[19]

On the thirteenth they crossed a relatively low divide to headwater creeks that would soon unite to form a river later travelers would know as the Lochsa, a Flathead word meaning "rough water." Though they were unaware of it as yet, their guide, Toby, had been confused by paths the Flatheads used to reach good fishing places along the upper part of the river. The main trail followed the ridge tops, but he was whipping his horse down rain-slippery hills into tangles of fallen timber. On the night of the fourteenth, much fatigued and ravenously hungry, the explorers experimented with some of the gummy portable soup Lewis had packed away in lead canisters long before in Philadelphia. Not liking it, they killed one of their colts for supper.

The next day they floundered along the riverbank until Toby realized his mistake: they should be on the top of the giant hogback that formed the northern border of the Lochsa's profound canyon. To get there they climbed four thousand feet up a precipitous side ridge—tight zigzags, rocks that cut the horses' ankles, loose, gravelly soil, and piles of jackstraw trees that had been felled by fire and wind. Among the horses that lost their footing and rolled down the hill was one that carried Clark's field desk. Although the desk was irretrievably smashed, the horses survived. Dark had closed in when they reached the top. No water there. But they were able to melt enough snow for thinning the portable soup. With colt bones added for flavor, it tasted better.

Try to visualize that narrow, gigantic ridge winding between a series of knobby peaks overlooking a seemingly endless wilderness of deep, winding, heavily forested troughs. Rough saddles separate knob from knob, so that the travelers were constantly dropping down only to have to toil despairingly up again. In a few places the dim trail cut along the steep sides of the ridge to reach water. But eventually the long string, made up of forty or so horses and an unknown number of hikers, had to seek out the top again, to resume slogging from knob to wearying knob.

On the morning of the sixteenth they awoke on a side hill "astonished" to find their beds under six inches of snow, its whiteness dulled by thick fog. In order to find the trail, Clark walked along, head bent, leading his horse. Snow shaken from the weighted branches soaked them all, until, in Clark's words, he was "as wet and as cold in every part as I ever was in my life, indeed I was at one time fearfull my feet would freeze in the thin Mockirsons which I wore." Those who had cloth tore it up to wrap their feet. Sacagawea? The baby? No one says.

The low point came when Clark fired at a deer and heard the hammer click uselessly because of a loose flint—or so he wrote. Whitehead says the gun fired but the shooter missed.[20] As morale sagged in the afternoon, Clark hurried ahead with one man along the side of the ridge. On reaching water near a sheltering copse of balsam, he built huge fires to warm the others when they came up, numb and downcast. That night they killed a second colt, ate half of it as a side dish for portable soup, and kept the rest for the next day's breakfast.

They had to turn the horses loose that night to graze. In the morning the hungry animals were badly scattered, partly because the mare whose colt had just been butchered had gone back along the trail looking for it. The delay caused by gathering the animals and excessive slipperiness resulting from melted snow held the cavalcade to a meager ten-mile advance. At suppertime they butchered the last colt, and again saved half. The skimpy supper left the thirty-five adults almost as voracious as if they hadn't eaten. In desperation the captains decided Clark should press ahead the next morning with six men (but without Toby for some unexplained reason) and try to find food to send back.[21]

After twenty miles of rocky, up-and-down riding, the advance party climbed a knob later named Sherman Peak. Far ahead the rumpled forest at last leveled off. Broad, tan openings broke the black look of the spiked trees. Surely there would be game there, and perhaps Indians to lend help. But the plains were still forty or more rugged miles away, and that involved going without food until late in the morning of the nineteenth, when they spotted a stray Indian horse. It was not fat, and Jefferson had been emphatic about respecting Indian rights. But the men begged hard, and Clark consented. After eating a hearty breakfast, they left the rest of the meat for those who followed. Sustained by that one meal, they reached Weippe Prairie late the next morning, September 20.

Three Indian boys, seeing the seven strangers riding toward them among the widely spaced ponderosa pines, dived into the tall grass to hide. Dismounting, Clark gave his gun and horse to one of the men to hold and searched through the grass until he found two of the youngsters curled up and trembling like rabbits. Reassuring them with a piece of ribbon, he and his companions followed the excited pair to a village of about thirty lodges made of mats woven of withes. Here the newcomers were surrounded by scores of apprehensive women and children and a few old men. The chief and most of the braves, Clark learned through signs, were away on a war excursion. They told him, as nearly as he could understand the word, that they were Cho-pun-nish. They were a likely people, he thought, of a somewhat darker complexion than the Flatheads. The men were portly, the women small but "handsome featured." He noticed their ornaments: white shells, blue beads, and brass rings. Some were worn in their noses. For these native people were indeed of the Pierced Nose tribe, the Nez Percé, later its pronunciation anglicized, unfortunately, into "nezz purse."

The mobile village had been located on the prairie because this was the best place and season for harvesting the bulbous roots of the camas lily—women's work. Mounds of roots stood here and there on the prairie and in the village. Close by were pit ovens for drying the vegetables so they could be pounded into flour for making soup or bread. When the new arrivals asked for food, the Indians plied them with dried salmon, raw camas roots, cooked roots, and bread of camas flour. Although the whites ate copiously, they wanted more solid food, both for themselves and for Lewis's expectant group. Sending hunters out for deer, Clark rode to a neighboring village, for he understood it might be near a navigable river. The town was not on a river, however, and he had no luck finding meat. Neither did the hunters. But again they were fed generously on fish and roots.

All seven were miserably sick during the night, the result, they thought, of overloading their hunger-weakened stomachs with unfamiliar food. Nevertheless, the men went hunting again in the morning, while Clark delved for information. Obligingly the principal chief of the town drew a map for him. Half a day's march away, on an island in the river Clark wanted to see, was the fishing camp of an influential person whose name the captain translated as Twisted Hair. A little distance below Twisted Hair's camp, his river and another came together. A little farther on, more streams added their water to the flow. After a distance of many sleeps, this big river broke through the mountains, creating in its passage a huge waterfall. Below the fall some white men lived, a remark the captain recorded without comment. He had heard a similar rumor way back among the Shoshoni.[22]

The hunters returned in the afternoon, still empty-handed. So roots and dried salmon would have to do for both his men and Lewis's. Clark bought as much as the Nez Percé would sell for the knickknacks he had in his pockets. Loading the food onto a packhorse, he entrusted it to Reuben Field for delivery. Still feeling miserable ("I am verry sick to day," he wrote, "and puke which relive me"), he set out for Twisted Hair's river camp to doublecheck the information he had received. After a long ride through the dark with an Indian guide hired for a red handkerchief, the explorers reached the top of a line of tall bluffs bounding a large stream. After inching cautiously downward, they located the camp shortly before midnight and were made welcome. Sick and weary though he was, Clark went through the requisite ceremonies, explained the American purpose as well as his knowledge of sign language allowed, and after bestowing a medal on the chief—"A Chearfull man of about 65 with apparent siencerity"—he tumbled into bed at about one in the morning.

Far back on the Lolo Trail, Lewis picked up his pen and resumed his journal writing. It was a doleful tale. The twenty-eight people with him were showing signs of malnutrition, perhaps even of scurvy—cramps, thin diarrhea, skin rashes.[23] Weakness, the difficulties of the trail, and constant trouble with the horses kept them to a snail's pace, even though they wanted to hurry. On September 18, the day Clark's party pushed ahead, they rode eighteen waterless miles, coming after dark to the head of a ravine down which they were able to lead the horses to a spring. After drinking deep and dining on a bit of soup, bear oil, and a few tallow candles, the wayfarers lay down beside approximately forty horses and managed to pass the night "on this Sidling Mountain."

The next day the rough ridge trail led them to the top of Sherman Peak. There they, like Clark, looked out to the distant prairie "with inexpressible joy." A little farther on, the narrow trail slanted high across the face of an almost perpendicular slope. There Robert Frazer's horse, loaded with two boxes of powder and ball, fell a hundred yards down the hill (200 feet, Ordway; 100 feet, Whitehouse) and crashed into the brushy creek bottom.[24] Amazingly, the men were able to salvage both the ammunition and the horse, "the most wonderfull escape," Lewis said, that he had ever seen.

Another wonderful experience was finding, the next day, the

slaughtered horse Clark's advance party had left for them. That sustained them for thirty more hours, when they were able to put together a meal of a bit of horse meat, three grouse, one coyote, and some crayfish taken from the stream beside which they camped.

It is a measure of Lewis, perhaps, that throughout this time the entries in his trip journal stayed as voluminous as ever—much longer than Clark's. He devoted pages to distinguishing between the eight varieties of evergreens they passed and describing new birds they saw: a black-and-white jay (Canadian jay), and three varieties of grouse. As altitude dropped and the temperature warmed, he noted the changes these factors brought to the vegetation. But after they had met Reuben Field toward noon on September 22, had devoured the food he brought, and had gone on to make camp beside the nearest Nez Percé village, he wrote one flowery sentence about "the pleasure I now felt in having tryumphed over the rockey Mountains," and then laid down his pen. With one three-day exception (November 29 through December 1) he did not make another journal entry until the new year.

Clark, limping from the effects of a fall from a horse he had borrowed from Twisted Hair, rejoined the party that same evening. He bore glad tidings. No more rocky trails. No more horses to struggle with. They were within fifteen miles of a branch of the river that would carry them to the ocean.

He also warned them against eating too much. Wasted breath. Those were starving men. During a day's layover, while the captains held the usual council and handed out gifts, including an American flag for the grand chief who was absent, they absorbed as much dried salmon and camas root as they could hold. The next morning nearly everyone was violently ill. They blamed the ailment on their radical change of diet. The experience of later explorers and fur trappers tends to confirm the belief.[25] In spite of the extreme unpleasantness of the affliction, however, the captains determined to press on: they had no time to lose building canoes, reaching the ocean, and establishing winter quarters.

It was a ghastly march, attended by crowds of Indians. "Capt. Lewis," Clark wrote, "scercely able to ride on a jentle horse which was furnished by the Chief, Several men So unwell that they were Compelled to lie on the Side of the road for some time others obliged to be put on horses." The hunters Clark had left at Twisted Hair's camp—they were sick, too—had killed only two deer, and so the temptation to eat salmon and camas root continued. Clark handed out every type of medicine the expedition had: Rush's thunderbolts, salts, and "Tarter *emetic.*" On they dragged through heavily forested country and down beside Twisted Hair's river (the north fork of the Clearwater) to the main fork, or, as the captains called it, the Kooskooskee. On September 26, they managed to cross the main stream and set up what they named Canoe Camp in a likely grove opposite the mouth of the north fork.

They stayed there eleven days. Considering their circumstances, they wrought mightily. When the hunters proved unable to bring in enough deer, they ate a horse. That finished, they turned reluctantly to fish and roots, the latter of which "filled us [the two captains] so full of wind, that we were Scercely able to Breathe all night." Despairing, some of the crew followed the example of the French rivermen and began buying and eating fat Indian dogs.[26]

At Canoe Camp the crew was divided into five groups. With axes hardly big enough for the work, they began hacking away at five huge trees, probably red cedar though heavy ponderosa pine was more common in the area, from which they hoped to fashion five river-worthy boats. Once the trees were down, they saved labor by building fires along the tops, Indian fashion, and then scraped out the ashes and charred wood with their chisels and adzes.

They dried and repacked their possessions. They branded and cut the forelocks off their thirty-eight surviving horses so the animals could be easily recognized, and entrusted them to Twisted Hair to watch until they returned. They cached their saddles and some powder during the dark of the night. There were four big canoes—no journal keeper reported their length, width, or depth—and one small one designed to run ahead of the others and check the state of the water. They planned on thirty-seven passengers: the original thirty-three, which included Sacagawea's infant, plus Toby and his son, and Twisted Hair and a fellow chieftan, Tetoharsky. The latter two had agreed to come along as interpreters while the travelers were still in Nez Percé country. And then there was Seaman.

On the night of October 6, Clark fell ill again. No matter. Lewis was even more debilitated. So it fell to Clark, the next morning, to supervise the hurly-burly of breaking camp, loading the canoes, and lashing in the bundles, for they knew rough water foamed ahead. Finally, toward noon, uncertain of their own strengths and certainly uncertain about their new boats, they swung into the current. For the first time since leaving the junction of the Ohio and the Mississippi, Meriwether Lewis and William Clark were going with the flow of a river instead of against it.

FIFTEEN

Wild Water

After so many days of plodding, the discoverers must have felt a heady exhilaration when the swift current of the Clearwater, as the river is called today, whipped their loglike dugouts downstream toward the Pacific. But the water was also low in October, and every so often clusters of black rocks rose ominously above tangles of frothing waves.[1]

The first wreck, which can typify the rest, came just one day after the launching. They had successfully passed "fifteen rapids, four islands, and a Creek." Perhaps they were cocky. Anyway, the boat Sergeant Gass was steering, either with a sweep oar or a big, Indian-style paddle, banged into a boulder and tossed him overboard. One side of the dugout split open, letting water pour in. Fortunately, that part of the river, though swift, was only waist deep and salvage was possible. Clark described it: "the men, Several of which Could not swim hung onto the Canoe. I had one of the other Canoes unloaded & with the assistance of our Small Canoe and one Indian Canoe took out everything & toed the empty Canoe on Shore, one man Tompson a little hurt."[2]

Most of the cargo was soaked, of course, and had to be spread out to dry while the canoe was repaired—under guard, for many Indians, alert for anything loose, had gathered quickly during the rescue work. At that point the two Shoshoni guides, Old Toby and his son, vanished, either because they feared being ducked in some later rapid or they had decided there were too many strange Indians around for comfort. Actually the defection did not matter much, for the two Nez Percé chiefs, Twisted Hair and Tetoharsky, had already taken over as river guides and ambassadors of good will among the stream-side Indians.

What did matter was the way the river was forcing the captains into a familiar dilemma of the Western world: lose time by hurrying. "we should make more portages," Clark admitted, "if the season was not so far advanced and time precious with us." They tried to compromise by adding precautions. On approaching an unusually heavy rapid—they were warned either by their Nez Percé guides or by the deep-throated roar of the water—Lewis and Clark would signal for the flotilla to land while they walked ahead with the guides and the steersmen to read the water. If it looked particularly rugged, they would have the nonswimmers walk to the foot of the tail waves, carrying what they could. Men able to swim would then take their chances with the partially lightened craft. Generally no more than one or two boats went through such stretches at a time. This precaution left the others perched in handy eddies, ready to dart out if rescue operations became necessary. As they did—at least five times during the first ten days. "we have great cause to lament," Clark wrote after one of the wrecks, while the salvaged goods were drying, "as all our loose Powder two canisters, all our roots prepared in the Indian way, and one half our goods [are lost]." To say nothing of time.[3]

As they bobbed and twisted downstream, the nature of the country changed radically. The Clearwater was breaking out of the last foothills of the Rockies and entering the bowl-shaped Columbian Plain in an area where, because of the rain shadow cast by the coastal Cascade Range, precipitation averaged less than ten inches a year. Pine trees disappeared from the hills, as did all vegetation, except stunted willows and weeds, from the stream margins. "Barren and broken" became the common words in the journals for the lands stretching out beyond the canyon walls. Prickly pear cactus covered the wind-scoured ground, but that and spaciousness were the only traits the region shared with the High Plains bordering the Missouri. There were no great, clotted herds of buffalo, elk, deer, or antelope. Food was limited to salmon, most of it dried, and to roots, and a slowly increasing number of dogs, all purchased from the stream-side Indians with articles reluctantly drawn from the expedition's shrinking supply of trade goods.

Stalks, twigs, and bits of driftwood served as fuel, and often had to be purchased. The captains, heedful of Jefferson's admonition about treating the Indians fairly, were scrupulous about paying for everything that was not clearly offered as a gift. But one night, after yet another wreck had left them cold and hungry and with a canoe-load of sodden goods in need of drying, they did break into a cache of unguarded wood they stumbled across. We know because all the journal keepers admitted to the theft, perhaps to exorcise their guilt by confessing it—or perhaps to help readers understand how dire their straits had become.[4]

Yet how marvelous those crystal rivers were! Five days out of Canoe Camp, they were hurried by the Clearwater into a stream more than a quarter of a mile wide, its water a faint, translucent green as it surged out of the south. The Nez Percé called it Kimoo-enim. After recalling his explorations of the Salmon River and remembering his many talks with Indians about the lie of the land, Clark decided this "new" river was actually a reappearance of the Salmon, swollen now by many tributaries. Lewis's River, he had named it—the great South Fork of the Columbia as postulated on their maps.

His only mistake was not realizing that Lewis's River, instead of being the main stream, was actually a tributary of the majestic Snake. Right then, however, the error was irrelevant. For as the captains knew from the Indians, a bigger river than the Kimoo-enim lay only a short distance ahead. This newest one had to be the main fork of the Columbia, which the Corps still identified with Alexander Mackenzie's Tacoutche Tesse. Riding a surge like that, they would surely reach the Pacific in short order. Or so they must have joyfully believed, pleased meanwhile that their guess-work geography, born of many hours of speculation, was turning out to be correct—except in the one vital matter of a short portage across the Rockies.

On October 16, having traveled by Clark's calculation 3,714 miles from Camp Wood at the mouth of the Missouri, they reached the Columbia. It was one of the great rivers of North America and a primary goal of the expedition, yet the journals record no elation. The matter-of-factness has baffled some commentators. But exhilaration had come to the explorers two months earlier, after the crossing of Lemhi Pass, where most of them, stooping beside a small rivulet, had first "tasted the water of the Great Columbia." This last encounter, however welcome, was no more than a confirmation.

Still it merited a halt. The captains wanted to make observations

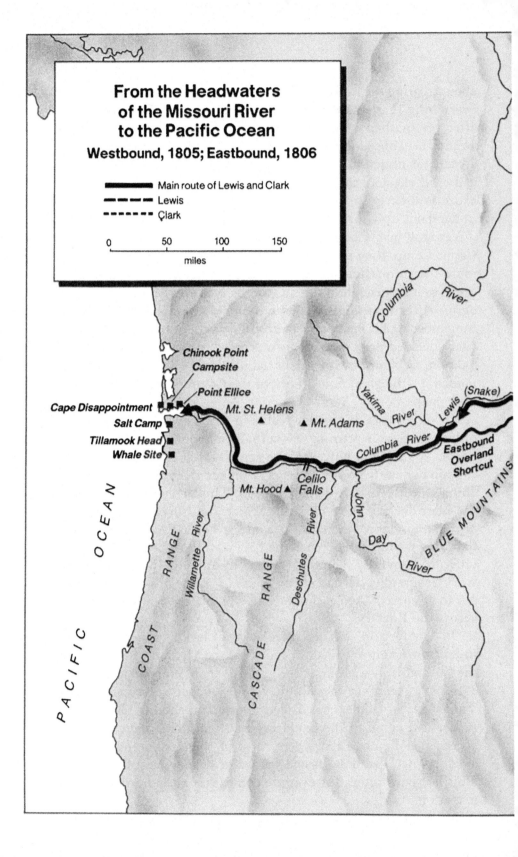

From the Headwaters of the Missouri River to the Pacific Ocean
Westbound, 1805; Eastbound, 1806

Main route of Lewis and Clark
Lewis
Clark

0   50   100   150
miles

Columbia River

Chinook Point
Campsite

Point Ellice

Cape Disappointment

Salt Camp

Tillamook Head

Whale Site

Mt. St. Helens ▲

▲ Mt. Adams

Yakima River

Lewis (Snake)

Columbia River

Eastbound
Overland
Shortcut

Celilo Falls

Mt. Hood ▲

Columbia River

John

Day

River

BLUE MOUNTAINS

OCEAN

PACIFIC

COAST RANGE

Willamette River

CASCADE RANGE

Deschutes River

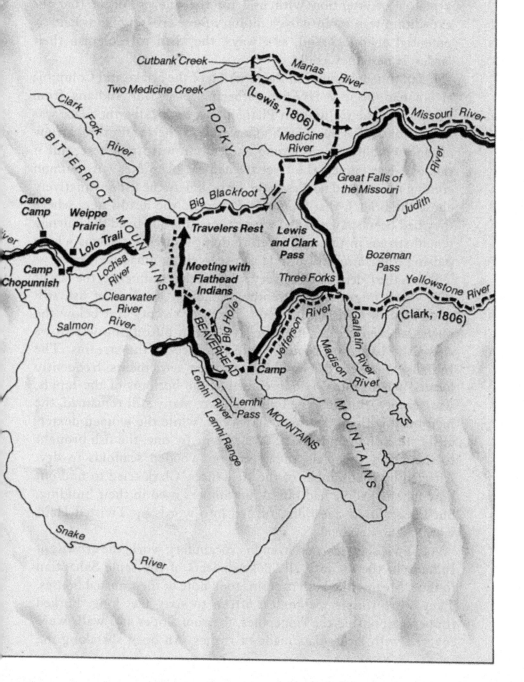

for latitude. (They again sidestepped the tricky calculations involved in computing longitude.) Lewis was anxious to collect comparative vocabularies, and Clark hoped to explore upstream toward another tributary he had heard of, today's Yakima. The men needed to mend their clothes and put their arms in order, "always a matter of attention with us," for they never forgot that the expedition was, essentially, a military force crossing lands held by potential enemies. And, as always, they had to replenish their larder as best they could.

From time immemorial the junction of the Snake and Columbia rivers had been a favorite gathering place for Indians from throughout the Columbian Plain. Topographically, the place was not dramatic, for the river bluffs were low there, affording a view of empty scablands stretching endlessly toward nowhere. But if the land was empty, the river teemed each summer with salmon coming in repeated hordes to the forks. There the fish instinctively chose the branch that would lead them to the headwaters where they had been spawned and where those that survived the journey would spawn in their turn before dying—intense swarms whose pulsing, thrashing magnitude can scarcely be imagined today.

When the Corps of Discovery reached the confluence, the last of that year's migration was ending. Though myriads of fish still undulated in transparent water fifteen to twenty feet below the boats, an even greater number lay dead in putrefying windrows along the banks or floated on the surface of the streams. The Indians, too, were leaving. Many of their settlements, frequently located where salmon congregated at the bottoms of the rapids, were empty. But, like the living salmon, many still remained, the men busy with spears, nets, and weirs, while the women dexterously slit in half and disemboweled, one by one, the fish brought to them and then laid the pieces on wooden scaffolds to dry. Amazed by the number of the structures, Clark tried to find out how far the people had rafted the timbers used in their building, but his gestured questions, turned into words by Twisted Hair, were not understood.

As Lewis soon learned from his vocabulary work, the crowds of Indians in the vicinity all spoke dialects of the same Sahaptian tongue. Meanwhile both captains took note of the unusual houses. They were simple rectangles, fifteen to sixty feet long. Forked timbers supported the ridgepoles; the roof slopes and walls were covered with large mats made of rushes. An open slit along the entire ridge top of each dwelling gave egress to smoke from fires built along the center of the interior. The gap, said Clark, "proves to me rains are not common in this country."⁵ Several families, each with its own fireplace, occupied each house.

The Nez Percé of the foothills, the captains found, were more "dressy" than their relatives at the junction. The former's hide garments were garishly decorated, as were the twin braids of the men's hair, which hung forward over their chests. The women of the Clearwater wore belted dresses that reached to their ankles, and they were far more modest than the men about *"secreting the parts* [emphasis by Clark]." The women downstream, however, eschewed ornaments and long dresses and wore only "a pece of leather tied around them at their hips and drawn tite between their legs and fastened before So as barly to hide those parts which are so sacredly hid & s[e]cured by our women."

These benighted people, the captains agreed, seemed happy. They had many horses; the men shared more tasks with women than was customary in most tribes. Monogamy was the rule; age was respected. But there were problems. One widespread affliction was sore eyes and, often, blindness—the result, the captains thought, of the sun's unbroken glare on water during the fishing season and on snow during winter. Many teeth were worn to the gums or missing entirely. The whites explained this by saying the grit of unwashed roots ground away the teeth. More recent theories suggest that both the trachoma and gonorrhea forms of conjunctivitis should bear most of the blame for the ailing eyes, and that sand worn from mortars and pestles during the grinding of food (roots were generally washed, Clark notwithstanding) accounted for the bad teeth.⁶

The Indians returned the whites' curiosity in full. The afternoon the Corps arrived at the confluence, they were greeted by two hundred natives, singing and pounding on their drums. They formed a half-circle around the visitors, smoked a little, and made what they could out of gestures concerning trade and universal peace. Chiefs were "made," and small gifts distributed. Acquiring food from the Nez Percé who lived along the river continued to be an all-important problem. With the greatest politeness, the captains turned down the salmon that were offered them, for they feared some of the fish might have been picked up dead or dying and be contaminated. But they did purchase an amazing heap of forty dogs. Unless the unfortunate creatures were bought already dressed and in individual transactions, the barking, howling, teeth-bared massacre must have been too gruesome even to contemplate.

At four o'clock in the afternoon of October 18, the explorers again took to their boats, still accompanied by Twisted Hair and Tetoharsky. The next day the wide Columbia, which had been running south, veered west through the Wallula Gap into new canyons. Barren, dark brown cliffs of basalt, the result of ancient lava flows, climbed higher and higher. There were more snarling rapids to run. More Indians to contact, including one group Clark inadvertently frightened out of their wits.

The episode occurred near the bottom of a rush of white water two miles long. He and some others walked ahead to lighten the boats for the passage. It turned out to be slow, and to kill time Clark climbed to the top of a two-hundred-foot cliff to see the view. Far to the west he made out, with what must have been a spark of excitement, a tall, snow-covered peak. Mount Saint Helens, he thought, named in 1792 by the British naval captain George Vancouver, who had sighted the mountain from the mouth of the Columbia. If Clark's identification was correct, the continental gap had been closed: two inquiring humans, separated by only a few miles and years, had stared in wonder at the same dazzling object, albeit from different sides. (Actually, the identification was not accurate; Clark had sighted a huge new peak later named Mount Adams. Mount Saint Helens was only twenty-five miles farther west, however.) The ocean lay *just yonder*, tangible at last. Englishmen had been there; the American Robert Gray had entered the river with his ship *Columbia*. But though part of the coast was known, the dark interiors of the land could still be frantically primordial, as William Clark learned on his return to meet the boats.

The setup was this. The smallest of the dugouts had reached the foot of the rapids, but the larger ones were still upstream, having trouble. Nor was Clark the only watcher. Across the river from where he settled down to wait were five long houses. Their inhabitants, who evidently had not noticed Clark as he descended the cliffs, were scattered out on ledges, staring at the fleet. At that point Clark half-negligently snapped a shot at a crane flying overhead, barely visible against fleecy clouds. A lucky hit: the bird dropped with a puff of feathers into the river. Instantly the Indians across the way, who never before had heard a gun, fled in panic into their long houses.

Not connecting the incidents but wanting to keep all Indians on a friendly footing, Clark called to Drouillard and the Field brothers, who were waiting nearby. Boarding the small boat, they rowed across the river. Along the way Clark shot at a duck. It, too, fell into the river.

Arrived at the closest house, the whites shoved aside the upright mats that blocked the doors and entered. Abject terror greeted them. Thirty-two men, women, and children crouched on the floor, heads hanging as they wailed and moaned and wrung their hands. The thought crossed Clark's mind that he could go among them tomahawking each in turn without encountering resistance.[7] It was an instinctive, bloodthirsty reaction born in his own dark, unexplored interior, and psychologists might like to play with it. In the event, however, Clark simply took each person by the hand and offered trinkets and bits of ribbon. As the people calmed, he sent his men to the other lodges to repeat the performance.

To seal the peace, he produced his pipe and loaded it with tobacco prior to passing it around for a ceremonial smoke. Sunlight falling through the slit in the roof led him to light the tobacco with a burning (magnifying) glass—no pocket matches in those days. At that the terror returned full force. Fire drawn by a demigod from the sun!

Realizing what he had done, Clark retreated outside and sat on a rock, holding the pipe in a welcoming position. No one ventured out, however, until Lewis arrived with Twisted Hair and Tetoharsky. The two Nez Percés jabbered questions. The Indians explained. They had heard roars like thunder; dead birds had fallen from the sky. Clearly the white man was from the sun. Twisted Hair clucked. No, this was the way of it. But what really wiped the fears away was the sight of Sacagawea coming up the hill with her eight-month-old son in his carrier on her back. "This . . . confirmed those people of our friendly intentions, as no woman ever accompanies a war party of Indians in this quarter."[8]

As the miles fell away, the desolation of the land increased. The lava-rock precipices, particularly those bordering the north side of the river, climbed hundreds of feet high. Over the eons they had shed huge chunks of basalt into the water. These dark, forbidding rocks split the river into many fretful channels, some stirred in places by whirlpools as if with a giant spoon. And these were but preludes. From the natives the explorers kept hearing the word *timm*, spoken in deep tones to imitate the roar of unseen falls ahead. As for the Indians, most continued to be of Sahaptian stock —Nez Percé and their relatives. Here and there, however, the whites began coming across squat, unkempt, loose-haired, bandy-legged members of the Chinookan language group.

The Chinookans were true flatheads. Foreheads, molded when infant bones were soft, sloped backward without indentation from the tip of the nose to a pointed cranium. Protrusions at the back of the head were also flattened out, to intensify the peaked-head look that among the Chinookans signified beauty and nobility. Two or three of the Columbia Chinookans had blankets of red and blue cloth; one wore a sailor's jacket. The articles clearly came from the mouth of the river. But did the whites who had traded the merchandise live in permanent posts, as the Indians seemed to indicate, or did they simply make occasional visits by ship to the coast? At that point the destitute explorers probably did not care greatly either way, so long as ship or post, even if manned by Britons, was well stocked with supplies.

On October 22, after speeding down a roaring channel between the south shore and a long island spiked with fantastic towers and pinnacles of basalt, they came to the brink of a massive, perpendicular, twenty-foot waterfall—*timm* water, shrouded in mist. If Lewis felt any resurgence of the awe that had gripped him at the Great Falls of the Missouri, it is not mentioned. Nor does Clark reveal anything more than a concern to get on down the river as efficiently as possible. Aesthetics and adventure were losing their savor.[9]

Because this was a heavily traveled Indian route, the captains had no trouble planning procedures. Accompanied by an old Indian, they located a rough, twelve-hundred-foot portage across solid rock and windblown sand. By hiring a few horses for transporting the heaviest bundles and letting the men carry the rest, they completed moving their cargo by nightfall and camped near "5 lod[g]es of natives drying and prepareing fish for market."

The steep, winding route would not do for the heavy dugouts, however. So the next morning Clark and the greater part of the men rowed the boats to the south side of the river and, with great difficulty, "hauled" them a quarter of a mile through the debris of a recently abandoned fishing camp. The fleas swarming there infested the men. Frantic, they tore off their hide clothing and worked naked so they could brush away the vermin as opportunity allowed. They could not abandon their overrun clothing, however, for they had nothing else to wear. So they took the fleas with them on a swift ride through a narrow channel that ended at the top of a snarling cascade whose total drop was about eight feet. The pitching banks allowed no room for portaging big dugouts, and the tremendous surge of the water created a maelstrom unsafe for the men to ride. Finding perches on rocks above the fury, the men lined the empty craft through with elkskin ropes. One broke loose and was pounced on by Indians waiting below the falls; ransoming the boat was costly. The full drop of falls and cataracts, a unit later called Celilo Falls, was, by Clark's calculations, thirty-eight and a half feet.

Another bit of foresight here. In a back eddy below the falls the captains saw two beautiful canoes different from any they had witnessed before. Tapering gracefully at both ends, they were unusually wide in the middle. Their sides, "dug thin" in Clark's words, were strengthened by crossbars; these also served as handles for lifting the relatively light vessels out of the water onto the shore. The bows were decorated by fanciful figureheads. Such canoes, they learned through their Nez Percé interpreters, were constructed to ride high waves and carry huge burdens. Since the Corps dugouts most assuredly could not do those things, Lewis sought out the owner of one of the vessels and, after much bargaining, obtained it in exchange for the expedition's small dugout plus a hatchet and some trinkets.[10]

A couple of miles below Celilo Falls, a massive black promontory thrust into the stream as if trying to touch a shorter span on the opposite bank. Accompanied by several Indians who lived near the obstruction, Clark climbed to its top to study what he later called the Short Narrows. It was awesome—the entire Columbia pouring into a gap forty-five yards wide as if into a high-pressure nozzle. Yet avoiding the stretch by portaging the heavy dugouts across the steep, broad obstruction was impossible.

After studying "this agitated gut swelling, boiling & whorling in every direction," Clark and Pierre Cruzatte, the principal boatman, decided it could be run. Presumably the captains sent all nonswimmers, including Sacagawea and her baby, and the most valuable goods around the cauldron. *But* he doesn't say so, as he does every other time the group is divided, and the exception tantalizes. Did *everyone* run the gut—a rougher run, Clark admitted later, than he had anticipated and one that amazed the Indians watching from the rocks above? After clearing the agitated whorls, the boats raced on through a slightly wider slot to a "very bad place, the current divided by two islands." *There,* at the Short Narrows, nonswimmers did carry the expedition's most valuable "papers Guns & amunition" by land while the dugouts took on the "very bad place" without casualties.

Between the Short Narrows and the next rapid, which Clark named the Long Narrows, stood a strong village of Wishram Indians, a Chinookan band. Called Nixluidix, the town consisted of twenty-one long, plank houses, their foundations dug deeply into the earth—the first wooden town the captains had seen since leaving the Illinois country. Along with a settlement of related Wascos located on the southern shore (a village the captains did not visit), Nixluidix dominated the twelve-mile stretch of furious water later named La Grande Dalle de la Columbia, or, more simply, The Dalles.[11]

From mid-April to mid-October, salmon of several species could be taken in almost unlimited numbers as they struggled upward toward their spawning grounds. Cleaned, dried, and pounded into a powder, the catches were stored in big baskets lined with fish skins. The storage baskets were then stacked in pyramids, seven below and five above. Mats were wrapped around the stacks and cinched tight with cords. Clark counted 107 stacks scattered around the environs of Nixluidix—by his estimate, ten thousand pounds of "neet" fish (fish unmixed with other substances). The fish meal, he was assured, would stay edible for several years and was a principal source of winter food. The odorous region—fish entrails, excrement, and decay in general—also attracted innumerable fleas and polecats.[12]

Nez Percés and other Sahaptian groups from higher up the Columbia came to the area to increase their own supplies of fish and also to swap their furs, hides, bear claws, bear grass (used in making baskets), and dried meat with Chinookan visitors for dried clams, tools whittled out of wood, cloth and metal items from ship traders who stopped by the Columbia's mouth, and choice dentalium shells that trickled south along the coast from Vancouver Island. The shells were about two inches long and curved like tiny walrus tusks. Chinooks liked to wear them in their noses, and a few Nez Percés imitated the custom, just as some Sahaptians flattened their children's heads according to the Chinookan style. Other exchanges at the great mart consisted of folk stories, dances, and whatever was staked on the interminable gambling games.

The Wascos and Wishrams who lived along The Dalles were as intent on retaining control of the Indian commerce that flowed through their part of the gorge as the Teton Sioux had been in mastering the trade of the middle Missouri. Of the two groups at The Dalles, the Wishrams were the more belligerent, and it was among them that Lewis and Clark camped during their descent of the river. The Indians were suspicious. Just what did these strangers want? According to Twisted Hair and Tetoharsky, the villagers were even planning to attack the expedition. No problem, the captains said, but made a show of examining the men's arms and issuing enough ammunition to give each soldier a hundred rounds.

Evidently the demonstration had its effect. The Indians became civil. With Twisted Hair and Tetoharsky acting as representatives of the Nez Percés, the captains arranged a peace between the tribes. Pax Americana, just what President Jefferson wanted, even out here where his nation exerted no sovereignty—as yet. From this moment on, Clark wrote with astounding naiveté, "those two bands or nations will be on the most friendly terms." In celebration Pierre Cruzatte fiddled and the soldiers danced, to the delight of the natives.

On October 25, the explorers successfully passed the Long Narrows, boiling and whirling just below the Wishram settlements. The thirty-five miles of relatively quiet water that followed served to take them out of the arid Columbian Plain into the humid rain forests of the coastal Northwest. The change was extraordinary. Average annual rainfall (which of course the explorers had no way of measuring) rises from fourteen inches at The Dalles to sixty-five inches—more than five feet!—on the western slope of the Cascade Mountains. Under the influence of the repeated deluges, the stunted pines and oak coverts the explorers had noticed at The Dalles gave way to Douglas firs, red cedars, spruce and hemlock of unbelievable size. Rioting underneath the high canopy of the branches were almost impenetrable tangles of lesser trees, brush, and giant ferns.

The Indians changed too. The Eneeshur band of Sahaptians, who lived near Celilo Falls, could not understand the Echeloot Wishrams who lived only half a dozen miles away.[13] Although salmon were an important part of the economy of the Sahaptians, and especially of the Nez Percé, their chief orientation was toward the grassy, untimbered land where their horse herds ranged. In the thick forests west of the Cascade Mountains, however, horses were useless. The Chinookans were people of the Pacific littoral and of its great rivers, and of fantastic canoes that were capable of riding across waves that would keep the cumbersome log dugouts of the Americans pinned to the shore for days at a time. They were a people of wood. They built plank houses covered with riven fir and cedar; they carved not only domestic utensils from the produce of the forest but also decorative figureheads for their boats and curious images of human forms to set up beside their wooden burial vaults.[14]

Lewis and Clark distrusted them. Part of the prejudice came from Twisted Hair and Tetoharsky, who accompanied the expedition through the Short and Long Narrows with great reluctance and then hurried home on horses they had purchased near Celilo Falls. One of the duties of the Corps, however, was to be friendly, so they could acquire, through observation and pantomime, knowledge that might some day be useful to their country. For themselves they needed to create a good will they could draw on while toiling back up the river the following spring.[15] Each day, accordingly, they smoked with most of the groups they encountered on the river, and at night entertained neighborhood villagers with the well-tested devices of fiddle music, the soldiers' dancing, York's exuberant jigging, and demonstrations of the airgun. They also needed to buy fish meal and edible dogs from the people they met, and so the underlying antipathy they felt did not surface visibly until they had reached the discomforts of the lower river.

The transition into wetness was complete by the time the Corps reached the infamous rapids that became known, during immigrant days, as the Upper and Lower Cascades of the Columbia—rapids that gave their name to the mountain range through which the river bored. (Today those once powerful and startlingly beautiful waters are buried underneath the reservoir backed up by Bonneville Dam.) Like the Short and Long Narrows higher upstream, both Cascades were compression rapids, the confined waters rushing "in a most horriable manner" among a clutter of boulders "both large and small." Clark promptly named the Upper Cascade the Great Shute (*sic*).

The Great Shute was so formidable that the captains decided they would have to portage the dugouts as well as the cargo around it. They accomplished the difficult feat by having the men place poles across the ragged crevices between the boulders littering the shore and then skidding the heavy boats across the timbers. The work, handicapped by rain and slippery footing, was so onerous that on reaching the Lower Cascade they decided to portage only their shrunken packs of merchandise and equipment and again risk the empty dugouts to the white turbulence. All five slammed through right side up.

A briefly joyful climax rewarded them. Just beyond the bottom of the last rapid, under the shadow of a stone pillar almost nine hundred feet high called Beacon Rock, they encountered the first tides of the ocean they were striving to reach. It would come as a shock to learn, gradually, that in spite of the fluctuations, the sea was still more than a hundred miles away.

They were miserable miles, even though the confining mountains soon gave way, in a stretch where the river ran northward, to broad, almost level forests broken by occasional prairies. For the days were short, fogs common, rains all but unending. Curious, light-fingered Indians were everywhere, some in high-prowed canoes that put the whites' clumsy dugouts to shame, others on the flat, tree-covered islands that dotted the widening river or in clearings on the shore. The natives carried guns, swords, sailors' clothing, copper and brass trinkets, and other articles that could have reached them only through white traders. And some of those traders, the Indians kept insisting, insofar as the Americans could read their gestures, lived in houses near the mouth of the river.[16]

The increasing ambivalence with which the two races regarded each other became evident on November 4, on what is now Sauvie Island near present-day Portland. (The Corps was skirting the north shore of the big island; as a result they did not see the many-channeled mouth of the Willamette River, which enters the Columbia from the south.) During the morning they landed at a village of twenty-five long houses. On the shore in front of the houses were fifty-two canoes, many very large and high in the bow. The inhabitants consisted of two hundred male Skilloots and their families, one of the many Chinookan bands. "We were treated very kindly by them," Clark wrote, "they gave us round root near the size of a hens egg roasted which they call *Wap-to* to eat." This was a happy introduction to a food more commonly spelled wapatoo (and known to later immigrants as swamp potato) that would serve the travelers well throughout the winter.

After purchasing four bushels of the roots, the Corps went on several miles before pausing to eat. Hard behind them came several canoe-loads of armed Skilloots dressed in garish combinations of sailor clothing and native garb. This meeting was not as pleasant as the earlier one. The Indians, who were armed, were "assumeing and disagreeable, however we Smoked with them and treated them with every attention & friendship." Taking advantage of the hospitality, the visitors adroitly purloined Clark's pipe tomahawk and a capote belonging to one of the interpreters. At that the captains' tempers slipped the leash. While the soldiers held their rifles at ready, Lewis and Clark searched both the persons and boats of the Indians.

In the captains' minds the effrontery was justified. "Finding us determined not to suffer any imposition . . . they showed their displeasure in the only way which they dared, by retreating in an ill humor to their village." But were the Indians pilfering as the word is defined by property-conscious Anglo-Saxons? Apologists say no and argue that the Indians were not appropriating the articles for personal gain, but to force the whites to notice them and enter into what one commentator calls "mutually rewarding reciprocal relations." All the Indians wanted was honest payment for the use of their territory, the theory holds.[17]

On November 7, three days and roughly eighty river miles from the Skilloot town, the explorers entered a broad indentation on the north side of the river. By then the Columbia, flowing mostly west again, was penetrating the Pacific Coast Range. The gentle banks that had prevailed farther upstream were gone. In their place were "high rugid hills with Steep assent the shore boalt [bold] and rockey, the fog so thick we could not See across the river." The tide was in, islands were numerous; without a hired Indian pilot, the travelers would have had difficulty finding the proper channel. (They also bought three dogs, some wapatoo roots, and salmon at the pilot's home village.) In the afternoon the fog lifted partially, though a light rain persisted, and they saw the great river of the West widening into what seemed an endless expanse of water. "Great joy in camp," Clark wrote. "we are in *view* of the *Ocian* . . . the great Pacific Octean which we have been so long anxious to See, and the roreing or noise made by the waves brakeing on the rockey Shores (as I suppose) may be heard distictly."

Technically he was wrong. Those waves were breaking on the steep shores of Gray's Bay, and the ocean was still about twenty direct-line miles away. And yet psychologically Clark was right. Gray's Bay had been named for the American ship captain Robert Gray, who, on the bright spring morning of May 11, 1792, had entered the mouth of the Columbia and a little later had anchored in that bay, the first white man to do so.[18] On entering the same bay from the east, the first whites to do so, the Corps of Discovery was finally tying the middle section of North America together.

There were other reasons to celebrate. Lewis and Clark had long since given up their initial plan, expressed in a letter of early April to President Jefferson, of returning at least as far as the headwaters of the Missouri before going into winter quarters. Now they were thinking in terms of the lower river. If a settlement, even a British settlement, did exist near the Columbia's mouth, as they understood the Indians to say, many of the problems of wintering in the storm-swept land, among natives of unpredictable moods, would be largely solved. If there was no settlement, as the captains were inclined to believe, at least a trading ship was likely to appear— perhaps the one commanded by a Captain Haley, whose name was well and favorably known to the Indians. They could replenish their alarmingly depleted store of trade goods; they could send messages, specimens, and copies of their journals to Jefferson, as he had requested. Above all, they would have the satisfaction of talking to others of their own kind, and of learning, in the language of home, what had been going on in the distant world during their long absence.

And so there was joy in camp.

Premature joy, as events developed. Because of frenzied weather and booming tides, they never did get their canoes to the river's mouth. Half of the group never did stand on the great north headland known as Cape Disappointment and look across the white-capped rollers that were pounding toward the coast, uninterrupted, all the way from the Kuril Islands north of Japan.

The miseries began in the very camp from which they peered with such joy at what they supposed was the ocean. The shore was so narrow they escaped high tide only by spreading their sleeping mats on heaps of round stones at the edge of the forest—in the rain, inevitably. The next day, November 8, they crept along the shore for a meager eight miles. The waves were high. The dugouts twisted and sheared and bobbed. Many of the crew—Clark listed Reuben Field, Peter Wiser, Hugh McNeal, and Sacagawea—vomited in agonized seasickness over the sides of the dugouts they were in. (What of the baby? No one says.) Giving up finally, they camped on a narrow shingle between the water and a hill too steep and brushy for the hunters to ascend in search of food.

That night the roar of the rising tide awakened them. Scrambling to the dugouts, they unloaded them in the rain-swept darkness and boosted the baggage onto log platforms. The next day they spent struggling to keep the tossing boats from being crushed by gale-driven driftwood trees two hundred feet long and up to seven feet thick. But, Clark said, the men were still cheerful, thinking of the nearby ocean.[19]

Whenever the gales slackened briefly during the next several days, the explorers reloaded the dugouts and rowed toward the next bay to the west—Baker's Bay, named by George Vancouver's men for a trader who had entered the Columbia only a few weeks behind Robert Gray. Trading ships often anchored there, or so the whites understood from Indian gestures. They might even find the rumored settlement. But the approach was blocked by a cliff-sided promontory later named Point Ellice. (Clark labeled it Point Dismal on his sketch map.) Each time the dugouts neared the obstruction, screaming winds and heavy seas drove them back to a landing that seemed worse than the one before. In one place they had to build their fires and lay their beds on a driftwood raft that during high tide was "all on flote." In another place they sought to protect their canoes from the waves by filling them with rocks and sinking them.

For eleven days and nights rain fell almost ceaselessly. Elkskin clothing and moccasins rotted. Tents and sails were in tatters. The Corps's merchandise, which was their only bank account, was constantly soaked and much was spoiled. Only occasionally were they able to spear a few salmon, shoot a few waterfowl, or buy a few roots from passing Indians. Otherwise they made their meals from the dry, pounded, tasteless fish they had laid by for emergencies far back at Celilo Falls. They watched enviously as the Indians rode as easily as gulls over the towering waves—"the best Canoe navigaters I ever Saw," Clark wrote. Resentment and frustration filled him: "the most disgreeable time I have experienced confined to a tempiest [tempestuous] coast wet, where I can neither git out to hunt, return to a better situation, or proceed on."[20]

Gradually, though, they did proceed. First Lewis and a small advance party managed to break around Point Dismal into the eastern part of Baker's Bay. From there they could see the full expanse of the five-mile-wide ocean gateway between Cape Disappointment on the north and Point Adams on the south.[21] Neither town nor ship was visible. But some of the beaches, though windswept, were broad and sandy. An abandoned Indian settlement of thirty-six plank houses stood nearby; the ruins were full of fleas, but the Corps could take away enough boards to build shelters at a safe distance. Also nearby were two camps of Indians who called themselves Chinooks—the first meeting of either captain with the dominant tribe of the area and one whose name soon spread generically to related bands speaking the same language. After sending a suggestion to Clark that the Corps move to this propitious spot as wind and tides allowed, Lewis continued west—on foot, because the waves rolling in from the sea were rougher than he wanted to attempt by boat. His intent: to investigate the bays on the coast north of Cape Disappointment (Vancouver's chart showed at least one) for possible ships and/or winter quarters.

By the evening of the 16th, the rest of the Corps were ashore in Baker's Bay, at a location northwest across the river from the present city of Astoria, Oregon. The men worked busily at creating the first decent camp, relatively speaking, they had lived in for more than a week. When Lewis's party rejoined the main group on the 17th, morale was up again.

Who else wanted a closeup view of the ocean that had been their goal across two-thirds of a continent? William Clark, born explorer and mapmaker, certainly did. He told all who wished to go with him to be ready at daylight on the 18th. At the appointed time he started hiking with Sergeants Pryor and Ordway; Shannon, Colter, Wiser, and Bratton; Charbonneau, and York. Joseph and Reuben Field, who had been with Lewis's party, went along for a second look. The rest of the Corps stayed put; they could see all the salt water they wanted from their new camp.

After climbing to the rocky top of the cape and watching, in astonishment, giant breakers exploding against the cliffs, they turned north. They walked and slept in intermittent rains, crashed through brush, traversed grassy slopes, and carved their names on trees, as their predecessors had done. Reuben Field shot a condor with an amazing wingspan of nine and a half feet. Reuben's brother, Joe, killed a hitherto unknown species of black-tailed deer; it provided, on the morning of the 19th, "a Sumptious brackfest of Venison which was roasted on Stiks exposed to the fire." That same day Clark named a distant, striking height of land "after my particular friend Lewis." Today it is known as North Head. They saw no ships, although they undoubtedly scanned the ocean's misty face as closely as Lewis's group had.

Perhaps they wondered, as some later critics have, why President Jefferson did not send a ship to succor them.[22] Yet why should he have? Supposedly the expedition had left St. Louis with all the equipment it needed. On April 7, 1805, at the time of departing from the Mandan villages, Lewis had written Jefferson that he expected to reach the Pacific and return at least as far as the headwaters of the Missouri before winter set in. He had said nothing about being short of supplies. Schedules could go awry, of course; indeed, the Corps might never reach the Pacific. In view of those uncertainties, exactly when should a reinforcing ship appear off the mouth of the Columbia? And would a Congress speckled with Jefferson's political enemies authorize outfitting a vessel—an expensive undertaking for an administration that trumpeted of economy—to circle Cape Horn on so tenuous a mission? Sensing these deterrents long in advance, Jefferson had provided Meriwether Lewis with the only reasonable escape available: the right to contact whatever trading vessels he saw for whatever he needed, even to returning home on one if such proved necessary.

The right, however, did not bring a vessel with it. That being true, what should be done now?

Making the decision seems to have plagued the captains more than any other problem they had faced so far. They hated to give up all hope of a vessel, and yet they could not stay in this estuary, exposed to an endless sequence of storms. A week's hard experience had showed them that they could not count on their guns to provide them with the food they needed, yet they did not have enough merchandise left to buy a winter's supply of food from the hard-bargaining Indians.

If they did not stay, where should they go? The men who accompanied Clark to the coast expressed a desire to winter near Celilo Falls.[23] The climate there would be dry—but cold and short of the kind of large animals from which clothing could be made. Another possibility was the Sandy River, which drained off Mount Hood into the Columbia a little west of the Lower Cascade. Meadows broke the forests there; deer would probably abound and the climate would be mild.

So there was talk. Yet after Clark returned to the Baker's Bay camp a little after midday on November 20, the days went by as though nothing serious pressed on anyone's mind. The captains made chiefs and distributed medals among the canoe-borne Indians who kept coming in and out despite a ferocious new storm. (Clark simply could not reconcile himself to such weather: "O! how horriable is the day waves brakeing with great violence against the Shore throwing the water into our camp &c. all wet and confined to our Shelters.") Red traders, impervious to the deluge in conical hats tightly woven of split twigs, hawked their wares. Both Lewis and Clark yearned for a luxurious robe of otter skins that one Indian would sell only for more blue beads, a valued medium of exchange throughout the Northwest, than the Americans could afford to dip out of the expedition's skimpy supply. Eventually they solved the problem by persuading Sacagawea to part with a belt of blue beads she habitually wore around her waist; in return they gave her a blue cloth coat that was more adaptable than her buffalo-skin robe.

Another trade article in great demand was produced by a Chinook madam, wife of a chief, who showed up with six of her daughters and nieces "for the purpose of gratifying the passions of our men." Clark's diary entries for November 21 grew puritanical. The young women's countenances, he admitted grudgingly, were pretty—if one ignored their slanted foreheads. But they were short of stature, their hair hung loose and long, they had "large swelled legs & thighs." Their limbs were tattooed. Venereal scabs were plain on some of them. They "sport openly with our men." But there was no use objecting: "we divided some ribin between our men . . . to bestow on their favorite Lasses, this plan to save the knives & more valueable articles."

What finally ended the indecision was the arrival, late on November 23, of seven Clatsop traders from the south side of the river. Undisturbed by the whites' refusal to buy the furs they offered for sale, the Indians cheerfully suggested their own territory as winter quarters. Over yonder, their gestures said, elk abounded, a source of food and of skins for clothing. The ocean and the Columbia's estuary were close by. The first meant the whites could prepare salt to improve the taste of their food. The second would allow them to contact, through the Indians, any trading vessel that dropped anchor in the river's protected bays. The one obvious drawback would be living for months in the dreadful weather, as the newcomers considered it, of the coast.

Reluctant to impose their own preferences on the men—nothing could be more damaging to already shaky morale—the captains called for a vote from everyone, soldiers, interpreters, black York and red Sacagawea. A few favored going to Celilo Falls; more declared for Sandy River. But the majority followed the captains in choosing the Clatsop lands, with this qualification: if, after an examination, hunting and living conditions proved inadequate, they could move up the river.[24]

On the 25th they started out. Not daring to risk the broad estuary in their log dugouts, they labored upstream to a narrower spot, crossed, and crept back along the shore to Tongue Point, a promontory about four miles long but only fifty yards wide at its narrowest section. They had succeeded in rowing around this obstruction when a new storm pinned them to its exposed ocean side.

On the 29th Lewis, always impatient, broke loose. The big dugouts might not be able to handle the huge swells, but the small Indian canoe he had purchased at The Dalles could. Accompanied by Drouillard, Reuben Field, Colter, Shannon, and Labiche, he explored the coast of what Clark would later name Meriwether Bay (now Young's Bay) in his honor. After considerable trial and error, he found an inlet into which the Netul River flowed. (Today it is the Lewis and Clark River.) The party followed its windings through marshy ground thick with small trees and brush, a mix they called "slashes." The knolls rising out of the slashes supported much larger evergreens, and when they came to one whose top was some thirty feet above high tide level and when they saw elk tracks everywhere around it, they decided this would do for their winter camp. On the morning of December 5, three of them started back to summon the others. Two stayed behind to hunt. Nothing was said, at least in the journals, about a two- or three-week examination before a final choice was made.[25]

Waiting for Lewis's return was another doleful experience for William Clark. Winds strong enough to blow down trees raged through the camp. Thick smoke from wet fuel hurt Clark's eyes. The roar of the sea depressed him more and more. It had assaulted his ears for "24 days Since we arrived in Sight of the Great Western; (for I cannot say Pacific) Ocian as I have not seen one pacific day . . . [just] emenc waves . . . tempestous and horiable."[26]

Though there were elk in the vicinity of Tongue Point, the hunters were rarely able to bring down one of the animals as they raced away among the thick trees and through the pelting rain.

Except for occasional hawks and waterfowl, their food again was fish meal boiled in salty water dipped from the ocean side of the point. Digestive disturbances left Clark and some of the men too unwell to eat even that. Deciding the salt water was to blame, he directed the cooks to use fresh water from the upper side of the point. It helped, he thought.

During the days of waiting he wandered around the vicinity, observing plants and wildlife and faithfully recording what he saw. It seems likely, too, that he passed some of the time reading from Alexander Mackenzie's account of his own crossing of the continent, with its climactic lines, "I now mixed up some vermilion, in melted grease, and inscribed, in large characters, on the South-East side of the rock on which we had slept, this brief memorial—'Alexander Mackenzie, from Canada, by land, the twenty-second of July, one thousand seven hundred and ninety-three.' "

With that in mind the American found a large tree and carved into its bark, "Capt William Clark December 3rd 1805. By Land. U. States in 1804–05." In thus imitating Mackenzie, he may have only been reassuring himself in his doldrums. Or he may have been announcing to all who read his words, which he copied in his journal, that Mackenzie's feat had been matched. Or the lines may have carried implications of national sovereignty to come, as Mackenzie's most certainly had.

Or perhaps all three motives were involved. Today there is no way to be sure.

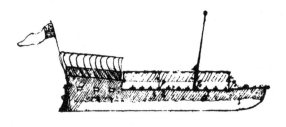

SIXTEEN

The Farthest Reach

With what must have been mixed feelings, the Corps toiled up the Netul past slashes and through a wide slough to the foot of Lewis's hill. Peering through the rain, Clark approved the choice, as most of the men probably did, by damning it with faint praise. "this is certainly the most eligable Situation for our purposes of any in its neighbourhood."[1] So what else was in the neighborhood?

After carrying their baggage up the slope out of reach of the tide, after setting up the tripods from which cooking pots would be suspended, each over its own fire, and after pitching what was left of their tents, the soldiers started clearing space for the quarters that would be named Fort Clatsop. It was to be square, fifty feet to a side, and consist of two parallel rows of rooms. Running north and south, the rows faced each other across a twenty-foot-wide parade ground where the troops could be reviewed.

The western row would hold four rooms, the largest of which was designated for the captains. It was to be graced by a wall fireplace whose chimney protruded into the parade ground, an arrangement that allowed more interior space for furniture crafted by Joseph Field—a table, chairs, and, for each officer, "a wide slab hued to write on."[2] York probably cooked for them on that fireplace. A roofed sentinel box stood outside the captain's door.

On either side of the captains' quarters were somewhat smaller rooms, each with a chimneyed fireplace in its center. Charbonneau, Sacagawea, and their child were to occupy one. The other, the orderly room, served as the office of the sergeant of the guard and his three men, a rotating assignment. It may be that York slept in the orderly room, where he could be quickly summoned by his owner. At the north end of the row was an even smaller room destined for the smoking and storing of meat.

The row on the opposite side of the parade ground held three rooms, each with a center fireplace. One was eighteen by fifteen feet; the other two, sixteen by fifteen—hardly roomy, yet each housed eight men.

The ends of the parade ground were walled off by sharpened pickets. The main gate faced south toward the boat landing. The stockade at the other end of the courtyard contained a small gate that gave egress to a freshwater spring only about thirty feet away. (The water in the slough was brackish.) There were two latrines, locations not specified. The state of the weather considered, one hopes they were provided with roofing of some sort.

The walls of the cabins were built "of the streightest and most beautifullest logs" (Clark's phrase) and daubed with mud.[3] Planks served for roofs and floors. The first trees felled for that purpose —whether Douglas fir or Sitka spruce cannot be determined— rived easily into boards up to ten feet long and two wide. But they seem to have soon run out of that wood, for Clark wrote on December 17, "The trees which our men have felled latterly Split verry badly." On the 19th, accordingly, he sent Pryor with eight men in two dugouts to a vacant Indian long house on the shore of Meriwether Bay, there to help themselves to as many boards as they could load on. Poor boards, Clark grumbled later.[4] But they were free. No Indian objection is recorded.

At first only about half of the Corps were involved in clearing away trees and pulling stumps from the site of the fort. On December 8, the day after the landing, twelve hunters departed in two canoes in pursuit of elk. (How different from stalking buffalo on the dry plains!) That same day Clark set out with five more men to blaze a trail to some site beside the ocean where a crew, yet to be appointed, could obtain salt by tediously boiling off the water. The assignment was necessary because too much salt had been cached beside the Missouri, awaiting the return journey. Of what remained, the last grains had disappeared along the lower Columbia, leaving the men with no savoring for their insipid diet of pounded fish, boiled roots, and overly lean elk. A physiological need may have also been involved. The men worked hard, per-

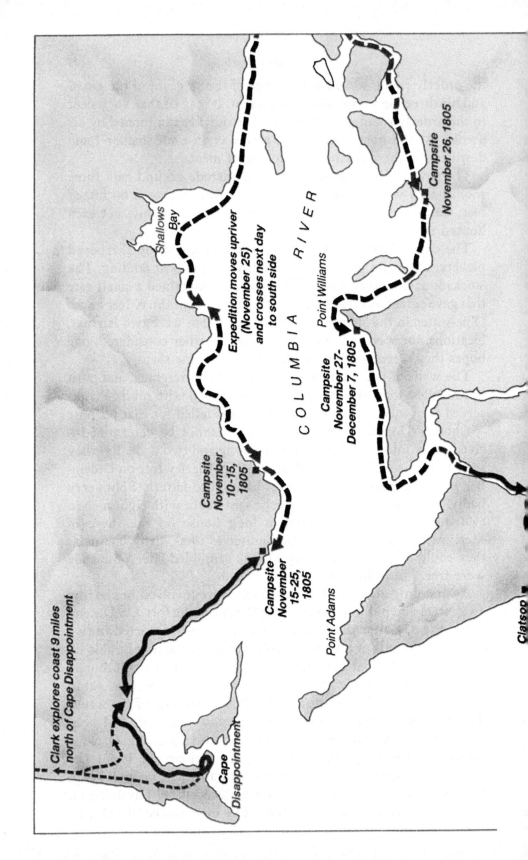

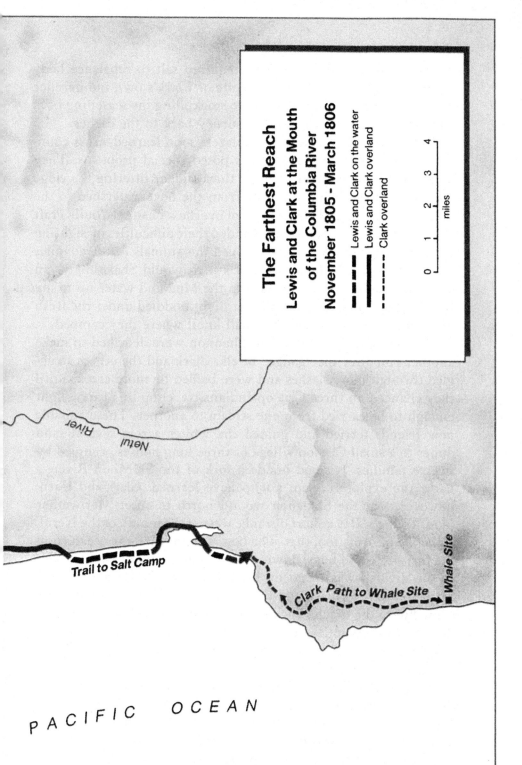

The Farthest Reach
Lewis and Clark at the Mouth
of the Columbia River
November 1805 - March 1806

Lewis and Clark on the water
Lewis and Clark overland
Clark overland

0   1   2   3   4
miles

Netul River

Trail to Salt Camp

Clark Path to Whale Site

Whale Site

PACIFIC OCEAN

spired profusely, and may have required salt to rebalance body chemistry. In any event and in spite of Clark's own indifference to salt, the captains gave priority to stockpiling the seasoning both for the stay at the fort and the journey back to the caches.

As Captain Clark and his trailblazers soon learned, cross-country travel in a watery wilderness posed special problems. They scrambled arduously through the thick timber littering the ridge that divided the Netul drainage from the next watershed to the west, became entangled in a maze of overflow channels, built a raft to cross a deep creek, and compounded their difficulties by sighting a large "gange of elk." They pursued the animals for three miles "through bogs which the wate of a man would Shake for ½ an acre, and maney places I Sank into the Mud and water up to my hips." They killed one elk and that night huddled under the fresh hide while rain drenched the small knoll where they camped.

The next day Drouillard and Shannon were detached to make another run after the "gange" of elk. Clark and the others struggled through more slashes and were baffled by more creeks until they chanced on three Clatsop Indians traveling in a canoe light enough to be carried from one stream to another. These amiable new friends ferried and guided the whites across several sand dunes to a small Clatsop village of three long houses occupied by twelve families. It stood beside a fork of the Skipanon River, a name the explorers seem not to have learned. Clark did learn, however, that the Skipanon wound north to enter Meriwether (now Young's) Bay a short distance west of the mouth of the Netul. Valuable information, that. The best way to reach the ocean from the fort—to avoid bogs, down timber, and the wind-swept ridges of the divide—was to go by boat down the Netul and up the Skipanon to the village and then walk a few hundred yards over a low hill to the beach. The savings in effort would be well worth the increase in miles—a tantalizing thought as the explorers slogged back cross-country to help Drouillard and Shannon carry the meat they had procured to the fort builders.[5]

Because Drouillard and Shannon were the Corps's best shots, they were soon sent out again, this time up the right fork of the Netul, to kill as many more elk as possible. (Salt making was delayed; everyone was busy at other things.) On Friday the 13th —no bad luck there—the two hunters rowed back with word they had killed and butchered, at widely separated spots, eighteen of the high-horned animals. This feat, a Fort Clatsop record, served to introduce Clark to rainy-season elk hunting in northwestern Oregon, and he did not relish the experience.

The general practice was for hunters chosen by the captains to go by dugout along one or another of the sluggish, twisting waterways to areas that, for the most part, were assigned them. On reaching the designated spot, the nimrods beached their boats and pushed afoot through heavy timber to the edges of the bogs and into the more open slashes where hunting was likely to be best. Having killed an animal, they skinned it, disemboweled it (it would spoil quickly if not gutted), quartered it, and then lugged the pieces and the valuable hide back to the dugout, a carry that might range in length from a few hundred yards to two or three miles. Whenever sizable numbers of carcasses were involved, the hunters rowed back to the fort for help.

On December 15, while Lewis supervised construction, Clark went with sixteen men in three dugouts to retrieve the eighteen dismembered elk slain by Drouillard and Shannon. No one, not even Clark, was exempt from the carrying, and he also cooked at least one meal for the group. Darkness caught them before the boats were loaded. Rain was falling as usual. "when we lay down," Clark wrote afterwards, "the water soon Came under us and obliged us to rise." They sat up the rest of the night, shivering under elkskins, as the salt party had.

The next morning he filled two dugouts with the parts of thirteen elk. Then, leaving seven men to fetch the remaining carcasses, he headed for the fort. A desperate trip. "The winds violent Trees falling in every derection, whorl winds, with gusts of rain Hail & Thunder, this kind of weather lasted all day, Certainly one of the worst days that ever was!" . . . plus, at the end, no little danger from the high waves the storm kicked up on the river. For the next few days, he said, several of the men went around complaining of having hurt themselves while handling the meat.[6]

Those rain-forest elk were not as satisfactory a food as one might think. The animals at that season were lean, and their flesh was stringy. The weather, moreover, was mild and would stay that way, except for several days late in January and early February when snow fell and ice dulled the surface of the sloughs. In such a climate, meat grew tainted before it could be brought to the smokehouse, and even there it did not always stay fresh until consumed.

The point came home at Christmas. There was double cause for celebration: the day itself and the fact that the fort was near enough completion that the men had moved in out of the rain the day before. Everyone tried to be merry. The enlisted men roused the officers at daylight (not very early at that season) with a volley of rifle fire, a cheer, and a song. Presents were exchanged. Clark does not say what he gave, just what he received—articles of clothing from Lewis, a pair of moccasins from Whitehouse, a small Indian basket from Goodrich, and two dozen white weasel tails from Sacagawea. The captains divided half of the expedition's remaining tobacco among the smokers; nonsmokers, a decided minority, received silk handkerchiefs. To which Clark added, "The day proved Showery wet and disagreeable." By all rights they should have feasted, "had we any thing either to raise our Sperits [i.e., liquor] or even gratify our appetites, our Diner consisted of pore Elk, so much Spoiled that we eate it thro' mear necessity, Some Spoiled pounded fish, and a few roots."[7]

The tasteless diet, the captains probably realized, was also unhealthful. (We know today that lean elk, dried fish, and wapatoo bulbs were low in caloric intake for active workers.)[8] Debilitation was to be avoided partly because it interfered with daily work but more because it would sorely handicap the four thousand-mile dash for St. Louis that Lewis and Clark hoped to begin as soon as spring came. Accordingly they set about trying to improve the quality of the daily meals as much as their limited resources allowed.

Their main dependence had to be on foods brought them by the Indians. From that standpoint, Fort Clatsop, isolated by several miles of forest and stream from the native villages scattered along the Columbia estuary to the north and the ocean beaches to the west, was not well situated. Members of the expedition seldom visited the towns, but waited for the Clatsops and the more distant Chinooks and Cathlamets to come to them by canoe, as a small but steady stream of natives did. As word of the whites' needs spread, they began bringing in, for sale, furs for clothing and occasional edible dogs, sturgeon, and, more frequently, wapatoo roots. Like shrewd bargainers everywhere, the Indians enjoyed haggling and had sharpened their wits in their dealings with the trading ships that now and then dropped anchor inside the Columbia's mouth. Quickly realizing how much Fort Clatsop depended on them, they jacked their prices beyond what the captains considered reasonable and certainly beyond what they could afford to pay, day in and day out, from their shrunken stores of merchandise.

Wapatoo furnished a prime example. The plants did not grow near the coast but were harvested from inland swamps and the bottoms of shallow ponds and lakes. Women did the work. They paddled small canoes to a likely gathering place, slid over the edge of the craft into the water, often neck deep, and worked the bulbs loose with their feet.[9] They—women often traded as well as harvested—took whatever surplus they accumulated to the Columbia's estuary, where they traded the roots to the coastal Indians for manufactured goods—blankets, cloth, buttons, sheet metal, knives, kettles, beads, and mirrors—which the latter had picked up from passing ships. The exchanges put a lot of edible bulbs in the hands of the coastal tribes—roots they hoped, opportunistically, to sell at a profit to the unexpected white newcomers from the east. Unaware of the complexities of the trade, the captains felt they were being exploited beyond reason, and they resented it.

Whenever an opportunity arose for them to act on their own, independent of middlemen, they seized it vigorously. Shortly after Christmas they directed Joseph Field, William Bratton, and George Gibson to establish the delayed salt works at the nearest suitable place on the Pacific coast, a project that would make tainted elk more palatable and thus move the Corps closer to self-sufficiency. At about the same time traveling Indians brought word that a whale had been beached in the estuary. Immediately Lewis prepared to take a crew there, thinking that fried blubber and roots cooked in whale oil would be highly nourishing, as, indeed, they were—consider the Eskimos. Unhappily, the effort was defeated by several days of high winds.

A second chance came early in January with the report that an exceptionally large whale had been washed ashore near a village of Tillamook Indians, some thirty-five miles south of the fort.[10] This time it was Clark who put together a small bundle of trade goods in the hope of buying a part of the beached creature from whoever owned it. He selected twelve men to go with him in two boats, enough to hold large quantities of blubber. Just before departure, Sacagawea begged to go along. She had not visited the great water during Clark's trip to Cape Disappointment and beyond. Now that there was a monstrous fish to see, she felt it would be hard not to view the combined marvels. He acquiesced, although it meant she would have to float rivers, thread swamps, and climb mountains with her child, not yet a year old, riding in his carrier on her back.

Although stormy water kept the blubber seekers from reaching the Skipanon River, as Clark wished, they were able to duck into a parallel creek that took them in the general direction they wanted to go. When night fell they ate most of a freshly killed elk for supper and then camped comfortably beside a roaring fire of driftwood, under—rare treat—a clear sky luminous with the light of a full moon. The next day they left their canoes beside landmarks Clark recognized from his earlier trip to the coast, clambered over sand dunes to the beach, and turned south until they reached the salt camp. It was well located between tide pools and the fresh water of today's Necanicum River. Wood from the nearby forest kept five large iron kettles boiling night and day, evaporating water from good, pure white salt, some of which the mess cooks at the fort were already using. Also close by were four large, plank houses occupied by a mix of Clatsop and Tillamook Indians. The natives had been kind and attentive, the salt makers said. On the strength of that recommendation, Clark hired one to guide the party across the towering promontory now called Tillamook Head.

The trail was so steep in places "we were obliged to Support and draw our selves up by the bushes & roots." The view from the top was tremendous—waves breaking into towering jets of spray around the huge, detached rocks in the sea near the base of a series of headlands. Off to the north the mouth of the Columbia sprawled, dotted with islands and fed, particularly on its south side, by a maze of crooked, timber-girt streams. The travelers did not sightsee for long. Still ahead stretched an even more arduous traverse where "if we had unfortunately made one false Step we Should eneviateably have fallen into the Sea and dashed against the rocks in an instant." As a consequence they went slowly and yet reached, in midafternoon, what was left of the whale.

The leviathan had washed ashore near a settlement of Tillamook Indians. They had gone to work on it immediately, cutting off big chunks of blubber they piled in a wooden trough with hot stones that cooked out part of the oil. The liquid was stored in containers made from the whale's own bladder and intestines, and the partially prepared blubber was set aside for later eating. Before the villagers were well started on their butchering, other Indians from throughout the area appeared, drawn by the seemingly instantaneous intertribal communications network of canoes. By the time the whites arrived, nothing was left of the whale but a skeleton that Clark estimated, perhaps overenthusiastically, as being 105 feet long.

As first on the scene, the Tillamooks had harvested well. Clark thought they should have been generous with their riches. Instead they were parsimonious (in his eyes), parting with only three hundred pounds of blubber and a few gallons of oil in exchange for his entire stock of trade goods. To these gleanings he painstakingly added his usual ethnographic and geographic notes, a work briefly interrupted when an Indian stranger in the town reportedly sought to kill Hugh McNeal for his blanket.

The next morning, loaded with parcels of blubber and oil in addition to the bedding and personal gear in their knapsacks, the party faced with a "Shudder . . . the dreadfull road on which we have to return." They reached their boats at sunset, very fatigued. But the tide was favoring and Clark insisted they go ahead. At 10:00 P.M. they were at the fort after what must have been a spooky ride through the mist with little more than the sound of surf on the beach to guide them. The blubber, doled out among the messes with great care, lasted until January 29.

By that time the captains and men were operating under two new procedures laid down on January 1, 1806, shortly after the fort's completion. Meriwether Lewis, who for long periods had kept no records other than rough field notes, was now the official keeper of the journals. And security measures concerning visiting Indians had been tightened considerably.

The change that held the greatest significance for the future was the extraordinary number of essays Lewis poured forth day after day in keeping with Jefferson's directive that the explorers note for posterity as many physical and cultural characteristics of the distant land as possible. What is strange about this performance is that Clark, busy with his maps, apparently—but only apparently—copied down, almost verbatim, each of Lewis's long journal entries, day after wearisome day. As spelling and phrasing indicated, Lewis never copied Clark during this period.

The two men kept their diaries in separate notebooks. But when Reuben Gold Thwaites edited and printed the complete journals in 1904–5 as part of the centennial observation of the historic crossing, he coalesced the entries. He put Lewis's entry of January

1, 1806, first and followed it with Clark's duplication. So it went, every day, Lewis and then Clark. Now, why did this rigamarole come about? Why didn't Clark keep his own diary, filling it with his own pungent observations?

The probability is that he did keep a set of running notes like those that elsewhere have been identified either as field notes or first drafts. In the main, however, he was involved at Fort Clatsop with collating his many sketch maps and the astronomical observations he and Lewis had taken at key points along the way. That done, he incorporated the results, in scale, into the big map of the West he had begun drawing at Fort Mandan during the spring of 1805. The potential importance of this carefully drawn map to the expansionary forces of the young United States hardly needs emphasis.

The map work was finished, by and large, on February 14.[11] Studying the results focused the captains' attention on what they needed to do during their return journey. Most important, the map showed clearly that their Shoshoni guide, Old Toby, had been right when he had said that travelers could cross the Continental Divide from Traveler's Rest near the mouth of the Flathead River (now the Bitterroot) to the junction of the Dearborn and Missouri above Great Falls, in four days. That route would be at least five hundred miles shorter than the hairpin curve the outward bound expedition had followed south along the Missouri to Lemhi Pass and then north again. The water along the new path might not be navigable, but it needed checking anyway. Also Lewis wanted to take another look at Maria's River, to learn how far north it really did extend. Finally, they had promised, when writing Jefferson from Fort Mandan, that they would explore the Yellowstone, a trip Clark could make while Lewis was on the Maria's.

The separation of the captains would subject the single journal Lewis was keeping to possible destruction. Hoping to guard against such contingencies, Jefferson had ordered that duplicate records be kept. And so, at some unstated date after his maps had been completed, Clark began his dreary chore as copyist. He was still at it when the expedition left Fort Clatsop.[12]

He was not entirely slavish. At times he nodded a little and got blocks of text slightly out of order. He omitted occasional sentences. Now and then he added material from his own notes. He made slight alterations. For instance, Lewis wrote at one point concerning their diet, "I have become so perfectly reconciled to the dog that I think it an agreeable food and would prefer it vastly to lean Venison or Elk." Clark could not swallow that. He omitted the sentence and wrote in its place, "as for myself I have not become reconsiled to the taste of this animal as yet."[13]

It is unlikely, also, that Lewis wrote each day's long entry under the date ascribed to it. What he did do was jot down a brief summary of each day's events, including in it, repetitively, such lugubrious phrases as "rained last night as usial," "not any occurences today worthy of note," and "everything moves on in the old way." He then used the short opening paragraph as a not-always-relevant hook on which to hang a discourse dealing with one of the broad variety of topics Jefferson had directed him to consider. He lovingly described the plants he and Clark had seen west of the Rockies (sagebrush, Oregon grapes, ferns, licorice, rushes, many varieties of berries, including cranberries, whose hard wood the Indians used for making wedges to hollow out canoes); trees (long-needled pines and short-needled firs, hemlocks, and spruces, including one fir 36 feet in circumference and 230 feet tall); birds (condors, woodpeckers, grouse, swans, and on and on, at least fifty species altogether); domestic animals (horses and Indian dogs); fishes and reptiles. Many of the life forms he dwelt on were new to the science of his time.

His eye for detail was sharp, whether he was discussing the form of a leaf, the length of a bird's beak, or the way a mule deer ran. He was attentive to Indian culture—their plank houses and hats of bark and bear grass, their scanty clothing, their foods, domestic utensils, funeral customs, and, in particular, their canoes. He commented on the place of women and old people in the social structure, and dutifully noted how the former were isolated during their menstrual periods. In many places he included rough drawings to illustrate his descriptions.[14]

He was prescient. Jefferson, it will be recalled, had hoped the expedition would discover routes over which the furs of Canada and of the headwaters of the Columbia could be diverted, by short land portages and canoes, to the Missouri and thence into American hands. The unexpected height of the Rockies and the lack of navigable streams near the Continental Divide had erased that hope. But in reviewing what Clark and he had seen west of the Rockies, Meriwether Lewis glimpsed another avenue for commerce. Fine horses, easily acquired, thrived among the Shoshoni and Nez Percé. "This abundance and cheapness of horses," he predicted, "will be extremely advantageous to those who may hereafter attemt the fir trade to the East Indies by way of the Columbia River and the Pacific Ocean"[15]—an exact reverse of what had been originally promulgated. In John Jacob Astor's hands, a similar concept would lead, a few years later, to the founding of Astoria, the first (and short-lived) American settlement on the Pacific.

The Indian tribes of the lower Columbia were cheerful, hospitable, tranquil, and, except for habitual pilfering, almost devoid of spirit—or so the captains reported.[16] The enlisted men liked to socialize with them. Lewis and Clark got on with them equally well and varied their bargaining sessions by handing out small medals and mentioning, in such Clatsop phrases as they were picking up, the glories of the United States.

This easygoing situation did not accord with military regulations as laid down by an army that since the Revolution had been employed mainly in waging intense battles against tribes resisting the loss of their homes east of the Mississippi River. Nor did distance reduce the need to heed authority. As soon as Fort Clatsop was completed, Lewis and Clark brought procedures into line by issuing an order of the day whose relative mildness would have won Jefferson's approval, while at the same time its strictures against fraternizing would satisfy the military's habitual suspicion of all aborigines.

No member of the garrison, the captain's directive read, should abuse, assault, or strike the natives, unless provocation came first from the Indians. However, the soldiers could refuse to let troublesome natives enter their rooms. Above all, no Indian could stay inside the fort's gates after sunset.[17]

At first the Indians resented being herded outside into the rain as darkness fell. Later they seemed to accept the exclusion as part of the strangers' strange way of doing things. And the captains did soften the sting by ordering exceptions in the case of small groups containing women and children and/or a chief of local importance. But whenever a potentially dangerous situation arose, military prudence ruled. Such was the case of Tahcum, a principal chief of the Chinooks, who stopped by the fort on February 20 with twenty-five armed men. In spite of the Indians' weapons, the visit was intended as a get-acquainted call, and the captains were glad to see the group. The Chinooks were the dominant tribe of the area, but because they lived on the north bank of the Columbia, the Americans had had little contact with them since moving to the south bank late in November. As a matter of national diplomacy, therefore, Lewis and Clark plied the group with smoke and afterwards fed them lavishly, although twenty-six extra mouths were a drain on their limited stocks. They gave Tahcum the standard medal and no doubt extolled the virtues of peace and American trade, as they almost always did. But at sunset they ejected the visitors.

Afterwards Lewis felt called upon to explain the action. "We all know," he wrote in his journal, "that the treachery of the aborigines of America and the too great confidence of our countrymen in their sincerity and friendship, has caused the destruction of many hundreds of us." As military men, Lewis and Clark believed that statement. Forts had been captured and ships burned by natives whose shows of friendship had lulled the whites into relaxing their guard. (The Indians might have considered their actions sound strategy rather than treachery.) No such entrapment must be allowed to develop at Fort Clatsop. Out the Chinooks went, and, in all probability, the enlisted men received another lecture on the virtues of alertness.[18] The point here, however, isn't only white arrogance, although frontier America was imbued with that trait. Rather, it is the ability Lewis and Clark possessed, in spite of their training and prejudices, to keep their trigger fingers and those of their men under control. When Lewis, writer of the apology for the treatment of Tahcum's Chinooks, did at last resort to violence, there was provocation. But that is getting ahead of the story.

The days dragged, wet, boring, sickly. Colds, coughs, fevers, and an ailment Ordway spelled "enfluenzy" were common. Fleas continued to be maddening. Once again, venereal complaints brought the Corps's supply of mercury out of the medicine chest. The poison cured a couple of the men before the drug itself could kill them—at least Lewis thought it did. He believed, too, that the physical unattractiveness of the available women reduced the number of contacts with the soldiers, so that Fort Clatsop was less afflicted by sexual diseases than Fort Mandan had been. Still, he was alarmed when the old Chinook bawd who had produced her retinue of daughters and nieces for the gratification of the Corps on the Columbia's north bank suddenly reappeared on the south with the same group. Gathering the enlisted men together, he wrung a vow of chastity from them: Let's stay in shape for the trip home. The bored, husky young men kept the promise, Lewis reported later.[19]

The salt makers wound up their work late in February after producing enough seasoning to satisfy the cooks at the fort and also fill twelve small, ironbound kegs for the return journey. Health had been bad at the salt camp, too. Gibson had to be carried back on a stretcher, but responded to treatment. William Bratton, whose pain centered severely in his lower back, did not, and a baffled Lewis confessed to worries about whether the man would ever recover.[20]

One tasty change from the monotonous fare of elk and wapatoo roots came on February 25 when Comowool, chief of the nearest Clatsop village, sold the Corps half a bushel of a smallish fish the captains called anchovies. After declaring them the most savory fish he had ever tasted, Lewis described them carefully in his journal, while Clark embellished the copy he later made with one of his better-known illustrations.[21] The "anchovies" were so rich in oil that they would actually burn after being dried and so became known, later, as candlefish. Scientifically they were a species of smelt named eulachon. Whatever the name, Pryor and others of the force were hurried to the river with trade goods to buy as many as possible from the Cathlamets, whose south-bank villages were strategically located near the head of the estuary. They returned with, we are told, thousands of "anchovies." But the little fish (about ten inches long) spoiled quickly unless smoked at once, and before long the Corps was again depending on elk. Because of constant hunting, these animals were becoming more and more difficult to track down.

Shortly after settling in at Fort Clatsop, Lewis and Clark had chosen April 1 as the date for starting home. Some carefully pondered guesswork accounted for the timing. A primary motive for selecting the Fort Clatsop site had been the hope that sooner or later a trading ship would sail into the Columbia, and they did not want to give up that chance for relief until they had to. On the other hand they could not afford to stay so long that the Missouri would freeze before they could reach St. Louis—a joy they anticipated even more than they wanted a ship. The points of balance were the snowy Columbian Plain, where not a stick of wood existed for fires, and the massive snowdrifts of the Rockies. Under the circumstances, how soon was soon enough? April 1, they decided.[22]

The plan was toppled by too much rain, too little poor food, homesickness, and a general malaise of body and spirit. Fort Clatsop became, quite simply, unendurable. Shortly before the middle of March the captains decided to start east as soon as the necessary logistics could be put together. First they wanted to store up a supply of meat. As events turned out, the hunters—even Drouillard—were not able to get ahead of daily needs. They decided to go anyway, moving slowly while hunters ranged ahead in search of each night's supper. If emergencies arose, they would fall back, cautiously, on their trade goods—so few fishhooks, beads, small knives, little files, burning glasses, and trinkets that the material could be wrapped up in two handkerchiefs. Beyond that they could count on odds and ends of clothing and a few kettles. But at least, they thought, they could keep moving.[23]

They wanted Jefferson to learn as soon as possible that they had reached the Pacific, and yet they were unwilling to hand over their single extra copy of the journals to local Indians for delivery to the first trading vessel that arrived. They did consider, briefly, leaving the document with two or three of their own men in a camp beside the estuary, but rejected the notion. They had outlined so many investigations for their return trip that they could not afford to reduce their strength, especially with Bratton still incapacitated by his back problem. In the end, therefore, they wrote and gave to the Indians for delivery several short summaries of their crossing, each embellished with a rough map and a list of the expedition's personnel.[24]

(As chance would have it, one of the documents fell, during early April, into the hands of Captain Samuel Hill of the Boston-registered brig *Lydia.* Traveling by way of China, the news reached Philadelphia in January 1807. Clustered about this episode are bits of Lydian mythology that are glanced at in Appendix III.)

Another acute need was for boats. Of the five craft they had brought to Fort Clatsop—four big dugouts built beside the Clearwater and the small Indian canoe Lewis had purchased below Celilo Falls—only three had survived. All three were ponderous dugouts. Seamed with cracks, they needed to be caulked and waterproofed with resin gathered from nearby evergreens and melted for the job, a procedure delayed again and again by the incessant rains. Efforts to buy supplementary Indian canoes were frustrated by high prices until Drouillard, the all-purpose man, picked up a small one in exchange for Lewis's laced uniform coat and half a carrot of the Corps's vanishing tobacco. The price mirrored the regard in which the coastal Indians held their canoes. A lover generally gave one to his sweetheart's father as the price of the girl's hand. So the cost was not exorbitant. Nevertheless Lewis remained disgruntled. "I think the U'States are indebted to me another Uniform coat"—a bill he collected in due time.[25]

One canoe was not enough, and at that late date (March 17) the explorers lacked either the time or the willingness to build another. Instead they followed Drouillard's suggestion that they appropriate one from the nearest Clatsop village—the village whose chief, Comowool, the captains considered "the most friendly and decent Indian we have met with in this neighbourhood." Drouillard justified his proposal on the grounds that Comowool's Clatsops had made off with six elk carcasses the preceding February 6. The only redress the hunter had been able to obtain had been two small dogs. In his mind the payment was hardly adequate, although it may have seemed so to the Indians, once the dogs had been accepted and eaten.

The captains, breaking their own rule about not stealing from the Indians, authorized the taking of the canoe. On March 18 four men paddled surreptitiously around the water route to the village, removed a boat from among several resting on the village beach, brought it back, and hid it where Comowool, who happened to be visiting the fort with some of his people, would not see it. They were desperate, to be sure. And so a question of relative ethics arises: how desperate do you have to be to resort to pilfering from a friend who demands more for what you must have than you are able to pay?[26]

On March 22 the captains sent three hunters ahead to provide meat for the first camp on their outward journey. That same day Comowool dropped by. The officers handed him a parchment certificate attesting to his good character and helpfulness, and topped that by giving him title to Fort Clatsop. Were they salving their consciences by presenting his tribe with something that no longer had value to them? Had Comowool recognized the stolen canoe as belonging to his village? Was the gift of the fort a way of buying him off? The journals do not say, although the problem was not yet finished with.

At 1:00 P.M. on March 23, under clearing skies, they departed. Sergeant Gass looked back on their stay through a lens of statistics. From November 4, a day or two after they had emerged from the gorge, through March 24, the Corps had experienced only twelve days without rain and six of those had been cloudy. From December 1 through March 20, they had killed 131 elk. (Ordway raises the count for the period to 150 elk and several deer.) From those hides they had made 338 pairs of moccasins and an unspecified number of leather shirts and pants.

High winds and high waves almost swamped them as they rounded Tongue Point on their way to their first camp. The next day a different sort of obstruction arose. As they were passing a Cathlamet village (the Cathlamets and Clatsops were neighbors and friends) an Indian recognized the stolen canoe. Paddling out, he said it was his. "Having no time to discuss the question of right, we compromised with him for an elk skin."[27] With that, the last unpleasant link to their dreary winter quarters was broken. As they pushed up the swollen river, dodging the mats of driftwood that accumulated in the eddies, there wasn't a person among them who did not think joyfully that at the end of this journey, home beckoned. All that remained was to pass through the obstreperous Indians of the gorge, cross the divide, reach the Missouri, and along the way finish those tasks of exploration that had eluded them on their way west.

SEVENTEEN

Against the Flow

On the morning of April 1, a small fleet of Indian canoes swung into the overnight camp the explorers had set up on the north bank of the Columbia, well over a hundred miles from the ocean. The news the visitors brought was alarming. The annual salmon run had not yet begun, and the fishing villages in the Columbia's gorge were all but out of food. To escape starvation the visitors were paddling downriver in search of wapatoo, sturgeon, or anything else they could find to eat.

"This information," Lewis wrote, "gave us much uneasiness with rispect to our future means of subsistence." The captains had been counting on buying enough food at the villages to carry them across the barren Columbian Plain to the land of the Nez Percés. But if the Indians were hoarding what little they had, they would resent the intrusion of thirty-two hungry strangers and would ask exorbitant prices—assuming they agreed to sell any part of what they had.

What to do? The captains rejected the idea of waiting until salmon appeared. The delay might force them to spend another winter on the Missouri. The Nez Percés might leave on a buffalo hunt before the explorers arrived to claim the horses Chief Twisted Hair was guarding—horses absolutely necessary for taking personal baggage, specimens, and remaining trade goods across the Rockies. The only solution, the Americans decided, was to spend the next few days procuring and drying as many bundles of meat as possible under the still-cloudy skies. The hides they acquired could also be used in bartering.[1]

Early the following morning, April 2, another group of Indians rowed into the camp to learn what was going on. Because some of them were from a tribe unfamiliar to the explorers, Clark questioned them about their local geography as diligently as he could through signs and the smattering of Chinook trade jargon he had picked up. What he was after was information about a grand southern tributary of the Columbia that had to exist—if logic and Indian rumor picked up at Fort Clatsop were correct.

Envision the topography. A broad trough, sometimes called the Puget Trough, runs north and south between the high Cascade Mountains on the east and the low Coast Range on the west. The Columbia River breaks into the eastern (Cascade) side of the trough through its fabulous gorge. It flows west about thirty-five miles and then bends north for about the same distance. After picking up two sizable northern tributaries, known today as the Cowlitz and Lewis rivers, the augmented river veers west again through the Coast Range.

On their way downstream the previous spring, the captains had described what they saw of the trough as "a fertile and delightful country, shaded by thick groves of tall trees. . . . The soil is rich and capable of any species of culture." It looked fully as good when they reached it again in the spring. The land and the mild climate, they estimated, could sustain fifty thousand agriculturists.[2] Such information would delight Jefferson, but the data would not be complete until the southern tributary had been found and described. Strangely, however, the explorers had seen no sign of such a stream.

By drawing a map on a grass mat with a piece of charcoal, the visiting Indians explained the mystery. While following the Columbia through the trough, both upstream and down, the whites had hugged the north bank. A curtain of islands had shut off the view of the south shore where a large stream the Indians called Multnomah slanted in from the southeast. Today it is the Willamette, pronounced "wil-*am*-it."

While Lewis and most of the men hunted or built scaffolds on which to dry meat, Clark and seven others hurried downstream with an Indian guide to see as much of the Multnomah as time allowed. They, too, would need food for their trip, and when they saw, just before reaching the mouth of the new river, a large plank house with several small canoes out front, they stopped to buy roots.

The inhabitants were inside, perhaps in connection with some ceremony. When they did not respond to a call, Clark and a few men went in. The Indians rebuffed them. As they stood there frustrated, Clark perhaps recalled the commotion he had caused the previous fall by lighting his pipe with a magnifying glass in another plank house farther up the Columbia. Anyway, he took from his pocket a "port-fire match," a slim paper tube packed with gunpowder that artillerymen used for firing cannons. (The expedition's last swivel gun was cached with the white pirogue near the Great Falls of the Missouri. How did he happen to have a fuse with him on the Columbia? No one knows.) Sitting beside the fire, he dropped the match unnoticed into the flames. Simultaneously he held up a compass with its face toward the watchers and set the needle to spinning with a magnet.

The fuse sparkled, hissed, and smoked; the Indian women and children scrambled to hide behind the men, and all implored him to desist. They'd give him bundles of roots. The fuse died of its own accord. Clark pocketed the compass, paid for the wapatoo he took, and resumed his journey. When he told the story in his journal, he said nothing about the ethics of the performance. His men needed the roots, didn't they—just as they had needed to steal Comowool's canoe? Similar dilemmas—the means and the goal—would occur again and again during the rest of the transcontinental trip.

The Multnomah turned out to be as noble a river as rumor had said. The explorers camped about ten miles above its island-studded mouth on a crisp and glorious evening. Northward the snow-covered, volcanic peaks of Mounts Rainier and Saint Helens glowed with sunset light. Mount Hood rose spectacularly to the east. All three had been named fourteen years earlier by Vancouver's men as they probed about in their ships and longboat. But to the southeast, unrecorded on the Englishmen's charts, was another striking snow cone. Clark called it Mount Jefferson. Though he does not say so, he may have considered the action a retort to the British, just as carving his name and the date, December 3, 1805, on a tree near the Columbia's mouth had been a retort to Alexander Mackenzie. Americans, too, he was saying in effect, had their claims to this land.

The next morning he and his men went another two miles upstream. At a point that would later be included within the city of Portland, Oregon, they measured the Multnomah: five hundred yards wide and more than fifteen feet deep. Oceangoing vessels could dock there. Where, he wondered, did so big a river come from?

Its course, as he looked upstream, was a little east of south. Indians he met confirmed that the Multnomah continued in that direction even after it reached the Cascade Mountains. They named the many tribes that lived beside it and its tributaries, and mentioned that beyond the mountains was a great expanse of dry, open land—surely, he thought, a southern extension of the Columbian Plain.

His imagination jumped. A river as big as the Multnomah must rise a long distance away—as far, perhaps, as the central height of land he had indicated on his 1805 map, drawn largely out of conjecture at Fort Mandan. A height whose northern slope was the common fountain of the Gallatin, Madison, and Yellowstone forks of the Missouri on its northern slopes, of the Platte and Arkansas on the east, of the Rio Grande and Colorado on the south. And now the Multnomah on the west, completing the symmetry.

He was quite wrong. Western topography possesses no such intellectually pleasing order. Yet the compulsion that made Clark think so is rooted in human nature. As geographer John Allen Logan has pointed out, we are all inclined, when faced with the unknown, to press the familiar into it as a preliminary step toward understanding the challenge. The farther back the known rivers of the West could be extended, the smaller the blank spaces on the continent's map became. Nearly every one of Clark's western rivers, as first delineated, was too long.

Another comfort was his assumption, based on sign talk and murky interpretations of strange languages, that the Multnomah ticked the southern edge of the great Columbian Plain. Such a course would explain Shoshoni and Nez Percé tales of a big river in that direction, one on whose banks scattered bands of the widespread Shoshoni nation lived. The stream was actually the Snake, carving a long arc through what is now southern Idaho. The captains never would get that river straight, partly because Clark decided that the stream they kept hearing about was the Upper Multnomah.[4]

A curious historical irony flowed from the mistake. By early

1824, fur trappers had crossed the Continental Divide in today's Wyoming by way of South Pass, so-called to distinguish it from Lewis and Clark's North (Lemhi) Pass. The way up the Platte Valley to South Pass was so easy, according to an overenthusiastic article published in a St. Louis newspaper, that "loaded wagons can [some day soon] reach the navigable waters of the Columbia" —i.e., the Multnomah. And the Multnomah, according to Clark's map, published in Nicholas Biddle's 1814 version of the captains' journals, flowed gently through the Cascade Range to a valley capable of supporting fifty thousand farmers.

Dreaming of the wonder a half-mad Massachusetts promoter, Hall J. Kelley, proposed, in 1828, an Oregon Emigration Society of three thousand members who would first cross South Pass by wagon (when Kelley wrote no wagon had yet made that "easy" crossing) and then would load their horses, cattle, plows, furniture, wives, and children on Kentucky-style flatboats and "glide down current about 800 or 1000 miles at their ease to this 'Land of Promise.'" Impossible, of course, as several fur men quickly pointed out.[5] But for a while during the initial years of the Oregon fever that would eventually sweep the Pacific Northwest into American hands, it seemed that the transcontinental highway Jefferson so badly wanted did exist, thanks to the headwaters of a stream William Clark never saw but vividly imagined. Too vividly. The Willamette, fed by the heavy precipitation the Corps was still enduring in April 1806, needed no long run to build up its size. It rose grandly on the western slopes of the Cascades, hardly two hundred miles from where the captain had first encountered it.

On the evening of April 9, the reunited parties reached the base of the Lower Cascade rapids. During Clark's absence, Lewis's group had smoked enough elk meat to carry the expedition as far as Nez Percé land, provided they were able to supplement their rations with a few roots, dogs, and an edible horse or two along the way. But as they stared at what lay ahead, they felt other misgivings. The river, which spread out more than a mile wide behind them, was compressed up front, into a raging channel scarcely four hundred yards across. Its water, as nearly as they could tell, was twenty feet deeper than it had been the previous fall. The distance from the bottom of the lower cascade to the top of the upper, with a quiet stretch in between, was seven miles. They would have to portage their baggage most of the way and tow the boats up empty. But they had one stroke of luck. That night they were able to collect, close to their camping place, a large supply of resin oozing from trees recently burned. It would come in handy if the battered canoes needed waterproofing at the top of the torrent, as seemed likely.

The next morning the men were divided into three groups. One, armed with short-barreled Harpers Ferry rifles, were to pack the baggage to the midway point. Lewis and a few men undertook to guard the piles of equipment at either end of the portage trail. Clark's group was to handle the single rope of elkskin which was all they had for hauling their three big dugouts and two small canoes.

Indians who had been friendly last fall were hostile now, perhaps as a prelude to demands for toll, a custom that caused great trouble to later fur traders.[6] They crowded and jostled the porters. One threw stones down on them. There were individual scuffles here and there. The climax came when some of them lured Lewis's black Newfoundland dog away. Toll? To Lewis it looked like theft. Furious, he sent three armed men in pursuit with orders to kill if necessary—the first time (as far as the journals show) that such a command had been given concerning native peoples whom Jefferson wanted treated "in the most friendly & conciliatory manner which their own conduct will admit." Nor did the confrontation end there. The dog having been recovered without the need of violence, the captains assembled the Indians hanging around the baggage piles and warned them with unmistakable signs that anyone stealing any article or insulting any white man would be instantly shot. They then unceremoniously ordered the aggressors (as the explorers considered them) out of the camp.

The sternness had its effect. The next day the Indians kept a sullen distance, except for one chief who apologized profusely for his people and went along with the whites as a self-appointed bodyguard, actions that earned him a small medal as a reward. The clearing of the air was needed. The baggage still had to be lugged from the overnight bivouac to the top of the Great Shute at the head of the Upper Cascade. Again Clark took charge of the towing and spent a full day moving four of the craft into calmer waters above the rapids.

The activity injured the boats sorely. The next day—rainy, of course—Clark oversaw the repairs and the sealing of the joints with melted resin. Meanwhile Lewis and a fresh crew tackled the fifth boat, a heavy dugout. As they were straining to pull it around a projecting rock, the bow got too far out into the current. Hit broadside by the weight of so much water, the dugout tore loose from the workers' hands and vanished, end over end, into the foam. They didn't bother looking for the pieces.

For a little while after that luck improved. At a village a short distance above the Shute, Lewis purchased, as replacements for the lost dugout, two small, sound, easily maneuvered canoes. The cost: four elkskins and two far-traveled buffalo robes. Deerskins were exchanged for three fat dogs, and the hunters added more deer to the larder.

The area was populous. Each day more outsiders arrived to share the coming salmon run with the local Indians. Faithfully the captains added new lists to their vocabulary compilations and described the various native dresses and customs. Two items on which they dwelt at length were the Indians' procedures with their canoes and their mobile homes. Tribes that visited the gorge's fishing and trading grounds had to make at least two trips a year, one coming in and the other departing. Although their superbly built canoes could be carried, with difficulty, around the rapids, the effort was seldom resorted to. Those who lived below the Cascade Rapids would leave their boats where the white water feathered out and walk up the portage trail with their goods. At the top they rented other canoes for the rest of the trip to The Dalles; if they went beyond those rapids they frequently used rented horses for the portages. On returning downstream, they surrendered whatever they had hired to the owners and walked along the trails until they reached their own boats.

People who lived above or in the gorge of course reversed the process. Whichever direction they traveled, they transported their houses with them. The dwellings, made of boards covered with cedar bark, were easily taken apart for carrying, a labor shared equally by men, women, and older children. When assembled, these temporary houses were sometimes well over a hundred feet long and occupied by several families. Generally they rested flat on the ground. By contrast, the gorge's permanent residents wintered in smallish caverns dug as much as eight feet deep and roofed with timbers and earth. A hole in the top, equipped on the inside with a ladder, served both as entry and chimney. When warm weather arrived, the cave dwellers emerged to live in long plank houses like the ones the visitors used.

The natural setting of this teeming stretch of the Columbia was superb. A variety of flowers bloomed in April. The air near The Dalles, Lewis wrote appreciatively, was noticeably drier and more bracing than it had been near the coast. The wetland firs were gradually replaced by long-needled ponderosa pines and those, too, would soon disappear. High, dark cliffs of basalt lined the river's north bank. Cataracts swollen by rain and snowmelt dropped several hundred lacy feet down the forested slope to the south. Lewis, who worked hard over such scenes, tried to convey the spectacle in words: "mountains high and broken . . . romantic views occasionally enlivened by beautiful cascades rushing from the heights, and forming a deep contrast with the firs, cedar and pines, which darken their sides."[7] One of the waterfalls, today's famed Multnomah Falls, plunged seven hundred feet in two giant steps.

As the travelers neared The Dalles, they saw ten or twelve horses grazing near a cluster of plank houses. Twelve!—enough to carry their personal baggage, trade merchandise, pounded fish, roots, and dried elk meat (and William Bratton, who was still all but immobilized by pains in his lower back) to the foot of the Rockies, where their own animals waited. But the Indians at all the villages that had horses proved obdurate. No trade—not for anything the captains were able to offer.[8]

On the evening of April 15, the Corps camped on a prominent point below the Long Narrows. Several Indians visited them there, and those from the north bank said that if the Americans would come to their town the next morning, their people would sell. At 8:00 A.M., accordingly, Clark rowed across the river with eight men and Sacagawea, for the captain hoped that in so heterogeneous a gathering of natives there would be someone who understood Shoshoni. Lewis and the rest of the men stayed on the shore, confidently making twelve pack saddles and pack ropes for lashing down the loads that would be piled on them. Hunters ranging across the new grass of the plains brought in more meat to dry, and, all in all, things seemed more propitious than they had been for some time.

The euphoria soon faded. Although crowds gathered to see what Clark's detachment offered for sale, no one would part with horses. "Tanterlized" by the natives' on-again, off-again moods, Clark and his people moved slowly upstream, village to village, carrying their peddlers' packs on their backs after the water grew too rough for their canoes. During his second day of dickering, the captain bought, at exorbitant rates, three animals, only one of which he would have glanced at under different circumstances. That same day Toussaint Charbonneau, half-Indian himself and a canny trader, purchased a fine mare out of his private stock of ermine fur and elks' teeth. It is nowhere clear whether the interpreter let the expedition use the animal or retained it for his wife and child.

On the third day of trading, Clark resorted to ingenuity. Noticing painful sores on the skin of one of the chiefs in the crowd looking at the merchandise, he dipped into the medicines he had brought along and treated the eruptions. For good measure he applied camphor and warm flannel to the aching back of the chief's wife—"a sulky Bitch," he wrote out of his own ill humor. In return for the doctoring he received a promise of two horses.

By then he was nervously and physically exhausted. Because of mice, fleas, and bitter cold nights—he had not brought along enough blankets and he had passed beyond the tree line where wood was available for fires—he had scarcely slept for two nights. Leaving four men in charge of the sales merchandise, he and the rest of his crew led the few horses that had been delivered to them downstream to rejoin Lewis. There the normally equitable Clark hoped to get himself back under control.[9]

By that time Meriwether's group had crossed the river with their twelve new pack saddles and had arduously towed the expedition's two remaining dugouts and five canoes up the swift current to the bottom of the Long Narrows.* There, of necessity, they halted. Nothing, Lewis declared, could pass up or down that leaping fury without being portaged—and the two dugouts were far too heavy. Realizing this, the neighborhood Indians refused to trade even a single dog for vessels they expected would be abandoned. To spite them—and to warm themselves—the captains ordered the men to chop up the vessels, burn part of the pieces, and prepare the rest for portaging.

Aided by the horses, the men were able to get their baggage and the five canoes to the top of Celilo Falls by dark on April 19. Rejoicing Indians surrounded them. Salmon had at last arrived.

---

*The Corps had started from Fort Clatsop with two Indian canoes. They had bought two more to replace the dugout lost in the Upper Cascade. Somewhere, in an unrecorded transaction, they had acquired a fifth. The existence of five canoes is made clear in Lewis's journal entry for April 20.

Small pieces of the first one caught were divided among the village children, as tradition required. Prying horses from the celebrants was no easier, however. Only by collecting the animals promised by the doctored chief and by trading off all their iron kettles except one small cooking pot per mess—there were eight people in each mess—were the captains able to bring to nine the number of horses they owned. A Nez Percé who chanced to be visiting in the vicinity lent them another and agreed to accompany them to his homeland as guide.[10]

While Clark made a last futile effort to get more animals, Lewis prepared for the march to the base of the Rockies. When he discovered that Indians were pilfering from the different piles of baggage scattered about awaiting packing, he issued a warning through the chiefs. Shortly thereafter he caught one fellow trying to make off with the iron socket of a canoe pole. He dealt him several blows and had a few of his men give the culprit a bum's rush out of the camp. To everyone in hearing—a fairly large assembly—he announced that it was in his power to burn the Indians' houses, kill their people, and seize their horses if he so wanted. So take care. Stern words, but he was worried by these Indians. They were, he wrote angrily, "poor, dirty, haughty, inhospitable, parsimonious, and faithless in every respect. nothing but our numbers I believe prevents their attempting to murder us at this moment."[11] We have no way of knowing, of course, what the Indians thought of the whites.

They broke away from that exasperating land with its alarming delays on April 21, with their baggage lashed onto nine horses. The ailing Bratton rode the tenth. They piled the duffel that wouldn't go on the horses into two of their five canoes. Sergeant Gass and Reuben Field rowed one while John Colter and John Potts, who would become trapping partners a few years later, handled the other. Lewis sold two of the remaining vessels, along with some elkskins and pieces of scrap iron, for beads, a staple item of Indian currency everywhere. When the Indians declined to buy the third canoe, he cut it up for fuel.

They traveled on the north side of the Columbia, climbing each morning to the top of the encompassing bluffs in order to reach the open plains. In the evening they returned either to the river or to a tributary. There was no straggling; this was a military march. Some of the men led the loaded horses, no doubt to the accompaniment of blistering profanity, for the majority of the animals were ill-broken stallions, given to tantrums. The rest of the soldiers were divided into two detachments, each commanded by one of the captains. One squad marched in front of the pack string for a day, the other behind. The next day they changed positions. In some places the way was roughened by knotted sagebrush, prickly pear, and rocks. In other places their moccasins sank into sand. Because they had done little marching for several months, the men were soon complaining of sore feet and legs—a discomfort Lewis and Clark and perhaps some of the enlisted men relieved by bathing their extremities each night in cold water.[12] In spite of the aches, the short-grass openness of the plains, which had seemed forbiddingly barren the preceding fall, was now a relief after the confinement of the dense, wet coastal forests and soaring mountains.

They passed cavalcades of Indian families bound for the salmon fishing. Sometimes the natives made nuisances of themselves by riding into the middle of the line of march. In other ways they were godsends. They occasionally sold horses to the Corps for pewter buttons, pieces of brass, and strips of twisted wire. Using two of Sacagawea's "leather sutes," Charbonneau bought another mount for himself. By April 25 the captains were able to shift all their baggage onto horses, with two left over for the most sore-footed of the men to ride. They traded the two canoes (which they had once supposed they could swap for horses) for a few strands of beads—and then only after threatening to destroy the vessels unless the Indians came across with something. The migrating natives also sold them dogs, generally skinny, and wood or weed stalks for cooking them. Feeling bankrupt, the captains purchased only enough fuel for one small cooking fire each meal. Because their tents had long since disintegrated, they found the fireless nights uncomfortably cold.[13]

As they neared the point where they would have to cross the Columbia, they talked again of a land route on the opposite side —one that would do away with the long, north-sweeping arc they had followed down the Clearwater and Snake in October. According to maps Clark had drawn at Fort Clatsop, the shortcut would save about eighty miles—if those miles were, in fact, passable. But first they would have to find Indians who would help ferry them, their goods, and their horses across the swollen Columbia.

The necessary angel turned out to be amiable Yellept, a principal chief of the Walla Walla tribe. The explorers had met Yellept during their descent of the Columbia, but had been too hurried then to visit for as long as the chief wanted. They were hurried this time, too, but Yellept, recalling their promise to tarry on their return journey, was determined not to let them go until he had furthered his prestige by displaying them to his neighbors in the north, the Yakimas. To give the Yakimas time to arrive at the big party he planned, he declined to furnish canoes for ferrying the whites across the river until the next day. He made no objection, however, to their taking the horses over that afternoon, using a canoe belonging to an Indian whose injured knee Clark had treated. The passage was effected not by transporting the rebellious stallions one by one in the small unsteady boat, as is sometimes supposed, but by forcing two or three at a time into the water at the river's edge and then, after the animals had reached swimming depth, pulling them along behind the canoe with their halters.[14] Yellept topped all this off by giving Clark an "eligant" white horse. Afterwards he hinted he would like a kettle in exchange. Having none to spare, Clark substituted his sword and a hundred rounds of ammunition. Everybody ended up happy.

The party that night turned out to be quite an affair. Upwards of a hundred Yakima men, women, and children joined an even greater number of Walla Wallas in a big arc in front of the whites' camp to watch the soldiers do square dances and reels to the jigging tune of Cruzatte's fiddle. Afterwards the enlisted men taught the Indians a couple of American folk songs and then participated in a hop-and-chant dance with 350 or more natives of all ages. This time the music came from hide drums and rattles.

By the time the Corps bade farewell the next day to "the most hospitable, honest, and sincere people that we have met with on our Voyage," they had built up their horse herd, by purchase and gift, to twenty-three animals. Though the Indians assured them the trail across the high plateaus to Lewis's River (the Snake) wound through a country rich in game, they cautiously added twelve dressed dog carcasses to their commissary. A wise precaution. They saw little game along the way, and on May 3, when they dropped down from the high country to the Snake, seven miles below its confluence with the Kooskooske (Clearwater), they were hungry again.

Their immediate goals were two villages: that of Twisted Hair, to whom they had entrusted their horses, and of Broken Arm, the tribe's most influential leader. Broken Arm had been absent during their outward trip, but they had sent him a flag and medal. Now they wanted to talk to him, in council with other chiefs, about the wishes of the United States: peace among all tribes; locating sites for trading posts on the eastern side of the Continental Divide, in U.S. territory, that the Nez Percés could reach; and appointing delegates the Corps could escort to Washington to meet the Great Father.

The search for the villages presented problems. The winter had been severe, its snows deeper than usual. Many of the bands had run out of dried fish and roots; some of the people had been reduced, at times, to scraping lichen off certain pine trees and boiling it into a repulsive gruel—but they would not devour, except in extreme emergencies, any of the many horses they owned, for they were extravagantly attached to the animals. Even now, in May, the salmon had not appeared, and many of the bands, including the two they most wanted to see, had left the deep canyons for the plateaus. There the men, armed only with bows and arrows and disguised with antlers and buckskin over their heads and shoulders, searched for deer among the thin stands of ponderosa pines. While that was going on, the women dug and pounded into meal a root new to the captains: cowish, or cous. (The captains spelled it cows.) Because cous closely resembled water hemlock, a deadly poison, Lewis and Clark would not let their men risk digging it for themselves, hungry though they were.

They collected a large retinue as they traveled, still in military formation, up the rough canyons of the Clearwater, crossing back and forth over the surging stream in native canoes while the pack-horse and the few riding horses swam. Among the attendants was a brother of Twisted Hair, who volunteered as guide. Another was a Shoshoni prisoner who, with Sacagawea and Charbonneau, could act as interpreter during the coming talks. A third was a chief whose name translated as Cut Nose; although Lewis and Clark were not impressed, they gave him a small medal because of his station.

There were too many people. Along the way frictions developed. When the Corps halted for the night, Indians crowded around the fires in such numbers that completing the chores was difficult. Conversely, after the soldiers had been dismissed, they displeased the Nez Percé by pushing into their long houses, hoping to exchange their own trinkets for food. The constant search for dogs to eat created a potentially explosive incident. Dog meat was not a fare the Nez Percé relished. One noon as Lewis was sitting cross-legged at a meal of canine cutlets, a young show-off tried to win a laugh by scooping up a small, half-starved pup and dropping it almost onto the captain's plate. Furious, Lewis came up like a spring and—poor pup—flung the little creature back into his tormentor's face. Gesturing violently with his tomahawk, he then drove the fellow away and "we continued our Dinner without firther molestation."[15] But if the Indian had fought back and the tribe had chosen sides—well, there's not much use speculating about such things.

The Corps possessed one tremendous resource—Clark's reputation as a healer. Although Lewis had the better medical training, thanks to his pre-expedition crash courses in Philadelphia, Clark had established better rapport with Indians. During the Corps's western journey, he had relieved a few Nez Percés. As word of the whites' reappearance spread, groups of sick and ailing crowded into the camps for treatment—ignoring, evidently, the captains' inability to cure the semiparalysis of one of the expedition's own members, William Bratton. Soon Clark was treating as many as fifty patients a day for complaints ranging from "bad" eyes (the most common) through cracked bones, sore backs, rheumatism, internal disorders, depression, abscesses, and strains and sprains of many kinds. They mixed their own "eye water" from ingredients in their medicine chest. When they ran out of a soothing basilicon salve of lard and pitch they had brought with them, they concocted another out of pine resin, bear oil, and—of all things—beeswax. (There were no bees in the American West in those days. Clark, acting on impulse, had purchased this wax from a Tillamook Indian he met during his venture down the Oregon coast to buy whale blubber. Originally it had been part of the cargo of a Spanish ship that had gone aground and broken up on Nehalem Beach. The Tillamook Indians dug chunks of the stuff out of the sand for years.)[16]

When their own hunting failed, the whites traded Clark's medical skills for food. Well aware that the trust of the patients accounted for most of his cures, he justified the "deceptions" on the ground of the Corps's need, adding, "We take care to give them no article which can possibly injure them, and in maney cases can administer such medicine and sirgical aides as will effectually restore in simple cases." And though Lewis and Clark may have started the program cynically, they did not end that way. As their affection for their patients grew, they many times added to their records such statements as "I wish it was in our power to give releif to these poor aff[l]icted wretches."[17]

By using their diplomatic skills they brought about a healing of a different sort. Chief Cut Nose, jealous of the prestige Twisted Hair had gained as keeper of the expedition's horses, had sarcastically criticized Twisted Hair's methods. During the quarrel that erupted, nobody kept watch over the animals, and the captains feared they might have strayed beyond recovery. To make sure the search, so vital to their future, went smoothly, they and Drouillard adroitly patched up the quarrel. Twisted Hair then grew energetic and the horses were soon rounded up, except for the two Old Toby and his son had appropriated for returning to the Lemhi River. It developed, too, that when a flood had threatened to sweep away the saddles, Twisted Hair had intervened in time to salvage most of them.

The reconciliation of the chiefs took place on a high plateau west of the main fork of the Clearwater. (Because of the climb out of the canyon, the Corps missed seeing the place where they had built their five dugouts the preceding fall.) From this high ground they could see, to their dismay, the massive blanket of snow that covered the Bitterroot Mountains. They would not be able to cross, the Indians said, until the middle of June—"unwelcome intiligence to men confirmed to a diet of horsebeef and roots, and who are as anxious as we are to return to the fat plains of the Missouri, and thence to our native homes."[18] As if to underscore the difficulties, a storm that in the bottom of the canyons was rain dumped eight inches of snow on their exposed camp. It was May 10.

On they plodded, the snow balling up on the horses' feet and tripping them. About four in the afternoon they reached Broken Arm's "village." Like many other Nez Percé communities, it consisted of a single movable structure built of sticks, mats, and bundles of dry grass. Shaped like the roof of a house (an A-frame?), it was about 150 feet long, closed at the ends and with many small doors along the front. Undivided inside, it sheltered twenty-four fires and twice that many families. The noise of the women pounding roots sounded to Lewis (and to Clark, who, by and large, was still copying Lewis's journal) like a nail factory. In spite of the crowding, the captains declared, the Chopunnish (their name for the Nez Percé) "were more clenly in their persons and habitations than any nation we have seen since we left the Ottoes on the river Platte."[19]

They were hospitable as well. Broken Arm (Chief Tunnachemootoolt, as the captains spelled his Indian name) met them in front of the house, beside the American flag they had sent him— an exciting sight, that. He showed them where to camp and had some of the band's women erect a plains-style leather tepee for them and bring them roots and two horses for butchering. Because nearly all of the principal chiefs had gathered there to see the historic meeting, Lewis and Clark were able to arrange for a council the next day, May 11. In spite of the tedious chain of interpretation, they were able to urge peace, transmontane trade, and the sending of representatives East to see the strengths of the friendly white people. To indicate some of those strengths they fired the airgun and showed off the workings of their magnets, spyglasses, compasses, "and sundrey other articles equally novel and incomprehensible to them."

The next morning, May 12, the chiefs met privately to debate the whites' proposals. Peace? Of course it was advantageous. The tribe's feud with the Shoshoni, for instance, was costly in lives, but inasmuch as the Nez Percés had recently avenged the latest Shoshoni attacks, they were ready now to embrace their former enemies—especially since Lewis and Clark said they had also urged peace on the Shoshoni the previous summer.

The Blackfeet and their allies on the northern plains were different. Those implacable Indians had many guns. The captains had not yet spoken to them, and the Nez Percé were not certain what the answer would be. They were willing, however, to send some young men across the divide to the Missouri with the expedition, to learn the outcome of the meeting, if any. If the emissaries returned with word that peace had been arranged, then—and only then—would the Nez Percé feel safe in visiting the American trading houses of which the captains had spoken.

One point only, the sending of delegates to Washington, was left in abeyance.

Having decided on these responses in private, the chiefs summoned as many of the tribe as were within reach to vote on the issues. As was true with most Indians, unanimity among the males was necessary. After the chiefs had harangued the listeners, Broken Arm prepared kettlefuls of gruel. Those favoring the proposals should eat of the offering. Those opposed should abstain. Later a participant told Lewis there was no dissent: "all swallowed their objections, if any they had, very cheerfully with their mush." Not so the women. They had no vote, but they knew how many of their men had been killed or wounded by the tribes they were now embracing. Was this wise? As their answer, they "cried wrung their hands, toar their hair and appeared to be in the utmost distress."

Their decisions confirmed, the chiefs went in a body to inform the captains, who were sitting in front of the lodge the women had pitched for them. Two young men, acting as representatives of the nation, presented each captain with a fine horse. Lewis and Clark responded by giving each chief a flag, a pound of powder, and fifty rifle balls. (At that time the entire Nez Percé tribe probably did not possess more than half a dozen rifles, but the gift of ammunition slyly suggested there could be more if the new program succeeded.) The chiefs concluded by urging the whites not to be too precipitate about trying to cross the mountains, even though they would have young Indians with them who knew the trail, as agreed in council.[20]

Waiting in the vicinity of Broken Arm's village for the snow to disappear would place an undue burden on the hunters of both groups. The Corps therefore packed up and moved, on May 13 and 14, to a broad meadow in the canyon bottom across the river from and just below the site of present-day Kamiah, Idaho. There they placed their baggage inside what they believed were the remains of an ancient Indian fort but probably had been a winter pit lodge. Some thirty feet in diameter, the depression was three and a half feet deep and ringed by a low mound of earth. They covered the goods—and themselves—with shelters of brush and grass like those used by the Nez Percés and put together, a little distance away, a rough log corral in which their horses could be gathered as needed. Although the captains did not name this stopping place, historians of the expedition have taken to calling it Camp Chopunnish.[21]

They had about sixty-five horses then, including those they had retrieved from Twisted Hair. Many were stallions that kept the herd in turmoil with their kicking and biting. The Corps solved part of the problem by eating the most fractious of the studs. The rest they gentled by lassoing them, throwing them, and castrating them. Indians proved more adept at the surgery than the whites. One fine horse that Drouillard operated on became so badly infected that it was shot—and eaten.[22]

Medical work continued with both their own people and Indians. Most alarming was the illness of Sacagawea's son, by then about fifteen months old and cutting teeth. Infection swelled the lymph glands of his neck. An abscess formed under one ear; his fever soared. The captains—both were involved on this occasion —applied hot poultices of wild onions and later their homemade salve of resin, oil, and wax. When their favorite laxatives of cream of tartar and flowers of sulfur (the latter sometimes used now as an insecticide) proved inadequate, they resorted to an enema. The journals do not refer to his mother at any time during the illness, although her love, care, and diligence in keeping him clean (diapers consisted of moss or cattail fluff held in softly tanned animal skins that could be washed) were probably as effective as the soldiers' ministrations. During the next two weeks he gradually recovered.[23]

Those same days saw the case of the mysterious sweat baths. On May 22, Sergeant Ordway and Goodrich were sent to a village about five miles away to buy roots and bread made from pounded cous. There they watched some Nez Percé males strip themselves, crawl into a small sweat house similar to those used by native tribes throughout North America, and sit as long as possible in steam generated by sprinkling water on hot rocks. On their return to Camp Chopunnish the soldiers evidently talked about the process. This reminded John Shields, the gunsmith, of having seen white men with back trouble restored by "violent sweats." When Bratton asked that he be so treated, the captains authorized the digging of a hole deep enough to sit in. After the earth had been well heated by fire, the embers were removed and the patient was put into the pit on a chair, with a board at his feet and a vessel of water to sprinkle about. The cavern was sealed with blankets draped over bent willows. After twenty minutes, during which Bratton drank copiously of strong mint tea, "he was taken out and soddenly plunged into cold water twise and was then immediately returned to the sweat hole where he was continued three quarters of an hour longer then taken out covered up in several blankets and suffered to cool gradually." The next day he was walking with little pain.

On the day of that walk, several Nez Percé carried in a minor chief who had scarcely moved a limb for three years, and yet his bodily functions remained unimpaired. The captains had tried doctoring him with their concoctions at Broken Arm's village to little avail. Nevertheless, the man wanted more help—specifically a sweating after he had seen the effects of the treatment on Bratton. Since he was unable to sit, the hole had to be enlarged so that the patient's father could slide in beside him and hold him on the chair. The pains the chief felt were eased with laudanum. Although he needed more treatments than Bratton did, he was up and about when the expedition left the camp.[24]

Explanations? Modern doctors don't really have any. It has been suggested that Bratton may have been disabled originally by an inflamed sacroiliac joint or by an intervertebral disc that nature had about healed by the time of the bath. If the assumption is accurate, sweat was not a prime factor in the cure. The chief may have suffered from hysteria that yielded, psychologically, to the many subconscious suggestions attending the performance. But the main point, as far as the expedition is concerned, is the flexibility and ingenuity the captains showed in dealing with whatever problems, medical or otherwise, faced them.

The child and the soldier recovered when it was necessary they do so. The Corps of Discovery could stay no longer at Camp Chopunnish. Although the hunters had killed several deer and bear during the first days there, game had become increasingly difficult to find. Salmon, which by then were running up the Snake, did not visit the Clearwater. And the Snake was too far away to be depended on, as Sergeant Ordway learned. He, Wiser, and Frazer took a rough cross-country ride to visit both the lower Salmon and the Snake in the hope of buying fish. By the time they were back most of what they had purchased had spoiled. Meanwhile the Corps had run out of things to trade for food. Coat buttons, needles, thread, ribbon, fur, cloth, links of chain Shields turned into awls, old files, musket balls, and what not—all were gone.

Even so it had been a good camp. Relations with the Indians had been warm. (Years later several American army men in the Northwest ran into a light-haired Nez Percé who boasted that William Clark was his father.)[25] The weather in the canyon bottom had turned summer hot. There had been leisure for Lewis to add appreciably to his natural history notes and for Clark to work on his maps. The enlisted men had made saddles, saddle pads, and lash ropes. Everyone's health had improved. To build up stamina for the crossing of the Bitterroots, the captains had launched a fitness program—footraces with the Indians and such contests between teams of the soldiers as prisoner's base.

On June 9 the horses were brought in and inspected. (By that time the expedition must have had seventy or more.) On the 10th they set out in high spirits, each man well mounted and leading a second, lightly loaded animal. They had supplementary horses for eating if the need arose. Their goal was the west end of the Lolo Trail at Weippe Prairie, where they had first met the Nez Percés in September 1805. There, if plans materialized, the hunters would bring in enough meat to carry them across the mountains. What they lacked, and what Lewis no longer expected to see, was the peace mission to the Blackfeet that Broken Arm had said would be along as soon as a council of chiefs selected them. (Its young members could double as guides along the Lolo Trail.) By contrast, Clark, who was the last to talk to the chief about the matter, was confident the men would appear in due time.

The trail to Weippe was taxing, first a long climb out of the Clearwater and then a breakneck crossing of a tributary canyon. But when they reached the prairie—two thousand acres of grass rimmed by trees—the camas lilies were blooming so profusely the meadows looked like lakes. An amazing progression of seasons: summer in the canyons and spring on the prairie, while up ahead, as they could plainly see, the remnants of winter still clung grimly to the land.

They camped near the site of the village where they had first met the Nez Percés and where eating camas roots had made them so sick. (The village, being transportable, had been carried by its occupants down into one or another of the canyons for the winter.) Their schedule called for them to hunt vigorously until June 15, when they would take to the trail. In spite of the snow their spirits stayed high. For they fully believed that their intense desire to reach home would be sufficient to guarantee success.

EIGHTEEN

Peace Mission
to the Blackfeet

June 15. After impatiently sitting out a morning of heavy rain, the explorers started up the steep, slippery Lolo Trail without guides, counting on the long days of approaching summer to let them make up for the late beginning. They were right. In spite of laborious progress through thick forests littered with fallen timber, they covered twenty-two miles.

The next morning they were on the way by six o'clock, rejoicing briefly in grassy glades spangled with violets, columbine, and bluebells. This illusion of springtime did not last. Soon the horses were lunging "though intolerable bad fallen timber over a high Mountain on which great quantity of Snow is yet lying." In places that snow was eight to ten feet deep, or so the captains estimated from the depth of the cavities surrounding the tree trunks—cavities created by sun warmth reflected off the wood. When they reached Hungry Creek, on whose banks Clark's advance party had killed a deer the previous September, they were confronted with a raging torrent of snowmelt. Rather than enter the flood to skirt the base of projecting cliffs, they forced their horses up and over the obstructions. Rough going. A full day's exertion advanced them only fifteen miles.[1]

In one sense the deepening snow was an advantage, for it had settled enough to hold a horse's weight while covering the dense windfalls and jagged rocks that had plagued the animals at lower elevations. But the snow also covered the trail. Missing the way by taking a wrong turn along one of the many densely timbered, snow-shrouded ridges ahead of them could be disastrous. They needed guides who knew landmarks and, if necessary, could find the way from tree to tree by following scratches on the bark caused by the frequent passage of loaded packhorses. Perhaps such guides, chosen as promised by the Indian council, were already hurrying after them. But perhaps not. To cover the contingency, the officers decided to send Drouillard and Shannon back to Broken Arm's village with incentives: a good, short-barreled Harpers Ferry rifle for anyone who would conduct them across the Lolo Trail to Traveler's Rest. If two or three Indians would continue as far as the Falls of the Missouri, acting as both guides and peace delegates to the Blackfeet, they would receive ten horses plus still more guns. The party would wait for the guides (if any) at some meadow below the snow line where they could find food for themselves and the horses.

Reluctant to risk losing valuable instruments and papers while scrambling back down the killer terrain they had just crossed, the officers directed the crew to build a scaffold by tying poles between trees and flooring it with a deerskin. On that platform they placed their valuables and as much dried meat, roots, and baggage as they could get along without during the next few days. Then back they turned—the first retreat the captains had called since the trip began. "The party were a great deel dejected," Lewis admitted, "tho' not as much so as I had apprehended they would have been."

After a two-mile descent made late in the evening, they stopped at a small opening where grass was beginning to show. It did not satisfy the hungry horses. During the night they strayed so far and wide over the steep, thickly forested hills, searching vainly for food, that the party had to spend most of the next morning rounding them up. As soon as Drouillard and Shannon were mounted, they hurried ahead. The others followed into a dreadful day. While Potts was clearing trail with a "big knife"—we would probably call it a machete—he cut a deep gash across the inner part of one leg. Blood gushed, and this time it was Lewis whose medical competence was tested. Fortunately he was well enough grounded in anatomy to know a vein leading toward the heart, and not an artery, had been severed. By whittling a wooden "cushion," greasing it with fat, and pressing it *below* the wound with a tight bandage, he stanched the flow. He then sewed flesh and skin together, probably with an ordinary needle and thread, and got Potts back onto his horse.[2]

A little farther on, as the company was fording Hungry Creek single file, Colter's horse fell. The flood rolled rider and mount downstream, over and over among the rocks. Both eventually crawled out, bruised but not seriously hurt. The likelihood of such an accident explains why the captains had preferred leaving their papers unwatched in the forest.

To avoid fighting downtimber all the way to Weippe Prairie and back again with the guides, if any, they camped on the same meadow, under the same cloud of mosquitos, they had chosen on the night of the 15th. Unfortunately the hunters could find no game there, and so, two days later, they rode another twenty-two miles to their original starting place. Along the way they encountered two young Nez Percé warriors, each leading two extra horses. The pair had not been appointed as guides by the council but were on their way to gossip with the Flatheads on Clark's River concerning events of the past winter and learn the allied tribe's plans for the summer. Clearly they would be handy to have along if no appointed guides showed up, and so Lewis and Clark persuaded them, perhaps with small gifts as well as sign talk (clumsy signs with Drouillard gone), to delay their journey two days.

Although frequent Indian hunting at Weippe had made the deer very shy, the riflemen found a way to lure the does. The females were, at the time, giving birth to their young. By bleating in imitation of a fawn, the men drew targets within easy range. During June 22 and 23 they killed twelve. To this they added four bears, so that the larders were well stocked when Drouillard and Shannon appeared on the afternoon of the 23d with three men who had agreed to go as far as the Great Falls in return for two guns. The captains knew them—a brother of Cut Nose and two braves "of good character and respected by their nation." St. Louis by fall! Eagerly each man caught up the horses assigned to him (somebody must have helped Potts, whose inflamed, infected leg was being treated with poultices of pounded cous roots) and picketed them nearby for an early start in the morning.[3]

The first night out the Indians went through a ceremony they said would guarantee good weather for the trip. At dark they set fire to the dead, dry boughs that hung thickly below the green branches of several tightly grouped firs. The needles caught the flames and whooshed them up the trees, sparks exploding against the night sky—"a beatifull object in this situation," Lewis wrote.[4]

The charm worked; the weather held. At the scaffold cache, where they reloaded their goods, the snowpack had shrunk until it was "only" about seven feet deep. In spite of that still-considerable blanket, the Indians were able to go unerringly, each evening, to untimbered, south-facing slopes where patches of bare ground shimmered with tender new grass for the horses. Then back to the winding ridges for another day of progress along sun-crusted snow hard enough to support the animals. From a high knob on the main hogback dividing the drainage of the North Fork of the Clearwater from the Lochsa the whites looked out in awe across stupendous canyons and "mountains principally covered with snow from which to one unacquainted with them it would seem impossible ever to escape. . . . these fellows are most admirable pilots."[5]

By keeping to the main ridge the pilots avoided the detour along the Lochsa and up Wendover Ridge that Old Toby, the Shoshoni, had mistakenly followed the previous September. Now, in June, they needed to save every possible mile and hour. Running out of meat, they ate roots cooked in bear oil. The hungry, weary horses fared little better. But good guidance made the difference. On June 29 they dropped off the ridge, bade "adieu to the snow," and early in the afternoon reached a cluster of hot springs at the foot of low, massive gray cliffs. They had been too hurried on their outward journey to pause there, but this time they made the most of the phenomenon. Over the course of the years Indians traveling back and forth along the Lolo Trail had dammed the outlet of one of the cooler springs to form a bathing pool. (Some of the springs were too hot to endure. Ah, but this one!)

Lewis, always meticulous, timed his own immersion: nineteen minutes, a dunking that left him sweating profusely. Clark stayed ten minutes. The others fooled around at will, the soldiers luxuriating in what was probably their first bath in many months. They did not follow the example of the Indians, who "after remaining in the hot bath as long as they could bear it ran and plunged themselves into the creek [Lolo Creek] the water of which is as cold as ice can make it; after remaining here a few minutes they return again to the warm bath, repeating the transition several times but always ending with the warm bath."[6] A good evening. Joseph Field killed a deer to go with their roots, Potts's leg was healing at last, the violent headache that had afflicted Clark along most of the ridge had abated, and the horses were in surprisingly good shape. Best of all, perhaps, was the knowledge that in six days, and in spite of the snow, they had covered a trail whose previous crossing had taken eleven days.

On June 30 they pushed hard to reach Traveler's Rest, close to what they called Clark's Fork River (today's Bitterroot). There they gave themselves and the horses a two-day rest. Renewal: the spring vegetation was aglow with its own exuberance. Fat deer abounded. "this," Clark exulted, "is like once more returning to the land of the liveing a plenty of meat and that very good." Lewis botanized almost frenziedly. He rattled off the names of birds he saw—doves, larks, robins, blackbirds, cranes, jays, crows, and various members of the sparrow, woodpecker, and swallow families. He collected and pressed samples of flowers and shrubs to take East and show Jefferson—wild roses, serviceberries, chokecherries, lady's-slippers, flags, two kinds of wild clover, and, most especially, the dazzlingly beautiful, pink-hued bitterroot, another useful Indian plant food that few whites learned to like. Later the bitterroot would be named *Lewisia rediviva* and be designated as Montana's state flower.

During the layover Shields repaired all the guns. The five Nez Percés and the American soldiers ran footraces and horse races. "Those are a race of hardy strong athletic active men," Lewis wrote admiringly of the Indians. In between contests the horses stuffed themselves as they had not been able to do for a long, long time. Yet even paradise had its drawbacks—mosquitos such as the explorers had not seen since toiling along the upper Missouri the year before; the captains could not sit still and write except under netting, and the desperate horses crowded into the smoke of the fires. Goodrich and McNeal, whom Lewis thought he had cured, were very sick again with syphilis picked up from the Chinook women of the coast.[7]

During this rest stop, Lewis and Clark refined the plans they had made at Fort Clatsop for their return journey. The party was to divide, at Traveler's Rest, into two groups. One would explore north to, and along, the Maria's River, the other south to, and along, the Yellowstone. As each unit proceeded, it would be further divided into subgroups, each assigned a specific task.

Lewis undertook the northern and more dangerous ride. How it came about that he was the one chosen we do not know. First of all, he would strike as directly east as possible to the vicinity of the Great Falls of the Missouri. He knew, from the Indians and from celestial observations he and Clark had taken along the

Lemhi Pass route, that this new trail would be from five hundred to six hundred miles shorter than the other. But what, exactly, were its characteristics? Would it serve for transportation and communication between the United States and the Pacific?

Having reached the White Bear Islands above Great Falls, his party would open the caches there and repack the material for transport down the Missouri. That done, the captain and six men would cut across country to Maria's River and determine, if they could, how far north it actually extended—the old dream: a siphon for furs from the Saskatchewan. During this period three men would watch over the goods at White Bear Island until they were joined by one of Clark's subgroups, coming down the Missouri with the dugouts and other material retrieved from the cache at the eastern foot of Lemhi Pass. The combined groups, helped by horses, would transport the baggage around the falls to Portage Creek. After refitting the pirogue hidden there, they would rejoin Lewis somewhere near the mouth of Maria's River. During this time, Clark would take the rest of his group from the Three Forks of the Missouri to the Yellowstone, whose course he would explore by horseback and boat to its mouth. There he would join the other parties.[8]

Lewis's route would take him almost immediately into the canyon later called Hellgate because of its use as an ambush by the three confederated tribes of Blackfeet (Siksikas, Bloods, and Piegans) and their allies, the Atsina, whom the captains generally called the Minitaris or Gros Ventres of the Plains, although the Atsina had no blood or linguistic connection with the Minitaris (Hidatsas) of the Missouri, neighbors of the Mandans. After running the Hellgate gauntlet, Lewis's party would continue to White Bear Islands, drop off the three men delegated to stop there, and then turn north into the heart of Pahkee country, a blanket name for all the marauding groups. A risk, yes. But exposure to the Pahkees was what Lewis wanted (or had thought he wanted, back at Fort Clatsop) for the sake of intertribal peace and American commerce. The five Nez Percés who had brought the expedition across the Lolo Trail would, he hoped, help him reach his goal by continuing with his party at least as far as the Great Falls.

Unfortunately the five were already spooking themselves about the dangers involved. They nervously identified certain tracks they discovered near Traveler's Rest as left by the Pahkees. Suddenly they decided they wanted to go home, and it was only with difficulty that the captains persuaded them to continue far enough to put Lewis on the right "road to the buffalo."

Because the mission was dangerous, Lewis asked for volunteers. Several men stepped forward. First he chose, inevitably, George Drouillard and Joseph and Reuben Field. To them he added, as sergeant for the group, Patrick Gass, and then Robert Frazer and William Werner. The three men delegated to handle matters at the White Bear Islands were named arbitrarily: John Thompson and the syphilitic sufferers, Hugh McNeal and Silas Goodrich. Theirs was the easiest of the tasks; during intervals of rest, the ailing pair could "use the mercury freely," to quote Lewis.[9]

Clark's men divided from Lewis's early in the morning of July 3, 1806. "I could not help feeling much concern," Lewis admitted, not so much for himself or Clark, one feels, as for the success of the entire expedition. For at that moment, with the homestretch lying ahead, the Corps was disintegrating on purpose.

Bear with us now, for we run into a confusion of names. Lewis's group—ten whites, counting himself, and five Indians—started north, down the Bitterroot. (The whites called it Clark's Fork.) After riding about five miles they came abreast of the point where today's Clark Fork (their East Fork of Clark's River) joined the Bitterroot. Lewis wanted to cross the Bitterroot so he could follow the north bank of the Clark Fork through Hellgate Canyon to the Big Blackfoot River. Lewis called that stream "The River of the Road to the Buffalo," or, in Nez Percé, the Cokahlarishkit.*

The whites built three rafts for this crossing—three because the only dry driftwood they could find was small and crooked. Disdaining flotation, the Indians rode across the stream, towing their gear in sacks of deerskin manufactured on the spot. Shouting and throwing sticks, the whites chased their seventeen horses into the water. Once started, the animals swam on across the stream after the Indians. Altogether, the crossing took three hours, for the small rafts had to shuttle back and forth several times. During the process the boats drifted downstream more than a mile. By the time Lewis and the remaining men started over, they had reached a place of fast current. They paddled frantically, only to run into

*The U.S. Board of Geographic names eschews apostrophes in proper names—e.g., Clark Fork River, not Clark's Fork. This may be the place for us to drop the apostrophe from Maria's River, as the board has, even though Lewis himself, the namer of the stream, always wrote it Maria's and undoubtedly pronounced it that way, too.

some overhanging brush on the far side that knocked Lewis overboard. He floundered ashore unharmed. His erstwhile companions, unnamed but identified as poor swimmers, flailed mightily with their homemade paddles before managing to land.

That was the last notable adventure on the way to the Great Falls, unless struggles with fading morale can be called adventures. The next morning (July 4: no celebration that year) the Indians halted. No Hellgate for them. After giving Lewis directions to a pass across the Continental Divide, they smoked a pipe together, and the Indians grieved, "confident the Pahkees would cut us off." Then they parted, "these affectionate people [showing] every emmotion of unfeigned regret at separating from us." After that it was hard to pass old war camps, as the whites did nearly every day, and not feel uneasiness. July 6: "we expect to meet with the Minnetares and are therefore on our guard both day and night"—an awkward way to feel about people they had once wanted to find and turn into friends.[10]

No confrontation occurred. After crossing the divide at gentle Lewis and Clark Pass, which Clark never saw and Lewis did not name, they came down the Medicine (our Sun) River to the Missouri. It was July 11. Old Toby, the Shoshoni, had said the traverse would take four days. The Nez Percé had suggested five. The whites had spent a little more than eight, partly because they had sat out a rain and had taken time to hunt. Small matter. Last year's journey by way of Lemhi Pass had taken almost two months. (But if they hadn't gone that route they might never have found the horses they needed.) Their spirits soared. "the morning was fair and the plains looked beatifull the grass much improved by the late rain. the air was pleasant and a vast assemblage of little birds which croud to the groves on the river sang most enchantingly." The animals felt the joy, too. By Lewis's estimate, there were no fewer than ten thousand buffalo in a two-mile circle around the White Bear Islands. "it is now the season at which the buffalo begin to coppelate and the bulls keep a tremedious roaring we could hear them for many miles."

By evening they had killed, skinned, and butchered eleven of the massive animals, for food and for hides to be used in making boats, tents, many pack ropes, and other gear. As soon as the boats were finished, they crossed the river and set up camp close to where they had stayed while making the portage the year before. While wolves howled and circled around them at a cautious distance, they

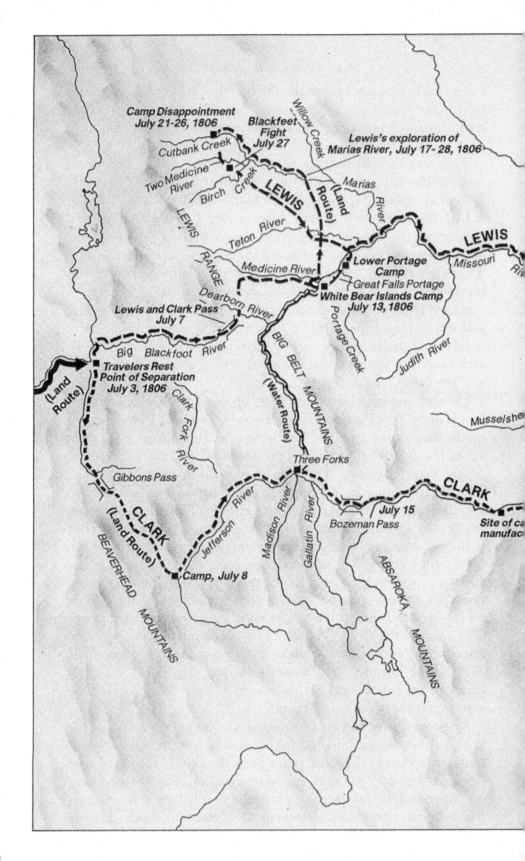

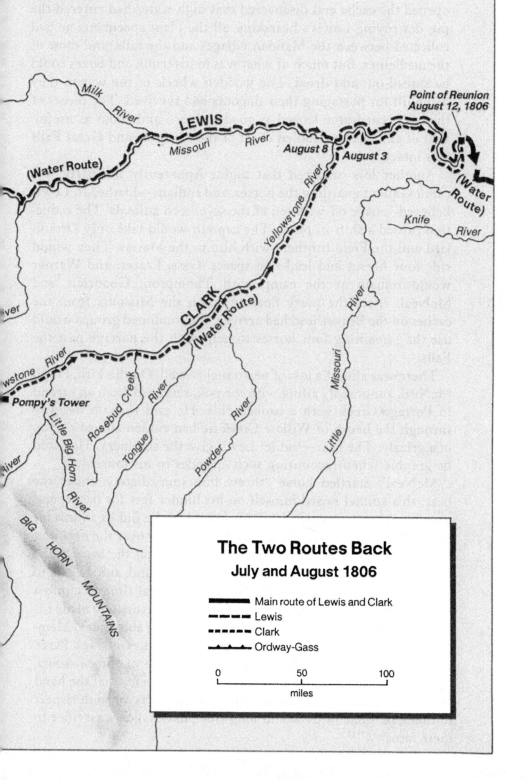

CANADA

Milk River

LEWIS

(Water Route)

Missouri River

August 8

August 3

Point of Reunion
August 12, 1806

(Water Route)

Yellowstone River

Knife River

CLARK
(Water Route)

Missouri River

wstone River

Pompy's Tower

Little Big Horn River

Rosebud Creek

Tongue River

Powder River

Little Missouri River

BIG HORN MOUNTAINS

The Two Routes Back
July and August 1806

——————— Main route of Lewis and Clark
– – – – – Lewis
▪▪▪▪▪▪▪ Clark
▲▲▲▲▲ Ordway-Gass

0   50   100

miles

opened the cache and discovered that high water had entered the pit, destroying Lewis's bearskins, all the plant specimens he had collected between the Mandan villages and the falls, and most of the medicines. But much of what was in his trunk and boxes could be spread out and dried. The wooden wheels of the wagon they had built for portaging their dugouts had survived. The pieces of the iron boat frame looked as good as ever—and about as useful. Best of all, Clark's detailed chart of the Missouri and Great Falls was intact.

Another loss occurred that night. Apparently the party was careless about guarding the horses, and Indians—Flatheads, Lewis believed—made off with ten of the seventeen animals. The reduction caused a shift in plans. The captain would take only Drouillard and the Field brothers with him to the Marias. They would ride four horses and lead two spares. Gass, Frazer, and Werner would remain at the camp with Thompson, Goodrich, and McNeal. After the party floating down the Missouri from the caches on the Beaverhead had arrived, the combined groups would use the remaining four horses to help with the portage past the Falls.

There was almost a loss of personnel as well. On the 15th, Hugh McNeal, supposedly ailing with the pox, returned from an errand to Portage Creek with a broken rifle. He said that on his way through the brush of Willow Creek he had ridden almost on top of a grizzly. The bear—but let Lewis give the summary. He could be graphic when recounting such episodes in his journal.

McNeal's startled horse "threw him immediately under the bear; this animal raised himself on his hinder feet for battle, and gave him time to recover from his fall which he did in an instant and with his clubbed musquet he struck the bear over the head and cut him with the guard of the gun and broke off the breech, the bear stunned with the stroke fell to the ground and began to scratch his head with his feet; this gave McNeal time to climb a willow tree which was near at hand and thus fortunately made his escape." The adventure put Lewis to ruminating about luck. Members of the expedition had killed several grizzlies in Nez Percé country, but none had been a match for those of the Missouri. "these bear are a most tremenduous animal; it seems that the hand of providence has been most wonderfully in our favor with rispect to them, or some of us would long since have fallen a sacrifice to their farosity."[11]

On the 16th, with no remarks about providence, Lewis, Drouillard, and the Field brothers started north, planning to intersect the Marias near the point where Lewis had turned back from his exploration of the river the previous year. On the 18th they reached the stream about six miles above their target point. They had seen Indian sign along the way and were very much on the qui vive as they jogged ahead for five days, sometimes out on the treeless plains. On reaching the junction of Two Medicine and Cut Bank creeks (their mingling forms the Marias River), they turned north along the Cut Bank. The gravelly soil, alternating in places with clay made rough by herds of buffalo, hurt the horses' feet. There was no sign of the migratory buffalo themselves, however. What little meat the quartet obtained had to be stretched out with pounded cous roots they had brought along for emergencies.

Lewis had assumed that Cut Bank Creek might bring him as high as the fiftieth parallel of latitude, close to major tributaries of the South Saskatchewan, as shown on British maps. The stream veered west, however, and by July 22 the party was close enough to the spectacular stretch of the Rockies later called the Lewis Range that he could see the gap by which the creek left today's Glacier National Park and entered the plains. Clearly it did not head nearly as far north as he had hoped.

Still, it was good to learn even unpalatable truths. The day might come, moreover, when boundary negotiators dealing with Great Britain about the upper limits of Louisiana Territory might find it useful to know just how far north he had penetrated into a key area of the Missouri River's drainage system. So he had the party camp beside Cut Bank Creek, intending to make his celestial observations the next day.

It rained the next day. It either rained or was cloudy until July 26, when Lewis grudgingly decided they could wait no longer but must return to the Missouri and join the other groups of the fragmented expedition. After naming the bivouac where they had stayed *Camp Disappointment* (Lewis's emphasis), the quartet rode south to Two Medicine Creek. Drouillard pressed down the stream to hunt. Lewis and the Field brothers climbed, on their horses, out of the creek's deep trench for a look at the plains, which in that area were rough and broken.

Through his spyglass the captain saw, with a jolt, eight Indians and about thirty horses on another hill about a mile away. Run? He resisted the impulse. The eight Indians had already noticed

him, and there might be more out of sight in the folds of the hills.
Fleeing would simply invite a chase by people whose horses were
probably fresher than his party's. And certainly the whites were
outnumbered. The best reaction, he decided, was to hold the Pahkee peace meeting he had talked so glibly about in the councils of
the Nez Percé.

Stiffly, like strange dogs coming together, the groups approached each other. The Indians, he noted, had only two guns
among them but a full complement of bows and arrows. When no
one made a threatening move, all relaxed. Lewis passed out gifts
to the three men who he was told by signs were the Indians'
leaders. He understood them to say they were Minitaris of the
Plains. If his interpretation was correct, they were lying; Canadian
traders who heard the story of the encounter from the Indians
themselves identified the eight as Piegans, a Blackfoot tribe.

Telling them he had much to say, he prevailed on them to camp
with him in the river bottom. The spot he chose was a tight
meadow between almost unscalable bluffs broken here and there
by stubby box canyons that he called niches. Close to the only
three cottonwood trees in the meadow the Piegans erected a large,
semicircular shelter of dressed buffalo skins (a windbreak? a sort
of half tepee?) and invited Lewis and Drouillard, who had been
fetched back to join the assembly, to sleep there with them. The
Field brothers spread out their blankets close to the fire, which was
built near the shelter. Each group, seeking perhaps to bluff the
other, said it had many friends nearby. Then, over their pipes, they
conversed in signs through Drouillard. In answer to a question
about commerce the Indians said they traded wolf and beaver skins
for arms, liquor, blankets, and so on at English forts on the Saskatchewan, six days' ride away. At that Lewis trotted out, with full
embroidery, his Pax Americana talk. He had been to the great
waters where the sun sets, he said. Along the way he had convinced many nations of the advantages of living at peace with their
neighbors. He had spread the word that the Americans would soon
build trading houses on the Missouri that all Indians could visit
without fear of attack. Would his listeners, or a delegation summoned by them, ride with him to the mouth of the Marias and
meet his men? (By then, he was figuring, the six soldiers he had left
at the Great Falls would be on hand with the white pirogue and
its swivel gun. Perhaps the nine men Clark was dropping off at the
Beaverhead would have joined them with their five canoes. Every-

body armed. Magic things to see. That ought to impress the Indians.) To those who made the trip, he said, he would give ten horses.

"To this proposition," he wrote laconically in his diary, "they made no reply."

That night he took the first watch. On being relieved by Reuben Field, he crawled into the shelter where Drouillard and the Piegans were sleeping. Lying down fully clad, as the others were, he fell into a deep slumber.

At dawn someone built up the fire outside. The Indians crowded around it while the whites, except for Joseph Field, who was then on guard, still luxuriated in their blankets. Lulled by the apparent friendliness of the Piegans, Joseph thoughtlessly laid his rifle on the ground beside Reuben's. Reuben was just beginning to stir and stretch.

The Piegans noticed not only the unattended guns but the general unreadiness of all the whites. Speaking quickly and openly, for no one knew their language, they planned a concerted attack. One warrior would make off with both of the Field brothers' guns. Two others would seize the rifles in the shelter—those lying beside Drouillard and Lewis. The other six Piegans should lay hold of the whites' six horses. There seems to have been no intent, right then, to kill the Americans. Such a battle might cost a Piegan life, a loss that all Indian raiders were reluctant to face. Bringing home white mens' guns and horses without harm to themselves would give them prestige enough. Besides, the Americans, left unarmed and afoot on the plains, would soon die anyway.

Someone flashed a signal and the attack began. Lewis's people responded faster than the Piegans anticipated. Joseph yelled at his brother and raced after the man burdened with their two guns. As they grappled, Reuben rushed up and stabbed the thief to the heart. As he withdrew the knife blade, he heard air whistle through the wound from the punctured lung. Drouillard meanwhile wrested his gun from the man who attempted to spirit it away. Their shouts and scuffles aroused Lewis. Drawing his pistol from its holster, he took after the brave who had his gun, yelling, "Drop it!" The man could not understand the words, but the meaning was clear and he could see that plans had backfired. Meekly, he complied.

During the excitement the American and Indian horses had mixed together and were galloping away in two bunches, the Piegans assigned to them racing after them afoot. Drouillard and the two Fields sprinted after the larger herd. Lewis pursued the two men hazing the smaller bunch. In the confusion some of the horses peeled off to one side or the other. The rest ran into one of the box canyons, or niches, opening into the main trench of the stream.

End of race: there was a blank wall ahead. Realizing this, one of the Piegans jumped behind a jumble of rocks. The other wheeled and took aim at Lewis, who, after three hundred yards of running, had pulled within thirty steps of the pair. Although he was gasping for breath, he managed to fire first. His hand held steady and the bullet hit the Piegan in the stomach. He dropped to his knees, caught himself, and fired back. The bullet passed so close to Lewis's bare head that he said he felt the breath of it. The wounded man then crawled away to join his companion among the rocks. Unable to reload—his shot pouch was in the shelter—Lewis decided he really did not want to follow the horses into the niche, where one hale Indian crouched, bow and arrow ready.[12]

One way or another, the Americans retrieved as many horses as they needed—a bargain, since four of them had belonged to the Piegans and were better than the ones the whites had been using. While the soldiers hurriedly packed and saddled the animals, Lewis threw most of the abandoned Indian baggage onto the fire. Seeing that the peace medal he had given to the dead man the night before was still around the corpse's neck, he left it there "that they might be informed who we were," for he still believed more Indians were nearby.

Fearing that the fleeing Indians would stir their yet nearby tribesmen to furious pursuit, the whites galloped from the scene in a hurry. Stopping only occasionally to eat, nap, and let the horses graze, they covered 120 miles, by Lewis's estimate (and he was pretty close), in little more than twenty-four hours. They were stiff and sore as they rode through the morning light onto the edge of a steep slope overlooking the Missouri, but they soon forgot the aches. By happy coincidence both of the groups that had been descending the Missouri hove into sight aboard the white pirogue and five dugouts. Behind them came Gass and Willard with the four horses they had been using at the portage around Great Falls. That portage had been hard work in deep mud, under clouds of mosquitos, but it had only taken four days to complete. And along the way both groups had passed through Edens of game, notably "beaver Sign and lodges without number."

The rivermen saluted the fleeing quartet with shouts and rifle fire. On reaching the water's edge, the men threw their saddles into the river and turned the horses loose. Hurriedly, for Lewis was still afraid of pursuit, he urged the boatmen on to the Marias, to retrieve as swiftly as possible the red pirogue and the goods that had been cached there the year before.

Though the caches were, for the most part, in good order, the red pirogue was too decayed to repair. After stripping it of its nails and ironwork, the explorers resumed their downriver dash, the men plying the oars with a will. Not until then, soothed by the rocking of the boat he was on, did Lewis relax with the belief that he and his men had passed well beyond the reach of any retaliation the Indians could mount. He never learned, as we have through the hindsight of history, that the eight Piegans had been alone and there had been no pursuit. He never learned either, for he died young, of the disastrous results that flowed from his extemporized incursion into Blackfoot diplomacy.

The Indians' first reaction to that murderous little fight—Lewis's target at the niche had also died—was a desire for revenge, a response normal to most North American tribes. Only blood satisfaction could wipe away the hurt brought on by the spilling of a friend's or relative's blood. That satisfaction, moreover, could be achieved by inflicting harm on any member of the tribe or clan to which the original attacker belonged.

The great Canadian geographer, cartographer, and fur trader, David Thompson, saw the workings of the system in person. During the summer of Lewis's battle with the Piegans, Thompson had tried to cross the northern Rockies to reach the tribes of the upper Columbia River. The Blackfeet, who then controlled trade with the western Indians by means of guns and sheer terror, turned him back. In 1807, however, Thompson got through, because, as he wrote, "the murder of two Peagan Indians by Captain Lewis of the United States, drew the Peagans to the Mississourie River to revenge their deaths and this gave me an opportunity to cross the Mountains."[13]

But there was more to the antipathy than just revenge. Having obtained guns from Canadian traders some years before, the Blackfeet had driven several tribes westward off the plains into wilderness fastness beyond the Rockies. Except for annual hunts by large parties, they stayed off, as Lewis and Clark had learned during talks with the Shoshoni, the Nez Percé, and, to an extent, the Flatheads. Yet the captains supposed that a general peace promoted by the United States and sealed with gifts and demonstrations of wondrous technological devices would solve the problem and let Western Indians visit trading houses on the Missouri—all to the benefit of American mercantile interests.

Naively, Lewis had outlined the program to the eight Piegans. Probably the implication did not register on them at the moment. Probably simple plunder had been their motive when they grabbed at the guns. But when they rejoined their tribe, they told the full story. Alarm as well as anger ran through the listeners. Trading houses—guns—on the Missouri! Any such development would undercut Blackfoot power and threaten their position as middlemen for the whites of the Hudson's Bay and North West fur companies. So they began lurking along the river and its tributaries, and when the first American trapping/trading parties came upstream on Lewis and Clark's trail, they struck. It was the beginning of a series of guerrilla wars that would keep taking American lives until a smallpox epidemic of the late 1830s and the decline of fur trade reduced the tribe to near-impotence.[14]

Meriwether Lewis did not see those developments. William Clark did live through those years, however, dying in 1838, but whether he grasped the full panorama, even during his time as Superintendent of Indian Affairs, is unlikely. After all, the Corps of Discovery had merely been trying to carry out Jefferson's bidding, and if there had been trouble, the Piegans were the ones who, in a most treacherous manner, had started it.

This discussion is, of course, basically fruitless. If Meriwether Lewis had not clashed with Indians over the control of the newly acquired West, some other "advance agent of civilization" would have. And the Indians would have fought back. That's the way the American frontier was.

Trigger fingers kept busy during the long run from the mouth of the Marias to the Yellowstone, where Clark's detachment was expected. Lewis now had twenty men to feed. Their appetites were huge, game abounded, and the hunters slaughtered exuberantly, taking only the choicest cuts of the animals they killed. Lewis also wanted elkskins for use as shelters against the deluges that were soaking them. The hunters (chiefly Drouillard, the Field brothers, and Collins and Colter) obliged with piles of hides. The soldiers draped them around the poles of abandoned tepees they occasionally found in the bottomlands and perhaps over log frames they erected themselves. Once Lewis had a crude hide awning stretched over the deck of the white pirogue. More shooting attended his request for the skeletons and woolly coats of mountain sheep that he could take East as specimens of Western wildlife. Grizzly bears furnished irresistible proofs of prowess, and by that time the Corps knew how to go about killing them. One monster they bagged measured nine feet from the tip of its nose to the end of its stubby tail. Finally, hides, bear claws, and elk teeth could be used at times as mediums of exchange in the Indian towns farther down the river.

So most of the hunting can be classified as necessary. Still, the size of some of the body counts Lewis recorded in his journal lead to a suspicion that many animals were shot just because they were there. On July 30, the nimrods brought in nine bighorns, two buffalo, two beaver, and one elk. The next day, fifteen elk, fourteen deer, two bighorns, and one beaver. Between the morning of August 2 and the evening of August 3, the Field brothers slew twenty-nine deer. Lewis did say on occasion that they rowed past game without pausing to kill it, as though the restraint were noteworthy. "Game," he wrote on August 6, "is so abundant and gentle that we kill it as we please." The American frontier was that way, too—joyfully exploitive in the presence of seemingly boundless resources.[15] The sadness and the feeling of loss came later, when the good things were hard to find.

About 4:00 P.M. on August 7, the detachment reached the mouth of the Yellowstone. From the remnants of a note once attached to a piece of elk horn, they learned Clark had arrived there on the 3d but had drifted on, looking for buffalo and, if possible, freedom from mosquitos. Unhurried now that he knew where Clark was, Lewis halted his little fleet a short distance below the river junction to repair the dugouts and let the men, who were nearly naked, make clothes out of deerskin. Then on they went until midday, August 11, when they spotted a herd of elk in a willow thicket on an island.

Landing, several of the men scattered out for a little shooting. Lewis, dressed like the others in buckskin, went with them. He had killed one elk in the brush and was pursuing another he had wounded when a bullet slammed into his left buttock. The lead ball passed completely through without striking a bone, grazed a deep groove across the right buttock, and lodged in his trousers. He yelled at Pierre Cruzatte, from whom he had recently separated, got no answer, remembered the Blackfeet, and jumped to the conclusion that Indians were lurking in the willows. He stumbled to the pirogue. Gathering as many men as he could, he prepared to comb the thicket. Then shock and pain and the blood running down his legs made him give up.

His men found no Indians. They did find Pierre Cruzatte, who admitted, with great trepidation, that he may have fired the shot. Satisfied that the accident did not deserve punishment even on the grounds of carelessness, Lewis let the matter drop and with Sergeant Gass's help turned to the torturous process of dressing the multiple wounds.[16]

Pain and fever kept him awake most of the night. Nevertheless, when the bowman of the pirogue spotted a riverside camp at eight o'clock the next morning, Lewis insisted on pulling over and interviewing the two trappers who stepped to the shore to wave at them. They were Joseph Dickson and Forest Hancock, residents of Illinois—the first American trappers to penetrate that high up the river and the first white men the Corps had seen since leaving the Mandan towns. "I pointed out to them," Lewis wrote later while lying on his stomach, "the places [on the Missouri] where the beaver most abounded." During the talk Collins and Colter, who had been separated from the main company for several days while hunting, reappeared with tales of having killed thirteen deer and five elk—and with the skins of thirty-one beaver. Excited by what they had seen and heard, Dickson and Hancock decided to return to the Mandan towns with the explorers and persuade one of the French-Canadian voyageurs who lived nearby to help them reach the fabulous fur grounds at the head of the river.[17]

At one o'clock that same day the fleet overtook Clark's party. Once more the crews banged away at the sky with their rifles, "being rejoiced to meet all together again," Ordway wrote. Lewis was not in sight, however, and Clark was alarmed until he found his friend stretched out stomach down in the white pirogue and heard his wan assurance that he would soon be on his feet once more. To speed the process Clark took over the painful task of dressing the wounds. Before long and still lying on his stomach most of the time, Lewis began trying to turn his abbreviated field notes into finished copy for his journal. The task proved too demanding and he quit—but not before he performed a last botanical duty by describing in detail the stem, leaf shapes, blossoms, and berries of "a singular cherry" Clark discovered and brought to show him.[18]

From then on, as far as we know, the chore of keeping the trip diary was entirely Clark's once again. He added the new copy without a break to what he had already written about his detachment's adventures and misadventures since parting from Lewis's group at Traveler's Rest.

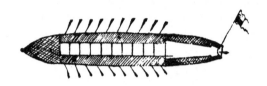

NINETEEN

Hurrying Home

As Lewis and Clark prepared to go their separate paths from Traveler's Rest to the Missouri, they began to wonder, inevitably, about ways to rescue the diplomatic assignments whose completion had eluded them on their way up the river. Except for their hard-earned horse herd they were dirt poor and could offer the Indians few shiny, colorful, mechanically helpful manufactured goods and inducements. How, then, could they persuade Hidatsa and Mandan chiefs to visit Washington with them? How could they persuade the belligerent Teton Sioux to quiet down and let the expedition pass safely along the Missouri with its Indian delegations, if any? How, indeed, could they purchase what they themselves would need for this last leg of their journey home?

Horses—perhaps they could provide the answers.[1] Horses could be traded for food and merchandise at the Hidatsa-Mandan villages. Properly manipulated, they might even be the key to making peace with the Sioux—if the Canadian fur trader, Hugh Heney, could be induced to come to the Americans' aid. A native of Montreal, Heney had become associated in the fur trade with another Canadian, Regis Loisel, head of the Spanish-licensed Missouri Company, operating out of St. Louis. In the strangely intricate ways of commerce, Heney also was connected with the North West Company of Canada. His base, when Lewis and Clark had encountered him at the Mandan villages during the winter of 1804–5, had been one of the Nor'Westers' trading posts on the Assiniboine River.

He had been very cordial with the captains. He had showed Clark Indian maps of the country west of the Mandan towns. He had given Lewis a plant reputedly useful as an antidote to the bites of rattlesnakes and rabid wolves—a specimen so curious that Lewis had sent it to Jefferson, with a special note, when the keelboat went back down the river in April 1805.[2]

During the Corps's recuperative pause at Traveler's Rest, June 30 through July 2, 1806, Lewis composed a long letter to Heney while sitting under a net to protect himself from mosquitos. The letter offered Heney a job pacifying the Teton Sioux, whom the Canadian knew well through his trading. If he succeeded—that is, if he freed the Missouri from harassment by the Sioux—he could look forward to being appointed U.S. Indian agent, salary $111 a month, at a trading post to be built at the mouth of the Cheyenne River, assuming the government followed Lewis and Clark's recommendations. As a part of the pacification program, Heney should persuade several influential Sioux chieftains to accompany the captains "to the U. States, where they will have an ample view of our population and resources . . . and on their return convince their nations of the futility of an attempt to oppose the will of our government."[3]

That was where the horses came in. As soon as Clark's detachment reached the Yellowstone and no longer needed the animals, they would be entrusted to several soldiers under Sergeant Pryor for delivery to the North West Company post on the Assiniboine. Heney could use twelve of them for purchasing the presents needed to win the good will of the Sioux. He could use three more for mounting himself and whomever he hired to help reach the Sioux camps. He would receive a dollar a day salary and all expenses while he was on this mission, regardless of whether or not he won the Sioux over. The captains would use whatever animals were left over for their own needs.

What the letter did not say, though Heney could fill in the silence well enough from his own knowledge, was that the Hidatsa and Mandan emissaries the captains hoped to enlist for a downriver trip would be more willing to go along if they knew the Sioux had embraced American peace overtures. And then the letter did say that the expedition had reached the mouth of the Columbia and that its planned exploration of a river they had named Maria's would soon push the American presence close to British claims along the Saskatchewan. The United States, in other words, was on the move and Britain's fur traders should know it. Yet they expected Heney to cooperate on an American plan concerning the Sioux. There always was a certain naiveté in Lewis and Clark's diplomatic thinking.

Clark was to carry the letter to Heney with him until he needed to hand it over to Sergeant Pryor for delivery, along with the horses, to the Canadian trader. (At the time of Pryor's departure, which would occur somewhere along the Yellowstone, Clark would make a copy for his records.) Between them Pryor and Heney would decide on a place for meeting the expedition and reporting on results—perhaps even in the country of the Teton Sioux.

Arrangements completed, Lewis started north down the Bitterroot River toward Hellgate. Clark's much larger party reined north up the stream, riding and driving a total of forty-nine horses and one colt. In his group were black York, Charbonneau, Sacagawea, and her eighteen-month-old son Jean Baptiste, called Pomp by Clark. On this trip Charbonneau achieved a role of his own. Clark identified him not just as an interpreter but, specifically, as an interpreter for the Crows, the only major tribe with whom the expedition as yet had had no contact. Until the Crows received the American message, the explorers' survey of the upper Missouri River basin would not be complete.

It was a beautiful season for riding along the Bitterroot Valley. To the east were the high, rhythmic swells of the Sapphire Range; to the west, the jagged summits of the Bitterroot Mountains, culminating in what became known as Trapper's Peak. At 10,153 feet above sea level it rose more than a mile higher than the lush, well-watered valley floor with its "great variety of Sweet cented plants, flowers, and grass." The only disruptions to the serenity were the swollen streams that plunged out of the western range. The water was so swift that when the riders forded the creeks, the current hit the horses broadside with such force that it billowed over the backs of the smaller animals, wetting the baggage and causing more of what by then must have seemed interminable stops to dry the contents.

Late in the afternoon of July 5 they reached Ross's Hole, the lovely basin where they had met the Flatheads the year before. At that time the Indians had told them of a trail across the Continental Divide to the Beaverhead that would eliminate the arduous crossing to the Salmon River and the long ride to Lemhi Pass. Though it was a cold shortcut—hard frosts at night in July—it confronted the riders with neither steep, rocky climbs nor down timber, and it saved them two days of riding, by Clark's estimate. The enormous vistas of the Big Hole Basin were stimulating, the camas lilies were beginning to touch the meadows with spots and streamers of blue, and Sacagawea, who as a child had visited the region with parties of Shoshoni root diggers, was able to point across the blue distance to gaps in the hills through which the explorers should make their way. On the afternoon of July 8, after covering 164 miles in six days, they reached the pond in which they had cached their dugouts the preceding August before tackling Lemhi Pass.

The first order of business was a frenzied unearthing of the caches by those who chewed tobacco, Clark among them. They'd not had a chew since leaving Fort Clatsop and the strain, Clark admitted, had been severe. After they had unearthed a few carrots of the stuff, Clark gave each man a tangled strand two feet long; the rest was boxed for carriage in the dugouts down the Missouri to the portage at Great Falls and, eventually, to a rendezvous with Lewis's equally tobacco-starved group somewhere near the mouth of the Marias.

Comfort restored, they dragged the boats out of the pond. They had wintered well and repairs were quickly made. A high wind dried out the wood overnight, and on the frigid morning of July 10—three-quarters of an inch of ice on a cooking pot—down the Beaverhead they went, some in the dugouts and some coursing the banks with the horses. In spite of sore-footed animals, headwinds, the snakelike windings of the river, and a pause to make paddles out of the dugout Clark had abandoned beside the stream the year before, the two units reached the Three Forks of the Missouri almost simultaneously at midday on July 13. The men must have bandied joyful remarks about the swiftness. The descent of the river from the caches had taken three and a half days; ascending the same stretch the previous year had required two and a half weeks.

They paused at Three Forks only long enough to rearrange the baggage according to destination. At 5:00 P.M. Ordway and nine men left in the dugouts for the Great Falls. At the same time Clark and eight volunteers, together with York and the Charbonneau family, turned the horse herd up the Gallatin toward the Yellowstone, or, as Clark persistently wrote the name, the Rochejhone, his version of the French Roche Jaune. As they traveled, he noted several buffalo and Indian trails leading toward a pronounced gap in the mountains eastward and some eighteen miles distant from where they were. He asked Sacagawea if they should go that way. She said no, the pass they wanted lay farther south—Bozeman Pass, to use its current name. A "great service," Clark commented. From that and a few other expressions of appreciation has sprung the overblown legend of Sacagawea the pathfinder. More statues, most of them showing her with her child on her back and her index finger pointing ahead, have been erected to her, it is said, than to any other American woman. These remarks are not intended to depreciate her charm and patient fortitude as a person.

The next day they floundered through a welter of marshes created by the overflowing of beaver ponds, worked up a fork of the Gallatin River into the mouth of the pass, and camped.[4] At two in the afternoon of the following day they reached the Yellowstone slightly below the gateway where it breaks swiftly and spectacularly out of the mountains. When Shannon killed a fat bull buffalo twenty-four hours later, Clark devised a way of shoeing some of the sore-footed, far-traveled horses. He had the men cut the hide into pieces and make round bags for fitting over the hoofs of the lamest animals.

It had been the party's intention to make dugouts out of cottonwood trees as soon as they reached the river. The trees in the bottomlands were too small, however. They discussed making substitute boats out of buffalo hides and flexible willow poles, like those they had seen Hidatsa and Mandan women paddling up and down the Missouri near their villages. But the Yellowstone's current looked dangerously swift, capable of carrying them without warning into rapids they could not manage in the fragile craft. So on they rode, driving the extra horses with them, looking for suitable trees and finding none, but marveling at such staggering numbers of buffalo, antelope, elk, and deer that Clark gave up trying to estimate how many. The tally was "increditable. I shall therefore be silent on the subject further."[5]

The problem of boats came to a head on July 18, some seventy-five miles down the river from the point where the cavalcade had first struck it. While running full speed after a buffalo, Charbonneau's horse stepped into a badger hole and catapulted the rider to the ground. He was not seriously hurt, but might have been. How would they have transported him then? Later that day,

George Gibson forced the question. As he was trying to mount after killing a deer, his horse whirled and he fell backward onto a snag whose fire-blackened point drove two inches into "the Muskeler part of his thy." Clark dressed the wound, almost as rough a procedure as the piercing, and that night pain kept Gibson from sleeping. The next morning he could not ride, though the men padded his saddle with a buffalo robe and blankets and put him on the gentlest horse in the bunch. If the party was to avoid a long delay while he healed, they would have to build a boat in which he could stretch out.[6]

A diligent search through the groves in the nearby bottomlands revealed no cottonwood big enough for the dugout Clark had in mind. (While combing the woods, the searchers did see a plume of smoke in the distance, but paid it little heed.) Of necessity Clark turned to what was available and had his axmen hew out of smaller trees a pair of canoes twenty-eight feet long, sixteen inches deep, and from sixteen to twenty-four inches wide. When the slim little craft were finished, he had them lashed together for greater stability.

The horses were sloppily guarded at night during the construction period, in spite of the smoke plume. On the morning of July 21, the camp awoke to find half the animals gone—stolen by Indians who knew their business, for they had either led or driven the horses in almost total silence across land so dry and hard their tracks could not be followed. Well, at least enough still remained to fund Heney's work with the Sioux.

While the canoes were being loaded, Clark made a copy of the letter to the Canadian trader and then handed the original to Sergeant Pryor for delivery. Privates Shannon and Windsor were assigned to help him drive the herd first to the Mandan villages and, if necessary, on to the Assiniboine. Three men, it developed, were not enough for the job. Most of the horses had been trained by the Shoshoni and Nez Percé for buffalo hunting. Whenever they saw a herd of the shaggy beasts, they took after them pell-mell. Totally exasperated, Pryor and his men drove the horses back to the river, intercepted the dugout, and asked for an additional man who could ride far ahead of the remuda to chase buffalo out of the way. Hugh Hall, who could not swim and was nervous in the crowded double canoe, volunteered for the job. He was practically without clothing, a lack that would do on the river but not on horseback. So Clark gave him "one of my two remaining Shirts a par of [hip-high] leather Legins and 3 pr. of mockersons," and sent him on his way.

It was not a way that was calculated to reduce Hall's fear of water. Two days after the quartet had left the main group, Indians stole the rest of the horses. Desperate, the four whites pursued the raiders afoot, gave up, and returned to their camp. Packing their gear on their backs, they struck for the river. Their first plan was to build a single leather boat, the hair still on the hide, that all four men could crowd into with their bits of baggage. But if that boat overturned and dumped them, their rifles, and their powder into the water, they would not be able to hunt for food. So they decided that in spite of their hurry to catch Clark, they had better construct two bull boats and divide themselves and their essential possessions between them.

Shannon produced the buffalo. From the skins they cut out circular pieces of hide big enough to form basins seven feet three inches in diameter at their tops. Each was sixteen inches deep. They tied inch-thick willows together to form, for each boat, two hoops, one for the top rim and a smaller one for the bottom. They crisscrossed fifteen inch-thick, flexible willow sticks to form the frame. They tied the pieces of frame to the rim and to each other where they crossed with leather thongs. They then waterproofed the surfaces with melted buffalo fat mixed with ashes. The sealing was not impervious; every night they would have to take the boats out of the water and turn them upside down to let the leather dry.

Down the Yellowstone they went, two men in each craft. The man in front knelt, reached over the rim, and drew his crudely whittled paddle toward him rather than working it off to the side. Paddles were used, too, to keep the round vessels from spinning. The second man, though also equipped with a paddle, acted mostly as ballast. Undoubtedly the men changed places from time to time, and one assumes Hugh Hall quickly learned how to manage his fear of water. They bobbed without trouble down one rapid where Clark, still far ahead, lined his double canoe through with ropes. Their only adventure came one night when a wolf slipped into the camp, bit the sleeping Pryor in the hand, and was swinging around to attack Windsor when Shannon awakened, grabbed his rifle, and put an end to that. Reading of the episode today, one suspects rabies. Pryor, however, showed no such symptoms, and his hand healed cleanly.[7]

His party reduced to nine persons by the departure of the

horses, Clark's wooden dugouts floated briskly ahead on a fast current. The day after the parting from Pryor, he spotted a flat-topped butte rising in isolation from the bottomlands. Landing, he and the others walked through the tall grass and among the scattered trees to look it over. Sacagawea's baby was of toddling age by then, but she probably carried him to keep him from holding her back, for she was curious and wanted to see everything, just as she had wanted to see the beached whale on the Pacific shore. The butte, an odd erosional remnant, turned out to be four hundred paces in circumference. Its sides were gray, gritty cliffs two hundred feet high and unscalable except where they were broken on the northeastern side by a steep gully.

Clark clambered up the break with an unspecified number of his crew. Just below the rim, where Indians had left many petroglyphs, he carved his name and the date into the soft stone. (The graffiti, protected now, is still visible.) On top he found two Indian cairns and a delightful prospect of distant mountains and of "the extensive country around, and the emence herds of Buffalo, Elk and wolves in which it abounds." Did Sacagawea toil up that far with little Baptiste on her back? It is impossible to be sure. Still, it is intriguing to try to read Clark's mind at that particular moment. Lewis and he had already named streams for Charbonneau and Sacagawea. One or the other of them had named, or soon would name, other landmarks for every member of the expedition, including themselves and the dog Seaman. And suddenly William Clark thought "This rock . . . I shall call Pompy's [*sic*] Tower." Today it is called Pompey's [*sic*] Pillar through vague association with Pompey's Pillar in ancient Egypt. But William Clark meant Pomp, his nickname for little Jean Baptiste Charbonneau, of whom he had grown very fond. It is also the nickname he used many years later for one of his own sons.[8]

On they went, "glideing down this Smooth Stream passing maney Isld. and Several Creeks and brooks." The noise of buffalo at night so disturbed the men's sleep that they would jump up with shouts of rage and fire guns to scare the beasts away. They filled Clark with alarm lest the marching columns of them trample their boat to pieces. Occasionally the travelers had to sit on the banks while herds miles long swam across the river ahead of them. Elk were almost as numerous. Although Clark's count of the game killed is not always as specific as Lewis's, it is clear that in the presence of such animal wealth his party was equally unrestrained.

They killed to get skins for shelter, for clothes, for trade. And for fun. Why not? They were living off the country, and all their exuberance after so many hungry days west of the divide was not making the slightest dent in the vast, rich life around them. Yet like frontiersmen throughout the continent they were helping create, bit by bit, an American attitude with each unnecessary shot they fired. One thinks of Africa today.

Each evening Clark wrote down his impressions of the countryside they had passed. He made detailed sketch maps of the part of the Yellowstone they covered. He noted seams of coal that might be useful sometime in the future. (This was near the Powder River, where many years later gargantuan machines would tear the ground apart, strip mining for energy.) He collected botanical and zoological specimens. One day he walked so far up the tributary Bighorn, wondering about its course, that on his return to camp he went straight to bed, too fatigued to eat. In anticipation of meeting roving parties of Crow Indians, he prepared an elaborate "Children" speech for them. His goal was to lure some of their chiefs to join him—and, he hoped, some Mandan and Hidatsa chiefs as well—for a visit to the great father, Thomas Jefferson, "and receive from his own mouth his good counsel and from his own hands abundant gifts."⁹ No Crows rode to the riverbanks to greet the whites, however, for probably members of the tribe were the ones who had stolen the whites' horses and they were keeping out of sight. Their absence left a disappointing gap in the expedition's surveys.

On August 3, they entered the Missouri. There was no sign of Lewis. Strangely, there were no buffalo in the vicinity, either. But there were excruciating swarms of mosquitos. Looking for a place where the party could find more of the one and fewer of the other while they waited for Lewis, they drifted on.

At 8:00 A.M. on August 8, Clark was astonished to see Pryor and the horse herders come bobbing around a bend in two skin boats. With growing dismay he listened to their story. So much for Hugh Heney and the plan to quell the Sioux. And for the captains' hope of using the extra animals for buying from the Mandans corn, beans, and whatever else they needed for the rest of the trip to St. Louis. The only bargaining substitutes for the horses he could think of were deer- and elkskins. In order to provide as many as possible, he decided to lay over for a day and turn his hunters loose. He also built, at another camp farther down the river, a rack on which meat could be dried, for that commodity, too, had some trade value.[10]

Disturbing portents continued to pile up. On August 11, the contingent met the Illinois trappers, Forest Hancock and Joseph Dickson. From them Clark picked up information that the wounded Lewis must also have learned but for some reason had failed to record. The pair said that they and a trader whose name Clark recorded as Ceautoin had spent the winter with the Tetons and had been ill treated. So that band was as bad as ever. The Mandans and Hidatsas, the trappers went on, were fighting with the Arikaras again. So much for the peace the captains thought they had established between those tribes during the spring of 1805. So much, too, for their hope of persuading influential Mandan and Hidatsa chiefs to run the Sioux gauntlet with the Corps in order to reach St. Louis and Washington. The mess looked bad, at least as the trappers described it. Yet the explorers had to tidy it up somehow, or the ambitious Indian program they had believed was in their grasp a year ago would evaporate. Well, at least they would have Lewis's persuasive oratory to rely on, or so Clark thought.

That comfort, too, collapsed when he rejoined Lewis's party and saw how disabling his friend's wounds were. Clearly Lewis would not be able to participate in the councils Clark felt had to be held when they reached the Hidatsa and Mandan villages a few days thence.

Indians riding along the bank saw them coming and spread the word. By the time the little fleet hove in sight, the river's edge was lined with crowds. Salutes of gunfire rattled back and forth. After pausing at the two lower Hidatsa towns to greet friends and prepare groundwork for the meetings, the whites moved on and camped between the clusters of dome-shaped, earth-covered huts that made up the Mandan towns. When the grand council assembled, Clark delivered the usual pitch about going "to see their great father and hear his good words & receve his *bountifull gifts* [Clark's emphasis]." The chiefs were amiable and heaped the visitors with gifts of corn. But whenever Clark thought one was on the point of agreeing to take the trip, minds changed. They feared the Sioux, they said, and did not believe Clark's insistence that he would keep them safe, both during the trip down and on their return.

His nerves tightening, he scolded the Hidatsas for sending war parties against the Shoshoni in violation of their promise to be peaceful. (But where, except on the warpath, could a young man prove himself?) He was mocked in turn for boasting, during the Corps's first visit to the villages, that the Americans had won promises of good behavior from the allied Sioux and Arikaras when, in fact, warriors of those tribes had attacked people from the Hidatsa towns as if nothing had changed. (Could old alliances and ingrained hostilities be changed by words from the outside?)

In a final attempt to sway Le Borgne, the grand chief of Big Hidatsa town, Clark fired off the swivel gun that had once been mounted on the keelboat but had proved unsuited to the white pirogue. He then ceremoniously gave the weapon and some powder to Le Borgne. The chief was delighted, but still declined to join the fleet. Clark must have felt totally frustrated. Were the failures somehow his? There is no evidence that Lewis attended any of the councils (as yet he could not walk) or that he would have made any difference if he had. The two cultures, red and white, were talking on different levels.

At some point during the verbal seesawing, Clark may have created trouble for himself by making a reckless promise to Toussaint Charbonneau. He told him that if any Hidatsa chiefs joined the expedition, he would hire Charbonneau as interpreter. Charbonneau, furthermore, could bring Sacagawea and his son Pomp along. If he chose to remain near civilization at the end of the trip, Clark would help him find employment. Sacagawea merited a reward for her services to the Corps, and "As for your little Son (my boy *Pomp*) you well know of my fondness for him and my anxiety to take him and raise him as my own child." When no Hidatsas would agree to go along, the proposal died. Clark, however, offered to take Pomp down without his parents, educate him, and help him become a trader. It was an obtuse statement for him to make at the time, for he must have noticed that the child, in keeping with Indian custom, was not yet weaned though nineteen months old by then. The parents declined. Next year, perhaps. . . .[11]

Quite possibly, that rascally trader to the Mandans, René Jessaume, learned of the proposal. Anyway, he was prepared when Clark, trying to salvage some crumb from the councils, asked his help in persuading a Mandan chief to join the trip. If René was successful, he would be hired to go along as interpreter. Jessaume responded with a vengeance. He won over Sheheke (Big White), a chief of the lowest village and a friend from the days of the

Mandan wintering, by promising that the Americans would transport not only Sheheke and his wife and son but also Jessaume's wife and two children. "we were obliged to agree," Clark wrote angrily, with no way of foreseeing that a few years later the bargain would help bring about Meriwether Lewis's death.

One last parting remained. The trappers Dickson and Hancock had followed the explorers to the villages, hoping at first to prevail on some French-Canadian voyageur to join them as helper. The plan shifted when they talked to John Colter. Stirred by his stories, they asked whether he could obtain an early discharge from the army and join them as a partner. Forgetting the joys of civilization, which perhaps were not joys to him, Colter said he'd try. The captains, feeling his exceptional work on the trip had earned him this opportunity, agreed—with one proviso, which they explained at a meeting of the men. Colter would be free to go if no other enlisted man asked for a release before the expedition arrived at St. Louis. The soldiers shouted compliance; everyone, Lewis and Clark included, chipped in to give the new civilian traps and supplies, and away he paddled with his new friends. Where the trio wintered is unknown. Dickson and Hancock vanish from the records, but during the next few years John Colter became one of the heroic figures in that surge of trappers and traders —the mountain men—who were the true pathfinders of the American West.

On August 17, having fastened two dugouts together with poles and having perhaps put a platform on the poles as a houseboat of sorts for Sheheke's and Jessaume's families, the Corps of Discovery left the villages, bucking high waves created by the unremitting winds of the plains. The 19th turned out to be a red-letter day. "Capt. Lewis'es wounds," Clark wrote, "are healing very fast, I am in hope of his being able to walk in 8 or 10 days." Later, when the party camped, Jessaume, after eyeing an approaching rain cloud, loaned Clark a piece of a tepee. The two Indian women "Stretched it over Some Sticks, under this piece of leather I Slept dry, it is the only covering which I have had Sufficient to keep off rain Since I left the Columbia." The next morning, following a downpour at dawn, he boasted smugly, "all wet except myself and the Indians."[12] Sleeping wet and cold during four months and more than fifteen hundred miles of travel through frequent and often violent storms—of such glum realities are high adventures made.

They were moving fast now. On the 21st, a short distance upstream from the Arikara towns, they met three French traders, one of whom, a mere lad, they let join them as an oarsman. From the others they learned that, yes, Joe Gravelines had taken an Arikara chief downstream on the keelboat in the spring of 1805, as scheduled. Rumor said the chief had died somewhere in the United States; anyway, he had not returned home. Bad news, but in spite of it the captains were determined to meet Jefferson's instructions by rounding up a few more Arikara chiefs to travel East with them, for the Arikaras occupied strategic sites along the riverbanks and, unless they were turned into allies, could cause trouble to future traders. After ordering the men to check their guns, on they went to the Indians' towns.

It was another fruitless meeting despite considerable puffing of smoke and exchanging of gifts. Both the Arikara chiefs and Big White, the latter speaking for the Mandans, blamed the Sioux for breaking the peace. But, they all said solemnly, their ears were open now; they understood what the Americans were saying; there would be no more trouble. As for visiting the Great Father, not yet. First they wanted to talk to the chief who had been there. Clark carefully refrained from mentioning the rumor he had heard, and found solace by spreading the Corps's message to a band of wild Cheyennes from the Black Hills who were visiting the Arikaras to trade. No, they'd not visit the Great Father, either. But they had many beaver in their land and would be glad if Americans visited them.[13] That, at least, was a small gain.

On the 22d Lewis walked for the first time; on the 27th, pushing himself too hard with characteristic impatience, he broke the wounds open and was immobilized again. So when they sighted the first Teton Sioux on August 30, Clark had to set the whites' course of action alone, except for the assistance of Cruzatte and Labiche, who knew a smattering of the Sioux language. There were eighty or ninety of them, mounted, silhouetted strongly on the skyline across the river from the explorers' anchored boats. Clark meant to keep them at a distance, but he also wanted them to know how he regarded them: they were the spoilers of all he and Lewis had worked for on the upper Missouri. He rowed in a small canoe with his interpreters to a sandbar in midstream. Several Indians rode to the water's edge on their side of the stream. Dismounting, three young men swam to the bar. Grimly Clark cut off their overtures. Using some of the signs he had learned and letting Cruzatte and Labiche supply such words as they knew, he used the trio as a conduit for roasting the entire tribe. Even Black Buffalo, who had acted with more restraint than any of the other Indians of the Teton band during the confrontation of two years ago, was unacceptable, and the encounter ended with threats, insults, and jangled nerves all around.[14]

Except for a brief meeting with some noisy Yankton Sioux, it was their last significant encounter with Indians. Travel grew tiresome, partly because of the crew's own impatience to reach home. The heat was often suffocating. Repeatedly Clark complained to his journal, "Musquetors troublesom." Lightning storms flared. Buffalo disappeared; deer and elk, whose presence could not always be depended on, became the main source of food. The Indian passengers fussed; the children cried. But by September 9, "My worthy friend Cap Lewis has entirely recovered... can walk and run nearly as well as ever he could."[15]

As they neared and then passed the mouth of the Platte, they encountered increasing numbers of traders whom they hungrily asked for news of the outside world. On September 12, at about the point where the city of St. Joseph, Missouri, now stands they met a party of old friends. Joe Gravelines was one; Pierre Dorion, the Sioux interpreter whom they had commissioned to take some Yankton Sioux, Omaha, Oto, and Missouri chiefs to St. Louis and Washington, was another. The third was Robert McClellan, an army scout who had gained a deserved reputation for derring-do during the Indian wars in the Ohio country.* The three were associated in a common project that spelled one more defeat for Lewis and Clark.

Gravelines told the story. After a debilitating illness and fits of indecision in St. Louis, the missing Arikara chief had gone to Washington with twenty-seven other Indians, traveling by rented horse, boat, and stagecoach. No, those others had not been the Otos, Missouris, Omahas, and Yankton Sioux Dorion had collected for the trip. Dorion's Indians, stranded in red tape, some of them ill, and all of them bored, had finally left St. Louis for home. Better if the Arikara had followed suit. He died during the Washington jaunt. Worried about the repercussions this might have on the tribe, Jefferson had sent Gravelines back up the river with a

---

*Robert McClellan first heard of the Columbia from the captains that September, as did Ramsay Crooks, a young Scot whom they would meet a week later at La Charette. In 1811 both Crooks and McClellan went to the Columbia on a nearly disastrous trip with a group of overland Astorians.

letter of condolence to the tribe and three hundred dollars' worth of presents for the chief's family and influential friends. Dorion had been hired to help Gravelines pass the unruly Teton Sioux and, if possible, recruit new chiefs to replace those who had dropped out in 1805. McClellan was going along with a few soldiers as bodyguard. He was instructed to search for some trace of the Lewis and Clark expedition, of whom nothing had been heard for more than a year.[16]

The newly found captains had no way of foreseeing, of course, how these frayed Indian junkets they had been instrumental in launching would come back to haunt them. After spending the night with their friends, the Corps rose early, downed a dram McClellan provided for everyone—they had been dry for a long, long time—and set out a little after sunrise, pummeled by headwinds as they worked through an "eme[n]city of Snags" and sawyers. More traders hailed them and, learning who they were, offered the soldiers all the liquor they could drink, which was considerable. Hunting grew poor. Soon they had no food other than a few "buiskits" and papaws they gathered in the hot bottomlands. Then only papaws remained. Never mind: home was close: "the party appear perfectly contented, and tell us they can live very well on papaws."

Endless sun glare on water: on September 20, three of the crew were unable to row "from the state of their eyes." Accordingly the captains abandoned the double canoe Clark had built on the River Rochejhone and put the three ailing members in other dugouts. Their companions, "being extreemly anxious to get down ply their oars very well." As they neared La Charette, westernmost village on the Missouri River, "we saw cows on the bank [plain, ordinary, wonderful cows] which caused a shout to be raised for joy." Springing to their oars, they soon reached the village itself and swung in beside five trading barges tied to the bank. Because the men were in the army still, they requested permission to fire a three-round salute, with cheers. Granted. Villagers poured to the docks, dumbfounded. Back from the Pacific! "every person, both French and americans seem to express great pleasure at our return"—but not so much pleasure that the tavernkeeper neglected to charge eight dollars, in cash, for two gallons of whiskey the captains bought for the men. An imposition, Clark grumbled to his diary.

Because another rain threatened, the citizens opened their doors to the soldiers. Lewis and Clark accepted the invitation of two Scotch traders, James Reed and Ramsay Crooks, who later became field manager of John Jacob Astor's American Fur Company, to share dinner with them and sleep in their tent.[17]

Clark does not say so, but there must have been endless questions. Places that before had been names too dim even to picture —upper Missouri, Yellowstone, Great Falls, Rockies, Columbia— what *were* they like? What of their plants and animals? Their people?

The rain thrummed on the canvas. The candle guttered. Those sky-filling peaks, snowy even in the summer, the buffalo herds, trees so big it was an affront to the listeners to expect them to believe what they heard, Indians skimming the stormy seas in a way to put white boatmen to shame—how was it possible to make them comprehend?

But somehow, and very soon, Meriwether Lewis and William Clark were going to have to find ways to tell President Jefferson and the American Philosophical Society, and, indeed, the whole nation just what was out there in the West.

TWENTY

Endings

The captains began their reportage with three letters whose differing contents and tones indicate careful thinking about how and to whom they wanted to spread the word of their discoveries. (Actually four such letters have survived. The first, however, dated September 21, 1806, and written in a wobbly hand that suggests it was composed on a moving boat, is very pedestrian and breaks off abruptly, as if the author, probably Meriwether Lewis, decided its style would not meet requirements.) The first of the other calculated letters was, not surprisingly, a preliminary report to President Jefferson.[1]

Dated St. Louis, September 23, 1806, it announced the party's safe arrival and stated that Lewis had held up the regular mail in order to dispatch the missive without delay. Its handwriting is shaky, too, as if Lewis had started composing it on the pirogue before the expedition reached St. Louis. Clark's journal fleshes out the skeleton somewhat. It says that after learning the mail for the East had already left, Lewis rushed a note across the river to Cahokia with a request that the postmaster there, John Hay, hold the rider for twenty-four hours. With the need for hurry somewhat relieved, the captains found storage space for their baggage and rooms for themselves. They then called on the Chouteaus and sat up late, talking and talking. "however we rose early [on the 24th, says Clark] and commenced wrighting our letters. Capt Lewis wrote one to the presidend . . ." after which the ever-dependable George Drouillard delivered the correspondence, posthaste, to Hay in Cahokia.

The first really informative letter about the new land—it couldn't cover everything. So what would Jefferson like to learn first?

We can imagine Lewis mentally reviewing the formal list of instructions Jefferson had handed him on June 20, 1803, more than three years before. We can imagine his memory latching onto this: "The object of your mission is to explore the Missouri river, & such principal stream of it, as, by it's course & communication with the waters of the Pacific Ocean, may offer the most direct & practicable water communication across this continent, for the purpose of commerce."

And so the second sentence of Lewis's letter reads, "In obedience to your orders we have penitrated the continent of North America to the Pacific Ocean, and sufficiently explored the interior of the country to affirm with confidence that we have discovered the most practicable rout which does exist across the continent by means of the navigable branches of the Missouri and Columbia Rivers." He described the route as modified by his return over Lewis and Clark Pass. Travelers should go by boat 2,575 miles up the Missouri past caving banks and difficult snags to the foot of the rapids below the Great Falls. There they would leave the river for 340 miles of land travel. Two hundred of those miles were not particularly difficult. But then came 140 miles across "tremendious mountains which for 60 miles are covered with eternal snow"— though not so eternal they couldn't be surmounted during the summer months. Fortunately the horses needed for the land section of the journey could be obtained from the Indians at trifling cost. The last leg of the journey consisted of 640 boat miles down the Clearwater, Snake, and Columbia rivers to the ocean, a stretch broken only by the three roaring cascades of the Columbia.

Lewis could imagine Jefferson's expression on reading all that. The president had presupposed an easy passage across a low continental divide to a short run down the Columbia, with no intervening falls, to the sea. The explorers had sent him nothing from Fort Mandan in April 1805 to prepare him for reality. And so Lewis tried to soften the blow. Although he granted that merchants handling bulky or brittle Oriental goods consigned to either the East Coast of the United States or Europe would continue using the sea lanes around the Cape of Good Hope, still "we view this passage across the Continent as affording immence advantages to the fur trade."

How valuable was that trade? Lewis dashed off what became the most frequently quoted sentence he ever wrote: "The Missouri and all it's branches from the Chyenne upwards abound in more beaver and Common Otter, than any other streams on earth, particularly that proportion of them lying within the Rocky Mountains." He also flattered Jefferson's perspicacity. The president had suggested in his secret message to Congress on January 18, 1803, the possibility of diverting Canadian furs to America's Eastern ports by way of the Missouri and Ohio rivers. His instructions to Lewis had, in effect, asked the explorer to study the feasibility of the idea. In the part of the letter that reported on the study, Lewis suggested reversing the pattern. A run of fewer than a thousand miles down the Columbia and its tributaries was preferable to one of four thousand or more miles down the Missouri and on across the Appalachian Mountains to the Atlantic. After all, one of the best markets for furs, as Yankee ship traders had learned many years before, was China and the East Indies. "If the government," he concluded, "will only aid, even in a very limited manner, the enterprize of her Citizens I am fully convinced that we shal shortly derive the benefits of a most lucrative trade from this source, and that in the course of ten or twelve years a tour across the Continent by the rout mentioned will be undertaken by individuals with as little concern as a voyage across the Atlantic is at present."

Lewis did not mention that Alexander Mackenzie was also proposing that the British government support a similar export route by way of the Columbia.[2] (He did not have to. Both Jefferson and he had read Mackenzie's book.) However, Lewis did warn the president about the expanded activities of Canada's North West Company on the upper Missouri. "The strides of this company . . . cannot be too vigorously watched nor too firmly and speedily opposed by our government." The more truculent Indians along the way, he added, also needed attention, a matter he would go into more fully when he saw Jefferson.

So there it was: the route, its potential value, and something of its problems. That letter on its way, he turned his attention to composing, with Clark, another letter aimed at different readers.

The best way to disseminate information in those days was through local newspapers. Jefferson might not see fit to show the press Lewis's letter to him, peppered as it was with anti-British sentiments. (Lewis already knew from what he had learned on the Missouri that relations between the countries were strained again.) But other recipients could be counted on to pass along a more circumspect letter to frontier editors they knew would be friendly. Accordingly Lewis drafted and Clark copied, also under date of September 23, 1806, a letter to "Dear Brother," an addressee who may have been either George Rogers Clark or Jonathan Clark, both of whom lived near Louisville, Kentucky. This letter repeated most of what Lewis had told Jefferson about the route but went into more detail about what they had experienced along the way. It mentioned the help given the expedition by some of the Indians, briefly described Fort Clatsop, and brushed off the return journey with a statement that familiarity with the land and people had greatly lessened the kind of hunger and fatigue they had experienced on the outward journey. There was no mention of either British competition or of Indian hostilities. Such a letter, landing in a Kentucky newspaper, would spread to other frontier papers and put pressure on the government as a whole to pay more attention to the feat than might otherwise be the case. More attention would mean more credit and perhaps greater rewards to all the Corps's personnel, captains and enlisted men both.

The third letter, written by Lewis under the date September 29, 1806, is much longer than the others and something of a mystery. The addressee is unknown, the original document has been lost, and only a garbled replica survives. Even so, it may reveal more about Lewis's fatal character flaws than its predecessors do.

The purpose of this letter almost surely was like that of the others—to bring the accomplishments of the expedition to the attention of a particular class of readers. The chief difference between it and the others is a long account of Lewis's experiences with Blackfoot Indians along the Marias River. In accounting for that bloody northern detour, Lewis does not refer even indirectly to the hope, dwelt on in his journals, of bringing about peace between the Blackfeet and the Western Indians. Instead he says he went there, "at every hazard," to find out whether the Marias River extended as far north as latitude 49°37'N.

Latitude 49°37' seems a curious figure to pop up here. It arose originally because of the geographic ignorance of the diplomats who, in 1783, hammered out the Treaty of Paris, which officially closed the American Revolution. After much haggling, the negotiators specified that the boundary between the United States and Britain's North American possessions should follow a complex of canoe waterways from Lake Superior to Lake of the Woods; "then through the said lake to the northwestern point thereof [later determined to be latitude 49°37′ and still later as 49°24′], and from thence on a *due west* course [emphasis added] to the river Mississippi." The south-flowing Mississippi would then serve as the boundary between the United States and Spanish Louisiana.

The trouble with this was that the headwaters of the Mississippi lay *south,* not west, of Lake of the Woods. Some day some kind of rectification would have to be made. Until that happened, the handful of Indian traders who ranged through the area would have to conduct their business as best they could, meanwhile suggesting lines of demarcation that would suit their own interests.

The North West Company wanted the boundary line drawn south from the northwest corner of the lake to the headwaters of the Mississippi—or at least as far south as the forty-ninth parallel of latitude. In 1797 the partners in that firm sent their great geographer and explorer, David Thompson, into the area to find the forty-ninth parallel and learn where the company's southernmost trading posts stood in respect to that line. For it seems the Canadian company had (or Thompson thought it had) an understanding with Spain that the forty-ninth parallel should serve as an arbitrary boundary separating the northern watershed of Upper Louisiana from the southern watershed of the Saskatchewan.[3]

Lewis and Clark must have learned many of these things during their frequent conversations with North West Company traders during the winter of 1804–5 while they were in the Mandan towns collecting information about the upper Missouri for Clark's map. Surely Lewis felt that as an official explorer of Upper Louisiana, he should follow through by discovering where the bounds of the territory were.

He had made a start of sorts when scouting the Marias in the summer of 1805 to determine whether it was the Missouri. On his return in 1806 he had crowded his luck to go there with only three companions on a double errand: to urge peace on the Blackfeet and to determine whether the Marias reached as high as 49°37′. If he found that some of the river's tributaries did reach that far north, he would peg the place on Clark's map. It would be a figure for negotiators to work with when deciding on the boundary between British and American holdings. If his finding was accepted as the line, it would bring the United States a little more territory than a line drawn along the forty-ninth parallel. Best of all, it would push his country close to the tributaries of the South Saskatchewan, which he had come to regard as a magic gateway to the prime fur country of northwestern Canada. Foreign pelts pouring through his native land for transshipment down the Columbia to the Orient and the rest of the world—that, too, would be part of the trade picture he eventually presented to Thomas Jefferson.

The Marias, however, did not reach that high. He candidly admitted as much in his letter to the unknown correspondent. Perhaps to assuage his disappointment, he let the addressee know his quest for truth had not been without peril. His small party, he wrote, ran into Blackfeet who "treacherously seized on & made themselves masters of all our Guns—in which Situation we engaged them with our Knives & our Pistol recovered our guns & killed two of them & put the others to flight, pursued them retook our Horses. . . . Fearing pursuit from 2 large Bands whom the Indians had informed us on the evening before were in our neighborhood, we hastened to the Rivers Maria & Missesourii."

The River Maria. The Missesourii. Lewis never used either form. He would never have made other mistakes in proper nouns, mileage figures, and so on that appear in the letter that has survived. In other words, the original had been copied by someone—probably by several people—before one of the duplicates landed in the hands of David Thompson, from whose papers in the public library of Vancouver, British Columbia, it was abstracted by researchers. Thompson and other Nor'Westers, incidentally, did habitually use the spelling Missisourie or slight variations thereof. Almost surely Canadians were among those who copied the original.

To whom was the original addressed? Donald Dean Jackson, close student of the expedition, has suggested, among others, John Hay, postmaster of Cahokia.[4] I agree. Hay, a former Canadian trader, was also a supplier of goods to fur traders working along the Mississippi and Missouri, many of whom had taken out American citizenship papers in order to obtain licenses. He had provided Lewis and Clark with translations, goods, and geographic information while they were preparing to embark from Camp Wood in 1804. Jackson, however, does not feel Lewis, aware of the anti-British sentiments of the time, would have given Hay a letter that might be passed on to Canadians. I wonder. Lewis had left a U.S.

medal hanging around the neck of one of the Blackfeet his party had slain so the Indians—and, inevitably, their white traders along the Saskatchewan—"might be informed who we were." Clark and he had carved their names on several trees on both sides of the Columbia's estuary so that whoever came along later would be informed of the American presence. I think he would have liked Britons to know he had been investigating potential boundary lines as a part of his assignment. American traders should know it, too, for they would expect that sort of information as they spread out through the fur paradise he was reporting. The third letter he wrote in St. Louis, then, may well have been intended for the trading fraternity, a group unlikely to be reached by his other initial correspondence concerning the expedition's accomplishments.

Letters, of course, contained only a small part of what the captains hoped to put before the public. They planned to draw from their journals one volume of narrative about their travels, another about the Indians of the West, and a third about their scientific investigations of the terrain, the climates they encountered, botany, zoology, and so on. Plus a large map drawn by Clark, showing details never before recorded about the American West and some of its contiguous lands. All this was in their minds when they left St. Louis for the East late in October. A big cavalcade accompanied them: various important Missouri figures; Sheheke's family (in Washington the chief and his wife would be called the King and Queen of the Mandans); Jessaume's family; a delegation of Osage Indians shepherded by Pierre Chouteau; and Ordway and Labiche in charge of a packtrain loaded with the party's baggage and whatever plants, seeds, bird skins, animal skeletons, and furs had not been ruined in water-soaked caches.

Clark and York halted in Louisville for a reunion with Clark's family; afterwards Clark continued to Fincastle, Virginia, north of Roanoke, to see how Julia Hancock, who had delighted him when she was a child of twelve, had developed. He had named the Judith River in Montana for her, which prompts an interesting speculation. How well had he known her when he was thirty-three and she had first made an impression on him? Had he heard her nickname Julie as Judy?

Lewis pressed on to his home at Ivy Creek, Albemarle County, Virginia, near Monticello. After spending Christmas with his mother, he continued to Washington, where Chouteau had already arrived with his Osages. Clark, his mind dazzled with thoughts of Julia, rejoined him in the capital city sometime after the middle of January. They had a great deal of business to do and debriefings to attend, though the sessions weren't called that then. There were fetes, banquets, balls, and less formal dances at which Lewis may well have consumed more liquor than was good for him.[5] Then came the climactic rewards. Like the enlisted men of the expedition, each captain (they would soon resign their commissions) received double pay while on service with the Corps—it came to $1,228 apiece. They also received warrants to 1,600 acres each as compared to the 320 acres awarded the soldiers. If they chose not to select their allotments from the public domain, they could sell the warrants for whatever land speculators would pay, sometimes as much as $2 an acre.[6]

Much more important was Clark's double appointment as brigadier general of militia and superintendent of Indian affairs for the Territory of Upper Louisiana. Lewis was named governor of the same territory.* The territorial secretary and, in effect, Lewis's lieutenant governor was Frederick Bates, whose brother, Tarleton Bates, had been a close friend of Lewis's during pre-expedition days. The appointments came through early in March 1807. On March 10, Clark and Bates left Washington for St. Louis by way of Fincastle and Julia Hancock's home. Clearly the brigadier general of militia was smitten by the young woman, by then sixteen or close to it.

Not so Meriwether Lewis. He caught a raging fever in Washington while helping nurse Jefferson's son-in-law, Thomas Randolph. On recovering he traveled to Philadelphia to find a publisher for his and Clark's joint venture into literary production. For a time the business went swimmingly. He obtained the services of a reputable publisher, C. and A. Conrad & Co., lined up the famed doctor and philosopher, Benjamin Barton, to act as editor of the scientific volume, and hired a battery of famous artists and naturalists to illustrate the animals, plants, birds, and natural wonders that would be discussed in the tome.

While he was engaged in those affairs and also sitting for at least three portraits, two other accounts of the expedition were announced. One was by Private Robert Frazer and the other by

---

*Missouri Territory would be carved out of Louisiana in 1812.

David McKeehan, who had purchased Sergeant Gass's journal and proposed to bring it out in refined, heavily edited prose. Lewis promptly defended his and Clark's interests by running paid newspaper stories depreciating all such efforts as being written by unqualified men. Nothing more was heard of Frazer's proposal, perhaps because of financial difficulties. McKeehan, however, responded with stinging sarcasm. "Did your Excellency never attend to the advice given those who have glass houses? Were you afraid that some persons affected by your publication might inform the public that you were not a man of science, that you were not a man of letters, and that you were not qualified for scientific research?"[7] And he went right ahead with Gass's book, pretty well drowning in long sequences of bland sentences whatever individuality the sergeant's rough-hewn account might have had.

McKeehan's long and scurrilous letter was printed in the Pittsburgh *Gazette* on April 14, 1807. Lewis may never have seen it. If he did, he took no public notice of either it or Gass's volume. And so probably it was not shock over this unexpected threat to his and Clark's plans that caused him to suddenly quit working on their joint project. For the sad truth is that Meriwether Lewis, having allowed a stirring prospectus to be issued about the forthcoming work, *never* provided the publishers with a single line of the promised manuscript.[8]

At first he may have been frozen by plain old writer's block, rising from a deep, inner fear of the inadequacies that McKeehan chanced to hit on without Lewis's being aware (probably) of the hack writer's charges. The same feelings of inadequacy may have kept him loafing around Philadelphia when he should have been following Clark to St. Louis, where his duties as governor awaited. Later, drink may have added its chains to his paralysis of will, for it is known that by 1809 he was indulging heavily. As far as that goes, he never had been a teetotaler.[9]

He was floundering during that unhappy summer, and he desperately sought a wife in the hope that matrimony might fill the restless, unquiet, indescribable void in his heart, as he put his despair to his friend Mahlon Dickerson. Nothing worked out. His cousin, Maria Wood, for whom he had named Maria's River, had married during his absence. One unnamed charmer put his head to spinning, but he found out she was already engaged. Something, we do not know what, ended his pursuit of a Miss E-B-y, "whose memory still remains provokingly *important* in spite of all my philosophy."[10]

Sometime late in July he drifted from Philadelphia to Washington and then on to Albemarle. Along the way he took deep offense at something Jefferson did or said—certainly Jefferson had reasons for scolding him about his book, about his delay in going to St. Louis, and perhaps about his drinking—and thereafter, during the rest of his life, he wrote only three or four curt business letters to the man who had done so much for him.[11] Toward the end of November he and his brother Reuben appeared in Fincastle, the home of Clark's fiancée. There Lewis was smitten by Letitia Breckinridge, whom Reuben declared was "one of the most beautiful women I have ever seen, both as to form and feature." Meriwether immediately laid siege, but he had scarcely begun to fight when off she went, leaving him with only one more memory to cling to. When William Preston, Julia Hancock's brother-in-law, later suggested he pay court to Letitia's sister Emily, Lewis rejected the plan: "Such was my passion for her sister that my soul revolts at the idea of attempting to make her [Emily] my wife."[12] Which sounds more than a little like overblown rhetoric from a man who, in his despondency, had decided not to risk being spurned again.

William Clark married Julia in Fincastle on January 5, 1808. Presumably Lewis hung around waiting for the ceremony, in which one supposes he played a major role. (Clark later named his eldest son for him.) What he did after the wedding is unknown. He did not reach St. Louis until March 8, 1808, a full year after his appointment as governor. For that matter, Clark did not return there until July. Territorial officials, it would seem, did not take their responsibilities very seriously.

Lewis should have. He had landed in a turbulent milieu. St. Louis was awash with opportunists of every sort. Politics was violently partisan. Indian unrest sent continual ripples of alarm down the rivers. Land speculation was rife; land titles were in a mess because of old Spanish grants. Dueling was common, violent crime all but unchecked. Lewis could maintain discipline in a company of soldiers when he had the weight of the army behind him. He could not do it in a disorderly community while being constantly undercut and sniped at by a jealous territorial secretary, Frederick Bates, who had grown used to being top dog during the year of Lewis's absence. Turning to the bottle, as Meriwether apparently did, simply compounded his problems.

His collapse was precipitated by the Mandan chief, Sheheke, whose trip to Washington was supposed to salvage something from the wreckage of Lewis and Clark's Indian diplomacy on the Missouri. Having been taken from their homes, Sheheke's and Jessaume's families had to be returned so the chief could spread word of the wonders he had seen. By the time Clark reached St. Louis, a military escort of fifteen men was on the point of setting forth. In charge was one of the Corps of Discovery's former sergeants, Nathaniel Pryor, promoted to ensign for this purpose. Among his fourteen soldiers were George Shannon and George Gibson, formerly of the Corps. Accompanying the soldiers were twenty-three traders bound for the Mandan towns. As soon as the new superintendent of Indian affairs appeared on the scene, the mission became his responsibility.[13]

Traveling ahead of Pryor's group was a larger party of traders led by Manuel Lisa, hurrying upstream to exploit, ahead of everyone else, the beaver streams revealed by Lewis and Clark. Lisa's passage alerted the Arikara Indians that a second party was following. The Arikaras were resentful still of the death of their chief in the United States and had abused Joseph Gravelines for bringing them the bad news. Now here came a live Mandan—a Mandan!—under the protection of the nation who had let the Arikara die. After some confused posturing and maneuvering by both sides, they and several Sioux allies attacked. They killed three whites and wounded seven, one of whom later died. George Shannon, who had been the youngest member of the Corps of Discovery, had to have a leg amputated because of his wound. (He later married and became a successful lawyer and a Missouri state senator.) Thoroughly shaken by the experience, Pryor reported that four hundred armed men would be needed to get Sheheke past the Arikaras. His letter about the incident caught Clark while he was on his way to Fincastle for his wedding. If Lewis was there, as he almost surely was, they undoubtedly talked the problem over.

Responsibility for the return now fell to Lewis.

Manuel Lisa arrived back in St. Louis from his own upriver excursion late in the summer of 1808, afire to raise enough capital for expanding his activities. As a means to this end he formed, during the winter of 1808–9, the St. Louis Missouri Fur Company, more popularly the Missouri Fur Company. He took in as partners a representative of every important commercial interest in St. Louis, plus William Clark and Reuben Lewis, brother of the governor. In order to obtain collateral for necessary loans he signed with Meriwether Lewis, acting on behalf of the United States government, a seven-thousand-dollar contract for escorting Sheheke, Jessaume, and their wives and children to their homes. Clearly a conflict of interests was involved that would not be tolerated today and was looked at askance even then.

The contract required the company to go upriver with no fewer than 120 men. Forty of them were to be a militia unit of expert American riflemen (not French voyageurs). Hunters, boatmen, and so on lifted the total to more than three hundred. They would travel, at intervals, in thirteen barges and on an unknown number of horses. To help the ponderous force get underway, Lewis signed a number of vouchers, some of them without proper bureaucratic authorization. Insofar as Sheheke was concerned, the effort was successful. The show of force cowed the Arikaras and Sioux, and the chief was delivered safely to his tribesmen, who did not seem to care very much, anyway.[14] Lewis, however, did not live to learn these things.

The new administration in Washington refused to honor some of his vouchers. Learning this and fearing he might face bankruptcy if all the vouchers were rejected, land speculators to whom he was indebted for about five thousand acres of supposedly get-rich-quick property closed in on him. Lewis panicked, whether rightly or wrongly cannot be said. Late in the summer he gathered together the papers he hoped would save his economic life and added to them his journals, bound by then in red morocco leather, as if he could belatedly use them for justifying his worth to his countrymen. Thus laden, he departed early in September 1809 for the East to plead his case before the new secretary of war, William Eustis.

Would such a man, who had helped lead a small expedition farther west than any other American had yet gone, commit suicide?

Yes, under a certain conjunction of circumstances: If he suffered chronically from melancholia, as Lewis did. If he could find no one to help fill the void he felt in his life. If the clarity of his mind and feelings were blurred by alcohol. And if, now that his great adventure was over, he dreaded the blackness of life more than the blackness of death. Psychiatrists tell us, furthermore, that such persons often reveal their proclivities, long before the event, by the reckless way with which they embrace danger.[15] Thus Meriwether Lewis. If Jefferson had not intervened, he would have taken a most risky winter trip to Santa Fe to compensate for his delays in reaching St. Louis in 1803. The Corps's expedition had barely gotten underway when he unnecessarily climbed a dangerous cliff beside a place called the Tavern and very nearly fell to destruction. He went alone past the Great Falls of the Missouri into country he knew was filled with grizzlies and came close to paying for his recklessness. With only two companions he forged ahead of the expedition's boats to find Shoshoni Indians and buy horses, although he had no idea how the tribe would receive the first white man they had ever seen. With only three companions he ventured into the country of the Blackfeet, although he had been forcefully warned not to. But so far death, if he really wanted death, however subconsciously, had eluded him.

On September 4, 1809, attended by his free mulatto servant, John Pernier, he caught a riverboat for New Orleans, intending to finish his journey East by sea. For some reason the trip south past the mouth of the Ohio was slow. Lewis had too much time in which to brood, drink—and twice attempt to take his life. It seems likely he was urged off the boat at Fort Pickering, Chickasaw Bluffs (now Memphis)—or so implied Major Gilbert Russell, the commander at that fort, into whose charge Lewis was delivered. Lewis himself says he landed because of an "indisposition."[16] Conceivably, another subconscious wish was involved. In 1797, as a young ensign, Lewis had supervised the building of, and had been briefly in command at, Fort Pickering. Did he welcome being put ashore in a blurred hope of again gaining command, this time of himself?

He needed help. He was incoherent and well soaked. Major Russell put him in whatever served the fort as sick bay and deprived him of all spirits except occasional sips of claret or white wine. Under solicitous treatment his remarkable constitution reasserted itself, and within a week he was chafing to continue his journey, this time by land, promising the while "never to drink any more spirits or use snuff again."[17] When James Neelly, Indian agent for the Chickasaw tribe, showed up, bound for the interior, and agreed to lend Lewis riding horses and pack animals and keep an eye on him, Russell reluctantly let the governor go. There was little else, actually, that he could have done.

Somewhere in the Chickasaw nation Lewis apparently got hold of more liquor and became incoherent again. They rested for two days and on either October 8 or 9 crossed the Tennessee River and intersected the once-notorious Natchez Trace. They turned north-east along it. At their first camp beyond the river, they lost two horses. Ever-restless Lewis: while Neelly hunted for the horses, the governor, his servant, and Neelly's servant (charged with watching the ailing man?) went ahead, after "promising to wait for me at the first house he came to that was inhabited by white people; he reached the house [and tavern] of a Mr. Grinder about sun set, the man of the house being from home, and no person there but a woman who discovering the governor to be deranged, gave him up the house & slept herself in one near it."[18]

Because no one saw what actually happened thereafter, circum-stantial reports of the killing vary in detail. Suffice it here to say that sometime during the night Lewis loaded his pistols and shot himself twice, first in the forehead and, after that ball had glanced off his skull without killing him, a little below the breast. All accounts agree he died slowly. In his agony he called for water but received none until dawn, when Mrs. Grinder, who had heard the shots and was in abject terror of him, summoned his and Neelly's servants from the barn where they had been sleeping.

Lewis died shortly after sunrise. During the day, Neelly reached the house, heard the stories of Mrs. Grinder and the servants, and buried the body as best he could beside the road. (There it stayed. Today the site is marked by a monument, erected in 1846.) Taking charge of Lewis's personal possessions, Neelly sent them with a letter, by Lewis's man, to Jefferson. There was no doubt in Jeffer-son's mind—or in Clark's, who heard the news in Louisville while on another trip East with Julia and their eldest son, the infant Meriwether Lewis Clark—that the death was suicide and not mur-der, a theory that keeps insistently cropping up to explain, in more palatable form, the death of a national hero.[19]

After learning of his friend's death, Clark continued to Fincas-tle. There he left his wife and son while he visited Jefferson and some of Lewis's family. Gathering up the journals, he went to Philadelphia to arrange with Nicholas Biddle to rewrite them in two volumes as a coherent, smooth-flowing narrative. After being given a final polishing by Paul Allen, they were issued in 1814, with Clark's map as a supplement. Although that chronic procras-tinator, Benjamin Barton, renewed his promise to edit the scientific volume, he died before getting around to it. With no one in charge of the specimens the captains had either sent back down the Missouri on the keelboat from Fort Mandan or had brought with them, the materials became scattered and many were lost.

Not long after Lewis's death, Charbonneau, Sacagawea, and Pomp, the child well weaned by then, came down the river to visit Clark. They stayed about a year. The parents then returned to the Hidatsa villages beside the Knife River, leaving little Jean Baptiste with Clark to be educated, as the captain had promised. His benefactions continued. Late in 1811, Reuben Lewis of the Missouri Fur Company built a post, named for Manuel Lisa, beside the Missouri River. Clark was well aware of this, of course, and it was perhaps through his influence that Charbonneau got a job at the new establishment as interpreter. He moved there with Sacagawea, who was pregnant, in early 1812. A daughter, Lizette, was born to them in August. Four months later, on December 20, Sacagawea died of what the post trader called putrid fever. She was about twenty-three.[20]

As soon as circumstances allowed, Clark assumed guardianship of the girl and, later, of Charbonneau's son Toussaint by a second Shoshoni wife. As for Jean Baptiste, he went back among the Indians in 1816 or so. In 1824, when he was twenty, he caught the attention of Prince Maximilian of Wied, who was touring the Missouri River country on an elaborate sightseeing junket. The prince took Pomp to Germany, where he stayed for five years before returning to the American West to make a commendable name for himself as a mountain man and army guide.

When Thomas Jefferson died on July 4, 1826 (his predecessor as president and sometime enemy, John Adams, died on that same day), America's fabled fur trade had been firmly and profitably established throughout the area Lewis and Clark had known as Upper Louisiana. Curiously, the man who had presided over the purchase of that territory had little to say about either the land or its burgeoning commerce, at least in public. In his introduction to Biddle and Allen's *History of the Expedition under the Command of Captains Lewis and Clark*, he outlined his own early interest in trans-Mississippi explorations, repeated the instructions he had given Lewis before Clark had been decided on as the party's co-commander, mentioned the excitement caused by the Corps's return, and closed by mourning Lewis's untimely suicide. That death, the president finished, had kept his fellow Americans from receiving from Lewis's own hands their first knowledge of "that vast and fertile country, which their sons are destined to fill with arts, with science, with freedom and happiness."

As to the United States' share of that vast and fertile land he was quite definite and quite conservative. His nation, he believed, should not make any effort to extend itself politically across the Continental Divide, the country's western boundary as arbitrarily established by the purchase itself. The communications of the time were too slow to allow the quick responses between voters and their government needed by a democracy, and Jefferson despised the thought of his country becoming masters of a distant colonial empire. The Oregon country should become, in his opinion, a neighboring nation "of independent Americans, unconnected with us but by the ties of blood and interest, and employing like us the right of self-government."[21] No more territory (except West Florida), he said in effect, not sensing the energy Lewis and Clark had helped impart to the westward dynamics of the young nation. If the British and Spanish—both of them empires—could be forestalled, that was enough.

Clark's concluding years were the antithesis of Lewis's. In 1813 he was named territorial governor and held that office until the state of Missouri was created in 1820. Though defeated in the first election for state governor, he continued as superintendent of Indian affairs. Whether dealing with whites or Indians or both together, he sought to settle controversies by conciliation. He was imposingly proportioned, dignified, trustworthy, and respected. Most Indians liked him, called him Red Head Chief and, whenever circumstances brought them to St. Louis, eagerly visited him and the Indian Hall he had erected on his estate.

Maintaining his contacts with traders and trappers, he utilized the information they brought him to regularly update his master map of the West. The white spaces shrank, the Indians retreated, the vast herds of game became mere ghosts of what they had been. When William Clark died peacefully in 1838, the face of the nation was changing at a rate that neither Lewis nor he could have imagined when they returned to St. Louis in 1806, bursting with news. Luck! That, too, was part of Meriwether Lewis's heritage, in spite of the manner of his death. The West was bound to be crossed sooner or later by—who knows, acting with what motives? But through good fortune Lewis, Clark, twenty-seven white soldiers, a black slave, an Indian woman, an infant, and a man of mixed races were the first. Acting for the government and hence for the people, and following plans laid down by the president of the United States, they saw the grandeur and space and felt the freshness, and returned successful. The imprint stayed. This was the people's West, the public domain, in ways not quite matched anywhere else. That domain has been sadly abused—and gloriously used—over the years, but the ideal, the sense of newness and promise with which the names Lewis and Clark have always been identified, has not yet been lost.

APPENDIX I

Jefferson's Instructions to Lewis

To *Meriwether Lewis, esquire, Captain of the 1st regiment of infantry of the United States of America:* Your situation as Secretary of the President of the United States has made you acquainted with the objects of my confidential message of Jan. 18, 1803, to the legislature. you have seen the act they passed, which, tho' expressed in general terms, was meant to sanction those objects, and you are appointed to carry them into execution.

Instruments for ascertaining by celestial observations the geography of the country thro' which you will pass, have already been provided. light articles for barter, & presents among the Indians, arms for your attendants, say for from 10 to 12 men, boats, tents, & other travelling apparatus, with ammunition, medicine, surgical instruments & provisions you will have prepared with such aids as the Secretary at War can yield in his department; & from him also you will recieve authority to engage among our troops, by voluntary agreement, the number of attendants above mentioned, over whom you, as their commanding officer are invested with all the powers the laws give in such a case.

As your movements while within the limits of the U. S. will be better directed by occasional communications, adapted to circumstances as they arise, they will not be noticed here. what follows will respect your proceedings after your departure from the U. S.

Your mission has been communicated to the Ministers here from France, Spain & Great Britain, and through them to their governments: and such assurances given them as to it's objects as we trust will satisfy them. the country of Louisiana having been ceded by Spain to France, the passport you have from the Minister of France, the representative of the present sovereign of the country, will be a protection with all it's subjects: And that from the Minister of England will entitle you to the friendly aid of any traders of that allegiance with whom you may happen to meet.

The object of your mission is to explore the Missouri river, & such principal stream of it, as, by it's course & communication with the waters of the Pacific Ocean, may offer the most direct & practicable water communication across this continent, for the purposes of commerce.

Beginning at the mouth of the Missouri, you will take observations of latitude & longitude, at all remarkable points on the river, & especially at the mouths of rivers, at rapids, at islands & other places & objects distinguished by such natural marks & characters of a durable kind, as that they may with certainty be recognized hereafter. the courses of the river between these points of observation may be supplied by the compass, the log-line & by time, corrected by the observations themselves. the variations of the compass too, in different places, should be noticed.

The interesting points of portage between the heads of the Missouri & the water offering the best communication with the Pacific Ocean should also be fixed by observation, & the course of that water to the ocean, in the same manner as that of the Missouri.

Your observations are to be taken with great pains & accuracy, to be entered distinctly, & intelligibly for others as well as yourself, to comprehend all the elements necessary, with the aid of the usual tables, to fix the latitude and longitude of the places at which they were taken, & are to be rendered to the war office, for the purpose of having the calculations made concurrently by proper persons within the U. S. several copies of these, as well as your other notes, should be made at leisure times & put into the care of the most trustworthy of your attendants, to guard by multiplying them, against the accidental losses to which they will be exposed. a further guard would be that one of these copies be written on the paper of the birch, as less liable to injury from damp than common paper.

The commerce which may be carried on with the people inhabiting the line you will pursue, renders a knolege of these people important. you will therefore endeavor to make yourself acquainted, as far as a diligent pursuit of your journey shall admit,

with the names of the nations & their numbers;
the extent & limits of their possessions;
their relations with other tribes or nations;
their language, traditions, monuments;
their ordinary occupations in agriculture, fishing, hunting, war, arts,
& the implements for these;
their food, clothing, & domestic accomodations;
the diseases prevalent among them, & the remedies they use;

moral & physical circumstances which distinguish them from the
tribes we know;
peculiarities in their laws, customs & dispositions;
and articles of commerce they may need or furnish, & to what extent.

And considering the interest which every nation has in extending &
strengthening the authority of reason & justice among the people around
them, it will be useful to acquire what knolege you can of the state of
morality, religion & information among them, as it may better enable
those who endeavor to civilize & instruct them, to adapt their measures
to the existing notions & practises of those on whom they are to operate.

Other object worthy of notice will be
the soil & face of the country, it's growth & vegetable productions;
especially those not of the U. S.
the animals of the country generally, & especially those not known
in the U. S.
the remains and accounts of any which may deemed rare or extinct;
the mineral productions of every kind; but more particularly metals,
limestone, pit coal & salpetre; salines & mineral waters, noting the
temperature of the last, & such circumstances as may indicate their
character.
Volcanic appearances.
climate as characterized by the thermometer, by the proportion of
rainy, cloudy & clear days, by lightening, hail, snow, ice, by the
access & recess of frost, by the winds prevailing at different seasons, the dates at which particular plants put forth or lose their
flowers, or leaf, times of appearance of particular birds, reptiles or
insects.

Altho' your route will be along the channel of the Missouri, yet you
will endeavor to inform yourself, by inquiry, of the character & extent
of the country watered by it's branches, & especially on it's southern side.
the North river or Rio Bravo which runs into the gulph of Mexico, and
the North river, or Rio colorado, which runs into the gulph of California,
are understood to be the principal streams heading opposite to the waters
of the Missouri, and running Southwardly. whether the dividing grounds
between the Missouri & them are mountains or flatlands, what are their
distance from the Missouri, the character of the intermediate country, &
the people inhabiting it, are worthy of particular enquiry. The Northern
waters of the Missouri are less to be enquired after, because they have
been ascertained to a considerable degree, and are still in a course of
ascertainment by English traders & travellers. but if you can learn anything certain of the most Northern source of the Missisipi, & of it's

position relative to the lake of the woods, it will be interesting to us. some account too of the path of the Canadian traders from the Missisipi, at the mouth of the Ouisconsin river, to where it strikes the Missouri and of the soil & rivers in it's course, is desireable.

In all your intercourse with the natives treat them in the most friendly & conciliatory manner which their own conduct will admit; allay all jealousies as to the object of your journey, satisfy them of it's innocence, make them acquainted with the position, extent, character, peaceable & commercial dispositions of the U. S. of our wish to be neighborly, friendly & useful to them, & of our dispositions to a commercial intercourse with them; confer with them on the points most convenient as mutual emporiums, & the articles of most desireable interchange for them & us. if a few of their influential chiefs, within practicable distance, wish to visit us, arrange such a visit with them, and furnish them with authority to call on our officers, on their entering the U. S. to have them conveyed to this place at public expence. if any of them should wish to have some of their young people brought up with us, & taught such arts as may be useful to them, we will receive, instruct & take care of them. such a mission, whether of influential chiefs, or of young people, would give some security to your own party. carry with you some matter of the kinepox, inform those of them with whom you may be of it' efficacy as a preservative from the small-pox; and instruct & incourage them in the use of it. this may be especially done wherever you winter.

As it is impossible for us to foresee in what manner you will be recieved by those people, whether with hospitality or hostility, so is it impossible to prescribe the exact degree of perseverance with which you are to pursue your journey. we value too much the lives of citizens to offer them to probably destruction. your numbers will be sufficient to secure you against the unauthorised opposition of individuals, or of small parties: but if a superior force, authorised or not authorised, by a nation, should be arrayed against your further passage, & inflexibly determined to arrest it, you must decline it's further pursuit, and return. in the loss of yourselves, we should lose also the information you will have acquired. by returning safely with that, you may enable us to renew the essay with better calculated means. to your own discretion therefore must be left the degree of danger you may risk, & the point at which you should decline, only saying we wish you to err on the side of your safety, & bring back your party safe, even if it be with less information.

As far up the Missouri as the white settlements extend, an intercourse will probably be found to exist between them and the Spanish posts at St. Louis, opposite Cahokia, or Ste. Genevieve opposite Kaskaskia. from still farther up the river, the traders may furnish a conveyance for letters. beyond that you may perhaps be able to engage Indians to bring letters for the government to Cahokia or Kaskaskia, on promising that they shall there receive such special compensation as you shall have stipulated with them. avail yourself of these means to communicate to us, at seasonable intervals, a copy of your journal, notes & observations of every kind, putting into cypher whatever might do injury if betrayed.

Should you reach the Pacific ocean [One full line scratched out, indecipherable.—Thwaites.] inform yourself of the circumstances which may decide whether the furs of those parts may not be collected as advantageously at the head of the Missouri (convenient as is supposed to the waters of the Colorado & Oregon or Columbia) as at Nootka sound or any other point of that coast; & that trade be consequently conducted through the Missouri & U. S. more beneficially than by the circumnavigation now practised.

On your arrival on that coast endeavor to learn if there be any port within your reach frequented by the sea-vessels of any nation, and to send two of your trusty people back by sea, in such way as shall appear practicable, with a copy of your notes. and should you be of opinion that the return of your party by the way they went will be eminently dangerous, then ship the whole, & return by sea by way of Cape Horn or the Cape of good Hope, as you shall be able. as you will be without money, clothes or provisions, you must endeavor to use the credit of the U. S. to obtain them; for which purpose open letters of credit shall be furnished you authorising you to draw on the Executive of the U. S. or any of its officers in any part of the world, on which drafts can be disposed of, and to apply with our recommendations to the Consuls, agents, merchants, or citizens of any nation with which we have intercourse, assuring them in our name that any aids they may furnish you, shall honorably repaid, and on demand. Our consuls Thomas Howes at Batavia in Java, William Buchanan on the isles of France and Bourbon, & John Elmslie at the Cape of good hope will be able to supply your necessities by draughts on us.

Should you find it safe to return by the way you go, after sending two of your party round by sea, or with your whole party, if no conveyance by sea can be found, do so; making such observations on your return as may serve to supply, correct or confirm those made on your outward journey.

In re-entering the U. S. and reaching a place of safety, discharge any of your attendants who may desire & deserve it, procuring for them immediate paiment of all arrears of pay & cloathing which may have incurred since their departure; & assure them that they shall be recommended to the liberality of the legislature for the grant of a soldier's portion of land each, as proposed in my message to Congress & repair yourself with your papers to the seat of government.

To provide, on the accident of your death, against anarchy, dispersion & the consequent danger to your party, and total failure of the enterprise, you are hereby authorised, by any instrument signed & written in your hand, to name the person among them who shall succeed to the command on your decease, & by like instruments to change the nomination from time to time, as further experience of the characters accompanying you shall point out superior fitness; and all the powers & authorities given to yourself are, in the event of your death, transferred to & vested in the successor so named, with further power to him, & his successors in like manner to name each his successor, who, on the death of his predecessor, shall be invested with all the powers & authorities given to yourself.

Given under my hand at the city of Washington, this 20th day of June 1803

Th. Jefferson
Pr. U S. of America

APPENDIX II

The Permanent Party

In Command

Captain Meriwether Lewis, First U.S. Infantry
Second Lieutenant (his official rank) William Clark, U.S. Corps of
  Artillerists

Sergeants

John Ordway
Nathaniel Pryor
Charles Floyd (died August 20, 1804)
Patrick Gass (replaced Floyd August 26, 1804)

Privates

William Bratton
John Collins
John Colter
Pierre Cruzatte
Joseph Field
Reuben Field
Robert Frazer (enlisted October 8, 1804, at the Arikara villages)
George Gibson
Silas Goodrich
Hugh Hall
Thomas P. Howard
François Labiche
Baptiste Lepage (enlisted November 2, 1804, at the Mandan
  villages)
Hugh McNeal
John Newman (discharged at the Mandan villages)
John Potts
Moses B. Reed (deserted, captured, and discharged)

George Shannon
John Shields
John B. Thompson
William Werner
Joseph Whitehouse
Alexander H. Willard
Richard Windsor
Peter M. Wiser

Interpreters

George Drouillard (generally spelled Drewyer in the journals)
Toussaint Charbonneau

Supernumeraries

York, Clark's slave
Sacagawea, Charbonneau's wife
Jean Baptiste Charbonneau (Pomp), their child
Seaman, a dog

APPENDIX III

Much Ado About Little—
The Case of the *Lydia*

In the spring of 1803, a trading ship hunting for sea-otter pelts sailed into Nootka Sound on the west coast of Vancouver Island, British Columbia. Resentful of several years of mistreatment by white traders, the Indians massacred all the crew except the ship's twenty-year-old, English-born armorer (blacksmith) John Jewitt, and the sailmaker, John Thompson. Those two languished as prisoners until rescued on July 19, 1805, by Captain Samuel Hill of the brig *Lydia*, out of Boston. The salvation was effected without bloodshed, and on departing for further trading operations along the Northwest Coast, Captain Hill said he would return to Nootka within a few months to pick up whatever pelts the Indians gathered during his absence.

Throughout his captivity, young John Jewitt kept a secret diary, using berry juice as ink. His entries, however, ceased with his rescue, and thereby hangs our tale. On finally reaching Boston by way of China late in the spring of 1807, Jewitt made arrangements for a printer to issue *A Journal Kept at Nootka Sound*. It was dull—terse because of necessity and vapid because the ill-educated sailor had "small capacity as a narrator," to borrow the words of Richard Alsop of Hartford, Connecticut, a rich merchant with literary ambitions. Alsop plucked the needed drama out of Jewitt bit by bit. Using *Robinson Crusoe* as a model, he then published in 1815 a *Narrative of the Adventures and Sufferings of John R. Jewitt*. Although the style is turgid and the tone elevated, the *Narrative* kept being reprinted until as late as 1975 (Robert F. Heizer, editor, *Narrative of . . . John R. Jewitt* [taken from the edition of 1820], published by the Bellona Press of Ramona, California). During those many decades it has become a standard item of students of the Lewis and Clark expedition for the following reasons.

As stated, Jewitt left off his diary with his rescue. His story was blood, thunder, and life with the Indians. English-born, he cared next to nothing about Lewis and Clark. Alsop, however, wanted to get his hero home to his loved ones. So he continued pumping Jewitt about the last stages of the story and in the process learned that during the course of sailing tediously back and forth along the coast, the *Lydia* had crept about ten miles into the Columbia estuary in search of a convenient stand of timber from which to cut a new mast and spars. While the traders were there, visiting Indians showed the mariners medals given them by Lewis and Clark, who, they said had arrived by land with a small party and then, only a fortnight earlier, had started home, again by land.

Alsop pounced. Lewis and Clark would certainly interest American readers, for in this year of 1814, when Alsop was interviewing Jewitt, Nicholas Biddle and Paul Allen had finally published their official *History of the Expedition under the Command of Captains Lewis and Clark, to the Sources of the Missouri, thence across the Rocky Mountains and down the River Columbia to the Pacific Ocean . . . during the Years 1804–5–6.* We can imagine Alsop digging away: how about some details? And we can imagine Jewitt shrugging. All that boring search for pelts from one foggy anchorage to the next—no blood and thunder in that. There were no details.

Well, then, when had the encounter with the Columbia River Indians taken place? Jewitt looked back across eight or nine years at the blur. No diary to refresh his memory. Another shrug. Maybe it had been in November, shortly before the *Lydia* had returned to Nootka, as promised, for more pelts. At least he thought the brig went back to Nootka in November.

And then? Again we can picture a shrug. Nothing much—more wandering along the coast—a pelt here, a pelt there—until mid-August, 1806, when Hill at last struck across the Pacific for Macao, China. He paused there to swap his furs for Oriental goods in demand in Boston. During the layover, Jewitt sent a letter to his mother by an earlier ship to let her know he was still alive—a small point for us to remember later.

Bridging the gap between Jewitt's rescue and his homecoming filled roughly two pages of Alsop's 160-page *Narrative.* Of those two pages two sentences were devoted to the encounter with the Indians who had the medals Lewis and Clark had given them—throwaway lines as far as Jewitt was concerned. But to American students of the expedition they were exciting. November! Why, from November 8 or so to the 25th, the explorers had been camping at various spots along the north side of the Columbia estuary, the same side where the *Lydia* had anchored. On the 25th the Americans had moved to the south side, where some of them had stayed until early December before going a couple of miles inland to build Fort Clatsop. How ironic! How dramatic! The Corps had been desperate for the kind of supplies the *Lydia* carried. They were eager to send specimens and reports to the president. And the ship had been there! Yet they had not seen it. They had not heard a word about it from the Indians. And the *Lydia* had learned nothing of them until after the whites had gone inland to settle at Fort Clatsop—a move the Indians represented as a departure for the East. How amazing!

Amazing is right. This blind leap at an offhand remark by Alsop/Jewitt put the historians who made the jump in an untenable position. (I admit to being one of them—Lavender, *Land of Giants,* New York: Doubleday, 1958, pp. 73–74—until I examined the entire context of the Jewitt *Narrative.*) While it is barely possible, given the state of the weather, that the Americans did not see the brig, it is inconceivable that the small parties of Indians who stopped by their camps every day to gossip and sell food and furs did not mention the ship—if it was in the vicinity. Some historians evade the issue, saying the Indians' silence was an enigma. Others have cooked up a conspiracy theory. The Chinooks from the many different bands, they say, had agreed to seal their lips as a way of taking revenge on the whites because Clark had threatened to shoot them for stealing from the Corps. Well, possibly they stayed silent while the explorers might still have reached the *Lydia.* But what about the nearly four months that followed? Several Chinooks visited Fort Clatsop during the period. Did none boast of the feat in order to watch the whites squirm? Members of other tribes, Clatsops and Cathlamets, also floated in and out. None mentioned the *Lydia,* ever. Such an unbroken veil of secrecy among the gossippy, far-traveling, curious Indians—remember how fast the news of the beached whales spread—passes credulity.

Conspiracy is a favorite refuge for those unwilling to face simple, direct explanations. Lee Harvey Oswald killed President Kennedy entirely on his own? No, no. There had to be conspirators in the background. Similar reasoning holds that all the Indians living around the Columbia delta agreed to stay silent about the *Lydia* in order to—well, discomfit Lewis and Clark, who actually would have traded eagerly with them for supplies, if they had been able to get the necessary goods from the ship. To suppose the shrewd-bargaining Indians did not realize this is to suppose they wanted to do themselves out of business for the sake of a small revenge.

There is a simpler explanation. From Meriwether Lewis's journal we know that shortly before the Corps left Fort Clatsop on March 23, 1806, Clark and he gave to several Indians a written notice of their crossing, together with a rough map of their route and a list of the expedition's personnel. They asked the recipients of these documents, some of whom had medals as well, to pass the papers along to the first trading ships that showed up. Their hope was to let Jefferson know as soon as possible that they had indeed reached the Pacific; after all, they might not get back, and history should be aware of their feat. Then off they went. Shortly thereafter, in April, the *Lydia* definitely did enter the estuary. Indians thronged around, and one of them gave Captain Hill one of the documents. He carried it to China, where he arrived in December 1806. Knowing he would be delayed there by his mercantile enterprises, he handed the papers to another ship captain for delivery. Almost surely the paper traveled to New England aboard the same ship that carried Jewitt's letter to his mother. And that indeed is irony, because the rescued blacksmith could have straightened out the matter then and there by mentioning the Lewis and Clark documents. But Lewis and Clark were nothing to him—so little, in fact, that when Alsop probed for details, Jewitt probably got his dates mixed up. He said that after cutting spars in the estuary, the *Lydia* had returned to Nootka, arriving there late in November. It is more likely, however, that the *Lydia* had gone to Nootka in April, after the Lewis and Clark papers had fallen into Hill's hands. It was an easy mistake to make, considering all the beating back and forth along the coast the ship had done during those winter months.

Of course it is possible that the *Lydia* also went to Nootka in November, after pausing in the estuary shortly *before* Lewis and Clark arrived there. Such a pause would account for the frequent mentions of a ship in the delta that the Americans heard as they descended the river, only to be greeted by empty water when they arrived. But whether or not the *Lydia* bracketed the explorers' months in the area or simply arrived in April, the main point is that there was no ship there during the Americans' stay. The matter would hardly merit mention if the legend weren't still being delivered to wide-eyed tourists in the Northwest as another item of great drama in real life.

Notes

Because Reuben G. Thwaites's *The Original Journals of the Lewis and Clark Expedition* is the basic reference book for the expedition itself, references to it are frequent and therefore limited, in all the following notes, to volume and page number. For an example, see note 12 below.

Chapter 1: Beginner's Luck

1. Jefferson to Lewis, February 23, 1801, in Jackson, *Letters*, 2–3.
2. Lewis to F. Claibourne, March 7, 1801, in ibid., II, 675.
3. Malone, IV, 40.
4. Dillon, 16.
5. Wistar to Marshall, January 20, 1792, in Jackson, *Letters*, II, 675–77.
6. Jefferson, "Life of Captain Lewis," in Biddle, xviii.
7. Malone, III, 109. Jackson, *Jefferson and Stony Mountains*, 157.
8. Jackson, *Jefferson and Stony Mountains*, 86–96, discusses Jefferson's library.
9. Boyd, IX, 218. Both Morse and Dwight are quoted in DeConde, 39–40. See also Smith, 10–12.
10. Quoted in DeVoto, *Course of Empire*, 416. For an analysis of Ledyard's proposal, 595–98.
11. Jackson, *Letters*, II, 668–69.
12. VII, 204.
13. Bakeless, *Lewis and Clark*, 86.
14. Ibid., 3–5. Burroughs, 2. DeVoto, *Course*, 608.
15. The army's authorized strength when Jefferson took office was 5,438 officers and men, but only a few more than 4,000 were actually in office. On March 16, 1802, the authorized strength was cut to 3,312. Malone, IV, 248. Ganoe, 104.
16. Jackson, *Jefferson and Stony Mountains*, 120. Malone, IV, 248.
17. Malone, IV, 248.

18. Ibid., 40.
19. Jackson, *Letters*, II, 667. "Jefferson's Analysis of Expenditures . . . ," in Mayo (ed.), 236.
20. Malone, IV, 40.
21. Padover, 115.
22. My account of the events leading to the Louisiana Purchase is based on DeConde; Malone, IV; DeVoto, *Course*; Sprague; Johansen and Gates; Morison and Commager; and McDonald, Decker, and Govan. More iconoclastic is Philbrick. For appropriate pages consult the indexes in the different books.
23. Quoted in DeConde, 87.
24. Malone, IV, 266.
25. The full letter, Jefferson to Livingston, is in Sprague, 362–63.
26. Jefferson's military preparations: Adams; DeConde, 132–37. There is a reference to the proposed fort at Cahokia in Jackson, *Letters*, 41 n. 4.
27. Jackson to Rush, February 28, 1803, in Jackson, *Letters*, 18–19.
28. This runs counter to the common convention that the expedition, with Lewis at its head, had been in Jefferson's mind for years. But the first actual step westward was taken as a *defensive*, not expansionist, measure. To quote Johansen and Gates, 93, "It was to counteract this [British] influence, to win over the Indians, and to conduct a military reconnaissance against a possible war that Jefferson originally projected the Lewis and Clark expedition." See also Adams, 174–75, 184–85.
29. Mayo, 249. Malone, IV, 272–73.
30. Nasatir, *Before Lewis and Clark*, 712–16.
31. "Jefferson's Message to Congress," in Jackson, *Letters*, 4–8.
32. Ibid., 12.
33. Ibid., 13.

Chapter 2: Preparing for the Future

1. Malone, IV, 278–81. McMaster, II, 448–99, 631–33. [Benton] *Abridgement*, 672–92, passim.
2. Manpower is given variously as between eight and twelve in Jefferson's letters to Barton, Wister, Rush, and Patterson, all of them members of the American Philosophical Society. (Jackson, *Letters*, 16–20.) See also Dearborn to Lewis, ibid., 70.
3. Ibid., 70.
4. Ibid., 38.
5. Quoted in Chuinard, 99.
6. Ronda, 8.
7. Jackson, *Letters*, 38.
8. Cutright, *Pioneering Naturalists*, 4.
9. I hypothesize this paragraph from Jefferson's letter to Robert Patterson, March 2, 1803 (Jackson, *Letters*, 21): "He [Lewis] has for some time been qualifying himself for taking observations of Longitude and latitude . . . but little means are possessed here for doing that; and it is the particular part in which you could give him valuable instruction."

10. Cutright, *Pioneering Naturalists*, 5, 25.
11. Theoretical geography and mapmaking therefrom are covered in fascinating detail in Wheat, I, and Allen, passim. See also DeVoto, *Course*, 51–79.
12. For Charlevoix, Du Pratz *et al.*: Allen, 14; DeVoto, *Course*, 199–200; Lavender, *Westward*, 23–24.
13. Carver, passim. Allen, 16–30, 91, 96 (the citations also cover map reproductions); Lavender, *Westward*, 50–64; Jackson, *Letters* II, 695.
14. For Gray: Boit, "Log of the Columbia," Howay, *Voyages of the Columbia*. For Vancouver's men on the Columbia River: Barry, "Broughton," and "Who Discovered the Columbia?"
15. Allen, 96–97.
16. This is DeVoto's contention in his foreword to the *Journals*, 1–lii. The whole foreword can be read with profit, even though (in my opinion) DeVoto is quite wrong-headed in some of his dogmatic declarations—for instance, his insistence that Jefferson was not surprised by the Louisiana Purchase.
17. Wood and Thiessen, 26–27, 42–47, and appendix, Table 1.
18. D. Thompson, 160–81.
19. Allen, 87–90. Portions of the Thompson, Mackenzie, and 1802 Arrowsmith maps are in ibid., 80, 84, 92.
20. Ibid., 87, 79. Fidler's copy of the Indian map is on 22. See also Wheat I, 178.
21. Jackson, *Letters*, 27–28.
22. For King's map, Allen, 100, 116. See 47, 96–104, 117 for a discussion of the relationship of the King and Arrowsmith maps. For Allen's belief that Lewis took the King map to the Pacific with him: 97–98, 132, and, by implication, 165–66.
23. Jackson, *Letters*, 63.
24. Ibid., 26.
25. Morton, 466–68.
26. Jackson, *Letters*, 19–27.
25. Ibid., 38, 44.

Chapter 3: Grappling with Logistics

1. Russell, 37–43, 278–85. Figures from Jackson, *Letters*, 70, 72.
2. Lewis's account of the boat building is by no means clear. Jackson, *Letters*, 39–40. For dimensions: Cutright, *Pioneering Naturalists*, 165; Biddle, II, 245.
3. Jackson, *Letters*, 43, and *Jefferson and Stony Mountains*, 135.
4. Jackson, *Letters*, 40.
5. Ronda, 9.
6. Jackson, *Letters*, II, 735. Chatters, 4–6.
7. Chuinard, 121–44.
8. Ibid., 68–69.
9. Cutright, "I Gave Him Barks." Jackson, *Letters*, 80, 88, 93.
10. Jackson, *Letters*, 53.

11. Ibid., 50.
12. Ibid., 28–31, 56.
13. Dickerson, "Diary," in ibid., 679–81.
14. Malone, V, 78–79.
15. Jackson, *Letters*, 53–54.
16. Ibid., 32–34.
17. Ibid., 34–36. Lincoln's suggestions "sharpened focus on the approach the expedition should take to the tribes, which in too many cases was roughshod and calculated to produce hostility." Ronda, 2, 7.
18. It is possible Lewis did not reach Washington until June 17, 1803. (See his letter to Clark in Jackson, *Letters*, 57.) However, he seems to have left Philadelphia before June 11. (Note dates referring to his trip in ibid., 54, 51.) A young man on horseback could easily cover the 130 miles separating Philadelphia from Washington in four days, and three if he pushed himself. A stagecoach, traveling by night as well as by day, would be still faster. So I imagine Lewis reached the White House by June 12 and "day before yesterday" refers to the day he penned the first draft of his carefully prepared letter to Clark (see next chapter) and not to the date, June 19, attached to the final draft.
19. The negotiations about Louisiana have been summarized in DeConde, 148–75; Sprague, 299–313; and Malone, IV, 286–96.

Chapter 4: Trial Run

1. DeVoto, *Course*, 397.
2. McMaster, II, 638–40.
3. Malone, IV, 324, 335. DeConde, 201–4.
4. Jefferson to Breckinridge, August 12, 1803, quoted in Sprague, 315.
5. Indian removal: Jackson, *Jefferson and Stony Mountains*, 112–13, and *Letters*, 152–54; Esarey, 69–73; Prucha, 213–17, 226.
6. Steffen. Bakeless, *Lewis and Clark*. Appleman, 52–55.
7. Lewis to Clark, in Jackson, *Letters*, 57–60.
8. The actual commission, a lieutenancy, contained a blank wherein Lewis could enter any name he chose. (Jackson, *Letters*, 104.) In Pittsburgh, as we will see, he came close to naming a regimental friend, Moses Hooke, rather than Clark.
9. Jackson, *Letters*, 103–4.
10. Lewis's dog was long called Scammon or Scannon because of errors made by Coues, Thwaites, Osgood, and others in reading the manuscript journals. The mistake was corrected by Jackson, "Call Him Good Old Dog." I assume, as do Osgood in "Our Dog Scannon" and many others, that Lewis bought the dog somewhere on the East Coast, paying twenty dollars. However, I have found no mention of him before the start of the trip down the Ohio, and Lewis may have picked him up in Pittsburgh.
11. Drawings made by Clark of a keelboat resting in a cove of the Mississippi show a high stern cabin and two masts. (Moulton, *Atlas*, maps 3a, 3b.) Later, near Cahokia, December 7, Clark reported that a

violent wind blew down one of the masts. (Quaife, entry for December 7.) This suggests the unusual second mast was another of Lewis's innovations.

12. Extracts from Cramer's *The Navigator* appear in Hulbert. See also Havighurst, *Long Horizons*, 165–70, and *River*, 135–36.

13. Jackson, *Letters*, 109.

14. Ibid., 110–15.

15. Ibid., 115–17.

16. Appleman, 49.

17. Lange, "Shannon." Colter may not have joined the expedition at Pittsburgh but at Old Limestone, now Maysville, Kentucky. See biographies of him: Burton Harris and the *Dictionary of American Biography*.

18. Lewis to Jefferson, from Wheeling, September 8, 1803, speaks of having hired "a waggon." Moses Hooke, the military agent who had to pay for the vehicles, says two. I follow Hooke. See Jackson, *Letters*, 119, 122.

19. I reconstruct the trip down the Ohio from Lewis's journal in Quaife and his letters to Jefferson, September 8 and 13 and October 3. Jackson, *Letters*, 121–31.

20. Jackson, *Letters*, 126–31. Havighurst, *River*, 131–32.

21. Havighurst, *River*, 136–38.

22. Lange, "Shields." Clarke, 53–54.

23. Jackson, *Letters*, 364–73.

24. Bakeless, *Background to Glory*, 242–48.

25. Ibid., 295. Quaife, 59–62. Jackson, *Letters*, 152.

26. Quaife, 169.

Chapter 5: Facing Reality

1. On December 19, 1803, Lewis wrote Jefferson that during his pause at Kaskaskia he had filled the expedition's roster. He was including the seven-man crew of the supply boat when he said that. (Actually, the boat crew lifted the count to twenty-six.) Jackson, *Letters*, 142, 145.

2. Ibid., 155. Innis, 254–55, outlines the travels of a trader named John Hay through the borderlands between central Canada and the United States in 1794–95. I suspect this is the same John Hay Lewis met in Cahokia. In any event, the Hay of Cahokia was able to make valuable corrections to that part of King's map depicting the regions west and northwest of the Mississippi's headwaters.

3. Jackson, *Letters*, 151.

4. Ibid., 142–43, 145–47.

5. Ibid., 147. Quaife, 63.

6. Jackson, *Letters*, 150–51.

7. Ibid., 148–55.

8. Osgood, *Field Notes*, 28.

9. My summary of events on the Missouri River preceding the arrival of Lewis and Clark in St. Louis rests on four works by the indefatigable Abraham P. Nasatir, two by Abel, and one each by Houck (vol. II) and

Williams. See bibliography for titles. See also Quaife, 186ff.: Ewers, "Indian Trade"; scattered references in Wood and Thiessen (consult index under "Evans," "Mackay," "Menard," "Jessaume," "Truteau," "Mandans"); and DeVoto, *Course*, 355–79.

10. Houck, II, 171.

11. Wood and Thiessen, 50.

12. DeVoto, *Course*, calls this "a lot of time." Lewis and Clark, however, spent about ten days more on the same stretch.

13. For Clark on Evans's sad realization: Jackson, *Letters*, II, 515.

14. For Evans's map: Allen, 143. For Ménard's wanderings: Wood and Thiessen, 30, 44–45.

15. Quaife, 197.

16. Scholars have spent years trying to determine just what maps Lewis and Clark drew on in St. Louis—a subject too complex to detail in my narrative. To pursue the matter further, start with Diller, Friis, and Allen, 68, 73–180. Evans died before Lewis and Clark reached St. Louis, but much of his material may have fallen into Hay's hands and have been passed on by him. (Osgood, *Field Notes*, 16; Jackson, *Letters*, 156–57.) For a fine summary incorporating the latest speculation, Moulton, *Journals*, I, 6–7.

17. "Because of subsequent changes in the channel of the Mississippi, this site is now on its west side. . . . The mouth of the Missouri has also shifted and is presently some [four miles] farther to the south." Appleman, 287–90, 366 n. 2.

18. Osgood, *Field Notes*, under date January 3, 1804.

19. Ibid., 16–27. Although Clark hardly sounds well in his field notes, he kept a stiff upper lip when writing his brother-in-law, William Crogan, on January 15. "I am in tolerable health. . . . My situation is as could be expected in the woods and on the frontier." (Jackson, *Letters*, 164.)

20. Osgood, *Field Notes*, 21. Allen, 160–67.

21. Biddle, 2, flatly states the keelboat had twenty-two oars. Clark's sketch of the boat clearly shows twenty. (Osgood, *Field Notes*, 37, 41.) Completely conclusive, it seems to me, is a mention of twenty oars by a Canadian trader, Charles McKenzie, who saw the keelboat at Fort Mandan. (Wood and Thiessen, 238.)

22. For early St. Louis, the Chouteaus, and the transfer of flags see McDermott, Scharf, and Foley and Rice.

23. Jackson, *Letters*, 157–61.

24. Ibid., 64, 165–66.

25. Ibid., 167–68.

26. Dillon, 93–94.

27. Details of this and the following transfer come from Scharf, 250ff., and articles by Shoemaker and McDermott. Legend attests that after the Spanish flag was lowered in St. Louis, the French tricolor replaced it briefly, as had happened in New Orleans. However, the tale did not pop up until 1876 and is open to doubt.

Chapter 6: Smoky Water

1. The date, April 18, comes from Ordway's letter to his parents (Jackson, *Letters*, 176–77): ". . . we are to Start in ten days up the Missouri River." The quickened activity that gripped Camp Dubois during the last days of March and the early ones of April also supports conjectures that April 18 or so was the original starting date. See Osgood, *Field Notes*, 27–31.

2. The orders concerning the division of the "permanent detachment" are in Thwaites I, 11–12. His list of men in the detachment is reproduced in Appendix II.

3. Scharf, 265.

4. I borrow the phrasing of this message and of later ones to the Iowas and Sioux from a speech Lewis later delivered to the Otos, a Missouri River tribe. (Jackson *Letters*, 203–8.)

5. Ibid., 196–98.

6. Ibid., 199.

7. Osgood, *Field Notes*, 30. McDermott, 335.

8. I, 36–37. Jackson, *Letters*, 197, 200.

9. Osgood, *Field Notes*, 37.

10. Jackson, *Letters*, 172–73, 179.

11. Clark to Biddle, ibid., II, 571–72.

12. Appleman, 67–68, 74–75.

13. I, 30–34.

14. See Lewis to Stoddard, May 16, 1804 (Jackson, *Letters*, 189–90), concerning the twelve-man limit, and ibid., 199, for Jefferson's remark.

15. Foley and Rice, 55, 107–08.

16. Grace Lewis, 480. Compare her figures with Jackson, *Letters*, II, 420–30.

17. Jackson, *Letters*, 180, 209n.

18. Ibid., 170–71, 180–83, 189–95.

19. Appleman, 79.

20. Lewis on the wounding: "I instantly supposed that Cruzatte had shot me by mistake. . . . I was dressed in brown and he cannot see very well." (DeVoto, *Journals*, 445.) True, a one-eyed man cannot see as well as one with two. The remark does not have to be taken as an indication of myopia, however.

21. My account of the trip is compounded from Thwaites, Clark's "River Journal" as it appears in Osgood's *Field Notes*, and the Biddle narrative, with addenda from Ordway's and Whitehouse's journals. There seems no gain in noting each source except where discrepancies appear or points of emphasis vary. Lewis, incidentally, seems not to have kept a journal between St. Charles and the Mandan towns. See note 26 below.

22. Osgood, *Field Notes*, 45.

23. DeVoto, *Course*, 613–14.

24. Allen, 187–91.

25. Osgood, *Field Notes*, 53.

26. The vexing problem of Lewis's missing journals (he left big gaps all the

way to the Pacific and back) is discussed in Jackson, "Some Advice"; Cutright, *History of Journals;* and Osgood's introduction to Clark's *Field Notes.* However, Clark often copied the rough field notes Lewis did make (Moulton, *Journals,* II, 19–21) and so the record is probably quite complete in spite of Lewis's lapses.

27. Moulton, *Atlas,* 4, describes Clark's mapping procedures. Osgood, *Field Notes,* and/or Thwaites print the daily compass readings and estimates of distances between sighting points.

28. Osgood, *Field Notes,* 61. I, 56–57.

29. Though Lewis and Clark were unaware of it, Loisel wanted to draw the boundary of Louisiana along the Missouri River in order to protect the trade his men conducted south and west of that stream. On reaching St. Louis, he sent an offer to Spanish officials to act as an agent in countering American activities in the critical region, which, he asserted, would open easy routes to Santa Fe. Meanwhile Spanish officials in Florida, Cuba, and Mexico had grown alarmed about the threat to New Mexico, and letters flew back and forth about stopping the expedition either by sending out troops or stirring up the Indians. The efforts failed. A useful summary is in Cook, 458–83, passim. For Loisel, see the introduction in Abel's *Narrative.*

30. Jackson, *Letters,* 262–63.

31. DeVoto, *Course,* 367, 375–76. Appleman, 93–94.

32. Moulton, *Journals,* II, 405–16. Osgood, *Field Notes,* 88ff.

33. Moulton, *Journals,* II, 429–33.

34. I, 96–97. Ronda, 17–18.

35. Moulton, *Journals,* II, 433.

Chapter 7: Emphasis on Indians

1. The talk is given in full in Jackson, *Letters,* 203–8.

2. For an introduction to the long history of medal giving, see Hodge, I, 829–36.

3. The notes on the council Clark wrote on the spot are not as specific about the Otos' fear of meeting with the Omahas as he made them when being interviewed by Biddle. Jackson, *Letters,* II, 514.

4. Clark quotation from Moulton, *Journals,* II, 478–79. For Blackbird, DeVoto, *Course,* 367, 375–76. Appleman, 93–94, 334.

5. Ordway in Quaife, 108–9.

6. Osgood, *Field Notes,* 109.

7. Ordway in Quaife, 108–11.

8. Ibid., 112.

9. Moulton, *Journals,* II, 492–96.

10. Ibid., 499–502.

11. Ibid., 504ff. Ordway in Quaife, 117.

12. White, 319–43, discusses the Sioux's westward migrations. Lehmer, *Middle Missouri Archeology,* 168–69, touches on the James River

rendezvous. Hodge, I, 227, 376–77, II, 736–37, 988–89, summarizes the early history of the Ojibway (Chippewa) and Dakota (Sioux) tribes, and the Teton and Yankton divisions of the Dakotas.

13. Jackson, *Letters,* 62–63, 116.
14. Osgood, *Field Notes,* 120. Ordway in Quaife, 117.
15. I, 126–31. Biddle, 50–55. Osgood, *Field Notes,* 123–28. Ronda, 24–26.
16. Abel, *Tabeau's Narrative,* 72n. Cutright, *Pioneering Naturalists,* 80, says Ordway may have been the first person to use the term "prairie dog." This may be true for the Corps's journalists, but not for the French, who saw the plains years before the Americans appeared. For more on the encounter with the prairie dogs, Osgood, *Field Notes,* 133–34.
17. Cutright, *Pioneering Naturalists,* 144.
18. I, 152–54. Biddle, 66.
19. Osgood, *Field Notes,* 135.
20. Ibid., 139.
21. Abel, *Narrative,* 107–20.

Chapter 8: Into Winter

1. For the Teton meeting: I, 164–71; Biddle, 71–81; Osgood, *Field Notes,* 153–54; Ordway in Quaife, 138–43; Gass; Whitehouse in VII, 61–65. Antoine Tabeau points up the jealousies existing between the chiefs in Abel, *Narrative,* 108–13. Ronda, 31–41, places the confrontation against a background of conflicting Sioux personalities and the realities of trade competition. Because the situation was often tense and confused, discrepancies appear in the accounts.
2. Ronda, 63. Meyer, 80. Kehoe, 99–103.
3. From the Bad River to the Arikara villages: I, 170–84; Osgood, *Field Notes,* 151–56; Ordway in Quaife, 143–48.
4. Truteau's journal (not to be confused with Tabeau's) is printed in Nasatir, *Before Lewis and Clark,* 259–311; Truteau's "Description of the Upper Missouri" is in ibid., II, 376–85. See also Thwaites I, 230.
5. Lehmer and Jones, *Arikara Archeology,* 83–84. Lehmer, *Middle Missouri Archeology,* 136–68. Meyer, 29 and 272–39.
6. Osgood, *Field Notes,* 153.
7. Ronda, 49–50.
8. Among the Arikaras: I, 170–84; Osgood, *Field Notes,* 152–56; Ordway in Quaife, 143–48; Biddle, 83–93; Abel, *Narrative,* 123–51; Ronda, 43–65.
9. Abel, *Narrative,* 146.
10. Frazer was one of those who kept a journal at the captains' behest. He may have decided to increase the manuscript's salability by completing the trip. On the Corps's return he issued a prospectus, but the book was not published and the manuscript has been lost. Jackson, *Letters,* 345–46, 400–1, and "Race to Publish."
11. This thesis is developed by Ronda, 56–112, passim.
12. Biddle, 92.

13. From the Arikaras to the Mandans: I, 190–207; Ordway in Quaife, 152–61.
14. Osgood, *Field Notes*, 155. DeVoto points out (*Course*, 451) that garments made from those hides were probably stiff and uncomfortable, for the men lacked the ingredients and time for careful tanning.
15. Cutright, *Pioneering Naturalists*, 100–101.

Chapter 9: The Grand Plan

1. Osgood, *Field Notes*, 169. Clark omitted his denigration of Jessaume in his official journal. Alexander Henry, who encountered Jessaume in 1806, was also unfavorably impressed. Coues, 333.
2. For the names of the tribes and the villages they inhabited—more names than I have given—consult Clark's notes to Biddle in Jackson, *Letters*, II, 522, 524–25. See also Hodge under "Mandan," "Hidatsa," etc., and Ronda, 67–70. Henry gives the locations of the villages in Coues, 322–24. Thompson, *Narrative*, 169n, says the towns were scattered along eleven and a half miles of the riverbank. Perhaps so as the river curved, but the distance from the lowest Mandan village, Matootonha, to Big Hidatsa could not have been much more than six miles in a direct line by land. The maps in Ronda, 68, and Appleman, 238–39, do not agree with Clark's map as reproduced in Moulton, *Atlas*, plates 29 and 61. I have followed Clark.
3. I, 210–13.
4. Jackson, *Letters*, 213–14. For American licensing provisions under Jay's Treaty: Phillips, II, 73–74, and Jackson, *Zebulon Pike*, I, 256. In spite of Jay's Treaty, foreign traders were excluded from the Missouri in 1805. (Jackson, *Letters*, 256–57.) The sentiment that led to the exclusion must have been noticeable in St. Louis when Lewis and Clark were studying trade problems there.
5. Although Bernard DeVoto says flatly that four of the French boatmen headed downstream in November, other students of the expedition are content to say their exact numbers cannot be determined. The issue is confused by two French trappers who met the Corps on its way upstream and continued to the Mandans with the American boats, hoping to recover some traps and furs the Indians had taken from them. DeVoto, *Journals*, 63 n. 4. Appleman, 367, 368 nn. 64, 66, 74. Jackson, *Letters*, 237 n. 7.
6. For the spellings and their meanings: Jackson, *Letters*, 316n; Appleman, 115–17. I follow Kenneth O. Owens, "Sacagawea," in Lamar, 1055, for her age.
7. Cutright, *Pioneering Naturalists*, 110.
8. I, 218. For the fort in general: Biddle, 113; Wood and Thiessen, 143; and the appropriate sections in Moulton, *Journals*, III.
9. Every day someone checked the expedition's thermometers at sunrise and at 4:00 P.M. The readings were relayed to the captains, who recorded the figures in their weather journals, along with data about wind, precipitation, cloudiness, etc. A line of remarks followed most weather

entries. The data are reproduced by the month in Moulton's edition of the journals, and are collected in a single entry and printed as an appendix in Biddle, III, 846–89.

10. I, 222ff. Osgood, *Field Notes,* 178. VII, 69. Ordway in Quaife, 164–66. Whitehouse counts the spoils as 34 deer, 10 elk, 5 buffalo; Ordway as 30 deer, 11 elk, 5 buffalo.

11. Osgood, *Field Notes,* 174n. Moulton, *Journals,* III, 234. VI, 104.

12. Ronda, 89–90. Osgood, *Field Notes,* 176–77.

13. For Lewis's diplomatic adventure: I, 227–29; Moulton, *Journals,* III, 241–49, passim.

14. I, 226.

15. Laroque, reprinted in Wood and Thiessen, 137, 140. Also Charles McKenzie, "Narrative," in ibid., 232–38; Coues, 349–50.

16. I, 229. Ordway in Quaife, 168.

17. I, 230–32.

18. Biddle, 121.

Chapter 10: Forty Below—and Far to Go

1. Temperature readings: Biddle, III, 852–55. Biddle prints a low of −45° for December 17, 1804; a photostatic copy of the actual tables (Large, 7) shows the low for the day to be −43°. Averages were calculated by Large, 6–10.

2. Ordway in Quaife, 169. For the hunts: ibid., 169–71; I, 235–37; Biddle, 122–24.

3. Ordway in Quaife, 174. Biddle, 138: "The blacksmith has become one of our greatest resources for procuring grain."

4. Moulton, *Journals,* III, 211. Whitehouse (in Thwaites VII), 72.

5. The New Year celebrations: I, 242–44; Moulton, *Journals,* III, 266–67; Ordway in Quaife, 174–75; Gass, 79–80.

6. Bowers, 315–19. I, 245. Jackson, *Letters,* II, 538. Biddle, 131–32. Biddle put part of the description of the buffalo ceremony in Latin to avoid offending the sensibilities of his readers. A translation can be found in Marx, 21–22.

7. Wood and Thiessen, 148.

8. Chuinard, 267–69. Cutright, *Pioneering Naturalists,* 114. Moulton, *Journals,* III, 271–72. Ordway in Quaife, 176. Whitehouse, VII, 74, says the boy was abandoned when he fell behind, and his father expected to find only a corpse on returning to seek his son. A few days later Whitehouse froze his own feet when spending a night in the open.

9. Biddle, 133.

10. Tomahawks: Russell, 284–86. Boat problems: Moulton, *Journals,* III, 284–303, and for rejection of Laroque, entry for January 31, 1805.

11. The hunt can be followed in Ordway in Quaife, 179; Moulton, *Journals,* III, 285–300. The fact that Lewis wrote his entries in the journal Clark had been keeping is a bit of evidence that although Lewis had been writing up field notes, he had not maintained the diary Jefferson had requested. (Moulton, *Journals,* III, 285n.)

12. I, 261. Moulton, *Journals,* III, 291.
13. Jackson, *Letters,* 315–16, 369.
14. Moulton, *Journals,* III, 301–4. Ordway in Quaife, 183–84.
15. I, 275–76.
16. Ibid., 285–86. Ordway in Quaife, 187–89.
17. Jackson, *Letters,* 231–42.
18. VI, 29–55. Clark's tables are in ibid., 60ff., and have been reproduced in Allen, 228–31.
19. Jackson, *Letters,* 222–25.
20. Stewart, 127–33.
21. Smith, chapter 11.
22. Laroque in Wood and Thiessen, 151.
23. The procedures employed in producing the 1805 map are summarized in Allen, 226–51; DeVoto, *Course,* 464–69; Wheat, II, 32–39. The map itself is reproduced (use your magnifying glass!) in both Wheat and in Allen, 231–39.
24. Ibid., 234. Data concerning Lewis and Clark's notions of rivers they would meet on the way West comes principally from Lewis's "Summary View of Rivers and Creeks" in VI, 29–55.
25. Jackson, *Letters,* 234.
26. I, 278–79. McKenzie in Wood and Thiessen, 239.
27. I, 281.
28. Ordway in Quaife, 189–90. I, 285–86.
29. I, 285.

Chapter 11: Hazards by Water

1. I, 301.
2. I, 285.
3. Fort Mandan to the Yellowstone River: I, 283–347; Ordway in Quaife, 190–203; Moulton, *Atlas,* plates 32–35 and 55–56.
4. Quotations about wind and sand: I, 333–34. About eyewash: II, 22.
5. Cutright's "Summary of Discoveries" at the end of each chapter in *Pioneering Naturalists* makes Lewis and Clark's achievements in this field easy to follow. For the Montana section of the trail, see also L. Thompson, 6–19.
6. Moulton, *Atlas,* as in note 3 above. Heckrotte, 20.
7. Allen, 253–54, 259–60.
8. Pierre Ménard, a French-Canadian resident of the Mandan-Hidatsa towns, reputedly went to the Yellowstone and perhaps up it some distance before 1800. What little information he brought back was collected by Jean Baptiste Truteau of the original Missouri Fur Company. Copies of part of Truteau's data were sent to Jefferson, who forwarded the material to Lewis. One assumes the lines about Ménard on the Yellowstone were not included, or Lewis would have been less positive about his being the first white man to see that river. For odds and ends on the problem, see Nasatir, *Before Lewis and Clark,* II, 381; Wood and Thiessen, 30–45; Jackson, *Letters,* 138–39; Brown, 15; Saindon, 4–10. For Lewis on the Yellowstone: I, 335–36; Ordway in Quaife, 201–2.

9. I, 338.

10. I, 361, 345.

11. Yellowstone to the Marias: I, 348, II, 112; Biddle, 171–211; Moulton, *Atlas*, plates 35–41, 43, 57–61.

12. Cutright, *Pioneering Naturalists*, 142.

13. I, 372. Murphy, unpaged, under date May 11, 1805.

14. I, 25. Moulton, *Atlas*, plates 50, 58. The incident of the nearly swamped boat is used by some scholars to explain Lewis's missing journals. He had been keeping a daily record, the argument runs, but did not feel the material was well enough polished to send to Jefferson with the other items that left Fort Mandan on the keelboat. He hoped to refine the journals and dispatch them to Washington aboard a pirogue scheduled to go downstream from the headwaters of the Missouri. In the meantime he substituted Clark's journal, though Clark also was embarrassed by his work's lack of polish. According to this theory, Lewis's journals were stored in the white pirogue and were among the few articles lost during the mishap of May 14. Neither Clark nor he mentioned the loss, however, which seems strange—if it happened. Immediately after the upset Clark began copying into his often-sparse record Lewis's long scientific discourses, as if duplicate copies would guarantee that a similar loss would not occur in the future. For fuller discussions of this largely bootless argument, see Jackson, "Advice," and Cutright, *History of Journals*.

15. II, 91, VII, 95. Ordway in Quaife, 221. Gass, 110. The alternate explanation, drowned buffalo, is in Wood, "Slaughter River."

16. II, 80, 84, 88.

17. II, 67. Allen, 265–66. Some of the isolated peaks the captains noticed were the Little Rockies and Bear Paws to the north and the Judiths, Moccasins, Highwoods, and Little and Big Belts to the south.

18. L. Thompson, 10.

19. Allen, 246–52. Ibid., 136, gives a reproduction of Clark's mileage chart.

20. II, 136. Allen, 273n. Moulton, *Atlas*, plates 32a, b, c.

21. The stay at the Marias: I, 112–46; Biddle, 212–24; Ordway in Quaife, 224–30; Allen, 268–78.

22. II, 136–37. Ordway in Quaife, 227–29. Gass, 115. Whitehouse in VII, 98.

23. II, 140. Cutright, "Barks and Saltpeter."

Chapter 12: The Great Portage

1. From the Marias to the reuniting of Lewis's and Clark's groups at the foot of the Great Falls: II, 146–65; Biddle, 224–36; Whitehouse in VII, 97–104. A concise description of the region's topography, with a good map and pictures, is in Appleman, 309–17.

2. It is hard to tell how far Lewis did walk on this stretch. Much of the time he was heading ravines, which would increase the distance between overlooks, but he was also cutting points, which would decrease it. Modern accounts say the two falls in question are separated by about five river miles. Gill, 8.

3. The easiest of the various reproductions of Clark's 1805 map to follow

with its rendering of the Medicine, Great Lake, and Tacoutche Tesse rivers is Moulton, *Atlas,* plate 32c.

4. Cutright, *Pioneering Naturalists,* 160–62, and "Barks and Saltpeter"; II, entries for July 11–15, passim; Chuinard, 288–91; Will.

5. II, 165–78, with map on 176. (These pages also include Lewis's record of events at the camp below Portage Creek.) Clark's survey figures: VI, 5–8; Biddle, 240–42.

6. II, 163.

7. A map of the portage route is in Appleman, between pages 310 and 311.

8. The portage: II, 178–220; Biddle, 238–57; Ordway in Quaife, 235–44.

9. Biddle, 251.

10. II, 183.

11. Whitehouse in VII, 107.

12. Stevenson.

13. II, 184. The account of the *Experiment* continues on and off through page 221. See also Gass, 122–28.

14. II, 180–216, passim. Cutright, *Pioneering Naturalists,* 166–68. L. Thompson, 11–12.

Chapter 13: The Great Divide

1. II, 230. Biddle, 264. From White Bear Islands to Three Forks: II, 232–79; Biddle, 263–86; Ordway in Quaife, 247–53.

2. See chart of distances in II, 233–34.

3. DeVoto, *Course,* 483–90, diligently points out the shortcuts the Corps might have taken if Jeffersons' instructions, the rigid set of the captains' minds, and the hope of horses had not held them to the Missouri.

4. II, 244.

5. Modern travelers coming upcanyon on waters impounded behind a dam are treated, at a little distance into the gorge, to an optical illusion. Slabs of rock running at right angles into the water from both canyon walls seem to meet and form a solid barrier. As one draws nearer, the slabs appear to separate, like sliding doors pulling apart. Tour guides call the spot the Gates of the Mountains, and it is an intriguing sight. There is no indication, however, that Lewis was talking about the illusion. To him the whole splendid gorge was the entrance into (or exit from) the Rockies—a gate on a scale appropriate to the rest of the setting. Lewis on the name is in II, 248.

6. Temperature charts in Biddle, III, 858.

7. Biddle, I, 280.

8. The pause at Three Forks: II, 275–81; Biddle, I, 284–II, 290; Ordway in Quaife, 253–55.

9. Allen, 161, for Clark's figure of forty-one miles between meridians. Ibid., 288, for the assumption the captains knew the proper location of Three Forks when they arrived there. Well, sort of. Clark's maps of the river from Fort Mandan to Three Forks, which were quite accurate, showed two sides of a wobbly triangle. By drawing a hypotenuse between the fort, whose longitude was known, and the forks and by keeping the

figure forty-one in mind (actually it wasn't all that accurate) he could reach a rough approximation of the forks' longitude. Lewis says, meanwhile, that he took observations to determine both the latitude and longitude of the site, but he does not record the figures for longitude (II, 284–85). The mathematics connected with lunar observations for longitude are complex, and Lewis generally jotted down the figures for solution by experts in the East. (They found his figures muddled.) At best, then, the captains had only an educated guess about how far west they really were. It was enough, however, to let them know the ocean was a lot farther off than they had been supposing.

10. From Three Forks to Lewis's crossing of the divide: II, 286–336; Biddle, II, 290–322; Ordway in Quaife, 262–64; Whitehouse in VII, 132–35. Ordway and Whitehouse were with Clark.

11. Thomas James, 29–35 and 46, gives a contemporary account of Colter's and Drouillard's (Drewyer's) deaths. Clark's statement that Wiser had been killed is in Jackson, *Letters*, II, 639.

12. II, 290.

13. Clark on the wrong fork: II, 312–17; Ordway in Quaife, 258–60.

14. II, 324.

15. II, 326.

16. II, 330. Bakeless, *Lewis and Clark*, 233–36. Ronda, 139–40.

17. Lewis's first crossing of the divide: II, 333–56; Biddle, II, 315. When rewriting the journals under Clark's direction, Biddle omitted Lewis's remark about attaining one of his great objectives. Perhaps they, too, wondered about how long Lewis had actually been committed to this goal.

18. Allen, 292.

19. Lewis's second crossing of the divide: II, 337–51, passim.

20. II, 353, 354.

21. II, 366.

22. Shoshoni background: Trenholm and Carley, 3–40.

23. II, 342.

24. II, 366.

25. II, 355. Biddle, II, 349.

26. The tippet: II, 356, 378; Charles Peale to Jefferson, January 29, 1808, in Jackson, *Letters*, II, 439. Unlike many objects collected by Lewis, Cameahwait's tippet survived. A wax statue of Lewis wearing it stood for many years in Peale's Philadelphia museum. Charles de Saint-Mémin painted a picture of the explorer in the same tippet. Cutright, *Pioneering Naturalists*, facing 240.

27. II, 356–58.

28. Clark to Biddle, Jackson, *Letters*, II, 518–19.

Chapter 14: Hunger

1. Biddle, II, 334.

2. Hodge, II, 557. Jackson, *Letters*, II, 554.

3. Biddle, II, 334.

4. II, 361–63. Cameahwait's remark, "If we had guns . . ." is in II, 380.
5. II, 364.
6. DeVoto, *Journals*, 205–6. Ordway in Quaife, 270. Whitehouse in VII, 138.
7. Lewis's self-evaluation: DeVoto, *Journals*, 206.
8. Lewis's ethnographic jottings are spread throughout II, 372–III, 32 (the material on venereals is on 372–73). DeVoto's condensation is in *Journals*, 207–27. Biddle presents the ethnographic data in a single unit, 367–84.
9. III, 13.
10. III, 14. Ordway in Quaife, 272.
11. III, 28.
12. Holding Cameahwait to his promise: III, 35–36; Ordway in Quaife, 274. Ronda, 153, who persistently faults Lewis and Clark for not evaluating the Indians according to modern ethnological standards, feels the "blast" Lewis gave the chief was too severe.
13. Clark's reconnaissance: II, 380–III, 47; Biddle, II, 342–55; Allen, 294–300. Peebles, 5–11, attempts a precise definition of trails and a location of each night's campsite.
14. Horse buying: III, 46–48; Ordway in Quaife, 275–76; Whitehouse in VII, 146. It is not possible to determine the exact number of horses the expedition had at any one time. (Appleman, 372 nn. 115 and 116.)
15. Jackson, *Letters*, I, 315–17.
16. Shoshoni to Flatheads: III, 50–53; Biddle, 382–86; Gass, 155–56.
17. The Flatheads, a Salish tribe, did not deform their skulls, but their tops looked flat compared to the peaked skulls created by other Salish and Chinookan tribes. (Brandon, 310.) Ronda, 155, says the name came from the sign-language designation for the tribe: hands pressed against the sides of the head in a flattening motion. See also Hodge under "Salish."
18. III, 58.
19. The Lolo Trail: III, 62–72; Ordway in Quaife, 284–87; Whitehouse in VII, 153–58; Peebles, 17–19; Space, 2–12.
20. Clark and the deer: III, 69; Whitehouse in VII, 157.
21. From September 18 through 22, Clark's and Lewis's journal entries alternate in III, 79–84 and Space, 12–19. Whitehouse in VII, 156–60 and Ordway in Quaife, 288–90, supplement Lewis. See also Peebles under appropriate dates.
22. Reaching the Nez Percé through the building of the canoes: III, 84–98; Ordway in Quaife, 290–94; Peebles, 23–26; Space, 19–22.
23. Chuinard, 320. Mirsky, 318.
24. III, 74. Ordway in Quaife, 288. Whitehouse in VII, 156.
25. Cutright, *Pioneering Naturalists*, 218–19.
26. Ordway in Quaife, 293.

Chapter 15: Wild Water

1. From Canoe Camp to the junction of the Snake and Columbia: III, 97–119; Biddle, II, 407–26; Ordway in Quaife, 295–99; Whitehouse in VII, 166–74. When Clark took over full responsibility for the journals on this stretch, he first prepared a rough draft, which generally included

compass readings and mileage estimates between prominent points. When opportunity allowed, he elaborated on the other data in the draft. Thwaites presents each day's drafts in sequence. One should read both versions since the trial drafts sometimes convey incidents and impressions omitted from the final copy.

2. III, 99. Biddle, II, 407. Whitehouse, in VII, 168.

3. III, 113. Biddle, II, 417.

4. III, 115–16.

5. At the junction of the Snake and Columbia: III, 119–30.

6. Sore eyes: III, 126; Biddle, II, 423; Cutright, *Pioneering Naturalists*, 223.

7. The thought of tomahawking the frightened Indians appears in Clark's rough draft, not in the finished one. (III, 133–36.) The run from the junction to Celilo Falls: III, 130–50; Biddle, II, 429–46; Ordway in Quaife, 100–104; Whitehouse, in VII, 174–87.

8. Sacagawea: III, 136. See also ibid., 111.

9. Celilo Falls through the Long Narrows: III, 150–58. See Clark's sketch maps, one as frontispiece of III, the other facing 158. Also Ordway in Quaife, 304–5; Whitehouse, in VII, 182–88; Biddle, II, 429–48.

10. III, 151.

11. Water roaring through compressed straits tends to wear the confining stone into relatively thin strata. These layers cracked into pieces that looked like flagstones (*dalles*) to French voyageurs who, after Lewis and Clark's time, took boats through the Columbia narrows for Canadian trading companies. Hence by association the rough-water stretch became known as The Dalles—a name applied to several other North American rapids. Still later, The Dalles, as a name, slid downstream to a mission station located just below the narrows. Today The Dalles is a town—the only one in the U.S. with "The" as a legal part of its name. The Dalles as white water have been lost under a reservoir's flat surface. For the area in Lewis and Clark's time: Josephy, 22–23; Ronda, 173–74; Hodge under "Wishram" and "Wasco."

12. III, 148, 155.

13. III, 164. For the transit from the narrows through the Cascades; III, 159–90; Biddle, II, 448–64; Ordway in Quaife, 305–7; Whitehouse in VII, 182–88. Whitehouse's diary ends, incidentally, after his entry of November 6.

14. III, 178.

15. Ibid.

16. The lower river to the estuary: III, 192–208; Biddle, II, 464–87; Ordway in Quaife, 307–9.

17. The Skilloot encounter: III, 194–99; Biddle, II, 465–68; Ronda, 172, 176.

18. Gray's Bay was named five months after Gray's discovery of the river by Lieutenant William Broughton of Vancouver's fleet. Broughton ascended the Columbia about a hundred miles in a ship's longboat during the latter part of October. By contrast, Gray had halted in the estuary; in Broughton's opinion that didn't count as far as establishing national sovereignty was concerned. He named Gray's Bay to emphasize his point: the American had gone no farther than that. Baker's Bay, just

west of Gray's Bay, was named for an English trader who entered the estuary a few weeks after Gray's departure. (See Fuller, 56.)

19. III, 211–14. For the problems of the estuary in general: III, 208–48; Biddle, II, 473–87; Ordway in Quaife, 309–14.
20. III, 223.
21. A good map of the estuary (but with inexact trails) is in Appleman, between pages 198 and 199. See also Clark's sketch map in III, facing 234. Cape Disappointment was named by the English trader John Meares in 1788. He had heard of a great river in the vicinity, but when he rounded the then-unnamed cape, he thought he was looking at another bay. The name reflects his feelings.
22. Bakeless, *Lewis and Clark*, 284. DeVoto, *Course*, 550. Dillon, 224.
23. III, 231.
24. III, 247–49, gives the votes and arguments, but contains several small, inexplicable inconsistencies.
25. Lewis kept a journal on November 29 and 30, and then ceased again. Details of his search for the campsite have to be surmised from what Clark saw and briefly commented on.
26. III, 263.

Chapter 16: The Farthest Reach

1. III, 270.
2. Clark's rough sketches of the layout are in III, 268, 298. See also 297n; Appleman, 195, 346; Cutright, *Pioneering Naturalists*, 248–49. Joseph Field's furniture making: III, 289, 291.
3. III, 279.
4. II, 285–86. Ordway in Quaife, 318.
5. Clark's salt exploration: III, 272–77.
6. The elk adventure: III, 279–84.
7. III, 290–91.
8. Will, 13.
9. III, 217–18, 340.
10. The first word of the second stranded whale was brought January 3 by Chief Comowool of the coastal village almost due west of the fort. The news was confirmed by Willard and Wiser, who had helped carry kettles to the salt camp; they brought a chunk of blubber with them, along with a keg of salt. A meal of the blubber persuaded the captains to try to get more. (Biddle, II, 503–4; Thwaites, III, 308ff.) Clark's account of the whale expedition: III, 314–35.
11. IV, 70–71. Allen, 324–25.
12. Dunlay, 6–8.
13. See the duplicate entries in Thwaites for January 3, 1806.
14. Discussions of Lewis's work as supplemented by Clark are in Cutright, *Pioneering Naturalists*, 246–75, and, especially for ethnography, Ronda, 181–213.
15. IV, 72, 74.
16. Biddle, II, 513, 517, 534, 540.

17. III, 302–4.
18. IV, 88–91.
19. IV, 16, 27, 170ff.
20. IV, 195.
21. IV, 102–3. Clark's illustration of the eulachon forms the frontispiece of IV.
22. III, 350.
23. IV, 168–76. Biddle, III, 591–92.
24. Jackson, *Letters*, I, 300.
25. Dickering for the canoes: IV, 173–77. Recompense for Lewis's coat: Jackson, *Letters*, II, 428.
26. IV, 38, 177, 179. Ordway in Quaife, 329. Ronda, 211, is scathing about the theft and connects it with Lewis's denigration of Indian character in general after he'd ordered Tahcum's Chinooks from the fort on February 20. The implication is that Lewis's dealings with Indians accord with Jefferson's directions and *not* with Lewis's own feelings.
27. Gass, 227, 229. Ordway in Quaife, 329. Biddle, III, 595.

Chapter 17: Against the Flow

1. IV, 227–28.
2. III, 201–2, IV, 220. Biddle, II, 470, III, 600, 611–12. Allen, 332–33. Ordway in Quaife, 333. The quotations in this section are from Biddle.
3. IV, 236. Clark's trip to the Multnomah: IV, 227–39; Biddle, III, 605–9.
4. The problem of the Willamette's source is discussed in Allen, 327–28, 336, 341, 394. See also the maps in 384–89, which, however, are hard to follow.
5. The "new" portages and Hall Kelley's part in the delusion are treated by F. N. Powell, ed., *Hall J. Kelley on Oregon* (Princeton: Princeton University Press, 1932). Also Lavender, *Westward*, 214–15.
6. The passage of the Cascades: IV, 259–68; Biddle, III, 619–21; Ronda, 216. George Simpson, governor-in-chief of the Hudson's Bay Company's territories in North America, passed through the Columbia rapids in 1824 and gives a lively summary of several years of Indian problems there. Simpson, 61–63.
7. As rendered by Biddle, III, 627.
8. Dickering for horses: IV, 283–94; Biddle, III, 626–28.
9. Again (see note 14, chapter 14) it is not possible to tell from the journals (IV, 294–308) how many horses the captains had at any point during the passage of The Dalles and Celilo Falls. Ordway is no help, and neither is Biddle, who omits entirely the exchange of medical treatment for mounts. See also Appleman, 374 n. 130.
10. IV, 304.
11. IV, 321.
12. The march: IV, 318–27.
13. With the Walla Wallas: IV, 328–36.
14. Bakeless, *Lewis and Clark*, 311. Although the journals do not describe how the men used a canoe for ferrying the horses, this author believes,

from experience on other rivers, that the method suggested in the text was the only one that would have worked.

15. Lewis's account of the incident is in IV, 368. Clark's version, copied almost verbatim, is in IV, 361.
16. Chuinard, 363. Coues, 768. Fuller, 44.
17. IV, 358–62, V, 27, 58, 77, etc.
18. V, 20.
19. At Broken Arm's village: V, 17–31; Biddle, III, 660–66; Ordway in Quaife, 355–57.
20. The council and its aftermath: V, 19–24, 78–84; Ronda, 225–27.
21. V, 35, 39, 52. Ronda, 227–28.
22. V, 58, 100, 104, etc. Ordway in Quaife, 357–63.
23. V, 56–100, passim. Chuinard, 370–76.
24. Sweat cures as in 23 above, plus Cutright, *Pioneering Naturalists*, 293–96.
25. Josephy, 14. Ronda, *Montana, the Magazine of Western History* V (Summer 1955).

Chapter 18: Peace Mission to the Blackfeet

1. The first attempt to cross the Lolo Trail: V, 136–56. Readers interested in determining trail locations and camping sites can consult Space and/or Peebles.
2. Chuinard, 377.
3. V, 157–58.
4. V, 159.
5. V, 164–65.
6. V, 170–71.
7. V, 173–82. Cutright, *Pioneering Naturalists*, 305. L. Thompson, 15–16.
8. V, 175–76, 179. Allen, 347–49.
9. V, 180.
10. V, 192. Incidental intelligence: for some unstated reason, Lewis gave his dog's name Seaman (*not* Scammon) to a creek they passed on July 5. (V, 191.)
11. V, 203–4.
12. The exploration of the Marias: V, 204–28; Biddle, III, 718–33. The fight: V, 223–25; Biddle, 730–31. Ordway's account as he received it from the participants is in Quaife, 382–83. See also Jackson, *Letters*, 341–42. In spite of all this coverage I have assumed a few details because Lewis, our main source, was concentrating on what was immediately under his nose, and certain peripheral matters need attention.
13. Thompson, 273.
14. Josephy, 651–53. Ewers, *Blackfeet*, 48. Ronda, *Lewis and Clark*, 244. Such fur-trade histories as DeVoto, *Across the Wide Missouri*, and Dale Morgan, *Jedediah Smith*, provide ample evidence of the implacability of the Blackfeet in the face of the whites' refusal to withdraw.
15. V, 240–42. Hunting statistics: V, 229–38, passim.

16. V, 240–42. Ordway in Quaife, 387.
17. V, 243–44. Ordway in Quaife, 388–89.
18. See chapter 19, note 10 below.

Chapter 19: Hurrying Home

1. I assume and perhaps oversimplify the steps by which the captains arrived at this idea. But since they do not say how the notion developed, "educated guesswork" seems to be the only substitute.
2. Jackson, *Letters*, 214n, 220–21. Nasatir, *Before Lewis and Clark*, 112–14.
3. Jackson, *Letters*, 309–13.
4. V, 260. Clark's journal says his party traveled 4 miles before camping. His "Course Distance" gives 6 miles. He estimates the distance from Three Forks to the Yellowstone as 48 miles. It is about 40. Throughout the Yellowstone exploration Clark overestimated distances, sometimes by as much as one hundred percent. (V, 262, 264; Brown, 35.)
5. V, 290.
6. V, 272–76.
7. V, 325–26.
8. Bakeless, *Lewis and Clark*, 349–50.
9. V, 299–301.
10. Clark tucks into the middle of his diary entry for August 10 an exact copy of the description of a "singular cherry," with which the wounded Lewis, lying on his stomach, closed his entry of August 12. Although the wording is definitely Lewis's, my hunch is that Clark spotted the plant ("I found a Sepies of Cherry . . ." he wrote) and took along a sprig to show his friend. Later, while bringing his notes up to date, he borrowed Lewis's botanical description of what was Clark's discovery. (V, 243–44, 328.)
11. The councils: V, 338–46; Biddle, III, 775–81; Ronda, 244–48. Clark's interest in Charbonneau's family: V, 344; Jackson, *Letters*, 315–16.
12. V, 348–49.
13. V, 349–57.
14. V, 365–68.
15. V, 380.
16. V, 382–83. Jackson, *Letters*, 242–43, 261. Lavender, *Fist*, 64, 72.
17. V, 389–90. Lavender, *Fist*, 78, 80.

Chapter 20: Endings

1. The four letters: Jackson, *Letters*, 317–43. Jackson's notes describe their appearance, provenance, and so forth. He is not to blame for my interpretations, however.
2. Lewis's suggestions raise the question of the effect the Corps of Discovery had on John Jacob Astor's plans for a vast fur-trade base, Astoria, at the mouth of the Columbia. It is true Astor was aware of

Lewis and Clark's crossing and wrote Jefferson about his intentions. For some years, however, the trader's orientation had been toward Canada. He knew of Alexander Mackenzie's drive to use the Columbia as the key point in a fur and fisheries plan embracing the entire Northwest. Before embarking on his own venture, therefore, Astor entered into arrangements with the Canadians that he hoped would preclude their competition—only to have the War of 1812 ruin his Pacific Fur Company. So, except perhaps for Wilson Price Hunt's harrowing overland trip, Lewis and Clark's example probably was no more than confirmation of plans already underway. (Lavender, *Fist*, 118–45, passim.)

3. Thompson, 131. Thompson, writing from memory, errs in saying that in 1792 the forty-ninth parallel formed the boundary between the British dominions and the United States as far west as the Rockies. The United States had no claims that far west until 1803.

4. Jackson, *Letters*, 343.

5. Jefferson to Major Gilbert Russell, April 18, 1810: "He [Lewis] was much afflicted & habitually so with hypochondria. This was probably increased by the habit into which he had fallen"—i.e., intemperance. Jefferson could have noticed the intemperance only during 1807, for he did not see Lewis after that. Apparently he did get occasional reports of it later on, but chronic alcoholism probably would have taken a while to develop.

6. Reimbursement affairs: Jackson, *Letters*, II, 377–84.

7. Ibid., 385–85, 394–97, 399–408. The McKeehan quotation: ibid., 406.

8. Jackson, *Letters*. See last sentence of C. and A. Conrad to Jefferson, 468–69. Also 459 and last sentence of Jefferson to Lewis, July 17, 1808, ibid., 445.

9. Ibid., 575n. Cutright, "Rest, Rest," passim.

10. Jackson, *Letters*, II, 720. See also Clark to Lewis, undated, 388.

11. Ibid., 444–45 and especially Jackson's note 1.

12. Ibid., 721.

13. Appleman, 237. Clark reached St. Louis either at the end of June or early in July 1807. Writing Dearborn, under date St. Louis, May [*sic*] 18, 1807, he says the party "will set out this evening." I cannot explain the contradiction in dates. For a summary of the affair: Oglesby, 50–54.

14. Oglesby, 69–76.

15. Kushner, 470–80.

16. Russell, "Statement," and Lewis to Stoddard, Jackson, *Letters*, II, 573–75, 466. It is said Lewis switched to land travel because he feared, given the international tensions of the time, that his ship from New Orleans might be seized by a British man-of-war. (Neelly to Jefferson, ibid., 467–68.)

17. Ibid., 748.

18. Ibid., 467.

19. Among those arguing, sometimes with great intensity, that Lewis was murdered are Elliott Coues, ed., *History of the Expedition under the Command of Lewis and Clark* (New York, 1893); Bakeless, *Lewis and Clark;* Vardis Fisher, *Suicide or Murder? The Strange Death of Meriwether Lewis*

(Denver, 1962); and Dillon. The case for suicide is put forth by Phelps; Kushner; Cutright, "Rest, Rest"; and Donald Jackson, who in his *Letters* moves from tentative to firm support of the suicide theory. (1962 ed., 486n; 1978 ed., 474n.)

20. I refer those who persist in believing, against all evidence, that Sacagawea lived to a ripe old age and is buried on an Indian reservation near Lander, Wyoming, to Irving Anderson, "Probing the Riddle of the Bird Woman," *Montana, the Magazine of Western History*, XXIII (Autumn 1973), 2–17.

21. Merk, 4–5, 116–17. The quotation is from a letter, Jefferson to John Jacob Astor, May 24, 1812, 117.

Bibliography

Abel, Annie Heloise, ed. *Tabeau's Narrative of Loisel's Expedition to the Upper Missouri.* Norman, Okla.: University of Oklahoma Press, 1939.

———. "Trudeau's Description of the Upper Missouri." *Mississippi Valley Historical Review* VIII (June–September 1921).

Abrams, Rochanne. "Meriwether Lewis with Jefferson, the Mentor." *Bulletin of the Missouri Historical Society* 1979.

Adams, Mary P. "Jefferson's Reaction to the Treaty of San Ildefonso." *Journal of Southern History* XXI (May 1955).

Allen, John Logan. *Passage through the Garden: Lewis and Clark and the Image of the American Northwest.* Chicago: University of Illinois Press, 1975.

Appleman, Roy. *Lewis and Clark: Historic Places Associated with Their Transcontinental Expedition, 1804–06.* Edited by Robert G. Ferris. Washington, D.C.: Government Printing Office, 1975.

Bakeless, John. *Lewis and Clark, Partners in Discovery.* New York: William Morrow & Co., 1947.

———. *Background to Glory: The Life of George Rogers Clark.* Philadelphia and New York: J. B. Lippincott Co., 1948.

[Benton, Thomas H.] *Abridgement of the Debates of Congress.* New York: D. Appleton & Co., 1857.

Barry, J. Neilsen. "Broughton on the Columbia in 1792." *Oregon Historical Quarterly* XXVII (December 1926).

———. "Who Discovered the Columbia?" *Oregon Historical Quarterly* XXXIX (June 1938).

Biddle, Nicholas. *History of the Expedition under the Command of Captains Lewis and Clark.* 3 vols. Reprint. Philadelphia and New York: J. B. Lippincott Co., 1961.

Billon, Frederick. *Annals of St. Louis, 1804–05.* Reprint. New York: Arno Press, 1970.

Boit, John. "Log of the Columbia." *Oregon Historical Quarterly* XXIII (December 1921).

Bowers, Alfred. *Mandan Social and Ceremonial Organization*. Chicago: University of Chicago Press, 1950.

Boyd, Julian P. *The Papers of Thomas Jefferson*. 16 vols. Princeton: Princeton University Press, 1950–61.

Brandon, William. *The American Heritage Book of Indians*. New York: American Heritage Publishing Co., 1961.

Brebner, John Bartlett. *The Explorers of North America, 1492–1806*. London: A. & C. Black, 1933.

Brown, Mark H. *The Plainsmen of the Yellowstone*. New York: G. P. Putnam's Sons, 1961.

Burpee, Lawrence J. *The Search for the Western Sea*. Toronto: Macmillan, 1935.

Burroughs, Raymond Darwin. *The Natural History of the Lewis and Clark Expedition*. East Lansing, Mich.: Michigan State University Press, 1961.

Carver, Jonathan. *Travels through the Interior Parts of North America* . . . Reprint. Minneapolis: Ross and Haines, 1956.

Cash, Joseph H. *The Sioux People*. Phoenix: Intertribal Council, 1971.

Chatters, Roy M. "The Not-so-enigmatic Lewis and Clark Airgun." *We Proceeded On* III (1973).

Chuinard, E. G. *Only One Man Died: The Medical Aspects of the Lewis and Clark Expedition*. Glendale, Calif.: Arthur H. Clark Co., 1979.

Clarke, Charles G. *Men of the Lewis and Clark Expedition*. Glendale, Calif.: Arthur H. Clark Co., 1970.

Cook, Warren L. *Flood Tide of Empire*. New Haven: Yale University Press, 1973.

Coues, Elliott, ed. *New Light on the Early History of the Greater Northwest: The Manuscript Journals of Alexander Henry . . . and of David Thompson*. Reprint. Minneapolis: Ross and Haines, 1965.

Cutright, Paul Russell. "I Gave Him Barks and Saltpeter." *American Heritage Magazine* XV (December 1967).

———. "Meriwether Lewis Prepares for a Trip West." *Bulletin of the Missouri Historical Society* XXIII (October 1966).

———. *Lewis and Clark, Pioneering Naturalists*. Urbana, Ill.: University of Illinois Press, 1969.

———. *A History of the Lewis and Clark Journals*. Norman, Okla.: University of Oklahoma Press, 1979.

———. "Rest, Rest, Perturbed Spirit." *We Proceeded On* XII (March 1986).

DeConde, Alexander. *This Affair of Louisiana*. New York: Charles Scribner's Sons, 1976.

DeVoto, Bernard. *The Course of Empire*. Boston: Houghton Mifflin Co., 1952.

———. *The Journals of Lewis and Clark*. Boston: Houghton Mifflin Co., 1953.

Diller, Aubrey. "Maps of the Missouri River before Lewis and Clark." In *Studies and Essays . . . in Homage to George Sarton*. New York: Schuman, 1946.

Dillon, Richard. *Meriwether Lewis*. New York: Coward McCann, 1965.

Dunbar, Seymour. *A History of Travel in America*. New York: Tudor Publishing Co., 1937.

Duncan, Dayton. *Out West: An American Journey*. New York: Viking Penguin, 1987.

Dunlay, Thomas W. "Battery of Venus: A Clue to the Journal-Keeping Methods of Lewis and Clark." *We Proceeded On* IX (August 1983).

Eide, Ingvard Henry. *American Odyssey: The Journey of Lewis and Clark*. New York: Rand, McNally and Co., 1958.

Esarey, Logan. *Messages and Letters of William Henry Harrison.* Indianapolis: Indiana Historical Commission, 1922.

Ewers, John C. "The Indian Trade of the Upper Missouri before Lewis and Clark: An Interpretation." *Bulletin of the Missouri Historical Society* X (1954).
———. *The Blackfeet, Raiders on the Northwestern Plains.* Norman, Okla.: University of Oklahoma Press, 1958.

Foley, William. "The Lewis and Clark Expedition's Silent Partners: The Chouteau Brothers of St. Louis." *Bulletin of the Missouri Historical Society.*

Foley, William, and David Rice. *The First Chouteaus.* Urbana, Ill.: University of Illinois Press, 1983.

Friis, Herman. "Cartographic . . . Adventures of . . . Lewis and Clark." *Journal, Washington Academy of Sciences* XLIV (1954).

Fuller, George W. *A History of the Pacific Northwest.* New York: Knopf, 1947.

Ganoe, William A. *A History of the United States Army.* New York: D. Appleton-Century, 1942.

Gass, Patrick. *A Journal of the Voyages and Travels of a Corps of Discovery under the command of Captain Lewis and Captain Clarke . . .* Edited by David McKeehan. Reprint. Minneapolis: Ross and Haines, 1958.

Gill, Larry. "The Great Portage . . . Around the Great Falls of the Missouri River." *We Proceeded On* I (Fall 1975).

Hafen, Ann W. "Jean Baptiste Charbonneau." In LeRoy and Ann Hafen, *The Mountain Men and the Fur Trade of the Far West,* vol I. Glendale, California: Arthur H. Clark Co., 1972.

Harris, Burton. *John Colter: His Years in the Rocky Mountains.* New York: Charles Scribner's Sons, 1952.

Havighurst, Walter, ed. *Land of Long Horizons.* New York: Coward McCann, 1960.
———. *River to the West: Three Centuries of the Ohio.* New York: G. P. Putnam's Sons, 1970.

Hawke, David Freeman. *Those Tremendious Mountains.* New York: W. W. Norton & Co., 1980.

Heckrotte, Warren. "Aaron Arrowsmith's Map of North America and the Lewis and Clark Expedition." *The Map Collector* (Summer 1987).

Hodge, Frederick Webb, ed. *Handbook of American Indians . . .* 2 vols. Washington: Bureau of American Ethnology, 1907.

Houck, Lewis, ed. *The Spanish Regime in St. Louis,* vol. II. Chicago: R. R. Donnelley, 1909.

Howay, F. W., ed. *Voyages of the Columbia to the North West Coast.* Boston: Massachusetts Historical Society, 1941.

Hulbert, Archer B. *Waterways of Westward Expansion.* Reprint. New York: Arno Press, 1971.

Hyde, George. *Red Cloud's Folk: A History of the Oglala Sioux Indians.* Norman, Okla.: University of Oklahoma Press, 1937.

Innis, Harold A. *The Fur Trade in Canada.* Rev. ed. Toronto: University of Toronto Press.

Jackson, Donald Dean. "Lewis and Clark among the Oto." *Nebraska History* XLI (September 1960).
———. "The Race to Publish Lewis and Clark." *Pennsylvania Magazine of History & Biography* LXXXV (April 1961).
———. *The Journals of Zebulon Montgomery Pike.* 2 vols. Norman, Okla.: University of Oklahoma Press, 1966.

————. "Some Advice for the Next Editor of Lewis and Clark." *Bulletin of the Missouri Historical Society* XXIV (October 1967).

————, ed. *Letters of the Lewis and Clark Expedition.* 2d ed. 2 vols. Urbana, Ill.: University of Illinois Press, 1978.

————. *Thomas Jefferson and the Stony Mountains.* Urbana, Ill.: University of Illinois Press, 1981.

————. "Call Him Good Old Dog, but Don't Call Him Scannon." *We Proceeded On* XI (August 1985).

James, Alton. *The Life of George Rogers Clark.* Chicago: University of Chicago Press, 1928.

James, Thomas. *Three Years among the Mexicans and Indians.* Reprint. Philadelphia: J. B. Lippincott Co., 1962.

Johansen, Dorothy O., and Charles M. Gates. *Empire on the Columbia.* New York: Harper & Row, 1957.

Josephy, Alvin M., Jr. *The Nez Perce Indians and the Opening of the Northwest.* New Haven: Yale University Press, 1965.

Kehoe, Alice B. "The Function of Ceremonial Sexual Intercourse among the Northern Plains Indians." *Plains Anthropologist* XV (1970).

Kushner, Howard I. "The Suicide of Meriwether Lewis: A Psychoanalytic Inquiry." *William and Mary Quarterly* (1981).

Lamar, Howard R. *The Reader's Encyclopedia of the American West.* New York: Harper & Row, 1977.

Lange, Robert E. "George Drouillard (Drewyer)." *We Proceeded On* V (May 1979).

————. "John Shields." *We Proceeded On* V (July 1979).

————. "Private George Shannon." *We Proceeded On* VIII (July 1982).

Large, Arlen J. ". . . It Thundered and Lightened: The Weather Observations of Lewis and Clark." *We Proceeded On* XII (May 1986).

Lavender, David. *Westward Vision.* New York: McGraw-Hill Book Co., 1962.

————. *The Fist in the Wilderness.* Garden City, N.Y.: Doubleday & Co., 1964.

Lehmer, Donald J. *Introduction to Middle Missouri Archeology.* U.S. Dept. of the Interior, National Park Service, Anthropological Paper no. 1. Lincoln, Neb., 1971.

Lehmer, Donald J., and David T. Jones. *Arikara Archeology: The Bad River Phase.* Smithsonian Institution, Publications in Salvage Archeology, no. 7. Lincoln, Neb., 1968.

Lewis, Grace. "Financial Records: Expedition to the Pacific." *Bulletin of the Missouri Historical Society* X (July 1954).

Lewis, Meriwether. "A Summary View of the Rivers and Creeks . . ." Printed in Thwaites, *Original Journals,* vol. VI, pp. 22–59.

Lewis, Meriwether, and William Clark. *A Statistical View of the Indian Nations Inhabiting the Territory of Louisiana.* American State Papers, Indian Affairs, no. 113, 9th Congress, 1st Session, Washington, 1806.

Loos, John Louis. "William Clark's Part in the Preparation of the Lewis and Clark Expedition." *Bulletin of the Missouri Historical Society* X (1954).

McDermott, John Francis. "Captain Stoddard Discovers St. Louis." *Bulletin of the Missouri Historical Society* X (1954).

McDonald, Forrest, Leslie E. Decker, and Thomas P. Govan. *The Last Best Hope, A History of the United States.* Reading, Mass.: Addison-Wesley, 1972.

McGee, W. J. "The Siouan Indians." In *The Sioux Indians: A Socio-Ethnological History.* New York: Sal Lewis.

McKenzie, Charles. "The Mississouri Indians." In L. R. Masson, *Les Bourgeois de la Compagnie du Nord-Ouest.* Quebec: 1889.

McMaster, John B. *A History of the People of the United States,* vol. II, *1790–1803.* New York: D. Appleton & Co., 1912.

Mackay, James. "Extracts from Capt. Mackay's Journal—and Others," edited by M. Quaife, *Wisconsin Historical Society Proceedings* LXIII (1915).

Mackenzie, Alexander. *Voyages from Montreal . . . to the frozen and Pacific Oceans, in the years 1789 and 1793 . . .* London: T. Cadell and W. Davies, 1801. (Many reprints since then.)

Malone, Dumas. *Jefferson and His Time,* vols. III, IV, V. Boston: Little, Brown & Co., 1962, 1970, 1974.

Marx, Walter H. "A Latin Matter in the Biddle Narrative . . ." *We Proceeded On* IX (November 1983).

Mayo, Barnard, ed. *Jefferson Himself.* Boston: Houghton Mifflin Co., 1942.

Merk, Frederick. "The Oregon Question." In *Essays on Anglo-American Diplomacy and Politics.* Cambridge, Mass.: Harvard University Press, 1967.

Meyer, Roy W. *The Village Indians of the Upper Missouri: The Mandans, Hidatsas, and Arikaras.* Lincoln, Neb.: University of Nebraska Press, 1977.

Mirsky, Jeanette. *The Westward Crossings: Balboa, Mackenzie, Lewis and Clark.* New York: Alfred A. Knopf, 1946.

Morison, Samuel Eliot, and Henry Steele Commager. *The Growth of the American Republic.* New York: Oxford University Press, 1942.

Morse, Jedediah. *The American Geography, a View of the Present Situation of the United States.* Reprint. New York: Arno Press, 1971.

Morton, Arthur S. *A History of the Canadian West.* Toronto and Buffalo: University of Toronto Press, 1973.

Moulton, Gary E., ed. *Atlas of the Lewis and Clark Expedition.* Lincoln, Neb.: University of Nebraska Press, 1983.

———, ed. *The Journals of the Lewis and Clark Expedition,* vols. II and III. Lincoln, Neb.: University of Nebraska Press, 1986–87. (Because of publication delays at the press and cataloging delays at the University of California, Santa Barbara, these were the only volumes of this monumental new edition of the journals that were available to me at the time of my writing this book.)

Murphy, Dan. *Lewis and Clark: Voyage of Discovery,* with photos by David Muench. Las Vegas: KC Publications, 1977.

Nasatir, A. P. *Before Lewis and Clark: Documents . . . of the Missouri, 1785–1804.* St. Louis: St. Louis Historical Documents Foundation, 1952.

———. "The Formation of the Missouri Fur Company." *Missouri Historical Review* XXV (October 1930).

———. "Anglo-Spanish Rivalry on the Upper Missouri," *Mississippi Valley Historical Review* XVI (December 1929. March 1930).

———. "John Evans, Explorer and Surveyor." *Missouri Historical Review* XXV (January–July, 1931).

Oglesby, Richard Edward. *Manuel Lisa and the Opening of the Missouri River Fur Trade.* Norman, Okla.: University of Oklahoma Press, 1963.

Osgood, Ernest S. *The Field Notes of Captain William Clark.* New Haven: Yale University Press, 1964.

———. "Our Dog Scannon: Partner in Discovery." *Montana, the Magazine of Western History* XXVI (Summer 1976).

Parish, John C. "The Emergence of the Idea of Manifest Destiny." In *The Persistence of the Westward Movement and Other Essays.* Berkeley and Los Angeles: University of California Press, 1943.

Padover, Saul K. *Jefferson.* New York: New American Library, 1952.

Peebles, John J. "Lewis and Clark in Idaho." *Idaho Historical Series,* no. 16. Boise, Idaho: December 1966.

Phelps, Dawson A. "The Tragic Death of Meriwether Lewis." *William and Mary Quarterly* 3d series XIII (July 1956).

Philbrick, Francis S. *The Rise of the West, 1754–1830.* New York: Harper & Row, 1965.

Phillips, Paul Chrisler. *The Fur Trade.* 2 vols. Norman, Okla.: University of Oklahoma Press, 1961.

Prucha, Francis Paul. *American Indian Policy in the Formative Years.* Cambridge, Mass.: Harvard University Press, 1962.

Quaife, Milo, ed. *The Journals of Captain Meriwether Lewis and John Ordway . . .* Madison, Wisconsin: Wisconsin Historical Publications, volume 22, 1916.

Ronda, James P. *Lewis and Clark among the Indians.* Lincoln, Neb.: University of Nebraska Press, 1984.

Russell, Carl P. *Firearms, Traps, and Tools of the Mountain Men.* New York: Alfred A. Knopf, 1967.

Saindon, Bob. "Old Menard." *We Proceeded On* XIII (May 1987).

Scharf, J. Thomas. *History of St. Louis City and County.* Philadelphia: Louis H. Everts & Co., 1883.

Schwartz, Seymour I., and Ralph E. Ehrenberg. *The Mapping of America.* New York: Abrams, 1980.

Shoemaker, Floyd C. "The Louisiana Purchase . . . and Transfer to the United States, 1804," *Missouri Historical Review* XLVIII (October 1953).

Simpson, George. *Fur Trade and Empire: George Simpson's Journal, 1824–25.* Edited by Frederick Merk. Cambridge, Mass.: Harvard University Press, 1931.

Skarsten, M. O. *George Drouillard.* Glendale, Calif.: Arthur H. Clark Co., 1964.

Smith, Henry Nash. *Virgin Land.* Cambridge, Mass.: Harvard University Press, 1950.

Space, Ralph. *The Lolo Trail.* Lewiston, Idaho: Printcraft Printing, 1970.

Sprague, Marshall. *So Vast So Beautiful a Land.* Boston: Little, Brown and Co., 1974.

Steffen, Jerome O. *William Clark, Jeffersonian Man on the Frontier.* Norman, Okla.: University of Oklahoma Press, 1977.

Stevenson, Elizabeth. "Meriwether and I." *Virginia Quarterly Review* XL (1967).

Stewart, Omer C. "Fire . . ." In William Thomas, ed., *Man's Role in Changing the Face of the Earth.* Chicago: University of Chicago Press, 1956.

Thompson, David. *Narrative, 1784–1812.* Edited by Richard Glover. Toronto: The Champlain Society, 1962.

Thompson, Larry S. *Montana's Explorers: The Pioneer Naturalists.* Helena, Mont.: Montana Magazine, Inc., 1985.

Thwaites, Reuben Gold, ed. *The Original Journals of the Lewis and Clark Expedition.* 8 vols. New York: Dodd, Mead & Co., 1904–5.

Trenholm, Virginia C., and Maurine Carley. *The Shoshonis: Sentinels of the Rockies.* Norman, Okla.: University of Oklahoma Press, 1964.

Wheat, Carl I. *Mapping the Transmississippi West,* vols. I and II. San Francisco: Institute of Historical Cartography, 1957–58.

White, Richard. "The Winning of the West: The Expansion of the Western Sioux in the Eighteenth and Nineteenth Centuries." *Journal of American History* LXV (1978).

Whitaker, Arthur P. *The Mississippi Question, 1795–1803.* New York: Appleton-Century, 1934.

Will, Drake W. "Lewis and Clark: Westering Physicians." *Montana, the Magazine of Western History* XXI (Fall 1971).

Williams, David. "John Evans' Strange Journey." *American Historical Review* LIV (January–April 1949).

Wood, W. Raymond. "Slaughter River: Pishkun or Float Bison?" *We Proceeded On* XII (May 1986).

Wood, W. Raymond, and Thomas D. Thiessen. *Early Fur Trade on the Northern Plains.* Norman, Okla.: University of Oklahoma Press, 1985.

Index

Agency Creek, 244
Allen, Paul, 385
American Philosophical Society, 3–4, 5, 6–7, 29, 64–65
anchovies, 312
Arapahos, 143–44
Arikaras: arrive at Fort Mandan, 177; council with the, 145–47, 151; D'Église's accounts of the, 79; description of the, 142–43; Evans-Mackay's adventures with the, 83; expedition meets with the, 144–45; gifts to the, 146, 368; and the Hidatsas, 155, 163, 178, 365; as horse traders, 143–44; location of the, 141; and the Mandans, 146, 152, 155, 165–66, 167, 178, 365, 382; peace mission to the, 155–67; relocation of the, 187; sexual practices of the, 146; and the Sioux, 142–43, 177–78, 368, 382; and smallpox, 142, 143; Truteau's account of the, 81; and the Washington trip, 368, 369–70; women of the, 145, 146, 147
Arrow Creek, 201
Arrowsmith, Aaron, 33–36, 39, 84, 87, 182, 192, 214–15
Assiniboins, 161–62, 175, 180–81
Atsina Indians, 341

Bad River, 88, 133
Baker's Bay, 292, 293, 294–95
barter system among the Indians, 78–79
Barton, Benjamin Smith, 45, 379, 385
Bates, Frederick, 379, 381–82
Beacon Rock [along the Columbia River], 289
bears, 197–99, 211, 215–16, 220, 227, 346, 353

Bear's Tooth Mountain, 35–36
Beaverhead River. *See* Jefferson River
Beaverhead Rock, 240–41
Benoit, Francis, 102
Biddle, Nicholas, 98, 129, 251, 320, 385
Big Belts [mountains], 230
Big Blackfoot River, 342
Big Bone Lick [Cincinnati, Ohio], 64–65
Big Hole Basin, 359
Bighorn River, 184
bighorn sheep, 203, 230, 240
Big Horse [Missouri chief], 118, 120
Big Man [Mandan chief], 166
Big White [Mandan chief], 149–50, 152, 165, 166, 168–69, 175, 184; and the trip to Washington, 366–67, 378, 382–83
Bissell, Daniel, 68
Bissell, Richard, 73
Bitterroot Mountains, 267–68, 330, 358
Bitterroot River. *See* Clark's River
Bitterroot Valley, 267, 358
Blackbird [Omaha chief], 80, 81, 82, 83, 119
Black Buffalo [Teton Sioux chief], 134, 135–36, 140–41, 178, 181, 368–69
Black Cat [Mandan chief], 152, 161–62, 163, 164, 171
Black Eagle Falls, 220
Blackfeet: and the ambush at Hellgate canyon, 341; destroy a fort at Three Forks, 237; Lewis meets with the, 348–53; Lewis's description of the meeting with the, 375–77; and the Nez Percé, 331, 335, 348; and Shoshoni, 244, 245, 248–49
Black Hills, 182–83, 202
Black Moccasin [Hidatsa chief], 162

Bois Brulés [Sioux], 132–38, 143, 178
Boit, John, 32
Boley, John, 92
Boone, Daniel, 10
boundaries: and the Maria's River
   exploration, 375–77; of Upper
   Louisiana, 244
Boyle Creek, 265
Bozeman Pass, 184, 360
Bratton, William: and bears, 198; and Fort
   Clatsop, 305; and Fort Mandan, 170,
   187; illnesses of, 312, 313, 323, 325, 329;
   recruited for the expedition, 67; repairs
   metal objects for the Mandans, 170;
   searches for Reed, 118–19; sees the
   Pacific Ocean, 293; and the sweat baths,
   333, 334
Breaks of the Missouri, 203
British traders: and Heney's letter,
   357–58; and the Hidatsas, 152–54,
   163–65; and the Mandans, 152–54,
   163–65; and the Teton Sioux, 132; and
   the Yankton Sioux, 126. *See also name of
   specific trader*
Broken Arm [Nez Percé chief], 327–28,
   330–32, 335
Broughton, W. R., 31–32, 35
Brown Bear Defeated Creek, 200
Buffalo Calling Dance [Mandans], 171–72
Buffalo Medicine [Teton Sioux chief], 134,
   136, 141
buffalo *pishkins*, 201
Bull Creek, 200
Burnt Lodge Creek, 200

Cahokia, 76, 92
Calumet Bluff, 124–25
Cameahwait [Shoshoni chief], 245, 246–50,
   252, 253, 256–59, 262
Cameron, Murdock, 178
Camp Chopunnish, 332–35
Camp Creek, 266
Camp Disappointment, 353
Canada. *See name of specific company or
   person*
Canoe Camp, 273
Cape Disappointment, 291, 293, 305
Cape Girardeau, 70–71
Carondolet, Francisco, 79–80
Carver, Jonathan, 5–6, 31
Cascade Mountains, 276
Cathlamets, 304, 312, 315
Celilo Falls [Columbia River], 285, 294,
   296, 324–35
Chaboillez, Charles, 153–54, 163–64
Charbonneau, Jean Baptiste: birth of, 176;
   future of, 366; goes to Germany, 386;
   illness of, 333; and the journey to the
   Pacific, 187, 189, 225–26, 264; returns to
   the Indian country, 386; and the return
   trip, 358, 363; stays with Clark, 386; and

Charbonneau *(cont.)*
   the Yellowstone River exploration,
   358–64
Charbonneau, Lizette [daughter], 386
Charbonneau, Toussaint: accidents of,
   191, 199–200, 234, 360; and bears, 204;
   boat assignment of, 189; Clark's
   promises to, 366; and the Columbian
   Indians, 324, 326; and the Continental
   Divide, 233, 258–59; as a cook, 190; and
   the *Experiment*, 221, 224; and Fort
   Clatsop, 298; and Fort Mandan, 187;
   future of, 366; and the Great Falls,
   225–26; and the Hidatsas, 162, 163, 164,
   181; hiring of, 158–59; illness of, 234,
   239; as interpreter with the expedition,
   164; and the Mandans, 166, 170–71;
   returns to the frontier, 386; and the
   return trip, 358; sees the Pacific Ocean,
   293; and the Shoshoni, 238, 252, 253,
   256, 257, 258; visits Clark, 386; and the
   Yellowstone River exploration, 358–64
Charbonneau, Toussaint [son], 386
Charlevoix, Pierre François Xavier, 30, 35
Cheyenne River, 141–42, 144, 182–83
Cheyennes, 143–44, 180–81, 368
"Children" speech [Clark], 364
"Children" speech [Lewis], 95, 116, 121,
   125, 134, 151–52
Chinooks, 31, 284, 286, 288, 293, 295, 304,
   310–12, 340. *See also name of specific tribe*
Chopunnish. *See* Nez Percé
Chouteau, Jean Pierre, 76–77, 78, 89–90,
   91, 96, 97, 101–2, 129, 372, 378–79
Chouteau, René Auguste, 76–77, 89–90, 91,
   97, 102, 372
Cincinnati, Ohio, 64–65
Claiborne, William C.C., 15–16
Clark, George Rogers, 6, 7, 9, 55–56, 69,
   375
Clark, Jonathan, 375
Clark, Meriwether Lewis [son of
   William], 66–67, 385
Clark's Ford, 342
Clark's River, 266, 267, 338, 340, 342–43,
   358
Clarksville, Indiana, 66–67
Clark, William: accidents of, 87, 109–10;
   attitudes toward Indians of, 330; and
   command of the expedition, 54, 56–57,
   60; death of, 352, 387; as governor of
   Missouri Territory, 387; illnesses of, 69,
   87, 149, 234, 271, 273, 297, 324, 339; and
   Jean Baptiste Charbonneau, 363, 386;
   learns about surveying from Clark, 68;
   and Lewis's death, 385; Lewis serves
   under, 9, 17; map at Fort Mandan, 243;
   mapmaking by, 182–86, 192, 214–15,
   243, 308, 326, 364, 387; marries Julia
   Hancock, 381; meets Jefferson, 55–56;
   military appointments of, 55, 57, 98,

Clark *(cont.)*
379; military service of, 55; personal background of, 54–55; personality/physical characteristics of, 66; and relations with subordinates, 86, 196, 206–8, 209; responsibilities on the expedition of, 76, 85–86, 109, 308; returns to Louisville, 378; Sacagawea's relationship with, 176, 210, 264; in St. Louis, 89–93; and the St. Louis Missouri Fur Company, 382–83; scientific talents of, 179; as Superintendent of Indian Affairs, 352, 379, 387; surveys the Great Falls, 219–21, 225–26. *See also* Lewis and Clark relations

Clatsop Indians, 295, 296, 302, 304, 306

Clearwater River, 273, 274, 275–77, 327, 328, 330, 335, 339, 373

Collins, John, 108, 187, 352, 354

Collot, George Victor, 13

Colorado River, 35–36, 49, 184, 319

Colter, John: and bears, 220; court martial of, 94–95; explores the coastal area, 296; and Fort Mandan, 187; horse stolen from, 133; insubordination of, 92; joins Dickson and Hancock, 367; leaves the expedition, 367; and the Lolo Trail, 258, 263, 338; and the Ohio River journey, 63; professional career of, 238, 367; recruited for the expedition, 61; and the return trip, 325, 338, 352, 354; searches for the Field brothers, 114; searches for Shannon, 125, 129; sees the Pacific Ocean, 293; and the Three Forks region, 237

Columbian Indians, 316–27, 321. *See also name of specific tribe*

Columbian Plain, 276, 280, 312, 319

Columbia River: arrival at the, 277; described to Jefferson, 373; Gray's discovery of the, 31; and the journey to the Pacific, 277–315; as a key point for the expedition, 34; multiplicity of claims for the, 32; portage on the, 284–85, 288–89, 320–21; and the return trip, 315–27; surveying along the, 277, 280; U.S. need to strengthen claim to, 18. *See also* Tacoutche Tesse

Columbia [ship], 27, 31, 282

Comanches, 143, 245

commerce: as *not* a purpose of the expedition, 38–39; as a reason for the expedition, 23, 48, 49

Comowool [Clatsop chief], 312, 314

Congress, 21, 23, 38, 65, 373

contiguity, principle of, 50–51

Continental Divide, 186, 215, 308, 319–20, 342, 358

Continental Divide. *See* Lolo Trail; Shoshoni

Corps of Discovery: cost estimates for, 19; expedition named the, 68; impact of the Louisiana Purchase on the, 50; importance of the, 93; initial planning for, 19–26; jealousy toward, 102; Jefferson's charges for the, 47–49; leaves St. Charles, 104; leaves the Wood River camp, 99; organization of the, 94; publications resulting from, 378, 379–80, 385, 386–87; purposes of the, 23, 38–39, 47–49, 54, 90, 164–65, 373; and reassessing the time/distance of the expedition, 88; rewards for the, 379; route for the, 26–37; secrecy about the, 38–39, 56; size of the, 23–24, 57–58, 74, 88, 99, 177; summary of results of, 148

Council Bluff, 114

councils. *See name of specific tribe; name of specific part of the council,* e.g., making chiefs

courts-martial, 94–95, 103, 108, 147

Cowlitz River, 317

Cramer, Zodak, 59, 62

Crooks, Ramsay, 371

Crows, 143–44, 180–81, 184, 245, 358, 364

Cruzatte, Pierre: and the boating accident, 199–200; on the Columbia River, 285–86; and the decision about the branchings of the Missouri, 206–8, 209; enlistment of, 103–4; as a fiddler, 108, 120, 170–71, 227, 287, 327; and Fort Mandan, 187; professional background of, 103–4; and the return trip, 368; searches for Indians, 113; and the shooting of Lewis, 104, 353–54; and the Teton Sioux, 133, 135, 140, 368

Cut Bank Creek, 347

Cut Nose [Nez Percé chief], 328, 330

Dakota Indians. *See* Sioux Indians

Dalles, 322–23

The Dalles [Columbia River], 286, 287, 322–23

dancing: and the Arikaras, 147; by the explorers, 108, 120, 171, 196, 209, 227, 327; and the Chinooks, 288; and the Columbian Indians, 287, 327; and the Mandans, 171; and the Shoshoni, 247; and the Teton Sioux, 137; and the Yankton Sioux, 125

Dearborn, Henry, 16, 23, 40, 57, 97, 98

Dearborn River, 308

Dearborn's River, 231, 267, 308

"Dear Brother" letter, 375

Delassus, Carlos Dehault, 71, 75–76, 91, 92–93

Deschamps, Baptiste, 99

Des Moines River, 126

Devil's Race Ground, 104, 106–7

Dickerson, Mahlon, 12, 46, 380

Dickson, Joseph, 354, 365, 367

Dickson, William, 46
diplomacy: as a purpose of the expedition, 54, 90–91; and the return trip, 356. *See also name of specific nation or tribe*
discipline, 86, 92, 97, 103, 108, 118, 154–55, 310
Dismal Swamp, 265
dogs: purchase of, 281–82
Dorion, Pierre, 111–12, 119, 123–24, 125, 127, 132, 137–38, 178, 369–70
Drouillard, George: arrival at Wood River camp of, 97; and bears, 198, 204, 227; boat assignment of, 189; and the boating accidents, 191, 240; and the branching of the Jefferson, 239; and the Columbian Indians, 283; death of, 237; delivers report to Hay, 372–73; and the *Experiment*, 224; explores along the Jefferson River, 241; explores the branchings of the Missouri, 206–8; explores the coastal area, 296; explores Maria's River, 342–53; explores the Yellowstone River, 193, 196; and Fort Clatsop, 302–3, 313, 314; and Fort Mandan, 160–61, 187; gets separated from the expedition, 107; goes hunting near Great Falls, 212; hired as an interpreter/hunter, 86–87; illness of, 174–75; kills a buffalo, 229–30; and the Mandans, 149; and the Nez Percé, 330, 337, 338; offered a job as civilian interpreter, 68; operates on horses, 333; and the recruits from South West Point, 68, 86; reports Shannon missing, 124; rescues Clark, 109–10; and the return trip, 337, 338, 342, 346–50, 352; searches for the Field brothers, 114; searches for Indians, 113; searches for Reed, 118–19; seeks supplies for wintering near the Mandans, 159, 160–61; and the Shoshoni, 238, 248, 249, 250, 252, 254, 256; and the Sioux, 174–75; and the Three Forks region, 237; trapping along the Cheyenne River by, 147
drunkenness, 86, 96, 97, 108

Église, Jacques D', 78–79, 148
Ellicott, Andrew, 42
"Estimate of Eastern Indians" [Lewis and Clark], 180–81
Evans, John Thomas, 81–85, 88, 150, 161, 184
expedition. *See* Corps of Discovery
Experiment [boat], 40–41, 41, 218, 221, 224, 226–28
explorers: promises to, 24; *See also* Corps of Discovery; recruitment; *name of individual explorer*; types of, 23–24

Fairfong [fur trader], 114, 118
The Feathers [Blackfoot Indian], 34–35
Federalists, 7, 17, 17–18, 22–23, 39, 48, 52–53
Fidler, Peter, 34
Field, Joseph: and bears, 207; bitten by a snake, 110; and the Columbian Indians, 283; and the *Experiment*, 221, 224; explores the branchings of the Missouri, 206; explores Maria's River, 342–53; explores the Yellowstone River, 193, 196; and Fort Clatsop, 298, 305; and Fort Mandan, 187; gets lost at Council Bluffs, 114; goes hunting near Great Falls, 212; and land travel near the Continental Divide, 231, 233; and the Lolo Trail, 339; recruited for the expedition, 67; and the return trip, 339, 342–53; searches for Shannon, 124; sees the Pacific Ocean, 293; shoots buffalo, 122; tells Clark about the Great Falls, 213, 217
Field, Reuben: and the Columbian Indians, 283; and the *Experiment*, 224; explores the branchings of the Missouri, 206; explores the coastal area, 296; explores Maria's River, 342–53; explores the Yellowstone River, 193, 196; and Fort Mandan, 187; gets lost at Council Bluffs, 114; illnesses of, 291–92; insubordination of, 92; and land travel near the Continental Divide, 233; on the Lolo Trail, 272; and the Nez Percé, 271; recruited for the expedition, 67; and the return trip, 325, 342, 346–53; searches for Reed, 118–19; sees the Pacific Ocean, 293
Flatheads, 266–67, 338, 346. *See also* Chinooks
Floridas, 13, 14, 15, 16, 19–20, 37, 49–50
Floyd, Charles, Jr., 67, 91, 94, 99, 120–21
Floyd's River, 121
Fort Adams, 16
Fort Atkinson, 114
Fort Cahokia, 16
Fort Charles, Nebraska, 82, 83, 85
Fort Clatsop, 298–315
Fort Greenville, Ohio, 55
Fort Jefferson, 69
Fort Kaskaskia, Illinois, 24, 57, 73
Fort Mandan: Christmas/New Year's at, 170–71; Corps winters at, 154–88
Fort Massac, 24, 59, 64, 67–68
Fort Peck Reservoir, 203
Fort Pickering, 384
Fox Indians, 95
France, 12–15, 22, 37, 38–39, 50, 92–93. *See also* Louisiana Purchase; *name of specific person or Indian tribe*
France, Baptiste La, 163

Frazer, Robert: court martial of, 94–95; enlists in the expedition, 145; and the *Experiment*, 221, 224; explores Maria's River, 342–53; and Fort Mandan, 187; gets sunstroke, 110; and land travel near the Continental Divide, 233; on the Lolo Trail, 271; in the Nez Percé country, 334; publication of journal by, 379–80; and the return trip, 334, 346–53; and the Sioux, 174–75

French rivermen, 94, 97, 99, 130–31, 155

fur trade: competition in the, 102; and Great Britain, 37; and the purposes of the expedition, 49; summary about, 373. *See also* British traders; *name of specific company or person*

fur traders: and the expedition, 20; and the Hidatsas, 152–54; and the Mandans, 152–54; mystery third letter meant for, 378; and the Teton Sioux, 365; and the trading house program, 20. *See also* British traders; *name of specific person or company*

Gallatin, Albert, 19, 36, 47–48, 102, 235

Gallatin River, 235, 236–37, 319, 359–60, 360

Garreau, Joseph, 79

Gass, Patrick: and the boat accidents, 275; and the branching of the Jefferson, 239; and the Continental Divide trek, 259; elected sergeant, 121; estimate of baggage by, 209; and the *Experiment*, 221, 224, 227; explores the branchings of the Missouri, 206; explores Maria's River, 342, 346–53; fixes boats, 125; and Fort Mandan, 187; illness of, 239; and the leaving of Fort Clatsop, 315; publication of journal by, 379–80; repairs metal objects for the Mandans, 170; and the return trip, 325, 342, 346, 350; and the search for Shoshoni, 238; and the shooting of Lewis, 354; and the Teton Sioux, 136

Gates of the Rocky Mountains, 232–33, 267

geographical studies: as a purpose of the expedition, 38–39, 109, 178–80

Gibbon Pass, 266

Gibson, George, 67, 187, 212, 305, 312, 360–61, 382

gifts: for the Arikaras, 146, 368; for the Assiniboins, 161; bought in St. Louis, 71; for the Columbian Indians, 281, 283; for the Hidatsas, 152, 365; and the initial planning of the expedition, 25, 42–43; for the Mandans, 152, 365; for the Missouri Indians, 117, 121; for the Nez Percé, 272, 332; for the Otos, 117, 121; purpose of, 25; and the return trip,

gifts *(cont.)*
356, 357; for the Sahaptian Indians, 281; for the Shoshoni, 253; for the Sioux, 125, 133, 134, 357

Goodrich, Silas, 174–75, 187, 212–13, 221, 224, 304, 333, 340, 342, 346

Grand River, 143–44

Gratiot, Charles, 91, 92–93

Graveline, Joseph, 145, 146, 147, 149, 155, 177, 178, 368, 369–70, 382

Gray, Robert, 18, 27, 31–32, 36, 51, 282, 291

Gray's Bay, 290–91

Great Bend of the Missouri, 190

Great Britain: as a claimant of the Oregon territory, 32; and the fur trade, 37; influence on Indians of, 80, 82, 83; interests in keeping France out of western territories by, 15; Jefferson's dislike of, 15; Mackenzie's influence on, 37, 38, 373; Spanish reactions to threat of, 79–80; as a threat to U.S. interest in the West, 16, 18, 22, 38; U.S. asks for passports through territory of, 38–39. *See also* British traders; *name of specific person*

Great Falls, 84, 185, 209, 212–28, 337, 338, 340, 346, 348, 350, 373

Great Lake River, 36, 214–15

Great Shute [Columbia River], 288–89, 321–22

Half Man [Yankton Sioux chief], 126–27

Hall, Hugh, 108, 187, 361–62

Hancock, Forest, 354, 365, 367

Hancock, Julia [Judy], 66, 202–3, 378, 379, 381, 385

Harpers Ferry, Virginia, 40, 47, 57–58

Hayden, Ferdinand, 190

Hay, John, 74, 77, 89, 97, 372, 373, 377

Heart Mountain, 35–36, 186

Heart River, 174

Hellgate Canyon, 341, 342, 358

Heney, Hugh, 179, 182, 356–58, 364

Hidatsas: and the Arikaras, 155, 163, 178, 365; barter system of the, 78–79; capture Sacagawea, 235–36; council with the, 151–53, 365–66; early French visits to the, 33; and foreign traders, 152–54; Jessaume lives with the, 150; location of the, 150; Mackay's information about the, 78–79; as neighbors of the Mandans, 150; nomenclature of the, 151; reticence toward U.S. of, 165; and the return trip, 365, 365–67; and the Shoshoni, 162, 235–36, 245, 365–66; and the Sioux, 163, 365; summary of information about the, 180–81; treating with the, 162–64; visit Fort Mandan, 174

Hidatsas, War Path of the, 205–6
High Plains, 127–28
Highwoods [mountains], 205
Hill, Samuel, 313
Hooke, Moses, 58, 60
Horned Weasel [Hidatsa chief], 162
Horse Prairie Creek, 241
horses: as a means of developing
    commerce in the West, 309–10; needed
    to cross the Continental Divide, 231,
    238, 243, 246; and the return trip, 316,
    332, 357, 361, 362; stealing of, 346, 361,
    362; to the North West Company, 357,
    358, 361, 364
horse trading: and the Columbian Indians,
    323–24, 326; and the Flatheads, 266–67;
    and the return trip, 356; and the
    Shoshoni, 242, 246, 247, 252, 253–54,
    256–58
hot springs, 339
Howard, Thomas, 187
Hudson Bay Company, 196, 352. See also
    name of specific person
Hungry Creek, 336, 338

Indian culture: artifacts to be sent to
    Washington, 178–81; Clark
    questionnaire about, 90; and the diary
    entries, 309; and "Estimate of Eastern
    Indians," 180–81; and information for
    use on the expedition, 77–85; as a
    purpose of the expedition, 45, 48–49,
    123. See also name of specific nation or tribe
Indian lands: in the Mississippi Valley,
    15–16, 20, 53–54
Indian relations. See name of specific nation
    or tribe
Indians: British influence on, 80, 82, 83;
    and the change of sovereignty, 90–91;
    development of good will among, 39,
    48–49; first contact along the Missouri
    with, 111–12; Spanish relations with,
    78–79; war as a way of life to the, 138;
    weapons traded with the, 79. See also
    name of specific nation or tribe
Indian trade fair, 126, 143–44
Iowa Indians, 95
Iron Banks [island], 69

Jackson, Donald Dean, 4, 377–78
James River, 122, 124, 143
Jarrot, Nicholas, 74
Jefferson River, 235–50, 348, 358, 359
Jefferson, Thomas: authorizes the
    expedition, 19; charges the expedition,
    47–48, 90; and the constitutional
    question concerning the purchase of
    foreign territory, 53; death of, 386;
    dislike of British by, 15; elected
    president, 8, 9; Francophilism of, 7;

Jefferson (cont.)
    hires Lewis as private secretary, 1, 9–10;
    importance of the expedition to, 65–66;
    instructions about Sioux Indians of,
    123; interest in the West of, 4–8, 10, 23,
    37, 386–87; and Lewis's death, 385;
    Lewis's relations with, 9, 65, 381; maps
    by, 28; meets Clark [William], 55–56;
    memoir of Lewis by, 4; Notes on
    Virginia by, 5, 28; personal
    characteristics of, 11–12; and the plans
    for the expedition, 41–42; predilection
    for secrecy of, 39; preliminary report
    to, 372–75; resettlement plans of, 53–54,
    69–70, 76–77; resigns as secretary of
    state, 7–8; as a scientist, 28–29; and
    secrecy concerning the expedition,
    20–21, 38–39, 373; views of Ledyard of,
    6; views of Lewis by, 4, 16–17, 386–87
Jessaume, René, 84–85, 150–53, 158, 162,
    163, 166, 171, 176, 366, 367, 378, 382
journals: given to Columbian Indians for
    arrival of next ship, 313. See also Lewis
    and Clark relations; name of specific
    individual
Judith's River, 202–3, 204

Kakawissassa [Arikara chief], 145–46
Kakoaksis [Hidatsa chief], 152
Kansas River, 182–83
Kelley, Hall J., 320
Kickapoo Indians, 78
Kimooenim River, 277
King mountain, 35–36, 186
King, Nicholas, 36, 87–88, 182, 192,
    214–15, 262
King, Rufus, 14
Kiowas, 143, 143–44
Knife River, 78, 83–84, 150–51, 154, 181
Kooskooskee River/North Fork of the
    Clearwater, 273

Labiche, François, 103–4, 118–19, 120, 133,
    135, 187, 252, 296, 368, 378
La Charette [village], 370–71
Laroque, François-Antoine, 163–65, 172,
    174, 179, 184
Laussat, Pierre Clement de, 91
Leclerc, Charles, 14
Lécuyer [trader], 81
Ledyard, John, 6
Lemhi Pass, 243, 244, 259, 277, 308, 320,
    340–41, 343, 358
Lemhi River, 245, 246
Lepage, Jean Baptiste, 154, 158, 187, 206–8
Lesser Missesourie River, 36, 184
Lewis and Clark Pass, 343, 373
Lewis and Clark relationship: beginning
    of friendship between, 9; and the diary
    entries, 264–65, 307–8; and the division

Lewis and Clark relationship *(cont.)*
of responsibilities, 76; prior to the
expedition, 56–57; while in the military,
55

Lewis and Clark River, 296

Lewis, Lucy Meriwether [mother], 2–3, 9,
378

Lewis, Meriwether: accidents of, 104;
alcoholism of, 379–85; as an agent of
American imperialism, 244; attitudes
about Indians of, 181, 288, 311, 325, 330;
birthday of, 120, 254; character of, 3,
16–17, 48, 63, 66, 254–55, 375; death of,
4, 383–85; depressions of, 1, 16, 41, 64,
254–55; dislike of English by, 153, 163,
373–74; as a failure in his own eyes, 65;
family background of, 2–3; as governor
of Upper Louisiana Territory, 379,
381–82; illnesses of, 68, 121–22, 209, 211,
238, 272, 379; Indian speeches of, 95–96,
115, 116, 121, 125, 134; Jefferson's
instructions to, 47–49, 90; Jefferson's
relations with, 9, 65, 381; military
service of, 4, 8–9; and the mystery third
letter, 375–78; physical characteristics
of, 66; political affiliation of, 10–11; and
the preliminary report to Jefferson,
372–75; as private secretary to Jefferson,
1, 9–10; proposes a trip to Santa Fe, 65;
relations with subordinates of, 67, 92,
196, 206–8, 209, 225, 238; responsibilities
on the expedition of, 76; romanticism
of, 215; scientific talents of, 28–29, 179;
shooting of, 104, 353–54, 365, 367;
teaches Clark about surveying, 68; and
women, 66, 70. *See also* Lewis and Clark
relationship

Lewis, Reuben, 381, 382–83, 386

Lewis's River, 262, 265, 266, 277, 317, 327,
358

Lewis, William [father], 2

Liberté [voyageur], 114, 118, 120, 148

Lincoln, Levi, 47, 48, 63, 66

Linnard, William, 47

liquor, 108, 117, 120, 121, 135, 160, 370

Lisa, Manuel, 102, 382, 386

Little Belts [mountains], 214, 217

Little Missouri, 190, 192

Little Thief [Oto chief], 118, 120

Livingston, Robert, 14, 15, 19–20, 37,
49–50, 52

Lochsa River, 268, 339

Logan, John Allen, 319

Loisel, Regis, 111–12, 126, 131–32, 356–57

Lolo Trail, 262–69, 271–72, 335, 336–339

Long Narrows [Columbia River], 286, 287,
323, 324

Lorimier, Louis, 69–70

Louisiana Purchase: and the ceremonial
transfer of Upper Louisiana, 91–93;

Louisiana Purchase *(cont.)*
completion of the, 52; and Congress, 65;
Federalists' reactions to the, 52–53; and
the French offer of selling all the
territory, 49–50; Livingston begins
negotiations with France for the, 15;
Monroe joins negotiations concerning
the, 19–20; national announcement
concerning the, 57; needed to be
confirmed by the Senate, 60;
negotiations concerning the, 37–38,
49–50; price for the, 52; Spanish
reaction to the, 53, 71

Lower Cascades [Columbia River], 288,
289, 320–21

Lydia [ship], 313

McClellan, Robert, 369–70

McCracken, Hugh, 152–53, 163–64

Mackay, Alexander, 27

Mackay, James, 77–85, 141, 184

McKean, Thomas, 11, 46

McKeehan, David, 379–80

Mackenzie, Alexander: and the British
claims to the Columbia River, 32;
importance of trip of, 31; influence on
British government of, 37, 38, 373;
influence on Lewis of, 19, 26–27;
Michaux learns about, 4; as a model for
Clark, 297, 318; publication of book by,
26–27, 37; route of, 18, 37; scientific
education of, 28; Tacoutche Tesse of,
215, 277; Thompson's influence on, 33

McKenzie, Charles, 163, 165, 174, 186

McNeal, Hugh, 187, 241, 242, 245, 247,
249, 291–92, 307, 340, 342, 346

McRae, William, 46

Madison, James, 11, 12, 13–14, 50, 235

Madison River, 235, 236–37, 319

Mahars. *See* Omaha Indians

making of chiefs: and the Columbian
Indians, 295; and the Hidatsas, 152; and
the Mandans, 152; and the Missouri
Indians, 116–17, 121; and Oto Indians,
116–17, 121; and the Sahaptian Indians,
281; and the Teton Sioux, 134; and the
Yankton Sioux, 125

Mandans: and the Arikaras, 146, 152, 155,
165–66, 167, 178, 365, 382; and the
Assiniboins, 161–62, 175; barter system
of the, 78–79; British influence on the,
80; council with the, 150–53, 365–66;
early French visits to the, 33;
Evans-Mackay's adventures with the,
78–79, 83, 84–85; expedition's first
sightings of, 148; expedition winters
near the, 154–88; explorers dancing for
the, 171; and foreign traders, 152–54;
hospitality laws of the, 84–85; location
of the, 150–51; medical work among

Mandans *(cont.)*
the, 173; meeting with the, 149;
pilfering by, 170; reaction to expedition
by the, 166–67; and the Red Stick
Ceremony, 171–72; and the return trip,
365, 365–67; sexual practices of the, 33,
171–72; and the Sioux, 142–43, 165–66,
167, 175, 365, 368; Thompson's visit to
the, 33; and the trip to Washington,
356, 366–67; Truteau's account of the,
80–81; women of the, 155, 171–72
Mandan villages: Clark's location of the,
182–83; distance between Wood River
camp and, 87; distance to the Pacific
from the, 88; Evans locates the, 84; as a
key point for the expedition, 34;
Thompson's location of the, 85, 87, 183
maps: inadequacies of, 71; Lewis learns
about, 28, 29–30, 42; as the major
purpose of the expedition, 48; obstacles
to making, 183–86; used for planning
the expedition, 27–37. *See also name of
specific person*
Maria's River, 208, 231, 308, 340, 341,
342–53, 375–77
Marks, John, 3
Marshall, Moses, 3–4
Matootonha [Mandan village], 149–50, 152,
165, 170–71, 175
medical supplies for the expedition, 24–25,
43–45
medical work among the Indians, 173,
329–30, 333, 334
Medicine River, 185, 214, 215–16, 220, 224,
231, 267, 343
Ménard, Pierre, 78, 84
Meriwether Bay/Young's Bay, 296, 298,
302
Michaux, André, 4, 6–7, 17, 26–27
military men for the expedition, 23–24,
130–31
military reconnaisance: as a purpose of
the expedition, 47–48
Milk River, 185, 197, 204, 205
Minnesota River, 83, 126
Mississippi River, 68–72
Mississippi Territory, 15–16
Mississippi Valley, 10, 13, 15–16, 20, 53–54
Missoula River, 267
Missouri Fur Company, 79–85, 126, 357.
See also name of specific person
Missouri Indians, 112–14, 116–18, 121
Missouri River: Arrowsmith's map of the,
34–35; Clark's map of the, 346; colors of
the, 99–100; Corps begins trip on the,
99; decision about the branchings of
the, 206–9; eddies/currents in the,
105–7; Evans's survey of the, 84; The
Feathers map of the, 34–35; as the
gateway to the West, 30; hazards in the,
100–101; King's map of the, 36; Lewis's

Missouri River *(cont.)*
views of the, 181; and the return trip,
364–71; tales/legends about the, 30–31;
Thompson's maps of the, 33, 34; three
forks of the, 233–37
Moncacht-Apé [Indian], 30–31, 36
Monroe, James, 17, 19–20, 37, 49–50, 52
Morales, Juan Ventura, 17
Mount Adams, 282
Mount Hood, 318
Mount Jefferson, 318
Mount Rainier, 318
Mount Saint Helens, 282, 318
Multnomah Falls, 323
Multnomah River. *See* Willamette River
Murphy, Dan, 199
Musselshell River, 202, 204, 205

The Navigator [Cramer], 59, 62
Necanicum River, 306
Neelly, James, 384–85
Netul River, 296, 298
Newman, John, 68, 146, 147, 154–55,
174–75, 177
New Mexico, 10, 79, 184
New Orleans, 13–14, 15, 17, 22–23, 46
Nez Percé, 259, 262–72, 277, 281, 327–35,
331, 332, 337, 338–43, 348
Niobrara River, 182–83
Nixluidix [Wishram village], 286
North Head, 293
North West Company of Canada, 181,
184, 196, 352, 357, 373, 376. *See also*
Mackenzie, Alexander; Thompson,
David
Nuptadi. *See* Rooptahee

Oglala Sioux, 143
Ohio River, 30, 61–66, 68–69
Old Toby [Shoshoni guide], 259, 262–69,
273, 275, 308, 330, 339, 343
Omaha Indians, 80, 82, 83, 112, 118,
119–20, 137–38
Ordway, John: and the *Experiment*, 221,
224; and Fort Clatsop, 311, 315; and
Fort Mandan, 160, 187; and the Great
Falls, 217, 359; and the Hidatsas, 162;
and hunting along the Cheyenne River,
144; journal entries of as copies of
Whitehouse's entries, 264; and the
Mandans, 170–71; and medical work
among the Mandans, 173; in the Nez
Percé country, 334; and Reed's
punishment, 120; responsibilities of,
101; returns to the East, 378; and the
return trip, 333, 334, 354, 359; sees the
Pacific Ocean, 293; sent to the Omaha
village, 119–20; as a sergeant with a
squad, 94; and the Shoshoni, 263–64;
and size of the expedition, 99; and the
sweat baths, 333; and the Teton Sioux,

Ordway *(cont.)*
140; and the Wood River camp, 91, 97; and the Yellowstone River, 193, 196
Oregon, 31–32, 36. *See also* Columbia River
Osage Indians, 78, 90, 91, 96, 97–98, 101–2, 129, 378–79
Osage River, 109, 182–83
Otis, Harrison Gray, 53
Oto Indians, 82, 112–15, 116–18, 121

Pacific Ocean: arrival at the, 290–91, 293
Padover, Saul, 12
Pahkees, 244, 341, 342
parchment certificates of good character, 117, 121, 134, 314
Partisan [Teton Sioux chief], 132, 134, 135, 136, 139, 140–41
Patterson, Robert, 45, 47
Pawnee Indians, 112–13
peace pipes, 126, 133, 283
Peale, Charles Willson, 45–46
Pernier, John, 384
Philadelphia, Pennsylvania, 42–47
Philanthropy River/Ruby River, 240
Pichon, Louis André, 12–14, 39
pilfering: by the Columbian Indians, 310; by expedition members, 277, 314; by Indians, 325, 346; by Mandans, 170; by Skilloots, 290
Pittsburgh, Pennsylvania, 58–61
Platte River, 109, 112–13, 182–83, 184, 319, 369
Point Adams, 293
Point Ellice/Point Dismal, 292
Pompy's Tower, 363
Ponca Indians, 81, 112
Portage Creek/Belt Creek, 219, 221, 224, 341, 346
Potts, John, 86, 187, 231, 237, 325, 337, 339
Powder River, 364
prairie dogs, 128–29, 211
Pratz, Antoine Simon le Page Du, 30–31, 36
principle of contiguity, 50–51
pronghorns, 128, 129, 147
Pryor, Nathaniel: explores the branchings of the Missouri, 206–8; and Fort Clatsop, 298, 312; and Fort Mandan, 187; and the Heney letter/horses, 357, 358, 361, 364; and the Mandans, 161; professional career of, 67; recruited for the expedition, 67; responsibilities of, 94, 122; and the return of Big White, 382; and the return trip, 357, 358, 361, 362, 364; sees the Pacific Ocean, 293; and the size of the expedition, 99; wolf bites, 362; and the Yankton Sioux, 124
Puget Trough, 317
punishments, 86, 108, 120, 146, 147

rabbits: jackass, 128
Rainbow Falls, 213, 219–20
rain forests, 287
Rattlesnake Cliffs [near the Jefferson River], 241
recruitment of explorers, 19, 23–24, 46, 57, 58, 60–61, 73–74, 86
Red River, 122
Red Stick Ceremony [Mandans], 171–72
Reed, James, 371
Reed, Moses, 118, 120, 145, 154–55, 155, 177
reports: and the "Dear Brother" letter, 375; Jefferson's preliminary, 372–75; and the mystery third letter, 375–78
resettlement plans, 53–54, 69–70, 76–77, 181
return trip: beginning of the, 315; by ship, 294; and the decision to leave Fort Clatsop, 312–315; and the initial plans for the expedition, 49; voting on route for, 295–96
rewards for the expedition, 379
Rio Grande, 49, 184, 319
River that Scolds at All Others. *See* Milk River
Robertson, John, 92
Rocky Mountains, 34–35, 84, 88, 205, 211–12
Rogers, Robert, 5–6, 31
Rooptahee/Nuptadi [Mandan village], 150, 152, 171
Ross's Hole, 358
Rumsey, Nathan, 96
Rush, Benjamin, 25, 43–45, 90
Russell, Gilbert, 384
Russia, 18, 79–80

Sacagawea: background of, 158–59; boat assignment of, 189; and the boating accident, 200; as a calming influence on Indians, 283; captured by Hidatsas, 235–36; Clark's relationship with, 176, 210, 264; and the Columbian Indians, 295, 323; on the Columbia River, 285; and the Continental Divide trip, 258–59, 267–68; death of, 386; and the *Experiment*, 221, 224; finds roots to eat, 191; and Fort Clatsop, 298, 304, 305–6; and Fort Mandan, 187; future of, 366; gives birth, 176; goes to Great Falls, 225–26; illness of, 209, 210, 216–17, 218–19, 291–92; and the Lolo Trail, 267–68; and mapmaking, 183; responsibilities of, 189–90; and the return trip, 358, 359, 360, 363; and the Shoshoni, 233, 250, 251, 252, 253, 256, 257, 258, 264; visits Clark, 386; and the Yellowstone River exploration, 358–64
Sahaptian Indians, 280–81, 287–88
St. Charles, 101–4

St. Joseph, Missouri, 369–70
St. Louis: and the ceremonial transfer of Upper Louisiana, 91–93; Clark in, 89–90; description of, 74–75; Indian relations in the, 95–96; as a key point for the expedition, 34, 71; Lewis in, 74–78; Lewis to camp near, 65–66; as a source of information about the Louisiana territory, 76–77; supplies from, 71, 94, 96. *See also name of specific person*
St. Louis Missouri Fur Company, 382–83
St. Peter's River. *See* Minnesota River
Salmon River. *See* Lewis's River
Sandy River, 294, 296
Santo Domingo, 12–13, 14–15, 22, 37, 50
Sapphire Mountains, 358
Sauk Indians, 95, 97
Sauvie Island, 289
sawyers, 100, 370
scientific inquiry: along the Cheyenne River, 147–48; along the Columbia River, 317, 323; and the diary entries, 309; along the Great Bend, 192; in the Great Falls area, 227; Lewis gains knowledge about, 26–27; Lewis sends specimens to Washington, 102–3, 178–79; and Lewis' studies with Philadelphia professors, 45–46; along the Lolo Trail, 272; along the Missouri River, 108–9; near the Continental Divide, 230; along the Ohio River, 64–65; as a purpose of the expedition, 23, 38–39, 49; in the Three Forks region, 235; in the Traveler's Rest area, 340; along the Yellowstone River, 354–55, 364
Seaman [dog], 58, 63–64, 69, 111, 122, 187, 191, 200, 227, 232, 235, 238, 321
Shannon, George: and the *Experiment*, 224; explores the branchings of the Missouri, 206; explores the coastal area, 296; and Fort Clatsop, 302–3; and Fort Mandan, 187; future of, 382; gets lost, 124–25, 129; and the Nez Percé, 338; and the Ohio River journey, 63; recruited for the expedition, 61; rejoins the expedition, 130; and the return of Big White, 382; and the return trip, 338, 360, 361, 362; sees the Pacific Ocean, 293
Shawnee Indians, 69
Sheheke. *See* Big White
Sherman Peak, 269, 271
Shields, John: court martial of, 94–95; and the *Experiment*, 221, 224; explores the branchings of the Missouri, 206–8; and Fort Mandan, 187; gets separated from the expedition, 107; and the Mandans, 170; as a metalworker, 170, 334;

Shields *(cont.)*
personal background of, 67; recruited for the expedition, 67; and the return trip, 340; scouts along the Jefferson River, 241; searches for Shannon, 124; and the Shoshoni, 242, 248, 249; and the sweat baths, 333; and the Wood River camp, 92
Short Narrows [Columbia River], 285–86
Shoshoni: ask for guns, 252; bargaining with the, 263–64; and the Blackfeet, 244, 245, 248–49; council with the, 252; and the Crows, 245; dancing with the, 247; eating habits of the, 248; first meeting with a, 242; gifts for the, 253; and the Hidatsas, 162, 235–36, 245, 365–66; horse trading with the, 242, 246, 247, 252, 253–54, 256–58; location of the, 215; looking for the, 229–42; meeting with the, 244–59; and Nez Percé, 331; and Pahkees, 244; sexual customs of the, 255–56; as a source of information, 253, 259; summary of the, 245–46, 255; and weapons, 245–46; women, 244, 245, 247, 255, 256–57
Shoshoni Cove, 241–42, 247–48, 250
Sioux: and the Arikaras, 142–43, 177–78, 368, 382; attack members of the expedition, 174–75; belligerency of the, 88; boast of attack on members of the expedition, 177–78; British influence with the, 112; Cameron selling guns to the, 178; and the "Children" speech, 95; Evans-Mackay adventures with the, 82, 83; gifts to the, 357; and the Hidatsas, 163, 365; Indians' fears of the, 112; Jefferson's instructions about the, 91, 96, 112, 123; location of the, 122–23; and the Mandans, 142–43, 165–66, 167, 175, 365, 368; overview of, 123; summary of information about the, 181; Truteau's account of the, 80–81, 81. *See also name of specific tribe*
Skilloots, 289–90
Skipanon River, 302, 306
Slaughter Creek, 201, 202
smallpox, 112, 142, 143, 352
Snake Indians. *See* Sioux Indians
Snake River, 259, 277, 280, 319, 334, 373
Soulard, Antoine, 76, 77, 91, 92–93
South Fork of the Columbia, 277
South Pass [Continental Divide], 320
South West Point, Tennessee, 24, 46, 68, 86
Spain: American settlement of lands owned by, 10; cedes Louisiana to France, 12–14, 38; as a claimant of the Oregon territory, 18, 32; difficulties of retaining the lands in the West of, 10; and the Evans-Mackay expedition,

Spain *(cont.)*
77–85; Indian relations with, 78–79; ownership of western territories by, 5; and permission for the expedition to cross territories of, 18; reaction to British threats in the Louisiana territory of, 79–80; reaction to the Louisiana Purchase by, 53, 71; transfers Upper Louisiana to the French, 92. *See also name of specific person*
Spirit Mound, 122
spoils system, 10–11
Squaw Creek, 263
"A Statistical View of the Indian Nations Inhabiting the Territory of Louisiana . . ." [Jefferson], 180
Stoddard, Amos, 73, 89, 91–93, 95, 96, 97, 103
Stone Walls [bluffs along the Missouri], 203
"A Summary View of Rivers and Creeks" [Lewis], 178–79, 185
"A Summary View of Rivers, Creeks, and Remarkable Places" [Clark], 178–79
Sun River. *See* Medicine River
sweat baths, 333, 334

Tabeau, Pierre Antoine, 132, 144–45, 167, 178, 179, 187
Tacoutche Tesse, 27, 31, 35, 215, 277
Tahcum [Chinook chief], 310–11
Tavern [caves along the Missouri River], 104, 384
technology, show of: and the Columbian Indians, 282–83, 318; and the Hidatsas, 366; during the Indian councils/ceremonies, 117; and the Mandans, 170; and the Missouri Indians, 117; and the Nez Percé, 331; and the Oto Indians, 117; for the Shoshoni, 253; and the Teton Sioux, 135, 136
Tetoharsky [Nez Percé chief], 273, 275–76, 282, 283, 287, 288
Teton Sioux, 123, 126, 131–41, 143–44, 181, 357, 365, 368–69
Thompson, David, 33, 34, 36, 85, 87, 100, 183, 351, 377
Thompson, John, 187, 275, 342, 346
Thornton, Edward, 34
Three Forks, 184, 185–86, 215, 233–37, 341, 359
Thwaites, Reuben Gold, 307–8
Tillamook Head, 306
Tillamook Indians, 305, 306–7, 329
Tongue Point, 296, 315
tow ropes, 105–6
trading house program, 20, 23
transfer of sovereignty: formal ceremony of, 91–93; and Indian relations, 97

Trapper's Peak, 358
Traveler's Rest, 308, 337, 340, 341, 356
Trudeau, Zenon, 78, 79
Truteau, Jean Baptiste, 80, 83, 141, 142, 184
Tunnachemootoolt. *See* Broken Arm
Twisted Hair [Nez Percé chief], 270–76, 280, 282, 283, 287, 288, 316, 327–28, 330
Two Medicine Creek, 347

Upper Cascades [Columbia River], 288, 321–22
Utes, 143, 245

Vallé, Jean, 141–42, 143, 144
Vancouver, George, 31, 32, 35, 282, 292, 318
Vancouver Island, 31, 286
Vérendrye brothers, 33
voyageurs. *See* French rivermen

Walla Wallas, 327
Warfington, Richard, 94, 99, 155, 177
War Path of the Big Bellies, 205–6
Wascos, 286, 287
Washington, D.C.: and the Arikaras, 146, 368, 369–70; and the Crows, 364; and the Hidatsas, 152, 356, 366; Indian visits to, 96, 178, 369–70; Jefferson suggests Indians visit, 90–91; and the Mandans, 152, 356, 366–67; and the Nez Percé, 328, 331; and the Osages, 90, 96, 97–98, 101–2, 129, 378–39; and the Otos, 121; trips as a purpose of the expedition, 48–49
Weippe Prairie, 269, 335, 338
Wendover Ridge, 339
Werner, William, 86, 187, 342, 346
Weuche [Yankton Sioux chief], 125–26
Wheeling: West Virginia, 63
Whelen, Israel, 42
Whiskey Rebellion, 8, 55
White Bear Islands, 220–21, 224, 341, 342, 343
White Catfish Camp, 113
White Earth River, 184–85, 192–93
White Hairs [Osage chief], 102
Whitehouse, Joseph, 68, 99, 107, 125, 187, 225, 240, 264, 266, 269, 304
White River, 82
Willamette River, 289, 317–19, 320
Willard, Alexander, 108, 170, 187, 220, 350
Willow Run/Box Elder Creek, 221, 224, 226, 346
Windsor, Richard, 187, 206–8, 361, 362
Wisdom River/Big Hole, 240, 266
Wiser, Peter, 92, 187, 237, 237–38, 291–92, 293, 334
Wishram Indians, 286, 287
Wistar, Caspar, 3–4, 24, 29, 45

wolves, 128, 192, 201, 211
Wood, Maria, 208, 380
Wood River camp, 76, 78, 85–86, 87, 91, 92, 97, 99
Worrell, Stephen, 91, 92–93

Yakimas, 327
Yankton Sioux, 123, 124, 125–26, 369
Yellept [Walla Walla chief], 327
Yellowstone River: and the return trip, 308, 319, 340, 341, 353–54, 358–63, 364; and the trip to the Pacific, 84, 180, 181, 182, 184, 193, 196, 205
York [Clark's slave]: accidents of, 169; at Fort Mandan, 187; and the branchings of the Missouri, 206; and the Chinooks,

York [Clark's slave] *(cont.)*
288; and Continental Divide trip, 231; and the *Experiment,* 221, 224; as a favorite of Indian women, 146; and Fort Clatsop, 298, 299; and the Great Falls, 225–26; kills buffalo, 127; and the Mandans, 171; as a member of the expedition, 66, 87, 99; rescues men in a boating accident, 107; responsibilities of, 189–90; returns to Louisville, 378; and the return trip, 358, 359–60; in St. Louis with Lewis and Clark, 96; sees the Pacific Ocean, 293; and the Yellowstone River exploration, 359–63
Yrujo, Carlos Martínez, Marqués de Casa, 11, 18, 38, 39, 46, 53

Other titles by David Lavender
available in Bison Books editions

BENT'S FORT

CALIFORNIA
LAND OF NEW BEGINNINGS

THE FIST IN THE WILDERNESS

ONE MAN'S WEST

WESTWARD VISION
THE STORY OF THE OREGON TRAIL